CAPTURING CONTEMPORARY JAPAN

CAPTURING CONTEMPORARY JAPAN

Differentiation and Uncertainty

Edited by

Satsuki Kawano
Glenda S. Roberts
Susan Orpett Long

UNIVERSITY OF HAWAI'I PRESS
HONOLULU

© 2014 UNIVERSITY OF HAWAI'I PRESS

19 18 17 16 15 14   6 5 4 3 2 1

Library of Congress Cataloging-in-Publication Data

Capturing contemporary Japan : differentiation and uncertainty /
edited by Satsuki Kawano, Glenda S. Roberts, and Susan Orpett Long.
pages cm
Includes bibliographical references and index.
ISBN 978-0-8248-3868-3 (cloth : alk. paper) —
ISBN 978-0-8248-3869-0 (pbk. : alk. paper)
1. Japan—Economic conditions—21st century.
2. Japan—Social conditions—21st century.
I. Kawano, Satsuki, [date] editor of compilation.
II. Roberts, Glenda Susan, [date] editor of compilation.
III. Long, Susan Orpett, editor of compilation.
HC462.95.C365 2014
331.10952—dc23
2013031859

Designed by Julie Matsuo-Chun
Printed by Thomson-Shore, Inc.

CONTENTS

PREFACE

This book was conceived in a dark restaurant/bar on one late autumn evening in New Orleans in 2010, during the 109th American Anthropological Association (AAA) annual meeting. After a long day of attending panels, seeing colleagues, and inspecting new books, we needed to enjoy the music for which the city is known—jazz. The result was not a release from work, however. We competed with the drums and discussed what books we were using in our Japan anthropology courses. We agreed that students love narrative-driven books, yet a monograph usually focuses on a few key topics. We wanted a book that was engaging, readable, and rich in ethnographic details that covered many key topics, and it would be even better if the book consisted of never-before-published chapters. We concluded that we should create such a volume. This is the result.

This project would not have been possible without the strong support and enthusiasm of the volume's contributors—all anthropologists who study Japan but work in different parts of the world. We are fortunate to have these colleagues. We would like to express our sincere gratitude to them for sharing their passion for studying Japan and anthropology with our readers.

Earlier versions of some of the chapters were presented at the American Anthropological Association annual meeting in Montreal in 2011 and at the Association for Asian Studies annual meeting in Toronto in 2012. We would like to thank everyone who took part in the panels, attended our sessions, and provided useful comments on the presentations. We would like to express our gratitude to Dr. L. Keith Brown, who contributed to our AAA panel but who unfortunately was unable to take part in the book project. We are particularly grateful to Professor Annette Schad-Seifert of Heinrich-Heine-Universität in Duesseldorf for her insightful comments and helpful suggestions. We also appreciated the thoughtful questions raised by Dr. William Kelly during our panel presentations. The anonymous reviewers for the University of Hawaiʻi Press provided constructive comments and suggestions aimed at improving the quality of this volume. We also thank our cover photo team, James Nickum and Julian Roberts (the photographers); Catherine Miyuki Nakajima, who warmly agreed to accompany us to search for a soothsayer and have her fortune told on a wintry January night; and Ms. Mitsu Kubo, the oracle gracing our front cover, for graciously permitting us to take photos of her in action. Ms. Katsue Chiba provided the image of mothers and infants included in chapter 9. Yaesu Publishing Corporation, the publisher of *Hot-K Magazine,* kindly allowed us to use the cover image of the first issue in chapter 12. The remaining photos that accompany the individual chapters are by the contributors themselves. Bojana Ristich's careful copyediting improved the quality of this volume. Finally, we would like to thank University of Hawaiʻi Press editor Pamela Kelley, who provided encouragement and support throughout the review and publication process.

Note on Conventions

This volume follows a modified Hepburn style of Romanization of Japanese terms. Japanese names are given in the order they are used in Japan—that is, family name followed by given name. The bibliography follows standard style in the use of surnames and given names in English sources. When dollar amounts are indicated in the text, they refer to U.S. dollars in order to give a non-Japanese reader a sense of the approximate value of the yen amount at the time of the event described or at the time of the research.

INTRODUCTION

Differentiation and Uncertainty

SATSUKI KAWANO, GLENDA S. ROBERTS, AND SUSAN ORPETT LONG

How have people in Japan lived with the nation's growing instability and widening disparity during the 2000s? Japan was only beginning to recover from the economic recession of the 1990s and the effects of the bankruptcy of Lehman Brothers in 2008 when it was hit with the earthquake, tsunami, and meltdown at the Fukushima Nuclear Power Plant of March 2011. The tragedies of the tsunami and the Fukushima meltdown heightened the anxiety surrounding not only the status quo but also future directions the country might take. Politically the influence of the long-standing Liberal Democratic Party had waned, and the Democratic Party came into power, although it was unable to provide consistent leadership to guide the nation back toward prosperity. Economically Japan has seen a widening gap between the haves and have-nots, and the emerging discourse of *kakusa shakai* (disparity society) has redefined the ways in which people understand their place in society. The worldwide recession has further challenged certain practices and patterns of employment that were once considered legendary of Japan during the postwar period (1945–1989). Among these, for example, were the security of life-time employment; seniority-based wages; "corporate welfarism," such as the provision of spousal, child, and housing allowances; and bonuses and other benefits.[1] Such benefits used to be taken for granted in large firms, but in the aftermath of the economic bubble, even many large firms, which had been assumed to be unassailable, retrenched and reduced their workforces, bonuses, and benefits and drastically cut the numbers of new hires for regular employment.

1

Furthermore, there was a shift toward performance-based evaluations rather than strictly seniority-based wages (Osawa 2011), which we can see as a variant of the "self-responsibility" trend favored by government and business since the 1990s (Hook and Takeda 2007). Many firms increasingly globalized their operations, shifting production offshore to take advantage of cost savings. Employment and livelihood insecurities have hence increased steadily over the past two decades.

Recent decades have also seen a sharp increase in more precarious forms of employment, with many young people left out of stable jobs altogether and instead entering short-term contracts, dispatch work, or part-time work, none of which offer a stable livelihood (Fu 2012). These short-term, contract, dispatch, or temporary jobs—defined here as irregular or non-regular work— are characterized by low salaries, limited or no benefits, and almost no chances for advancement. Osawa (2011, 72) notes that among women, the ratio of non-regular workers to all workers rose from 32.1 percent in 1985 to 46.4 percent in 2002 to 54.2 percent in 2008. In 2011 it stood at 54.7 percent (Ministry of Health, Labor, and Welfare 2011b). For men, who have long been expected to be the main breadwinners in families, the proportion of those engaged in irregular jobs also rose, from 7.4 percent in 1985 to 11.7 percent in 2002 to 18.7 percent in 2008 (Osawa 2011). The 2011 share was 19.9 percent (Ministry of Health, Labor, and Welfare 2011b). The worldwide recession in financial markets (the so-called "Lehman Shock" in Japan) of 2008 only exacerbated these trends.

Japan's demographic decline, characterized by rapid aging and a birthrate well below replacement level, poses further challenges, such as the hollowing out of regional communities, strains on the pension system, and the looming question of health care for the growing numbers of senior citizens, including the extremely old *(chōkōrei)* (Coulmas 2007). The middle-class model of family in postwar Japan, consisting of a salaried white-collar worker/husband, a homemaker/wife, and two children, is neither easily attained nor necessarily ideal. Life courses have become increasingly diverse.

Recession, unemployment, the proliferation of precarious work, and demographic decline are problems shared by most advanced industrial societies today. But how have Japanese people in particular experienced and responded to such conditions? What opportunities and options have become available? What new identities or lifestyles have people created in an increasingly globalized Japan? What old themes and conceptions have been revived or persist in a new context? While many societies share the same challenges under globalization, one might argue that Japan's situation is more acute because of the rapid pace at which the society is aging, coupled with the fact that Japan is not a country of substantial immigration and so cannot expect an immigrant population to shore up birthrates or assist in economic revitalization or caregiving for the elderly (Roberts 2012; Vogt and Roberts 2011). All humans respond to situations based on some combination of new information, rational calculation, social relationships, and habits and values that carry symbolic meanings in their culture. Japanese today thus respond with a range of tools that incorporate past ideas and values as well as new concepts absorbed through globalization and subsequently modified to fit Japan's social and increasingly neoliberal economic environment. This book provides lively accounts of people's responses and experiences by featuring recent ethnographic research conducted during the first decade of the twenty-first century.

Toward Differentiation and Uncertainty

As we look back to the earlier postwar period of the 1960s and 1970s, we can describe the changes Japan has gone through by the 2000s as an objective and subjective shift toward differentiation and uncertainty.[2] Immediately after World War II came years of recovery, but from the late 1950s until the oil shocks of 1973–1974, the Japanese experienced an "economic miracle," with double-digit growth for much of that period, enabling the country to rapidly recover from the war and even thrive. While the oil shocks caused a slowing of growth, the economy revived and then barreled into the investment and consumption craze known as "the bubble" from the mid-1980s until the bubble collapsed in 1991. By the 1970s, backed by the strong economy, the white-collar middle-class urban model had taken a strong hold. For a man, rather than working on a family farm or in a family business, obtaining a diploma (preferably a university degree) and becoming a salaryman was the course leading to a stable lifestyle. For a woman, marrying such a man and becoming a full-time homemaker and mother of two children was seen as more desirable than joining a family farm or small business as an unpaid worker. Of course, not everyone was able to achieve such a goal, but it was the taken-for-granted standard in the mainstream society. Because of the nation's strong economy until the 1990s, the differences among classes did not become a major social issue; it was possible for blue-collar families to emulate a middle-class lifestyle, particularly if wives supplemented their husbands' incomes. The class ideology during the postwar period was that Japan was an "all-middle-class" society, and it reflected not only the society's improving economic conditions, but also minimized the differences in income, prestige, and power in pre-bubble Japan.

In contrast, present conditions in Japan can be understood in terms of the shift toward differentiation and uncertainty. The recession during and after the 1990s and the outsourcing of many manufacturing jobs decreased the number of regular jobs and replaced them with more irregular positions. It is no longer sufficient to obtain a degree from a university to find a regular job. A large number of young people cannot secure lifelong employment, thereby making it harder for them to realize the postwar ideal of salaryman or full-time homemaker. Since a stable job and a two-parent family remain desirable conditions for child rearing in Japan, lower incomes and unstable working conditions raise the bar for marriage and children. Meanwhile, the once taken-for-granted middle-class standard is increasingly being questioned. Do I really want to be a salaryman or a homemaker? What do I want to do with my life? What suits me or makes me happy? Such questions should not be dismissed as sour grapes but should be examined as emerging alternatives to the former ideals. In the current economic climate, a regular employee might be dismissed or a reputable company might go bankrupt. A homemaker might have to get a job if her husband's income is reduced. Divorce rates have risen, and marriage no longer provides "lifetime employment" to women. The middle class, which used to be backed by the thriving economy, is no longer as attainable, secure, or predictable, and this change certainly provides a context in which people have begun to reevaluate the postwar ideals. Moreover, as in other postindustrial societies (see Giddens 1991), self-realization and individuality have become much more important in today's Japan.

As noted, the growing socioeconomic disparities are commonly expressed in the discourse on *kakusa shakai,* a term that was coined during the 1990s and that had become one of the most popular expressions by 2006. *Kakusa shakai* indicates a shift in the way people think about their society, rather than strictly referring to objective structural shifts alone. In other words, as a postindustrial capitalist society, Japan has always had class stratification based upon differences in income and assets. Yet in postwar Japan, the dominant theme was that everyone belonged to the mainstream, or *ichioku sōchūryū* (Kelly 2002). Toward the end of the decade-long recession of the 1990s, there developed a recognition that the all-middle-class society had ended. *Kakusa shakai* thus conveys an amplified sense of uncertainty and insecurity.

This volume explores the diverse voices and experiences of men and women in contemporary Japan, where postwar middle-class ideals have become increasingly contested or inaccessible. The contributors draw on their rich fieldwork data to examine work, schooling, family and marital relations, child rearing, entertainment, lifestyle choices, community support, volunteering, consumption and waste, material culture, driving manners, well-being, aging, death and memorial rituals, divination, and sexuality. These topics are explored through the eyes of various social actors positioned differently in the Japanese social world, including schoolgirls, teachers, single women, career women, organic women farmers, mothers of young children, small business owners, middle-aged and older men and women, people with disabilities, and the frail elderly.

Work Conditions and Experiences

Once the economic bubble burst and ended the consumption-oriented affluence of the 1980s, Japan faced a long economic recession during the 1990s and a slow economy during the 2000s. By then, deregulation in the workplace dramatically increased the number of irregular jobs that supported the neoliberal regime, which required an ever-flexible labor force. Glenda Roberts' (chapter 1) story of Sachi, a blue-collar worker in her fifties, and her adult children in their twenties and thirties provides a stark contrast between Japan's economy before and after the long recession and its impact on working conditions and opportunities. Despite the fact that Sachi had only a middle-school education, a strong economy offered her a stable job in the early 1970s, and by working hard and well, she was able to keep it until she retired. With her husband, also a blue-collar worker with a regular job, she was able to buy a modest house and educate her children in private schools, thus achieving some aspects of a middle-class lifestyle. However, in Japan's slow economy, only one of Sachi's three adult children could find a steady job.

Despite the tougher economic climate that has overshadowed even the most well-known conglomerates, the corporate hierarchy still shapes workers' experiences in a significant way. Workers at prestigious large corporations continue to have better working conditions, higher incomes, and superb benefits, while those working for the subsidiaries and contractors of the large corporations are not so fortunate (see Kondo 1990). However, the Equal Employment Opportunity Law (EEOL), introduced in 1986, opened up career-track jobs to women. Formerly, as Sawa Kurotani notes in chapter 3, regardless of education or talent, new female recruits were given clerical-track jobs with limited opportunities for advancement; their main job was to support career-track men (see Ogasawara 1998). Although some women are still hired as clerical-track workers, others are now hired for the career track. Kurotani reveals that the corporate hierarchy has thus become more complex, involving not only a growing disparity among long-term female workers, but also a persistent inequality between male and female workers.

Employment insecurity is particularly the case for aging women workers, a situation examined by Lynne Nakano (chapter 6). There are many single women who are long-term workers in the labor force. Those in their thirties and forties during the 2000s were aware that as they aged, it would become more difficult to find a new regular job with benefits, and they keenly felt the need to keep themselves competitive by strategizing and developing new, specialized skills. In their struggles in the employment market, which continues to celebrate women's youth, docility, and ability to assist male career workers, these women have developed alternative values—"perseverance, independence, innovation, hard work, and initiative," as Nakano puts it. Many countries have experienced problems of inequality and youth unemployment during the economic downturn in recent years. In societies where timing is less emphasized, young people have a bit more flexibility in pursuing their futures. Furuichi Noritoshi notes that in Europe, young people have long had a "gap year" after graduating from university before they were expected to find work; however, Japanese young people face the (increasingly unrealistic) expectation that employment will immediately follow graduation (Furuichi and Toivonnen 2012, 20). Mary Brinton (2011) has pointed out that Japan experienced its heyday and a rapid downturn in a very short period of time. As a result, a deeper-than-normal generation gap between parents and adult children is not unusual. A newspaper article indicated that seminars are now available to parents of young people seeking jobs to give them the latest information regarding the job market (MSN Sankei News 2012). The article explained that many applicants turned down job offers from less prestigious medium-sized companies or newer, unknown companies because their parents encouraged them to reject such offers. These parents were typically the beneficiaries of the nation's past strong economy, and their expectations had not adjusted to the current reality of shrinking opportunities. We can hear the echoes of the resulting frustration in some of our chapters (e.g., chapters 1 and 2).

The decade-long recession and slow economy particularly affected young people negatively, increasing the number of "freeters" (frītā), young people in irregular employment. Some consciously took that path, while others failed to obtain stable jobs after graduation (Mathews 2003). How do young people in irregular positions see their jobs and themselves? Some of them ask an important question about personal happiness in today's Japan: Which is important—pursuing the lifestyle of a salaryman (seen as stable but uninteresting) or finding a job that is unstable and pays little but offers a promise of personal fulfillment? If one cannot have both security and personal satisfaction, one might take the latter. The personal "fit" with a job is increasingly important among young people, as shown in chapters 1, 2, and 4 below. The celebration of a personally satisfying career is not limited to young adults but is also found among some older individuals (chapter 2). While the large major companies still offer more secure jobs with superior working conditions and stability is still valued by many, as expressed by the accounts of older men and women interviewed by Gordon Mathews, doubts have also been expressed about the salaryman way of life (chapter 2). Personal satisfaction and compatibility are important not only in the choice of careers, but also in other life transitions, such as marriage and death, as we shall see below.

Some young people have consciously abandoned the middle-class mainstream path and explored new work possibilities. Nancy Rosenberger (chapter 4) describes a female organic farmer's attempt to be self-sufficient and environmentally responsible. Her lifestyle relies on a face-to-face exchange relationship with consumers, called *teikei,* and she delivers boxes of produce to customers who have signed up. Such a lifestyle not only challenges the salaryman way of life, but also contests the larger capitalist system of mass production.

While organic farming represents a radical departure from the salaryman model, Gavin Whitelaw (chapter 5) describes a less radical alternative that is still deeply embedded in the neoliberal economy: that of small business owners. Members of the merchant class in premodern Japan were historically known for their distinctive cultural ethos and pride; they lived an alternative lifestyle to that of the warrior class, which was in charge of running the local and national governments (see Umesao 1990). Theodore Bestor's classic ethnography, *Neighborhood Tokyo* (1989), delineates the ways in which postwar merchants during the late 1970s and 1980s strategically constructed "traditional" images of themselves as the old middle-class, juxtaposed against the new middle-class, the salarymen. Small-scale, self-employed business people were central to community affairs and local religious activities in neighborhood shrines until the mid-1990s (Kawano 2005; Kondo 1990). What are their lives like today? Whitelaw's account provides a glimpse into their lives in Tokyo: many specialized mom-and-pop shops used to grace Tokyo's streets in the late 1970s, but they have disappeared or turned into franchise convenience stores.

As their own bosses, small-scale business owners sometimes characterize themselves as more "independent" and "free" than their mainstream salary-man counterparts (Kawano 2005; Kondo 1990). It is not unusual for non-salarymen to criticize salarymen in order to construct a positive self-image. For example, day laborers examined by Tom Gill (2003) emphasized their "in-dependence" and "freedom," while they saw salarymen as tied down to their companies and suffering from long work hours that they could not control. Do small business owners have more "freedom"? Whitelaw reveals equally tough, or perhaps tougher, working conditions among convenience store owners in Japan's stagnant economy. By the 2000s many more convenience stores had opened, thereby increasing the competition and decreasing a store's profits. The exploitative franchise contract set by the convenience conglom-erates further decreases store owners' profits, making it harder to establish a new, successful convenience store during the 2000s. Uncertainty and inse-curity thus overshadow not only corporate workers' lives, but those of small business owners as well.

Consumption and Emerging New Services

Consumption is not simply for the meeting of daily needs; what, how, how much, how often, and why we consume reveal the social world in which we live. The flourishing of convenience stores in Tokyo's neighborhoods (chapter 5) points to fussy consumers who seek convenience, speed, and variety. Selling everything from underwear to tofu and allowing customers to send express packages, pay utility bills, and buy concert tickets, convenience stores in Japan are indeed convenient, and as such, they are as necessary as air to many peo-ple. They carry one-person food portions, thereby catering to the increasing number of single and couples-only households that do not need the larger portions sold at supermarkets. In particular, boxed meals or lunches (bentō) are extremely popular, and they account for a large share of a store's sales. Whitelaw reports that ordering too few varieties of prepared foods makes a convenience store unattractive to its customers, who look for a wide selec-tion, while ordering too much means many unsold items and reduced profits for the store owners. Store owners are forced to shoulder the cost of unsold food items under the current franchise contract. Wasteful practices are built into the state-of-the-art retail system and are thus unavoidable for the owners.

Many owners try to cut their losses by consuming expired food items or giving them to their employees, even though this is against the terms of the franchise contract.

As a business, the convenience store can be seen as the antithesis of the business model adopted by the organic farmer examined in chapter 4. As noted, she and her fellow organic farmers, who belong to the Japanese Organic Agriculture Association (JOAA), attempt to return to a local, self-sufficient economy in which people in a community grow and exchange food among themselves. It is hard to follow the JOAA ideal in a capitalist market economy. Consequently this alternative lifestyle implies living in a small house without consumer luxuries or the latest gadgets, in sharp contrast to the mainstream consumption-oriented lifestyle that many desire.

People consume not only to live, but in many cases they also live to consume. For example, young women participate in the consumer economy not only by buying cosmetics, brand-name accessories, and clothes, but also by investing in themselves to remain competitive in the job market (chapter 6). Consumption provides a way for unmarried women to construct something positive in their lives because they, unlike their married peers, are not taking care of others. Those living with their parents without making full-fledged contributions to household expenses can easily save for overseas travel or consumer luxuries. It is worth noting that single women are more often publicly criticized for their spending habits because the public feels they should be married and devoting themselves to family (Miller and Bardsley 2005; also see chapter 6). This is especially so because there is a substantial bachelor population, men in their late thirties whom these women could have married. As caring for others (in particular family members) was such a central aspect of femininity in postwar Japan (e.g., Jenike 2003; Lock 1993; Long 1996; Rosenberger 2001), it is not surprising that men are less likely to be criticized for remaining single and being dependent on their mothers for meals and other domestic tasks so long as they remain in the labor force.

Some of the consumption activities examined in this volume are individual, while others are explicitly aimed at social bonding. Laura Miller (chapter 10) describes contemporary divination, a bonding activity for making and maintaining social ties among schoolgirls and young women. There is a bewildering array of Web-based divination services, and they emphasize cute illustrations and aesthetics that appeal to young women. While older men and women also participate in divination, the new forms of divination are popular among younger women and are strategically packaged to target them. Miller notes that critics often dismiss divination as superstitious and unscientific, and its consumption is seen as a form of "addiction." Furthermore, even though the market for feminized divination is enormous, like the beauty industry (see Miller 2006), it does not receive the attention it deserves. Miller notes that the Ministry of Economy, Trade, and Industry does not even publish statistical information on the divination industry; the divination market generates some $8.5 billion per year (see also Brasor 2006). Like Nakano, therefore, Miller reveals negative views of consumption practices among women. While divination affords young women entertainment in a social setting, the consumption of a particular service or product does not necessarily produce social bonds. While the organic farmer examined in chapter 4 made an effort to form strong relationships with her clients to build an environmentally sound, self-sufficient rural community, her attempts were not always welcomed.

Joshua Roth (chapter 12) examines a new pattern of consumption among women and the use of gender metaphors in the world of automobiles. Since the late 1960s the number of female drivers has grown—from 17 percent of all drivers in 1969 to 42 percent by 2004—and it has made K-cars (*keijidōsha*, lightweight, small cars) popular. One might imagine that as driving was formerly a masculine activity, the increase of female drivers would have led to more gender-neutral images of driving. On the contrary: there developed feminized car interiors and driving manners. Women personalize their K-cars by adding pink and frilly décor and use them to fulfill their domestic duties, such as shopping for groceries or transporting children. Roth argues that the popularity of the K-car among women drivers in contemporary Japan thus fails to destabilize the mainstream gender ideology that assigns domestic roles to women and public roles to men.

Several chapters in this volume touch upon services for the socially dependent. Peter Cave (chapter 11) discusses the persisting popularity of private tutorial services and test preparation programs (*juku*). The dual education structure common in postwar Japan, consisting of regular schools and private after-school academic programs (see Rohlen 1980), has continued. Some of these programs are intended to help slower learners (also see chapter 1), while others aim to prepare students for high school or university entrance examinations. Cave notes that a typical exam-focused program for middle-school students, with three to five lessons per week, may cost ¥25,000–35,000 per month ($300–420 at $1 = ¥80). The market for after-school academic programs and tutoring is vast.

Compared with tutoring and after-school academic programs for school-age children, paid child care for preschool children is not as widespread. Kawano (chapter 9) has found that mothers of preschoolers in Tokyo are reluctant to use non-family caregivers. This reluctance is shaped in part by the state's definition of mainstream child care, offered at public child care institutions *(hoikuen)*, and in part by its limited availability; municipalities determine whether or not a child needs institutional care by evaluating, for example, his or her parents' working conditions and the availability of co-resident caregivers. Child care is provided to those who qualify rather than being chosen and obtained freely by consumers. Furthermore, perhaps it is considered acceptable to have tutors teach children in their homes while parents (or really mothers) watch over the children, but a paid babysitter—in particular a non-family caregiver—is not considered an acceptable substitute for a mother.

Unlike child care, however, elder care by non-family caregivers at home has become socially accepted and much more widespread in twenty-first-century Japan than in the past, when elder care too was a family member's—usually a daughter-in-law's—duty. However, the deregulation of social welfare diversified elder-care services during the 1980s (Adachi 2000). With the creation of a public long-term care insurance program *(kaigo hoken)* in 2000, older persons can obtain non-family care more easily as choosers of elder-care services rather than dependent receivers of welfare support. In contrast to child care, then, elder care by non-family caregivers has come to have a more neutral image (Jenike 2003; Kawano 2010). Despite these new developments, non-family care assistants have not completely replaced family caregivers, as allowing the elderly to live independently without family support was not the primary goal of the long-term care insurance. Nonetheless, the care insurance is intended to offer non-family support to those who are still able to live independently and to provide relief for co-resident family caregivers. (For recent studies of elder care and the long-term care insurance program, see, for example, Long 2008 and Long et al. 2009).

New services have also been developed for the ritual care of the deceased. Older persons commonly wish to avoid an overdependence on family as they age (Long 2005; Traphagan 2000; Wu 2004; also see chapter 13), and some also wish to avoid overburdening family members after their deaths (Kawano 2010). By the 2000s, new burial systems had evolved to assist those without descendants or who did not wish to depend on family caregivers to maintain their graves. These new options are provided by religious and non-profit organizations, and Kawano (chapter 13) examines one such system, ash scattering. In the late postwar period conventional internment typically required a family grave, which ideally accommodated the cremated remains of generations of married couples. In this system, only one child, or the successor (most likely the eldest son), remains in the natal family to perpetuate the family line by taking an in-marrying spouse, while non-succeeding children marry into their marital families, are adopted into other families, or form new branch families. Thus in a family grave, there should be remains for one married couple in each generation, although it sometimes accommodates a couple's deceased unmarried children. A family grave would be passed on to the successor, who would pay annual fees and hold memorial anniversary rites (typically Buddhist) to transform the deceased into benevolent ancestors. A grave without a family caretaker would be abolished, and the dead would become pitiable homeless souls. Due to demographic shifts, many elderly persons today have no culturally preferred successors who can continue to venerate the family dead. A married adult son who has a son is an ideal successor, while a son without children, a married-out daughter who took her husband's family name, and unmarried adult children are not considered preferred successors. Thus older persons' choices in mortuary matters must be understood in the current social and demographic context, where conventional practices no longer provide a sense of certainty and security.

The recent developments in expanded support services for the elderly to some extent parallel advances in support services for people with disabilities. As in the case of the elderly, although there are paid non-family attendants, people with disabilities are often cared for by family members. To reduce the sense of dependence, people with disabilities are encouraged to see their attendants as their arms and legs. They should not feel they have to thank their attendants every time they receive help, for example, with eating or having their wheelchair pushed. Yet Karen Nakamura asks (in chapter 8) whether people with disabilities have the right to receive assistance to meet their sexual needs. Formerly they were assumed to be asexual. The 2000s saw lively public debates concerning the sexual identities of people with disabilities.

Life Courses: Education, Marriage, and Aging

What changes have occurred in life course transitions in contemporary Japan? Among the major phases of life, the transition to school is still taken for granted, yet the average duration of schooling has grown longer, and the quality of one's post-secondary education has become even more important in making a successful transition to work. Unlike in the early postwar period, when the number of university graduates was comparatively small, by the 2000s the ma-jority of high school graduates proceeded to a post-secondary education. Such a step became possible in part following the establishment of more lower-level junior colleges and universities whose diplomas were of limited value on the job market (see chapters 1 and 11). In the current competitive job market, with a decreasing number of permanent, career-track jobs, a diploma from a mediocre university does not guarantee a regular job. Furthermore, with the EEOL educational credentials are now relevant to women as well; indeed going to a good high school and getting a degree from a prestigious university are much more important for female corporate workers, some of whom re-main employed until they retire (see chapter 3).[3]

How have school curricula and pedagogical approaches shifted? Cave shows that in the past twenty-five years several attempts have been made to change the educational system in Japan (chapter 11). To "internationalize" stu-dents, a limited number of English lessons were introduced in the primary schools, and to encourage exploratory, individualized learning, the number of hours spent on academics was reduced. However, declining scores in inter-national academic attainment tests led to a reconsideration of reduced hours; these were again increased (but not entirely). Small class sizes and differenti-ated learning via proficiency groups were also introduced in a limited man-ner. Despite these attempts at change, however, Cave maintains that a strik-ing number of practices have endured since the late postwar period. Primary schools continue to provide opportunities for learning in academics as well as socialization, centering on group participation and cooperation. In junior high schools, working together continues to be important, and despite the in-troduction of small class sizes and differentiated learning, students most likely experience little differentiation through their nine years of compulsory edu-cation. Some high schools use competitive exams to select talented students who want to get into the nation's most prestigious universities, while others (usually private) employ interviews and other methods to admit students re-gardless of their academic record. At the same time, graduates are ranked ac-cording to the schools they attended, a factor that in turn largely shapes their occupational choices and life trajectories.

Just because some pedagogical approaches persist does not imply that the meaning and value of schooling have stayed more or less the same. The me-dia have sensationalized students who refuse to attend school and problema-tized the *hikikomori*, or the young people who have socially withdrawn (see Borovoy 2008). In the postwar middle-class ideal, schooling was the path to mainstream success. Given the recognition of disparity and the declining value of a college degree in the job market, it is not surprising to find that some students are not motivated to do well. Cave makes the point that rather than looking ahead, the Japanese educational system has been driven by a longing for the idealized past.

During the 2000s, the transition from school to work, as well as to marriage and childbirth, has not occurred in some people's lives. Previous studies conducted during the 1970s and the 1980s (see Plath 1980) examined age-related ideologies defining life course transitions and the narrow age ranges for each life transition that were culturally acceptable. These studies noted that women were pressured to marry before they reached the age of twenty-five (see Brinton 1992). This was a culturally constructed "cutoff" date, after which, like Christmas cakes that are no longer desired after December 25, women became unwanted marital partners. However, the average age for first marriage has risen dramatically: from 24.2 to 28.8 years for women and 27.2 to 30.5 years for men between 1965 and 2010 (Cabinet Office 2011). Consequently, the proportion of unmarried people in the life stage formerly associated with childbearing and child rearing has increased dramatically. For example, in 2005, 32 percent of women aged between thirty and thirty-four and 18.4 percent of women between thirty-five and thirty-nine remained unmarried, as did 47.1 percent of men between thirty and thirty-four and 30 percent of men between thirty-five and thirty-nine (Cabinet Office 2011). Despite such changes, the age-related ideologies persist to some extent, and now thirty is considered a new "cutoff" date for single women, as evidenced by Lynne Nakano's account in chapter 6. The difference today, however, is that an increasing number of women never transition to wife- or motherhood.

While many single women are interested in marriage, compatibility with one's partner has become highly valued, and they are not willing to compromise (see chapters 3, 4, and 6). In their mothers' time, marriage was seen as a woman's permanent job and marrying a salaryman was the ideal. Today, however, marriage is not the only path, and an increasing number of women remain in the corporate world as long-term workers. Moreover, as divorce rates rise and men's jobs in the post-bubble economy are not as secure as they used to be, marriage no longer provides a permanent position for a woman (Ochiai 1997). In this context, young people have developed alternative values. Nakano states that the "personalities" *(hitogara)* of husbands matter a great deal to women, and they are not willing to marry unless a potential partner is "appropriate."

Some older people also value compatibility, companionship, and communication in marriage in today's Japan, as Gordon Mathews indicates (chapter 2). Personality and value differences, as well as inadequate financial support from husbands, are reasons for divorce. Marriages are no longer satisfactory when husbands and wives simply fulfill the social roles of breadwinner and homemaker, as defined in a social contract, and lead relatively separate lives (Alexy 2011; Borovoy 2005; Nakano 2011). Due to this shift in ideals, the couples described in Mathews' chapter seem disenchanted after years of marriage. In contrast, Roberts (chapter 1) examines a couple with a close, loving relationship at a time when marriage was seen as a social contract. It is thus important to note that the quality of marital relations varies, and we need further in-depth research on the variations.

In the early 1990s, Japanese women tended to hold a series of non-overlapping roles, moving sequentially from student to worker to homemaker (see Brinton 1992). In the twenty-first century, despite the growing number of women in the workforce, many women still prefer not to be students and mothers at the same time or full-time workers and mothers at the same time, particularly when their children are young. Student, worker, and mother are all full-time "occupations," and a person is expected to fully devote oneself to each job. A married man, too, is primarily seen as a breadwinner by his employer and co-workers, and his participation in family life is consequently limited. Such postwar middle-class expectations are still alive in the 2000s. Long work hours are taken for granted, making it difficult for regular employees to balance family and work. The media often state that more women work today, but this does not imply that there are more married women with children in regular employment. A more accurate picture is the bifurcation of women into unmarried, full-time workers and mothers with part-time or irregular employment. A mother should primarily mother, at least when her children are young, and if she also works, ideally the work should not interfere with her primary role of nurturing her children.

The expectation that a mother should devote herself fully to child rearing continues to discourage women from staying in the labor force during the child-rearing years. Kawano (chapter 9) examines some of the consequences for a woman in the transition from a full-time worker to a stay-at-home mother; among these are social isolation and a need to build a network of child-rearing support. As their husbands often work long work hours and non-family babysitters are neither common nor popular (Holthus 2011), metropolitan mothers are usually left with only their own mothers, if available, to count on. (In a way, the situation of new mothers that Kawano examines is similar to that of new retirees: they lack a strong peer network and reciprocal support [see chapter 2.) To improve the child-rearing environment and reduce the social isolation, in 2002 the state initiated *tsudoi no hiroba jigyō*, or the drop-in play centers project, for parents and preschoolers. By creating these centers, the state aimed to address the major demographic problem of declining fertility rates. Hovering around 1.3 children per woman for the past several years, low fertility rates are seen to threaten the long-term stability of Japan's social security. However, the current structure of employment continues to assume that it is men who are first of all full-fledged workers. Kawano maintains that the development of new community-based child-rearing support systems among women, therefore, does not destabilize the persistent gender asymmetry that assigns them a domestic role, volunteer work, or irregular employment.

As life courses have become differentiated, household composition has become more diverse as well. For example, the number of single-person households almost doubled between 1975 and 2009, from approximately 6 million to 12 million, and the proportion of such households increased from 18.2 percent to 24.9 percent (Ministry of Health, Labor, and Welfare 2011a). Moreover, as marriage rates are lower now, households consisting of parents and their unmarried adult children have also become more common. The adults living with their parents, who often fail to make adequate contributions to household expenses, are seen negatively as "parasite singles," a widely used disparaging term coined by the sociologist Yamada Masahiro (1999) that the media used to capture the phenomenon. Yet the prolonged dependency on parents by adult children must be understood in the increasingly precarious labor market, where the number of regular jobs has decreased. Several chapters in this volume include examples of single adult children still living with their parents, some of them already middle-aged (chapters 1, 2, and 6).

Households that include older adults have also become more diverse. Older adults, who commonly co-resided with an adult child in three-generational households in early postwar Japan, are now less likely to live in such households. In 2001, the International Survey of Lifestyles and Attitudes of the Elderly indicated that 22 percent of those aged sixty and older lived in three-generational households (compared with 2 percent in the United States) (Ogawa, Retherford, and Matsukura 2006), but the proportion of the elderly so doing had markedly declined from 37 percent in 1981. Three-generational households have not disappeared, but their proportion has markedly declined from 16.9 percent in 1975 to 8.4 percent in 2009 (Ministry of Health, Labor, and Welfare 2011a). As discussed in chapter 13, many older adults now prefer not to live with their adult children's families. Nonetheless, when older people become too frail or ill to manage on their own, the expectation remains strong that they will be cared for by a family member living in the same household. In 2005 approximately three out of four primary caregivers for the elderly were still family members, and two-thirds of them were living with the elderly person in their charge (Maruyama 2006, 52–53). With demographic and cultural changes, family caregivers are more diverse in the 2000s, with wives, husbands, sons, and daughters (rather than only daughters-in-law) more often giving hands-on care (Long 2008). In recent years an elderly person has been more likely to receive care from his or her spouse as prolonged life expectancies have contributed to the co-survivorship of older couples (Ogawa, Retherford, and Matsukura 2006). Unmarried women living with aging parents sometimes express concern about future care for their co-residing parents, reflecting the diversification of caregivers during the 2000s (e.g., see chapters 3 and 6).

Longer life expectancies allow a growing number of older persons to get to know their grandchildren and potentially even great-grandchildren as individuals. Susan Long (chapter 7) explores how the meaning of grandchildren and grandparents has changed in a society where life expectancies are exceptionally long and a growing number of the elderly live away from their adult children and grandchildren. She finds that the frequency and quality of interactions vary greatly; a few grandparents rarely see their grandchildren, while others are involved in their lives. Frequent interaction does not necessarily lead to strong bonds between them, however. At times frequent encounters led to a criticism of the grandchildren, but grandparents who were actively engaged with their grandchildren tended to have closer relationships with them. Grandparents had more positive ties with grandchildren if they had taken care of them when they were young, had grandchildren who visited informally rather than only formally on holidays, or traveled with them. However, the grandchildren also reminded the elderly that the world had changed around them. The grandchildren were more materialistic, had different tastes in food, preferred different TV shows, and had different ideas about free time. Nevertheless, the grandchildren were often sources of great pleasure and provided the grandparents with a significant sense of continuity in twenty-first-century Japan.

As life courses have become increasingly diverse, the posthumous trajectories have as well. In postwar Japan, the living family members' ritual efforts and maintenance of a family grave were essential to ensure the peaceful rest of the deceased. However, Kawano (chapter 13) describes the rise of a new mortuary practice of ash scattering, which enables a deceased-to-be to ensure his or her peaceful rest embraced in nature, rather than having his or her remains interred in a conventional family grave—the ideal destination for the postwar middle class.

In summary, the chapters in this volume collectively reveal the questioning of postwar middle-class ideals and the exploration of new identities as well as some enduring practices and values maintained through people's daily lives during the 2000s. The voices in these pages are diverse in gender, social class, occupations, and generations. It is hoped that through this rich diversity one can glimpse the cultural resources people use as they craft new means to adjust and live in these challenging times.

Notes on Research Methods

Many scholars in social and cultural anthropology, in which all the contributors to this volume specialize, value both in-depth qualitative data collected during fieldwork and individual interviews. Anthropological fieldwork typically consists of firsthand observations of people's behavior in natural social settings. This method is known as participant observation. If an anthropologist wants to study the importance of dance in a particular culture, he or she will conduct participant observation by going to a dance hall to collect data. He or she will observe dancers and talk to them. The researcher will even try to learn the latest steps from the dancers. When a researcher finds some aspects of the culture puzzling, he or she will ask informants about them. The researcher is thus a participant-learner who engages in a social situation. The process of anthropological fieldwork is to some extent similar to a child's being socialized in a given cultural setting. Socialization results in the accumulation of knowledge through concrete, face-to-face interactions in various social contexts. To some extent an anthropologist acquires knowledge about a culture in a similar way, though there are a number of important differences between the two modes of learning. For example, unlike with the socialization of a child, the process of participant observation is not meant to make the researcher a full-fledged member of the society he or she is studying. The researcher is more self-consciously involved in social situations to gather data and make sense of them.

In-depth interviews are well suited to explore people's experiences and perceptions of the world. For example, what does it mean for a woman to remain single in her thirties? By interviewing (say) forty unmarried Japanese women in that age group, an anthropologist can gain a complex, situated account. Unlike survey results from a large, nationally representative sample, the researcher cannot use the results of in-depth interviews with a relatively small sample to make generalizations about single women in Japan. Nonetheless, qualitative interviews offer rich, nuanced data that large-scale surveys cannot easily provide. By using observational and interview data, the contributors to this volume thus convey concrete, rich examples of people's real-life engagements and struggles.

Notes for Instructors

This book contains thirteen chapters, divided into five sections. Chapters that address certain similar themes are grouped together, although except for chapters 1 and 2, which shed light on long-term changes, it is not necessary to assign the chapters sequentially. To facilitate the adoption of this volume for the teaching of Japan-related classes, the following provides the key themes covered in each chapter.

Chapter 1 (Roberts): economic change, family, work conditions and opportunities, blue-collar employees, marriage, cultural capital, class reproduction, parent-child relations

Chapter 2 (Mathews): marital satisfaction, marital ideals, men's experiences, aging, retirement, divorce, religion, disability, child rearing

Chapter 3 (Kurotani): the bubble generation, female corporate workers, the EEOL, career women, gender and work, *habitus*

Chapter 4 (Rosenberger): organic farming, women farmers, alternative lifestyles, resistance, identity, food safety, environment

Chapter 5 (Whitelaw): work culture, moral economy, convenience stores, small-scale business owners and retail systems, consumerism, loss and waste, prepared foods, urban lifestyles

Chapter 6 (Nakano): single women, employment opportunities and strategies, marriage opportunities and choices, meanings of singlehood, values, life courses

Chapter 7 (Long): grandparents, grandchildren, generational relations, aging, longevity, the frail elderly, elder care

Chapter 8 (Nakamura): sexuality, sexual services, people with disabilities, prostitution, men with physical disabilities, welfare organizations, volunteering

Chapter 9 (Kawano): child-rearing support, young mothers, preschoolers, metropolitan communities, social networks, non-profit organizations, female volunteers

Chapter 10 (Miller): divination, the occult, young women and girls, social bonding, entertainment, consumption, technology, communication

Chapter 11 (Cave): education, elementary schools, middle schools, high schools, private tutorial and test preparation programs, academics, moral values, socialization, pedagogy, curriculum changes, educational reforms

Chapter 12 (Roth): car culture, K-cars, gendered driving manners, driving metaphors, femininity, masculinity, structuralism

Chapter 13 (Kawano): mortuary rites; ancestors; ash-scattering ceremonies; dependence and late adulthood; the elderly living alone; attitudes toward death, family ties, and burial; attitudes toward religion; afterlives

We intend this volume to be read by students in tandem with recently published handbooks, ethnographies, and collections on aspects of life in contemporary Japan. Chapters from this book could be assigned to complement these other books in order to give students a feel for the people behind the sociological narratives. In recent years several handbooks on contemporary Japan have been published, systematically explicating various facets of social life today (for instance, Bestor et al., *Routledge Handbook of Japanese Culture and Society,* and Robertson, *A Companion to the Anthropology of Japan*). There are also several multi-author volumes that deal with various issues facing Japanese society today, such as Mathews and White, *Japan's Changing Generations;* Matanle and Lunsing, *Perspectives on Work, Employment and Society in Japan;* Hashimoto and Traphagan, *Imagined Families, Lived Families;* Ishida and Slater, *Social Class in Contemporary Japan;* and Ronald and Alexy, *Home and Family in Japan.* In *Capturing Contemporary Japan,* social transformation during a time of increasing globalization and challenging economic circumstances is the plumb line, while the topics covered vary depending on the ethnographic research of each author. The volume strives to provide a slide show of people in diverse positions during the first decade of the twenty-first century, but it does not attempt to cover all the major themes or topics important to contemporary Japan. For instance, in recent years, Japan has seen an increase in international marriages, as well as in its resident foreign population. While accounts of these groups are certainly important, we ask readers to visit other works, such as Willis and Murphy-Shigematsu, *Transcultural Japan,* in order to understand these populations. In a way *Capturing Contemporary Japan* is reminiscent of Imamura's *Re-imaging Japanese Women* as it attempts to highlight the diverse experiences of Japanese people during the 2000s, although there are a number of differences in scope and approach. Gender is not the primary focus of this volume, although many chapters attempt to provide gendered accounts as well as age- and class-sensitive accounts of people's experiences. None of the chapters in the volume are reprints; all are newly crafted to feature ethnographic data collected during the 2000s.

Notes

1. Osawa (2011) points out that no more than 20 percent of Japanese employees benefited from lifetime employment, but the large firms that offered it became icons of the economic stability and success of the country.
2. The postwar period in Japan often refers to the period from the end of World War II to 1989.
3. Formerly, as discussed above, women exited the world of work to marry, and a woman's status was measured to some extent by the socioeconomic position of her husband. Therefore her educational capital was less directly tied to her status.

References Cited

Adachi, Kiyoshi. 2000. "The Development of Social Welfare Services in Japan." In *Caring for the Elderly in Japan and the U.S.,* ed. Susan O. Long, 191–205. London: Routledge.

Alexy, Allison. 2011. "The Door My Wife Closed: Houses, Families, and Divorce in Contemporary Japan." In *Home and Family in Japan: Continuity and Transformation,* ed. Richard Ronald and Allison Alexy, 236–253. London: Routledge.

Bestor, Theodore. 1990. *Neighborhood Tokyo.* Stanford, CA: Stanford University Press.

Bestor, Victoria, Theodore C. Bestor, and Akiko Yamagata. 2011. *Routledge Handbook of Japanese Culture and Society.* Abingdon, Oxon: Routledge.

Borovoy, Amy. 2005. *The Too-Good Wife: Alcohol, Codependency, and the Politics of Nurturance in Postwar Japan.* Berkeley: University of California Press.

———. 2008. "Japan's Hidden Youths: Mainstreaming the Emotionally Distressed in Japan." *Culture, Medicine, and Psychiatry* 32, no. 4:552–576.

Brasor, Phillip. 2006. "Weekly Magazines Joust over Trillion-Yen Fortune Telling Trade." *Japan Times,* March 12. Http://www.japantimes.co.jp/news/2006/03/12/ national/ weekly-magazines-joust-over-trillion-yen-fortunetelling-trade/#. UUS18hmkAhs. Accessed May 13, 2013.

Brinton, Mary. 1992. "Christmas Cakes and Wedding Cakes: The Social Organization of Japanese Women's Life Course." In *Japanese Social Organization,* ed. Takie S. Lebra, 79–108. Honolulu: University of Hawai'i Press.

———. 2011. *Lost in Transition: Youth, Work and Instability in Postindustrial Japan.* Cambridge: Cambridge University Press.

Cabinet Office, Government of Japan. 2011. *Heisei 23-nendoban kodomo kosodate hakusho* (White paper on children and child rearing). Http://www8. cao.go.jp/ shoushi/whitepaper/ w-2011/23webhonpen/html/b1_s2–1–2.html. Accessed July 12, 2012.

Coulmas, Florian. 2007. *Population Decline and Ageing in Japan: The Social Consequences.* London: Routledge.

Fu, Huiyan. 2012. *An Emerging Non-Regular Labour Force in Japan: The Dignity of Dispatched Workers.* London and New York: Routledge.

Furuichi, Noritoshi, and Tuuka Toivonen. 2012. "'Shizukana henkakusha' ga shakai o kaeru" ("Quiet revolutionaries" will change society). *Kotoba* 8 (Summer): 16–21.

Giddens, Anthony. 1991. *Modernity and Self-Identity: Self and Society in the Late Modern Age.* Stanford, CA: Stanford University Press.

Gill, Tom. 2003. "When Pillars Evaporate." In *Men and Masculinities in Contemporary Japan,* ed. James Roberson and Nobue Suzuki, 144–161. London: RoutledgeCurzon.

Hashimoto, Akiko, and John Traphagan, eds. 2008. *Imagined Families, Lived Families: Culture and Kinship in Contemporary Japan.* Albany: State University of New York Press.

Holthus, Barbara. 2011. "Child Care and Work-Life Balance in Low Fertility Japan." In *Imploding Populations in Japan and Germany: A Comparison,* ed. Florian Coulmas and Ralph Lüzeler, 203–226. Leiden and Boston: Brill.

Hook, Glen D., and Hiroko Takeda. 2007. "Self-Responsibility and the Nature of the Postwar Japanese State: Risk through the Looking Glass." *Journal of Japanese Studies* 3, no. 1:93–123.

Imamura, Anne, ed. 1996. *Re-imaging Japanese Women.* Berkeley: University of California Press.

Ishida, Hiroshi, and David H. Slater, eds. 2010. *Social Class in Contemporary Japan: Structures, Sorting, and Strategies.* London: Routledge.

Jenike, Brenda Robb. 2003. "Parent Care and Shifting Family Obligations in Urban Japan." In *Demographic Change and the Family in Japan's Aging Society,* ed. John Traphagan and John Knight, 177–201. Albany: State University of New York Press.

Kawano, Satsuki. 2005. *Ritual Practice in Modern Japan.* Honolulu: University of Hawai'i Press.

———. 2010. *Nature's Embrace: Japan's Aging Urbanites and New Death Rites.* Honolulu: University of Hawai'i Press.

Kelly, William W. 2002. "At the Limits of New Middle-Class Japan: Beyond 'Mainstream Consciousness.'" In *Social Contracts under Stress: The Middle Classes of America, Europe and Japan at the Turn of the Century,* ed. Olivier Zunz, Leonard Schoppa, and Nobuhiro Hiwatari, 232–254. New York: Russell Sage Foundation.

Kondo, Dorinne K. 1990. *Crafting Selves*. Chicago: University of Chicago Press.
Lock, Margaret. 1993. *Encounters with Aging: Mythologies of Menopause in Japan and North America*. Berkeley: University of California Press.
Long, Susan Orpett. 1996. "Nurturing and Femininity: The Impact of the Ideal of Caregiving in Postwar Japan." In Imamura, *Re-imaging Japanese Women*, 156–176.
———. 2005. *Final Days: Japanese Culture and Choice at the End of Life*. Honolulu: University of Hawai'i Press.
———. 2008. "Someone's Old, Something's New, Someone's Borrowed, Someone's Blue: Changing Elder Care at the Turn of the 21st Century." In Hashimoto and Traphagan, *Imagined Families, Lived Families*, 137–157.
Long, Susan Orpett, Ruth Campbell, and Chie Nishimura. 2009. "Does It Matter Who Cares? A Comparison of Daughters versus Daughters-in-Law in Japanese Elder Care." *Social Science Japan Journal* 12, no. 1:1–21.
Maruyama Katsura. 2006. "Kazoku kaigo no shakai hyōka to kaigo hoken riyō jōkyō no yōin bunseki" (Social evaluations of family caregiving and the factors related to the use of long-term nursing insurance). In *Kazoku no henyō to jendā* (Changing families and gender), ed. Tomita Takeshi and Ri Jonfa, 51–73. Tokyo: Seikei University Center for Asian and Pacific Studies.
Matanle, Peter, and Wim Lunsing, eds. 2006. *Perspectives on Work, Employment and Society in Japan*. New York: Palgrave Macmillan.
Mathews, Gordon. 2003. "Seeking a Career, Finding a Job: How Young People Enter and Resist the Japanese World of Work." In *Japan's Changing Generations: Are Young People Creating a New Society?*, ed. Gordon Mathews and Bruce White, 121–136. London: RoutledgeCurzon.
Mathews, Gordon, and Bruce White, eds. 2003. *Japan's Changing Generations*. London: RoutledgeCurzon.
Miller, Laura. 2006. *Beauty Up: Exploring Contemporary Japanese Body Aesthetics*. Berkeley: University of California Press.
Miller, Laura, and Jan Bardsley, eds. 2005. *Bad Girls of Japan*. New York: Palgrave Macmillan.
Ministry of Health, Labor, and Welfare. 2011a. *Kōseirōdō hakusho* (Ministry of Health, Labor, and Welfare white paper). Http://www.mhlw.go.jp/wp/hakusyo/kousei/11-2/kousei-data/pdfNFindex.html. Accessed June 13, 2012.
———. 2011b. *Hataraku josei no jitsujō* (Current conditions of working women). Http://www.mhlw.go.jp/stf/houdou/ 2r9852000002eac3.pdf. Accessed June 20, 2012.
MSN Sankei News. 2012. "Ko no shūshoku, oya ga samatage, shūkatsu ni ihen? Hogosha muke seminā zokuzoku" (Parents make it more difficult for their adult child to find a job: What is happening to the job-hunting process? Many more job-hunting seminars for guardians). February 28. Http://sankei.jp.msn.com/ economy/news/120229/ biz12022906440027-n1.htm. Accessed July 12, 2012.
Nakano, Lynne Y. 2011. "Working and Waiting for an 'Appropriate Person': How Single Women Support and Resist Family in Japan." In *Home and Family in Japan: Continuity and Transformation*, ed. Richard Ronald and Allison Alexy, 131–151. London: Routledge.
Ochiai, Emiko. 1997. *The Japanese Family System in Transition: A Sociological Analysis of Family Change in Postwar Japan*. Tokyo: LTCB International Library Foundation.

Ogasawara, Yūko. 1998. *Office Ladies and Salaried Men: Power, Gender, and Work in Japanese Companies*. Berkeley: University of California Press.

Ogawa, Naohiro, Robert D. Retherford, and Rikiya Matsukura. 2006. "Demographics of the Japanese Family: Entering Uncharted Territory." In *The Changing Japanese Family*, ed. Marcus Rebick and Ayumi Takenaka, 19–38. New York: Routledge.

Osawa, Mari. 2011. *Social Security in Contemporary Japan*. London and New York: Routledge. University of Tokyo Series.

Plath, David W. 1980. *Long Engagements: Maturity in Modern Japan*. Stanford, CA: Stanford University Press.

Roberts, Glenda S. 2012. "Vocalizing the 'I' Word: Proposals and Initiatives on Immigration to Japan from the LDP and Beyond." *Asien* 124 (July), S: 48–68.

Robertson, Jennifer. 2005. *A Companion to the Anthropology of Japan*. Oxford: Blackwell.

Rohlen, Thomas P. 1980. "The *Juku* Phenomenon." *Journal of Japanese Studies* 6, no. 2:207–42.

Ronald, Richard, and Allison Alexy, eds. 2010. *Home and Family in Japan: Continuity and Transformation*. New York: Routledge.

Rosenberger, Nancy. 2001. *Gambling with Virtue: Japanese Women and the Search for Self in a Changing Nation*. Honolulu: University of Hawai'i Press.

Traphagan, John. 2000. *Taming Oblivion: Aging Bodies and the Fear of Senility in Japan*. Albany: State University of New York Press.

Umesao, Tadao. 1990. *The Roots of Contemporary Japan*. Tokyo: Japan Forum.

Vogt, Gabriele, and Glenda S. Roberts, eds. 2011. *Migration and Integration: Japan in Comparative Perspective*. Munich: Iudicium.

Willis, David B., and Stephen Murphy-Shigematsu, eds. 2008. *Transcultural Japan*. Abingdon, Oxon: Routledge.

Wu, Yongmei. 2004. *The Care of the Elderly in Japan*. London: RoutledgeCurzon.

Yamada, Masahiro. 1999. *Parasaito shinguru no jidai* (The age of parasite singles). Tokyo: Chikuma Shobō.

Change Over Time

Part I introduces readers to the long-term socioeconomic shift since the 1980s through the eyes of the Fujiis, a blue-collar family living in Kansai and studied by Glenda Roberts (chapter 1), and middle-aged and older people studied by Gordon Mathews (chapter 2). Both scholars reinterviewed those who had participated in their earlier studies, thus giving a depth to their informants' accounts.

Glenda Roberts examines the marriage and work experiences of her female informant, Sachi, who is in her fifties. Hers is not a typical middle-class family, yet in the strong economy Sachi and her husband held regular jobs and achieved a secure lifestyle: they bought a house, sent their children to private schools, and qualified for pensions. Their three children (in their twenties and thirties), however, did not obtain regular high-paying jobs in the downward economy, even though they had more education than their parents.

Gordon Mathews explores the concept of manhood among his informants. For many of them work used to be the primary source of manhood twenty some years ago, but it is no longer sufficient for men to financially support their families to have fulfilling, satisfying lives. Communication and sharing the same values and interests with one's spouse have become much more important in the 2000s.

When reading chapter 1, which portrays a couple in a close, loving relationship, in tandem with chapter 2, wherein couples seem aloof, embittered, and disenchanted after years of marriage, one might wonder about the reasons for the differences. While it is tempting to try to draw conclusions, we feel it is difficult to do so given that we have no other detailed samples in our research of happily married couples with strong families and enduring ties. Suffice it to say that there are such couples out there, and Sachi's family is proof of it.

CHAPTER 1

Work and Life in Challenging Times

A Kansai Family Across the Generations

GLENDA S. ROBERTS

JAPAN HAS UNDERGONE many changes in the past thirty years. It became affluent in these years but then faced a huge economic downturn with the bursting of its property bubble in 1991 and again with the world financial crisis (known in Japan as the "Lehman Shock") in 2008. With the increasing costs of producing goods domestically, many large firms fled offshore. In 1999, many kinds of jobs were deregulated, a move that enabled firms to hire more people for more insecure positions at lower wages and with fewer or no benefits. Youth now struggle to find stable employment. These trends have caused a great deal of anxiety, as middle-aged people wonder whether their children will be able to maintain the stable and comfortable environment that they themselves afforded. The family I introduce in this chapter has come through this era. We find in it a portrait of how one nuclear family of blue-collar workers has lived the past three decades, experiencing upward mobility in the early years, as well as instability in the later years, compounded by the death of the husband/father, the early retirement from regular employment of the wife/mother, and the economic instability of the children as they try to establish themselves in a downward-facing economy. I begin with a central focus on the work and family history of Sachi, the mother, followed by accounts of the children's educational trajectories, occupational attainments, and values.

Although we cannot generalize the experiences of this one family to all Japanese families of the recent past decades, case studies provide us a rich context from which to make sense of people's lives.[1] As much as possible, I will point out how this family, the Fujiis, resembles or differs from other families. Above all, through the family members' narratives, we can discern what their lifestyle has been and what sorts of decisions they have made as they lived through a period that has brought opportunities as well as uncertainty and challenges. I have known this family, in particular Fujii Sachi, since I started my doctoral research of the Azumi lingerie factory in Kansai in 1983–1985. We are the same age (b. 1955), and she was kind and accepting of me from the beginning of my study there. We have kept up some correspondence and have met each other on an occasional basis in the ensuing years. When I asked her if I could interview her and her children for this mini-study, the Fujiis held a "family conference" and agreed. Although I knew about some of the major events in Sachi's life—the births of her children, her husband Masaji's chronic kidney illness and subsequent death in his early fifties, and her own early retirement from the firm at age fifty—I was not cognizant of the details. We did our interviews seated around a low table on Sachi's living room floor, in full view of a portrait of her deceased husband hanging above a small altar. Inside the frame of her husband's formal portrait, Sachi had tucked a picture of herself and her husband when they were quite young, standing in front of a cool-looking car. He is looking entirely happy, with his beautiful girl by his side. It was under these images that we conducted all of our interviews, and I could not help but feel the strong legacy of Fujii Masaji in all of our ensuing conversations.

In many ways, the Fujiis provide an atypical portrait of a blue-collar Japanese family. They worked for large and stable companies (while the majority of the populace works for medium-to-small enterprises with much less stability), and Sachi remained at her regular job throughout a long career despite marriage and childbirth (while the majority of women, then and now, quit by the birth of the first child).[2] From the Fujiis' accounts, we can learn a lot about the nature of the workplace and the challenges it presented. We can glimpse a busy young family, pioneering as dual-career blue-collar workers while starting a family of three children. We see Sachi struggling to keep her job and to climb the ranks in an era when very few women did so. We see them creating a warm and loving family environment that put few demands on the children and also gave the children little direction in life, other than a moral one. We understand there was a very strong, to some extent lopsided, bond of love on Fujii Masaji's part for his wife and this and the fact that he was chronically ill may have contributed in some part to his having done so much of the household labor. He was also a totally "hands-on dad," way ahead of his time.[3] Finally, we view the children, now adults, struggling to build their own livelihoods, full of hope yet also anxious about how they will manage in the future. First, to the story of that girl, that smiling guy, and the car.

Rural to Urban

Sachi was born in the mid-1950s in Fukui Prefecture of central Japan, the third of four daughters in a family of six children. Her family was not well off; her mother did piecework at home while her father was employed at a mill. When Sachi was in her first year of junior high school, her father's employer went bankrupt, a not uncommon occurrence among small firms. Her paternal aunt, who had married into a household that owned a steel factory in Kyoto, offered to employ Sachi's father and the rest of the family. Sachi's older brother, eldest sister, and second brother were already employed there, and when the remaining family moved to Kansai, Sachi's aunt arranged company housing, and subsequently rental housing, so that the whole family of eight could live together. Her mother joined the factory as a *pāto* cook, and her two older sisters and brothers, along with her father, worked making steel. ("*Pāto*" refers to a worker's status as an irregular employee, without the benefits associated with regular employees and with much lower wages.)

Sachi, moving from the Fukui countryside to urban Kansai, found the level of the local junior high to be much more difficult than that of her hometown. She could not keep up in her studies; more important, her family did not have the means for her to continue in school but expected her to start working upon junior high graduation, as had her older siblings. High school was out of the question.[4] One thing Sachi did know, however: she did not want to work in the steel mill. It was filthy work; her family came home every day covered in grease and grime. She wanted something else, but she knew she had to work: "I had quite a strict father, and I could not have stayed at home if I hadn't worked. I would be hit if I didn't listen to him. He hit us. He was the kind of guy who would overturn the dining table [resembles a low tea table] . . . a *ganko oyaji* [stubborn old man]. He was scary." So she asked her teacher to recommend a job to her. And the teacher recommended Azumi, a large, well-established lingerie firm in the locale. In this era the "school-to-work transition," wherein schoolteachers introduced potential jobs to their pupils, was well in place, ensuring a smooth entry into the job market. It is no longer so (Brinton 2011). While her father would not have brooked resistance from Sachi, he was willing to listen to the teacher's advice, and he allowed Sachi to start at Azumi. She entered in 1969, along with a large cohort of other girls. As she put it, "When I was recruited, there were a few hundred 'golden eggs'; that's what we were called.[5] Nowadays there are few regular employees and many dispatch workers [haken]."[6] Another big difference in this company since the mid-1980s is that it no longer hires anyone but university graduates as regular employees. Due to rising production costs, most of the manufacturing work has been shifted abroad or to less urban areas of Japan, and the urban workforce is mostly engaged in office or retail work.

Not only did Sachi find herself employed at a stable, clean job at a well-known manufacturer, but on her first day of work, the office at the company also asked her to recommend other women whom she might know. Within a month, both of her elder sisters were also at Azumi: "We were called the three sisters. We were all in different places: my eldest sister in shipping, my elder sister and I in the main factory [but different workshops]. She is still there—making patterns on the computer." Sachi's elder sister, also a junior high school graduate, never married, but with her earnings and benefits as a regular employee at Azumi, she was able to purchase a new house right across from Sachi's.[7] Her eldest sister is also still at the company, although she quit her regular position when her husband's company transferred the family to one of its distant branch offices. But she returned to Azumi later as a *pāto* and is still working there today.[8]

At age twenty, Sachi became a *shisutā*, the lowest level of supervisor at Azumi. At this time, she was in the sewing division, which was line work. Sachi reported that all the women in the sewing division were young. Most people quit at marriage, and nobody in the sewing division had children in day care. Perhaps fortunately for Sachi, she injured her knee on a machine operated by a knee-lever and was no longer able to sew, so she was shifted to the inspection and packaging division, where there were some married women with children. She had to step down from being *shisutā*, but she gained the possibility of staying employed. She also married at this time.

The Girl, the Smiling Guy, and the Car

Sachi met her husband, Fujii Masaji, when she was eighteen: "I met him on the street. He was on a big motorcycle. Wearing a big helmet. I nodded to him.

That was the beginning! I thought he looked cool, so I nodded my head. And he asked me to go out." At the time, however, she already had a boyfriend, so she turned him down. But Masaji was persistent. Eventually her boyfriend left her, and a friend of Masaji's convinced her to go with him to visit Masaji in the hospital, as he was having kidney surgery and might die. That was the start of their relationship. She was nineteen, he, twenty-one. They married in 1976, when she was twenty-one—three years earlier than the average age for a woman at first marriage at the time. The groom, too, was younger than the average groom. Sachi was the first among the sisters to marry. She noted, "I wanted to leave home as early as possible. . . . Because we had so many of us [in the family], in any case I wanted to get out. Back in those days it was popular in TV dramas to feature young brides. We called them *osanazuma*—young wives, right? So I wanted to marry early." Although Sachi was younger than average for her cohort, twenty-one was not an unusually young marriage age for someone who had been in the workforce since age fifteen. Furthermore, she had already passed the age of twenty, the legal marker of adulthood.

While in recent years desirable men have been described with the attributes of the "three c's" (cooperative, communicative, and comfortable)—and before that, the "three highs" (tall, high income, and high education)—Sachi was attracted to Masaji because he was kind and gentle *(yasashī)*: "That was my only thought: in any case, [I wanted] a gentle guy."

Although she had been earning a living since graduating from junior high school, Sachi remained living with her parents as was the custom (and still largely is the custom, especially for younger women). This practice was encouraged by the factory; it expected young women who could commute from home to do so, and it did not provide a dormitory for young women whose parents lived nearby. Masaji had been living in a company dormitory since his family lived in a distant prefecture, but Sachi's family lived near the factory, so the only legitimate reason for her to move out would be marriage. Masaji was a high school graduate from rural western Japan. He had come to Kansai to attend high school and then obtained regular employment at a large and well-established battery company after he graduated.

Sachi and Masaji had a wedding, but they did not ask their parents to pay for it: "From our parents we got a futon and an inexpensive kimono and dishes. . . . So we didn't get money. . . . The two of us saved our money. We saved ¥50,000 a month; he saved ¥40,000, and I saved ¥10,000. That was how we rented a place to live and bought furniture and paid for the wedding."[9] It was a prodigious sum for them to save. This would have been about $170 a month in 1974 at the average exchange rate of ¥290 per $1 (Economic Research 2012). Sachi's contribution represented 10 percent of her disposable income. She gave half of her income to her parents. Masaji was able to set aside much more because he lived in a company dormitory. Perhaps another benefit of his years in dormitories was his expertise at cleaning house and doing the laundry, skills that he willingly put to use after marrying Sachi.

Upward Mobility

Sachi hoped for two or three children, and she and her husband wanted a house of their own. Before marriage, they discussed their goal of becoming homeowners, but they did not discuss how they were going to achieve it. It would have been an impossible goal had she not kept her position as a regular employee. But she did keep it. Nobody in her family objected since they knew she was aiming to buy a house. And although it was not easy in the inspection and packaging division to have children and remain working at Azumi (Roberts 1994), as noted, Sachi was encouraged by the few senior women in that department who had kept on working after childbirth.[10]

Sachi was able to give birth and return after fourteen weeks' maternity leave each time. Her own mother lived close by and was willing to look after the babies for the first six months until they could enter day care *(hoikuen)*, so she paid her mother to care for the children and remained at work: "It was tiring. I didn't have much morning sickness, but it was the standing [that was difficult]. But if you sit, you get terribly stiff shoulders. I am still going to the chiropractor now. All that work looking down [in inspection]. . . . It was really tough work." We should note that she *paid* her mother for her services. Sachi and her siblings, growing up in a working-class family, were expected to pull their weight. Yet the Fujiis did not enforce this norm with their own children when they became employed, perhaps because they wanted to indulge them, and until Masaji passed away, they could afford to do so.

The three children, two girls and a boy, were born in the span of six years. Soon Sachi had all three children in different public day-care centers. She drove them all to their centers first thing in the morning, on a motorbike, with her son, the youngest, on her back. She would leave work an hour early, at 4:30 p.m., to pick up the children. I asked her why they did not have a fourth. She replied, "Probably I would have kept having kids until we had a boy—my husband really wanted a boy. Because I saw the disappointed look on his face when our second child was a girl. Everybody had been saying it looked from my shape that it would be a boy. I was taken aback, and I decided to keep trying. But after we had a boy, I thought, that's it for me!" Up until the 1980s, the preference to have at least one son was still strong, as sons were seen as important as the ones who would carry on the family line. Nowadays this preference has weakened, as daughters are seen as preferable to daughters-in-law as companions and caregivers in one's old age (Fuse 2006).

The couple bought their first house when Sachi was twenty-four, in 1979. (At this point her elder daughter had been born.) They took out a thirty-year loan for the house, with a down payment of $4,550, which they had saved. The house price (at ¥220 per $1) was $55,700 (Economic Research 2012). Then in 1984, in order to take advantage of the after-school day-care program in another neighborhood, they sold it and bought another house for $100,000 (at ¥240 per $1) and a twenty-six-year mortgage. Because of rising land prices, they were able to make a small profit on the sale of the first house. The new neighborhood was suburban, peopled with salaryman/professional housewife families. The home was a modest two-story affair on a very small lot with a carport but no room for a garden.

By this time, their son also was born. They had achieved their dream: they had completed their family, they had their house, and they were both working steadily. Sachi had the good fortune to be blessed with a very strong mentor, who asked her to take the test for the first level of promotion.[11] She passed it at age thirty-one. It was around this time, in 1986, that Masaji became gravely ill and had to start kidney dialysis. This was also the beginning of Japan's bubble economy.

Challenges at Work

Although Sachi was able to pass the first level of promotion, she took the test for sub-section chief (kakarichō), four times in subsequent years and failed it every time. Whereas with the first promotion, her mentor had taken her aside during lunch breaks and given her practice tests, by the time she went up for sub-section chief, this mentor had moved on. Sachi explains:

> In subsequent tests I had nobody helping me. They said, "Do it yourself!" Truthfully I don't much like to study. They handed me two books of topics to learn. They said, "Study these." I pasted things [on the walls] in the bathroom, I pasted them [on the walls] in the wash-room. . . . The kids were still little, and I would get up after putting

them to bed and study, but I couldn't learn it. . . . I didn't know how to study. I only had a junior high school education, and I had worked so hard on learning sewing machine techniques, I had totally forgotten how to study. For the first time in my life, I tasted test neurosis! I just couldn't memorize it. The fourth time I took the test, it was really bad [laughs]. . . . They made it more difficult each year. . . . I was about thirty-six at test number four. You have to give younger people a chance at the test. People who graduate from college easily climb, but those with junior high or high school backgrounds. . . . It seems difficult.

In other words, the exam itself became more rigorous each year, so by the time Sachi had taken it the fourth time, she realized with regret that the first time she should have easily passed.

At the very end of our conversation, in a low voice, Sachi said to me, "Look, Glenda, if you don't have the education, you can't get easy work. No matter how much you want to do it, you can't put it in words on the test. . . . Tests are written. That was the problem with the tests for sub-section chief. I couldn't write essays. [And in those days they had to be written long-hand.] That's my weakness." Here we see Sachi's lack of education hindering her upward mobility in the company. Sachi's encounter with a sympathetic mentor who fostered her potential was a godsend, but after he left, she never found another mentor to help her to prepare for promotional exams that assumed a level of knowledge that she lacked. Indeed, years ago she asked me to help her to study a book on basic management techniques, which she needed for this exam, because she found it too difficult to read. Although the company gave her some chances to climb, the exam, which might have appeared to be a fair assessment of potential, was in fact a glass ceiling to her advancement.

After her relocation to the shipping center, in 1991 Sachi was transferred to a sales office where she sent out product shipments to area stores. The job was very heavy work lifting boxes. Her fellow workers were almost entirely men. She noted she was told to accept the transfer or quit. She accepted. It is my impression that this transfer was in effect an attempt by the company to force Sachi out, but she persevered. It was here that she injured her back, an injury that still bothers her today. At this location, there were four irregular employees and two regulars, including Sachi. As a supervisor (as noted, she had passed the first promotion exam), she had a lot of trouble trying to keep the employees in line. She worked right along with them as supervisors often do in Japanese workshops: "They hardly worked at all. Their work was half-assed. They ate snacks all the time during work, and they made lots of mistakes. Someone wrote on one of the cases, 'Go home, you pig!' I cried when I saw it. Then I cut it out and took it home as a souvenir. But in the end, I made friends with that girl [who wrote the graffiti], and we got along fine. And I got them to move the regular employee who had been causing a lot of the trouble. Six months after that, the rest of them came around. I was even invited to the wedding of one of them." This story was repeated in almost every place where Sachi was transferred. At first she would meet with a lot of resistance but she would not back down, and eventually she would get the people to come around. She always kept her high standards, but at the same time she had a very personable way about her, which must have helped.

After ten years at the sales office, Sachi was again transferred to a shipping center located in a southern suburb, where she had to interface with another company to ship products. This time it took longer to get to work; she would leave home at 8 a.m. and return at 8 p.m. Furthermore, her predecessor had made a mess of the situation, alienating the people from the other firm. When she arrived at this job, Sachi was given the cold shoulder. She needed to use the shipping company's computer, but the employees would not give her access to it—they just sat there playing card games. Although she could sometimes use the computer in the general affairs section, she hated asking ("It was hard to go through the door [of that section]") because it was a "different world." She is referring to the fact that the people in the general affairs office were almost all university graduates, white-collar workers, a situation that made the office seem culturally a different world to her. The same was true of the cultural distance between the factory and the main office; factory workers considered the main office to be far beyond their purview. It was where the *erai hito* (important people) were located. "I did it [walked into the general affairs office], but I was so nervous. Nobody taught me anything [at that workplace]. There was no training. . . . That's why I loved making manuals. No matter where I went, I made a manual. Even where I am now. Manuals and *kaizen* [continual improvement in production through workers' innovations]. I'm always doing it. At first you ask people, but then it's a bother to people when you keep on asking. So I make manuals so that people can figure it out [without having to ask anyone]." Why did Sachi love manuals so? First, asking for clarification is a nuisance *(meiwaku)* to others, something Japanese children are taught to avoid doing at all costs. But also, reading a manual kept Sachi from losing face. She could avoid the discomfort she felt in having to go through the door of a different social space where the rules of interaction did not come naturally to her and where she might face embarrassment.

In the end, the young women who had given her so much trouble stopped their bullying and went out drinking with her once a month, for which she used her *shunin* (supervisor's) allowance. Two of the girls were from Nara, too far to make the train home after going out drinking, so Sachi used to have them stay at her home overnight on futons on the living room floor. It must have been difficult for Sachi to hold her own in this situation because although she was a regular employee and had been at the firm for her entire career, her educational status was low. The women she supervised were making only a fraction of her salary, yet most of them no doubt had higher levels of education. Sachi was one of a few in her cohort at this firm who stayed on and fought for her place when the norm was to quit and become a homemaker and later, after the children were older, an irregular employee. She was still a regular employee and hence a high-income earner, yet married with children and a supervisor despite her education; any of these things could have been a source of friction with her subordinates. As Sachi put it, "Women are pretty hard on each other."[12]

At her last Azumi job, Sachi returned to shipping center work, but eventually all the shipping functions were amalgamated into one center far from her home, and she was sent to supervise forty part-timers at a new work process. There was a lot of overtime, and she was not getting home until after 10 p.m. A single woman three years older than Sachi gave her a particularly hard time, so Sachi would wear ear plugs in order not to hear this woman's biting remarks. She commented, "At Azumi, there was a lot of in-fighting. Even to the end, there was someone who was awful to me. . . . Women are scary, aren't they?" She also alluded to having been ganged up on by several of the irregular workers who were her subordinates, out of jealousy. This time, however, Sachi did not have the time to turn the situation around because, exhausted from her husband's death a year earlier (in 2005) and completely stressed out psychologically from the problems of trying to manage forty part-timers on her own, she opted to take early retirement at the age of fifty:

> When I came home [from work] . . . , we did fight, but he did a lot
> of housework for me and he listened to me complain. Without my
> husband, if I had continued, I probably would have gotten ill from
> the psychological pressure. I didn't want to cause my children trouble
> with no father and a sick mother. So I decided to quit. I worried about
> it for a long time, but I was able to continue because he was there for

me. I thought, "Enough! It's enough, already!". . . I had said it before, but the supervisors were a rather eccentric lot, the number of regular staff had decreased, my work was mostly with irregular workers as the mainstays, and I was given a huge amount of responsibility. [If I had stayed], the pressure would probably have gotten to me.

Particularly disheartening to Sachi was the sarcastic comment of her boss when he learned that Masaji had passed away: "So now you've come into the money [hidari uchiwa]!"[13] That comment may well have been the last straw for Sachi. But before she quit, she voluntarily gave up her last ten days of paid vacation in order to make a big manual. To the end, Sachi was interested in improvements in the work process, and she wanted her successor to be able to do the job more easily, without having to figure it all out from scratch. Over her long career, Sachi had become an expert at the logistics of work flow and quality control, and it was this legacy that she passed on through her manuals.

Sachi had thirty-five years of service. Her last day at Azumi was March 31, 2006, and her last yearly income there was ¥6 million (about $52,000 at ¥116 per $1), more than that of the average male breadwinner in Japan.[14] She told me wistfully, "If he were still alive, I might still be at Azumi. I would be complaining to him. Remember, Glenda, you asked me whether we talked about the company at home. I would be telling him all about it—all just me talking [ippōteki]. . . . If he were still alive, I think I'd be telling him, 'Today this happened and that happened!'"

In the end, what exactly led to Sachi's early retirement? She seems to have made the decision based on three factors. One is the poor workplace envi- ①
ronment, where regular employees like Sachi must take on increasingly oner-
ous burdens, managing large numbers of irregular employees as cost-cutting
measures under the globalized neoliberal economy. Next, she suffered harass- ②
ment from some of those irregular employees under her management, as well
as from her immediate superior, who gave her no sympathy or support when
her husband passed away. Finally, the grief from Masaji's death was fresh, and
she could not bear the pressures of the job without him. ③

Life as an Irregular Employee

Most salaried employees in Japan who take early retirement do not retire from the labor market altogether. The national pension scheme for those in Sachi's age cohort does not start until age sixty-one, leaving a large gap in income if one retires very early, as Sachi did. Sachi took eleven months off after leaving Azumi, as she was able to receive unemployment benefits. (This practice is common, and in Japan those who voluntarily quit their jobs still receive unemployment benefits.) After that, she went to the government employment agency (Hello Work) and found a job at a dyer's, where her job was to sew yard goods. Because the working conditions were very poor, she stayed only one year and one month. In the end, as was her wont, Sachi improved the place before she quit, convincing the boss to make a number of renovations to the shop.

Sachi's next job, which she has held for three years, was at a boxed lunch (bentō) factory; she started it six weeks after quitting the sewing job.[15] Here she was an irregular worker, hired for ¥800 an hour on half-year contracts. She noted that there were no automatic raises, and although the irregular workers received a ¥6 increase after she complained, Sachi said the pay could also go down at any time. Nevertheless she remains there: "Now I think if you're going to be working in any case, you might as well be doing something where you can go home happily at the end of the day. More than pay, I am thankful for the workplace environment. I want money, but I don't want to feel miserable [mazushii kokoro]. I want to be an energetic, kind old lady! I want to be able to smile and say, 'Otsukaresama' [thank you for your hard work] at the end of the day."[16]

For a half year, Sachi worked eight consecutive extended day shifts (9 a.m.–6 p.m.) followed immediately by one night shift (12 a.m.–8 a.m.) in order to get enough work hours to pay into the national health and pension insurance schemes (for which are needed more than nineteen days of work and more than 170 hours in a month). After that, she dropped back to days only, but she works enough hours to continue to be eligible for insurance.[17] At the most, she earns about one-fourth of her Azumi income. The benefit of this job is that as long as she informs management in advance, she can take holidays of a week or even longer. Taking advantage of this possibility, she traveled to India with her elder daughter recently. This would have been impossible in her job as a regular employee at Azumi.

The boxed lunch factory work is tough on the body. Sachi is in charge of cooked dishes and fried foods, and the workplace is very hot. In addition, for reasons of safety and sanitation, she must wear long pants, long boots, long-sleeved shirts, a mask, and two caps. But this workplace has no harassment problems, so it is enjoyable, she noted. Sachi, because of her long years of training in a professional environment, cannot help but bring that training and expertise to this job as well. She told me that there are some workers who do not take sanitation seriously and who break the sanitation rules. This she sees as unacceptable, so she notified the management. (Recall Sachi's high standards!) Now management has asked her to be the sanitation leader, and she inspects the finished products. She laughed at how easy it is for her to spot anything that shouldn't be in the boxed lunch when others just cannot see it. She remarked, "They said, 'Wow, you were really something to find that,' but . . . I could see it so clearly! [Laughs.] . . . My body remembers. It's the strangest thing."[18] On her own initiative, she made a manual to explain the flow of work and all the important things to keep track of in the preparation process. She plans to stay at the boxed lunch factory until age sixty; any longer would be too much for her body to withstand.

What can we learn from Sachi's work history? First, she was and is a very hard worker, as well as a clever one, always figuring out how to improve the work flow. Moreover, her leadership skills were marvelous. Although her lack of education held her back from climbing very far in the ranks, that she was able to endure as a regular worker for thirty-five years is remarkable and a testimony to her strength of character, as well as to her strong relationship with her husband.

Family Life at the Fujiis

Generally, blue-collar workers engaged in shift work in Japan have more discretionary time after working hours than do their white-collar counterparts (Roberson 1998; Roberts 1994). The latter tend to spend much more time doing unpaid overtime (sābisu zangyō). Working hours for managers at Azumi were long, but blue-collar unionized employees tended to leave work after their shifts unless there was paid overtime to be done. Because of his illness, Masaji had only infrequent overtime duties, and when he was home, he spent a lot of time on housework, playing with the children, or taking the family out on the weekends. His job was actually less burdensome than Sachi's in terms of hours, as well as in terms of human relationships. Sachi noted that the family usually had dinner together:

SACHI: "When we had dinner, he would listen to my complaints about work."
GLENDA: "Did he do the same with you?"
SACHI: "No, he didn't. In men's workplaces there doesn't seem to be much of that. His workmates really liked him, and he was happy with his work.

They treated him very well, and even now [after he had passed away] his close friends would come over. He listened to me unilaterally!"

Masaji had one week of night shift every fourth week. When working the night shift, he could not participate much in the household labor, but during the rest of the month, he pitched in with every chore: changing diapers, doing laundry, shopping for groceries, cleaning, vacuuming, making repairs. Once he had to have dialysis, his company shifted him to desk work and took him off the night shift. Monday, Wednesday, and Friday he would have dialysis after work. Tuesday, Thursday, Saturday, and Sunday, he would make dinner and do everything for Sachi. Masaji had also been walking the dog when the children were in elementary school, but Sachi took over this task because it was becoming increasingly difficult for Masaji as his illness progressed. Instead of walking the dog, Masaji would make boxed lunches for the children, which they needed when they began junior high. Although making boxed lunches is iconically a mother's job (Allison 1991; Roberts 2011), Sachi was happy to relinquish this chore:

> He really made nice ones [boxed lunches]. He'd get up at 5:30 a.m. He took a little hand vac and vacuumed the steps on the way down to the kitchen. The most I ever did was wipe the steps with a tissue! I'd be sleeping in the morning and then hear the sound of the vacuum—so noisy, right?—rrrrrrr!!!! I'd think, "Oh! I'm trying to sleep [and there he is at it again!]." But he'd get up early, do the hand vac, and then make miso soup and the lunches and then go to work. He wasn't a total neat freak *[keppekishō]*, but he hated to see dust on the steps! On vacation days he would vacuum for me. I'm really in trouble now that he's gone. He did so much.

When I asked Sachi if they ever enlisted the children's help in household chores, she said they never did; they did it all themselves as a couple: "It's normal for the *wife [okusan]* to do it all. . . . Nowadays some wives and husbands do it together and children fold laundry. . . . *Now.* . . . But when my husband was alive, the kids didn't do it. They did nothing.[19]

Relationships between husbands and wives in Japan have often been portrayed as distant, with each partner maintaining his or her separate friends and pastimes, growing further apart as the years of marriage pass (Iwao 1993; Salamon 1975). Such was certainly not the case with the Fujiis. As Sachi relates, "We didn't do things separately. No. And we were really open [with each other]." Her favorite thing about being married to her husband was that they were blessed with children and that they were able to create a cheerful family. They were together on holidays, and they went on many family trips, singing in the car as Masaji drove. Even in illness, Masaji did not sit at home: "Even after he got sick, once every two or three months, when the kids were of high school age, we would leave them home and stay overnight somewhere. We'd take the car. Because he loved to go all sorts of places. To Kumamoto, to Shikoku. And we went swimming a lot with the children, in my hometown, and to festivals."

The children in the Fujii family adored their father. The older daughter called him "Masaji," which is quite unusual in Japanese families. The second daughter called her dad "Baldy." Only the son used "Dad" as an appellation. Between mother and dad, Dad was the children's favorite, and Masaji was a warm and indulging parent: "He'd do anything they wanted. Let's say they blew their noses and left the tissue over there. They wouldn't throw it in the wastebasket themselves. Their father would do it for them. Maybe he wanted to protect them. . . . He would always be on their side. The kids loved having him there!"

Sachi says they were not at all strict in teaching their children manners and only scolded them on occasion. The most serious incident of punishment Sachi could recall was when elementary-school-aged Ami and Yūji were misbehaving and wouldn't stop, so she sent them outdoors and closed the door on them: "I heard them say, 'Mother's mad!' I think Yūji peed his pants. I don't think I told them what to do very much. Maybe I just left them to their own devices!" *[handwritten margin note: mimamoru?]*

Most married couples have their disagreements, and the Fujiis were no exception. Although they quarreled quite often, they soon made up, and Masaji never raised a hand to Sachi or the children. Sachi noted the most angry she ever saw her husband was when he threw his rice bowl down onto the floor. But then he picked up the pieces himself and went off to work. Most of the quarrels she can remember had to do with money—her husband loved to buy motorbikes and take out loans for cars and fancy accessories to the cars, buying a new car every four years. Also, they fought about hospitalization costs after Masaji became ill. His supplemental insurance plan paid him a lump-sum condolence benefit only after he had been in the hospital for at least twenty days. Masaji, who could never keep still, hated hospitals and wanted to be discharged as soon as possible. (There was some leeway in negotiating an early discharge as doctors tended to favor longer hospitalizations even though they were not strictly necessary.) As he was often hospitalized in his final years, they fought a lot about the early discharge issue: "We argued over money. We didn't have any. . . . Even though tomorrow would be day twenty, he'd come home on day nineteen. 'You could have stood it for one more day!' I'd say. . . . He would say, 'Don't tell me that. I'm begging you; let me go home,' and he'd come home." As a result, after Masaji became ill, Sachi frequently found herself borrowing a bit of money (¥10,000 or so) from her parents until the next payday. When her husband was hospitalized, his salary decreased, so they could not make ends meet. That was why she fought him over the insurance issue. They also fought over giving their son video games. She opposed it, but she lost that argument. She told me she connects her son's failure to do well in school to his video game console.

From Sachi's narrative we can discern that Masaji was the more indulgent parent, and he was less careful about family finances as well. The Fujiis had separate bank accounts. Masaji paid for his hobbies—such as the expensive auto accessories—out of his own account, but from Sachi's description, it sounded as if he purchased what he wanted when he wanted it. While it is customary in many salaryman/professional housewife families for wives to manage the family finances singlehandedly, Sachi did not enjoy this total control.

Parenting, Cultural Capital, and Human Capital: Reproduction of Social Class in the Next Generation

Japan has been known as an education-credentialist society (*gakureki shakai*) but according to Kariya (2010), it is increasingly shifting to a "high-skill society," where workers need to train themselves and market their skills rather than to expect that a degree from a highly regarded university alone will set them up for life. People now, he stresses, need the ability to continually learn. This is called "learning competency," a kind of cultural capital (Bourdieu 1977), learned from a very young age through one's parents' attitudes toward learning, as well as from the setting they provide conducive to learning. Those whose upbringings do not provide them with either recognized educational credentials or learning competency are at a large disadvantage in the labor market.

While the Fujii children grew up in a very loving and indulgent environment, their learning competencies were not fostered. Using the terminology of Lareau (2003, 238), whose study was strongly influenced by Pierre Bourdieu's

theory of *habitus* (1977), one could say the Fujiis did not "concertedly cultivate" their children's talents, as do parents of higher social class backgrounds.
Lareau defines *habitus* as "the set of dispositions toward culture, society and
one's future that the individual generally learns at home and then takes for
granted" (2003, 276). In Japan, the tests to enter high school assume an extremely important place in determining one's chances for upward social mobility. These tests demand a great deal of concentrated preparation by rote
memorization, a task the Fujii children were not prepared to undertake. The
Fujiis wanted their children to grow *nobi-nobi*, without inhibition. Although
Sachi and Masaji did provide the children with some remedial cram school
(*juku*) classes and indeed afforded them private education when they were
not able to gain access to public senior high schools, junior colleges, or universities, the children did not seem to learn *how* to study or *where* that might
take them. Unlike children in households where parents have more education,
more understanding of the requirements to move up in the system, and more
time to shepherd their children through the educational process, the Fujiis
did not equip their children by (for example) helping them with homework or
pushing them to excel in school. Their family *habitus* encultured the children
to be uninhibited and carefree. With two jobs, the Fujiis had the economic means to afford excellent schooling for their children, but they lacked the
cultural capital to push them through the hoops.[20] Atsuko, the oldest child,
now wishes she had studied more when she was young, but it may be too
late to acquire further education, other than the training sessions provided by
her employer. Neither of the other two children ever made efforts in academics. Sachi told me that the children decided for themselves, with their friends,
where they would go to school. They as parents did not give guidance. As a
result, they wound up attending very low-level private schools, the sort that
required no exam preparation to enter. Although they then graduated with
credentials, they were not worth much on the job market. And with the recessionary state of the economy at the time of the children's entry into employment (1999–2004), the lack of prestigious credentials surely mattered. Atsuko
has done the best of the three children because the credential she earned, a
day-care worker's license, was recognized and in demand.[21]

All of the Fujii children enjoyed their early childhoods (1980s–early
1990s). Atsuko remembers being sorry to be the last child picked up at day
care, but otherwise there were only happy memories. They all attended the
same local public elementary and junior high school, sometimes having the
same teachers. None of them particularly enjoyed studying, and they reported

that they frequently gave the teachers a hard time in class by chatting, goofing off, and not paying attention. Yūji said his favorite subject was recess—as soon as the bell rang, he and his pals would be out of the door like a shot, grabbing a ball on the way. They had many friends and no problems with bullying, which is often featured in the media as a major problem in Japanese schools. Their parents sent the daughters to an academic after-school cram school when they were in junior high, but as Atsuko relates, "It was a waste of money. I didn't study a bit. I just attended. It was fun because a lot of my friends were going, but I didn't feel like studying." None of the children remembers doing homework except perhaps during summer vacation, when teachers require children to finish a certain amount before they return in the fall term. Junior high school was much tougher academically, and the children reportedly had difficulty understanding the subjects. Yet the children enjoyed junior high immensely. As Atsuko reports, "What was so much fun? The feeling of esprit de corps [danketsushin]. The feeling of solidarity. It was a lot of fun. I had [my friends] do everything for me. They helped me decide what to do next, how to write a resume; I had them do all my summer homework for me. I could really count on my junior high friends." Here we can see that Atsuko, while not the best student, was certainly a strong leader.

When it came time to enter high school, Atsuko told me she had to enter the easiest private high school because her teacher told her she could not pass the tests for any of the public schools. As most of her friends went on to public senior high schools, she was a bit lonesome. Her sister Ami followed the same pattern of coasting to the bottom in junior high, so she too attended the same private girls' high school as her older sister. For this private schooling, her parents had to pay about ten times as much the tuition of a public school. The son also ended up following the private school route. Because their parents were both in regular employment, this was financially possible. In a different longitudinal project in which I am engaged with families in white-collar salaried employment (Roberts 2011), some of the full-time working mothers are also sending their children to private schools for much of their education, and it is affordable for some families only because they have two good incomes. In these cases, however, the mothers are highly educated, and their children are attending elite private schools, often in large part due to the intergenerational support of grandmothers, who shepherd the children through the cram school and exam system. In the Fujii family, if Sachi had not been working as a regular employee, it is doubtful that they could have afforded private schools. Moreover, if Sachi had been a homemaker and had had the time to push her children to study, she may not have done so because she always said she wanted them to grow up carefree.

The desire to have children be carefree is not limited to the working class; I have heard many middle- and upper-middle-class parents voice doubts about forcing their children to prepare for public high school entrance exams. The difference is that some middle-class parents with means have more options to avoid the exam hell by enrolling their children in "escalator" private schools, which start at kindergarten and go through high school. Others put their children through the exam hell despite misgivings about it because the path to social status is narrow and this path worked for them. In the recessionary economy of the past two decades, however, some people no longer see this direction as a secure path to social class reproduction (see Gordon Mathews' chapter in this volume).

Atsuko: Determining One's Life Path (Shinro)

As noted, after high school Atsuko decided to attend a two-year *senmongakkō* (post-high-school two-year technical school) for day-care center teacher (*hoikushi*) training. She first thought of it because a friend said that was what she had chosen, but also Atsuko's aunt was in the field, and Atsuko read over the notebook her mother had kept for her when she was a day-care child. These various factors inspired her to try to become a day-care teacher herself. This was the first time in her life that she actually had to apply herself:

> It was a two-year course, extremely severe. The practical training was awfully tiring, and we couldn't take any time off. During high school, without telling my parents, I used to play hooky quite often—right up to where I almost didn't have enough attendance days. . . . I was pretty careful about regulating those, but at the tech school if you were out three days for each course, you couldn't get any credits. I realized I couldn't take time off, so I always went to school. Some of what we studied was interesting, some of it not so. I graduated at age twenty, and then, without getting a proper job I started doing *arubaito* [part-time work performed by young people who are either still in school or who have not yet secured a regular job] for a moving company.

Atsuko did not immediately look for a job in her field because her best friend from junior high suddenly died, probably a suicide, shortly after their coming-of-age ceremony (age twenty). When she attended the funeral, Atsuko talked with this girl's mother, who told Atsuko to do something that she liked to do, something enjoyable. This advice prompted Atsuko to take two years off and do as she pleased. She also noted that some of her friends were still attending four-year universities, whereas she had only gotten two years of post-high-school education, so she did not feel obliged to start working hard right away. In a sense, Atsuko felt entitled to the "four-year moratorium" that many of her friends were able to enjoy by entering universities rather than technical training schools. Her parents did not object. With the income from her working-class job, she saved her money and then took trips to do environmental volunteer work, or to do part-time work at rural lodges in picturesque spots. Atsuko spoke fondly of the days with the moving company. She was apparently quite good at the job, and by the end of four years, she was a leader, driving trucks and bringing along her own subordinates. She loved the personalities of the other, mostly male, workers, who she said "stank of humanity" (ningenkusai) and who were totally frank (omote mo ura mo nai; no "front stage" or "back stage" to them).[22] In fact by the end of her time with the moving company, her hourly wage was over $10 an hour in 2002 (¥1,300 per hour at ¥125 per $1; Economic Research 2012), a high wage for part-time work.

Then came Atsuko's turn to the day-care field. Her father had clipped a newspaper help-wanted ad for a day-care center worker and left it on her desk for her to see: "I thought he must want me to try for it. He had cut it out and put it right on my desk. So I decided to try for it."[23] After a few irregular positions, Atsuko landed her current position as an after-school day-care program (gakudō hoiku) teacher and has been there since age twenty-seven.[24] It is a regular position with benefits, and in total she can earn about $39,000 a year (¥79 per $1 in 2011; Economic Research 2012). This job is classified as an "associate public servant," or junkōmuin. When the city was in charge of day-care programs, the job would have been as a full public servant, and the salary and benefits would have been better and would have increased steadily with years of service. Ever since the bubble economy burst, however, local governments have tried to find ways to cut costs and deregulate public programs such as day-care. In this case, the city government still pays the salaries of associate public servants like Atsuko, but they are not hired directly by the city any longer; the after-school program is run by a private external body that is not under obligation to provide the excellent labor packages that public servants enjoy. Still, one must be licensed as a day-care teacher to become even an associate public servant in the day-care program. Furthermore, this is a stable position, and she will be able to take child-care leave if she has children. Atsuko has been chosen twice for special half-week training sessions, and she has obtained the certification as a "child welfare personnel." Her ultimate goal is to work for an orphanage if a position becomes available. She also wishes she could return to school to learn more about child psychology, but she notes it is not likely that she will have the means to do so. Although Atsuko's technical education has given her access to a stable position, there are few opportunities to increase her skills and move up. In her spare time, she is a volunteer at a nonprofit organization, working with children on Sundays: "I can give back to the children what I've learned up to now. My aim is to give back, whether it's to my own children or the children around me."

It was clear through our discussion that Atsuko, like her mother, is not a sycophant. She is serious about her work, concerned about the welfare of the children in her care, and speaks up if she sees injustice or abuse, even though in her workplaces she has often been the youngest staff member. She does not like the gossip and back-stabbing atmosphere that she sees in her current field, but she loves caring for children, so she puts up with it. She has little tolerance for slackers, and she is always seeking new programs to improve things for the children, but she sees her efforts as an uphill battle in a bureaucratic workplace where most employees are not trying to innovate. In this way, she resembles her mother, a leader who was and is always looking for a way to work smarter. As the eldest child and elder daughter, she is an active agent in her approach to life.[25]

Ami: Caught in the Middle, in Search of a Desirable Job (Yaritai Koto)

Atsuko's younger sister, Ami, is the middle child. At twenty-eight, slim and pretty, with her long hair dyed chestnut brown, she sat next to me on the floor of the living room, trying to answer the questions I put to her. She seemed much less self-confident than her elder sister and a bit shy. She has had a tougher time than her sister figuring out what she wants to do with her life.

Ami and her girlfriend both decided they would attend the two-year junior college affiliated with their private high school, although it was not particularly oriented toward anything she wanted to do; she just wanted to avoid going to work. She told me she had wished to enter the cosmetics or beauty field, but no one gave her any advice as to how to go about this, and the junior college was simply a repeat of easy technical courses she had taken in high school.[26] When she graduated, she tried working for a spa, but she did not last there longer than three days: "I think I was just yearning to be in that line of work, and that was the problem. . . . You had to talk with the clients, ask them what sort of [skin] problems they had, and give them counseling. . . . You had to touch their skin and do treatments of some kind." She watched the process and thought it seemed hard *(taihensō)*: "You had to work standing up, and you had to encourage the clients to purchase courses of treatment. I saw that and I thought, 'No way.' . . . I couldn't continue. So I went to a drugstore."

The drugstore job, only three days a week, was the first of several part-time jobs Ami would try. She loved that job, selling cosmetics to clients. Although she wanted to become a regular employee there, the management refused to hire her as a regular because it did not want to pay her insurance. She noted that most of the employees were housewives who worked as irregulars. She quit to look for a real job at age twenty-three. Her next job was full time, but with hourly pay, at a hot-stones spa. She enjoyed the work, but the place went bankrupt after a year. At age twenty-four she found her next job at a general store selling accessories and cosmetics. This too was an irregular job without benefits, and she quit after a year because the store manager was unpleasant, strict, and oppressive: "He was scary," she said with a laugh. "I couldn't take it!"

Ami's next job was at a small one-man retail shop downtown, where she did office work and earned about ¥2 million a year ($26,000 at ¥77 per $1).[27] Although she was a regular employee, her pay hardly differed from when she did part-time work, but her job was six days a week with Sundays and holidays off. She was lonesome in this job as she hardly interacted with anyone all day long, so she had no opportunity to use her brain. She told me she wanted to quit at the end of the month of our interview. Yet she had not lined anything else up. She remarked, "I can't stick with something. I don't know what it is that I want, and because I don't know, I can't stick to something. Because I haven't got any goals." Ami told me that she planned to always work, however: "Because I want to buy clothes and stuff. I want to buy clothes and cosmetics, so I want to work."[28] At the end of our conversation I ask Ami if there was anything in life she wished she had done differently. Eventually she said maybe it would have been good to have acquired a practical skill. I asked, "Like what?" The examples she gave me were all negatives. "Not a hair stylist. Not a nurse." She added, "Nobody I know has continued with a certain job and is happy with it. My parents never suggested any particular kind of work to me. They just told me to do as I pleased." Ami is the only child left at home now, as Atsuko and Yūji married in 2011 and 2012, establishing their own households.[29]

Yūji: A Light-Hearted Optimist

When I met Yūji on a sultry August night in his mother's home, I was surprised to see him saunter in. I had not seen him since he was perhaps eight years old. Medium height, with a powerful build and an Afro hairstyle, Yūji filled the room with his presence. He dutifully and perhaps a bit playfully answered my questions.

Like his sisters, when Yūji was young he loved to play, and studying was not his forte. As he put it, "I didn't study, and I couldn't do well. My tests were all marked up in red. I hardly studied and was always outside playing." Soccer, however, was his love throughout his school years. Even now, he plays when he can. While soccer was the only thing in school at which he worked hard, I definitely got the sense that it had been character building.[30]

Yūji did not prepare for high school entrance exams during junior high school, so he ended up attending "the worst high school in the city, a private school." His junior high school homeroom teacher told him it would be impossible to go anywhere else. He described the entry process to his private high school: "Usually you have a test, and it's a bit difficult, right? Say, if it's English, they'll have you write an essay or something. All I had to do was to write the alphabet. For math, it was multiplication. For Japanese, we just had to write easy characters. Ones that everybody knows. Like *kuni* [国 country]. That's about it. There was an interview. But mostly I just had to sit there and listen. Usually you'd expect an examiner to ask you a lot of questions. But they asked me, 'Is there anything *you* would like to know?'"

Sachi wanted Yūji to go to a four-year university because he was their only boy, the *chōnan* (and there was still at this time a cultural preference for sons' higher education over daughters'; see Brinton 1994). Yūji, taking after his father, loved cars and thought of being a car mechanic, but he failed the exam for a four-year automotive technical school in his home city. He ended up attending a university in Kyushu (where his father had grown up); his school recommended it to him, and it had an automotive course. There was no exam. The intake interview was easy. Although he felt lonely at first living in a dorm, he made friends quickly and enjoyed college life. Like his older sister, he found friends to help him when he could not do the academic work, and he also sometimes cheated on exams. In the summers he came home and played with his friends and did part-time work in Atsuko's moving company. Although he could have gotten an auto mechanic's license from his school, he graduated in 2006 without obtaining it.[31] When it came time to get a job,

Atsuko knew someone in the car sales business in their city, and through this introduction, Yūji got a job interview and was hired. This time, however, the interview was "for real": "The interview was tough. There were five senior guys asking questions. . . . I managed it, but I was frozen with fear [gachi gachi de]! [You wore a suit?] Yes, I certainly did. And my hair was perfectly slicked back. [Laughs.] I was awfully nervous. If there had been that kind of interview for junior or senior high, I would have been more used to it, but this was the first nerve-wracking interview I'd ever had in my life. I tried really hard. . . . Yes, I made it somehow."

Although Yūji obtained a regular position in this dealership, things did not go well for him. His job was to do door-to-door cold sales of Toyota cars. The economy was bad, so it was not an easy job. It was terribly difficult to handle people's sometimes angry rejections, he noted. Moreover, his family had always been a Nissan family, and to sell Toyotas took more cunning than he could muster. He just did not feel good about urging people to purchase a car he would not buy himself. In a half year, he told his boss that he wanted out. His boss told him to keep trying at least another half year. His parents told him not to quit, no matter what. "But with my personality, if I don't like something, it's just no good anymore. [Then did you get another job before you quit?] No, I didn't even think of that. I just wanted to take it easy! [Laughs.] I was just spoiled. Really spoiled. [But had you saved up that one year of income?] No, no; I had no money left. I used it all. On going out, going fishing. Really extravagant. I just kept causing [Mother and Dad] trouble. I'm going to hell! [Laughs.] Now I've reached the age where I have to be a good son. But I still can't do it! I have to try a bit harder."

After quitting that position, Yūji stayed home "playing around" for three months, when one day he saw a program on TV about craftsmen. He thought it looked like interesting work, so he went to the local employment agency to inquire. There he saw a help-wanted advertisement for a tree and shrub nursery. He followed up on it and was given a job at this one-man operation. He has been there for three years now as an apprentice, managing fields of trees and shrubs, learning to fertilize, spray, weed, and prune. His wages are paid by the day; if it rains, he has no work. There are no formal bonuses, and his monthly income in 2011 was $2,300–$2,860 (at ¥77 per $1; Economic Research 2012). By now, the owner leaves most of the work up to Yūji. His goal is to get a tree surgeon's license after five years, if he can pass the test: "It's hard to get it. You have to study a lot to get it. And I hate to study! . . . I can study if I like the subject, so I think it'll be okay." Yūji says that most of his friends work for large companies and have much better salaries than his, but even those who have similar monthly incomes to his have semi-annual bonuses, so they earn about $15,500 more per year than he does. He muses, "I wish I had studied harder. But I am satisfied with my current work. . . . My life now is fine, but I wish I had a bit more money. But that's probably an either/or thing. You go to a place with good pay even though it's work you dislike, or you do what you love doing, even though the pay is low and you try hard anyway. I want the money, but deep inside, I think the best thing to do is what I love to do and to put up with [not having much money]. You have to put up with some things, right? . . . It's better to go to work with a smile on your face than with a frown!" Yūji added that Atsuko had long ago told him to study, and if he studied, things would be easier for him later on and he could get a good job. But he questioned that: "Who knows if that would have been better? I'm satisfied enough, even though I didn't study. Not everybody who studies succeeds, right? So I don't care."

The economist Genda Yūji, who has carried out extensive studies on youth employment since the bursting of the bubble economy, might consider Yūji's initial employment problem one of "mismatch" (2005, 57). Genda notes that while it has become commonplace to blame youth for their lack of perseverance when they quit regular employment even after only a year on the job, in fact this is a reflection of recessionary times, when there is a lack of variety in job offerings, leading many young people to take jobs that were their third or fourth choices. Genda reports that it is indeed true that there is more "job churning," or turnover, of young people in employment now than in previous generations. Once in the job, they find it is beyond their capacity to endure. In turn, the lack of job offerings to younger generations is due to the fact that corporations are protecting the benefits and favoring the retention of middle-aged and older workers (53). In Yūji's case, had he graduated from a university in his city, he might have had an easier time finding regular employment that interested him. He settled for his sister's connection without realizing that the job would be in sales. When I said to Yūji that his parents were both regular salaried employees, he replied that that was true and that they had made a lot of money, but that was "in the old days," and he did not think it was possible anymore.

Yūji is being totally realistic. And he is making a reasonably balanced assessment of his current occupation. While it will not make him well off or give him high status, at least he enjoys it. The same can be said of his older sister. Neither of them have prestigious or lucrative jobs, but both of them are in work that they feel is worth doing. When they were young, they were not inculcated with the "new middle-class" values (Vogel 1971) of studying hard, climbing the educational ladder, and landing a conventional white-collar job with all of its perks. On the other hand, some of Yūji's protests that he is better off not having studied harder may also stem from a doubt that he could have succeeded even had he made the effort.

Of the three children, Atsuko has a credential that has afforded her steady employment, but due to the privatization trend in the neoliberal economy since the 1990s, her job as an associate public servant no longer pays as well as it once would have. And while Yūji did get his BA degree, he did not come out with a credential to repair autos, which was his intention going into the program. The auto dealership job he obtained through his sister's connections was a total mismatch for him, and he could not reconcile himself to it. Had he stayed in it, it would have paid a much better salary than his current job as a nursery gardener, but he chose happiness over money; in the end this may be a much sounder choice if he is willing to compromise on his other goals. Like the blue-collar factory men in James Roberson's 1998 study, Yūji prefers to work with his hands; he could not stomach door-to-door sales, pressuring clients to make purchases. Like many children of his generation and also as was culturally appropriate as the only son, Yūji lived at home after university graduation. He continued to rely on his parents' largesse, only seeking a job after his benefits had run out. As the youngest child and the only son of the family, too, he readily asked for and received indulgence from his family.

All the children were used to having a family on whom they could lean financially, but after Masaji's death in 2005, this dependency became increasingly burdensome for Sachi. Ami has gone from one low-paying irregular job to the next, and although her most recent position was as a regular employee, she quit it because she could not stand the tedium and isolation. She knew she would need to find another job, but what she really wanted to do was marry her boyfriend and become a professional housewife, a solidly middle-class aspiration but one that was unlikely to come to fruition, at least not with the current boyfriend. Ironically, the children all have much higher educational credentials than their parents, yet they are in much less secure and/or well-paying jobs. Like many youth of their generation, there is also an element of wanting to be in work that they *like* to do, that *suits* them, and some unwillingness to put up with a job that doesn't fit their criteria. None of the children has fared so well in employment, characteristic of the general trend in youth employment in Japan in the recession era (Brinton 2011; Genda 2005; Kosugi

2008). This is also a phenomenon affecting youth in most postindustrial economies of late (Thomas 2012).

Her children's somewhat bumpy transition to stable adulthood frustrates Sachi, who now blames herself for not having paid more attention to the children when they were growing up, for not fostering their potential better or finding more avenues for them to explore. But in fact there was a lot more going on here than her failure to foster the children's "learning competency." There were also structural issues at play. Sachi and Masaji had easily landed their well-paying, lifetime factory jobs when the economy was still in a high growth period. When the children went on the job market, however, there were rising bars to advancement in an increasingly global, neoliberal, and recessionary environment. The 1980s and 1990s saw an extension of education and credentials to a wider population (via an expansion in number but not quality of universities and an increase in enrollments) at a time that desirable job placements began to shrink. Moreover, the cultural capital the children acquired from their parents was not suited to desk work and test taking but gave them strong values of work, family, friendship, and enjoyment in life.

Toward the end of our interview, Sachi expressed her worries about the future. She worries about the children's failure to put money into the household accounts, and she does not understand what motivates their behavior. She is extremely anxious that Ami's boyfriend seems unreliable, and Masaji is no longer there to help her think about the situation. Sachi still keenly feels the loss of the companion with whom she could consult about anything. In summing up her anxiety about the future she says, "I don't think things are going in a good direction. Those marrying are fewer, there are fewer children, and we just get older. I can't see the future ahead. The people in the generation ahead of us got public pensions and are stable, but I don't know if we can get a pension when we reach pensionable age. Frankly, I'm worried."

The past two to three decades have brought enormous changes and challenges to the Fujii family, who have been amazingly resilient. Despite illness, death, setbacks, difficult jobs, and heartbreak, they remain a very cohesive and generally optimistic family. In the autumn of 2012 as we looked over Atsuko's wedding pictures and talked about the recent wedding, Sachi told me that she had used some of Masaji's death benefits for Atsuko's wedding, and she was sure he was happy about it. The legacy Masaji has left them is one of hope, endurance, love, and joie de vivre. This family's ties to Masaji, as well as to each other, are strong and enduring, regardless of the challenging times.

Update

Yūji married his college sweetheart, and late in 2012, their son was born. Yūji's employment circumstances, too, have changed. He was able to obtain a new job at a larger tree and shrub nursery, where he is a regular employee with bonuses and benefits. Ami has had two jobs since she quit her regular position in 2011; currently she is a part-time worker at a bridal attire rental shop. Sachi, however, lost her job at the boxed lunch factory as it went bankrupt. She has now found a new irregular position making hand-sewn local craft goods at a tourist shop in northern Kyoto, an hour's commute from her home. She is hoping to learn how to work the cash register and convince the company to hire her full time.

Notes

I would like to thank Minja Choe and Ronald Rindfuss of the East-West Center's Program on Population and Health and the NIH grant on Innovations in Early Life Course Transitions for their generous support of my research and writing for this chapter. In addition, I am grateful to my co-editors, as well as Peter Cave and two anonymous reviewers, for helpful comments on earlier drafts of this chapter. Most of all, I give my heartfelt thanks to the Fujii family for the time and trouble it took to make this chapter come to light.

1. For a comprehensive understanding of the place in social science of what Michael Burawoy terms the "extended case method," see Borowoy (1998).
2. For further reading on blue-collar workers, see Cole (1971), Kondo (1993), Roberson (1998), and Roberts (1994). In Sachi's day, most women quit upon marriage, but nowadays, many wait to quit at childbirth. For reading on the "M" curve in women's employment and women's position in Japan's political economy, see MacNaughton (2006), and Rosenbluth (2007). For reading on social class formation in Japan, see Ishida and Slater (2010), and in particular Slater's chapter, "The 'New Working Class' of Urban Japan," in that volume.
3. In my earlier study of blue-collar women workers in the mid-1980s, I did find that some of the women's husbands, in contrast to what we knew of white-collar men, did quite a lot of the household labor and child care. This was more than a decade before the Japanese government campaign to get men to actively participate as fathers (see Roberts 2002).
4. By the time Sachi graduated from junior high in 1969, most Japanese children were matriculating on to high schools rather than entering work. In 1970, the proportion of all new junior high graduates entering employment was 16.3 percent, while by 1975 it had fallen to 5.9 percent (Ministry of Education, Culture, Sports, Science, and Technology of Japan 2008), illustrating the trend for children to continue on in their education through high school as the economy improved. These statistics give us an indication that Sachi's family was struggling economically as compared with the majority at the time.
5. "Golden eggs" *(kin no tamago),* a term popular in 1964, referred to fresh junior

and senior high school graduates from the countryside during the labor-short high economic growth period (Hatena Kī-wā-do 2012).

6. *Haken* is one of the many types of irregular employment that enables firms to save on labor costs. According to Fu (2012, 19), "*Haken* workers are employed and dispatched by *haken* agencies to work at the facilities of client firms. They are remunerated by the agencies but receive day-to-day job supervision from client firms." (In English, a *haken* agency is a kind of "labor subcontracting agency.") Sachi's point here is that because *haken* workers are not trained within Azumi as regular employees, they are harder to manage and they have less loyalty to the firm.

7. It is a huge accomplishment that a single woman with a junior high school level of education could manage to achieve independent security and purchase her own home. It would be impossible at Azumi nowadays since the company no longer even hires high school graduates, and one could never afford a home with the wages and conditions of an irregular worker.

8. Hence she followed the typical "M" curve of women's employment and wound up earning a fraction of Sachi's wages, although with the same employer.

9. Although I did not ask Sachi directly, I got the strong impression from our conversation that she and Masaji did not want to ask her parents to cover these costs because her parents were not well-to-do. They wanted to do it themselves.

10. The presence of one woman who sets an example by taking maternity leave and returning to work is enormously important to others following later. I heard comments to that effect from women over and over again during my studies of white-collar women and work-life balance. See Roberts (2004, 2007).

11. This mentor, a division chief, also recommended that Sachi participate in several overnight trainings in the course of her years at Azumi; these, she reported, were extremely helpful to her in her work. But such opportunities were not systematically offered to all regular employees. Sachi's sister, a pattern maker, has had an equally long career at Azumi but has never had such an opportunity. Sachi noted that she learned a lot about work especially from this particular mentor and a few other people who were division chiefs. It is probably through such interactions and training sessions that Sachi became so enthusiastic about improving the work flow *(kaizen)*, something that she subsequently practiced at every job she ever took on and that undoubtedly led to her achievements at work.

12. I discuss women's difficulties in personal relationships on the factory floor in Roberts (1994, 105–108). See Ogasawara (1998) for an analysis of similar structural frictions among women in a white-collar setting.

13. This remark was in reference to the money Sachi would receive from her husband's life insurance policy.

14. One way to put Sachi's income in perspective is to consider the average yearly income for household heads aged 47.3 years in workers' households in 2010; it was ¥4.17 million. Note that household heads are overwhelmingly male, and women on average earn only 66 percent of what men earn in Japan (Ministry of Internal Affairs and Communications 2011).

15. Sachi had earned a qualification as a care provider for the elderly *(kaigo fukushishi nikyū),* for which she took Sunday classes for six months while her husband was still alive. After she finished at the dyer's, she had an offer to work as a care provider, but her children did not want her to do this sort of work. Nor did they

want her to do night shift work. They told her, "Why don't you work someplace where the work is easier?" She had thought of working at an after-school day-care program as a helper, but the hours are short and the income would be insufficient, she noted. She might consider that line of work after age sixty.

16. *Otsukaresama* is a standard phrase exchanged by colleagues or joint participants of some endeavor, after it has finished, to thank each other for their hard work.

17. According to Sachi, most of her co-workers, who are almost entirely irregular and female, work 21–24 days per month, and most are older than fifty-five, with the oldest being seventy. She noted that boxed lunch factory work is very attractive to older women because unlike most jobs, these do not have an age cutoff for hiring. But she noted it would be unusual for someone over seventy to work there because one has to write and remember, and there are many things one has to keep track of. Furthermore, one has to stand all day long on concrete floors.

18. Sachi's uncanny ability to effortlessly spot a defective product is an example of "embodying labor" in anthropology. See Pretence and Whitelaw (2008) for analyses incorporating this concept.

19. Sachi was stressing the word "wife," perhaps a bit sarcastically, to indicate that full-time homemaker wives in the postwar years did all the housework for their families themselves, as part of their bargain in the gendered division of labor in a salaryman household. She did not consider herself to be this sort of woman.

20. For a similar story of a youth whose social class background prevented him and his mother from understanding how to negotiate and adjust to the rigors of junior high school, see David Slater's "The 'New Working Class' of Urban Japan: Socialization and Contradiction from Middle School to the Labor Market," in Ishida and Slater, *Social Class in Contemporary Japan,* 137–169.

21. A day-care worker's license, like a beautician's license or a nursing license, is considered *te ni shoku,* a license that leads to a skilled job. In contrast, a certificate from a two-year junior college, such as the one from which Ami graduated, became increasingly less marketable as businesses ceased hiring such graduates in regular secretarial jobs as the economy worsened in the 1990s.

22. This is in stark contrast to the employees at Atsuko's government day-care job, who, she reports, are not at all frank and who are highly hierarchical and bureaucratic.

23. Atsuko's parents rarely told their children what to do or suggested possible pathways to follow. This seems to have been the first time her father gave her some career guidance—albeit in a very circumspect manner. Lebra (1987) mentions the importance of silent communication in Japan. Atsuko picked right up on it and realized that her father wanted her to get on with her career.

24. After-school day-care programs are provided at subsidized rates in some public elementary school districts to care for children whose parents are working. They generally care for children through the third grade, although some programs also allow older children to drop in to play. Their staffs hold professional credentials from specialized two-year colleges such as the one Atsuko attended.

25. Atsuko also concertedly made efforts to meet a mate through dating parties, through which she found her husband.

26. I recently learned that one way to become employed by a cosmetics firm is to obtain technical school training in cosmetology and hair styling. The Fujiis had no idea of this route.

27. Ami is able to get by on this income because she lives at home. She pays her

mother a token amount each month for board, Sachi told me. Neither Ami nor her brother has any significant savings, Sachi noted.

28. Ami's penchant for buying things may be a sore point with her mother, who told me that Ami has a wealthy girlfriend with whom she is always comparing herself and wanting to compete, although Ami does not have the means.

29. Atsuko, at age thirty-two, married a high school graduate who has contract employment at a factory; Yūji, at age twenty-seven, married his college sweetheart, who works as an irregular employee. Atsuko is about three years beyond the average age for women at first marriage (which was 28.8 in 2010), and Yūji is 3.5 years younger than the average age for men (30.5 in 2010) (Cabinet Office 2011). Atsuko took her time to marry because she had promised her father she would look after him and forgo marriage, but after he passed away in 2005, she gradually came to the realization that she was not strong enough to live alone for all her life. Masaji's death affected the Fujiis greatly, but I will leave that topic for another book.

30. The character-building aspect of sports illustrates the value of extra-curricular clubs *(bukatsudō)* in Japanese junior high schools and beyond. For an in-depth understanding of the *bukatsudō* system, see Cave (2004).

31. Graduating without a license is another indication of Yūji's easy-going nature. He would have had to study for a test in order to obtain this qualification.

References Cited

Allison, Anne. 1991. "Japanese Mothers and Obentōs: The Lunch-Box as Ideological State Apparatus." *Anthropological Quarterly* 64, no. 4:195–208.

Bourdieu, Pierre. 1977. *Outline of a Theory of Practice.* Cambridge: Cambridge University Press.

Brinton, Mary. 1994. *Women and the Economic Miracle: Gender and Work in Postwar Japan.* Berkeley: University of California Press.

———. 2011. *Lost in Transition: Youth, Work, and Instability in Postindustrial Japan.* Cambridge: Cambridge University Press.

Burawoy, Michael. 1998. "The Extended Case Method." *Sociological Theory* 16, no. 1:4–33.

Cabinet Office, Government of Japan. 2011. "Heikin shokon nenrei no suii." *Heisei nijūsannenban kodomo kosodate hakusho.* Http://www8.cao.go.jp/shoushi/ whitepaper/ w-2011/23webhonpen/html/furoku08–05.html. Accessed November 1, 2011.

Cave, Peter. 2004. "Bukatsudō: The Educational Role of Japanese School Clubs." *Journal of Japanese Studies* 30, no. 2:383–415.

Cole, Robert E. 1971. *Japanese Blue Collar: The Changing Tradition.* Berkeley: University of California Press.

Economic Research 2012. Japan/U.S. Foreign Exchange Rates. Http://research.stlouisfed .org/fred2/ data/EXJPUS.txt. Accessed April 20, 2012.

Fu, Huiyan. 2012. *An Emerging Non-Regular Labour Force in Japan: The Dignity of Dispatched Workers.* London and New York: Routledge.

Fuse, Kanae. 2006. "Daughter Preference in Japan: A Shift in Gender Role Attitudes?" Working Paper, Department of Sociology, Ohio State University. Http://paa2006. princeton.edu/ download.aspx?submissionId=60747. Accessed April 25, 2012.

Genda, Yūji. 2005. *A Nagging Sense of Job Insecurity: The New Reality Facing Japanese Youth.* Trans. Jean Hoff and Connell Hoff. Tokyo: International House Press.

Hatena Kīwādo. 2012. "Kin no tamago." Http://d.hatena.ne.jp/ keyword/%B6%E2%A4%CE%CD%F1. Accessed February 24, 2012.

Ishida, Hiroshi, and David H. Slater, eds. 2010. *Social Class in Contemporary Japan: Structures, Sorting and Strategies.* London: Routledge.

Iwao, Sumiko. 1993. *The Japanese Woman: Traditional Image and Changing Reality.* New York: Free Press.

Kariya, Takehiko. 2010. "From Credential Society to 'Learning Capital' Society: A Rearticulation of Class Formation in Japanese Education and Society." In Ishida and Slater, *Social Class in Contemporary Japan,* 87–113.

Kondo, Dorinne. 1993. "Uchi no kaisha: Company as Family?" In *Situated Meaning,* ed. Jane Bachnik and Charles Quinn, 169–191. Ithaca, NY: Cornell University Press.

Kosugi, Reiko. 2008. *Escape from Work: Freelancing Youth and the Challenge to Corporate Japan.* Melbourne: Transpacific Press.

Laureau, Annette. 2003. *Unequal Childhoods: Class, Race, and Family Life.* Berkeley: University of California Press.

Lebra, Takie. 1987. "The Cultural Significance of Silence in Japanese Communication." *Multilingua* 6, no. 4:343–357.

MacNaughton, Helen. 2006. "From 'Post-War' to 'Post-Bubble': Contemporary Issues for Japanese Working Women." In *Perspectives on Work, Employment and Society in Japan,* ed. Peter Matanle and Wim Lunsing, 31–57. London: Palgrave MacMillan.

Ministry of Education, Culture, Sports, Science, and Technology of Japan. 2008. *Monbutōkeiyōran, Heisei 20 nenkan.* Http://www.mext.go.jp/b_menu/ toukei/002/002b/ mokuji20.htm. Accessed February 24, 2012.

Ministry of Internal Affairs and Communications. 2011. *The Statistical Handbook of Japan 2011.* Http://www.stat.go.jp/english/data/handbook/c13cont.htm. Accessed April 20, 2012.

Ogasawara, Yūko. 1998. *Office Ladies and Salaried Men: Power, Gender and Work in Japanese Companies.* Berkeley: University of California Press.

Pretence, Rebecca, and Gavin Hamilton Whitelaw, eds. 2008. "Embodying Labor: Work as Fieldwork." Special Issue. *Anthropology of Work Review* 29, no. 3:53–77. DOI: 10.1111/j.1548–1417.2008.00019.x

Roberson, James. 1998. *Japanese Working Class Lives.* London: Routledge.

Roberts, Glenda S. 1994. *Staying on the Line: Blue-Collar Women in Contemporary Japan.* Honolulu: University of Hawai'i Press.

———. 2002. "Pinning Hopes on Angels: Reflections from an Aging Japan's Urban Landscape." In *Family and Social Policy in Japan,* ed. Roger Goodman, 54–91. Cambridge: Cambridge University Press.

———. 2004. "Globalization and Work/Life Balance: Gendered Implications of New Initiatives at a U.S. Multinational in Japan." In *Equity in the Workplace: Gendering Workplace Policy Analysis,* ed. Heidi Gottfried and Laura Reese, 305–321. Lanham, MD: Lexington Books.

———. 2007. "Similar Outcomes, Different Paths: The Cross-National Transfer of Gendered Regulations of Employment." In *Gendering the Knowledge Economy: Comparative Perspectives,* ed. Sylvia Walby, Heidi Gottfried, Karen Gottschall, and Mari Osawa, 141–161. London: Palgrave.

———. 2011. "Salary Women and Family Well-Being in Urban Japan." *Marriage and Family Review* 47, no. 8:571–589.

Rosenbluth, Francis M. 2007. *The Political Economy of Japan's Low Fertility.* Stanford, CA: Stanford University Press.

Salamon, Sandra. 1975. "Male Chauvinism as a Manifestation of Love in Marriage." In *Adult Episodes in Japan,* ed. David Plath, 20–31. Leiden: Brill.

Thomas, Landon, Jr. 2012. "For Youths in Britain, Few Jobs and Rising Anger." *International Herald Tribune,* global edition, February 17, 1, 15.

Vogel, Ezra. 1971. *Japan's New Middle Class.* Berkeley: University of California Press.

CHAPTER 2

Being a Man in a Straitened Japan

The View from Twenty Years Later

GORDON MATHEWS

IN 1989–1990, I intensively interviewed fifty Japanese women and men (between the ages of twenty and eighty) from all walks of life in Sapporo, Japan, about their lives and their notions of what made life worth living (Mathews 1996). From these interviews, I gathered a clear sense of how the men with whom I spoke derived their feelings of "being a man"; it was not, for most, in having different sexual partners, nor in engaging in daring pursuits beyond work, but simply in working hard to support their families (Mathews 2003). Work consumed the lives of most of the men between twenty-five and sixty. Nonetheless many expressed ambivalence about this—chained to their workplaces, most could neither live for their own personal pursuits, as some men sought to do, nor, more pivotally, for their families. A man living for his family was not a real man, many said or implied, but some longed to do so all the same if only they could.

In 2011, twenty-odd years later, I interviewed once again many of the people I had earlier interviewed; this chapter focuses on men and how they have changed in how they see their lives, as well as on their wives, ex-wives, and widows. Some of the men have retired, an event that has shifted the balance of power between themselves and their wives. Others have divorced, sometimes dumped by their wives after a history of disharmony. Others have gone from being young and single to middle-aged with children and spouses. In this process, the meaning of being a man has changed for these men, both because of their own aging and because of the aging and changing of Japan. The earlier mode of being a man in Japan, of men living for work in a way by which they both supported and neglected their families, has been eroded. In today's Japan, more tends to be demanded of husbands than their stable financial support—wives seek compatibility and communication. But these may be difficult, especially in marriages formed in an earlier Japanese era; men may contribute to housework and child care somewhat more than in the past, but full communication with one's spouse seems rare. Family, more than before, may indeed have become a major focus of "being a man" for these and other Japanese men, but it is an arena in which men may easily fail, judging from my interviews.

In conducting these reinterviews, I did not initially intend to discuss men and their lives. I focus on changing senses of being a man in this chapter because it seemed apparent from my interviews that the men I reinterviewed had markedly shifted in their attitudes because of changes in Japanese cultural norms. Men have been forced to change more than women, I found, and this is why I have focused on them in this chapter. The discerning reader may rightfully ask whether my small number of interviews is sufficient to make any larger generalizations. I think it is, in that the points I make concerning individuals are echoed in the Japanese-language and English-language social scientific and popular literature (as I discuss), showing that the men I interviewed are illustrations of larger trends. The men and women I discuss portray something beyond their own stories: they reveal the changing nature of what it is to be a man in Japan today.[1]

History and Life Course

Finding the people I interviewed in Sapporo in 1989–1990 was a daunting task during the summer of 2011. I had kept in touch with a dozen of them but not the rest, and many were impossible to find. Of the fifty people I had interviewed, at least eight had died. Others I simply could not find. In Japan, people cannot easily be found through Facebook or Google, both because many Japanese are concerned about privacy, and because many older people in Japan do not use computers. All in all, I managed to reinterview twenty-one of the original fifty people, eleven men and ten women. This is a small number, but this follow-up study is worthwhile because it can serve as a window into changing

Japanese concepts of masculinity, providing glimpses of the same people at different points of their lives, and at different points of recent Japanese history.[2] The stories I report upon are individual and idiosyncratic, but coupled with statistical and scholarly analyses, they can tell us something about some of the different ways of being a man in Japan today.

changes In a study of lives over time, there are two intertwining variables, those of history and of life course. Over twenty years, a man's life changes—a twenty-five-year-old's sense of being a man might be based on finding a girlfriend; a forty-five-year-old's might be based on his career accomplishments, on supporting his family through his job, or perhaps on his own dreams still unfulfilled; a sixty-five-year-old's may be based on his being with his wife as never before, or in pride in his grandchildren, or in pursuit of a hobby. These are matters of one's own life course, but they are linked to history.

One pivotal historical change has been Japan's economic decline. Japan has entered a new, more straitened era, it is now universally recognized. In some cases this change has had a direct impact on the men I interviewed: an employee in a large company that went out of business thereafter refused to believe that any job could ever be secure; a designer whose business collapsed in the economic downturn was forced to become a taxi driver to support his family, and it eventually led to his divorce. In other cases, this impact was more indirect. But in all cases, Japan's economic doldrums cast a subtle shadow over these men's lives, not necessarily foreclosing possibilities, but limiting them. To the extent that the sense of being a man may have been based on being able to support one's family, this task has become considerably more difficult. On the other hand, these economic doldrums have led, claimed some of those I interviewed, to a greater array of values in Japan—an expansion of possibilities as to how men, and women as well, might work and live.

Aside from economic changes, there have been other, more particular changes as well, in terms of family and gender roles. One very important such change is that the earlier gender division whereby in middle-class households men worked to support their families and women stayed home to do housework and raise their children, has largely given way. This shift has had a very significant effect on the marriages of the people I interviewed.

The Erosion of "Husband at Work, Wife at Home"

The idea that the husband should be the breadwinner and the wife the homemaker is not "traditional" in Japan but is of recent vintage, becoming standardized around 1960 (Yamada 2004, 129), following the postwar emergence of "lifetime employment" for white-collar male workers in large companies. The number of full-time housewives *(sengyō shufu)* peaked in 1975 in Japan (Yamada 2001, 160), with increasing numbers of wives in the oil-shock era of the 1970s and thereafter going to work in part-time jobs, both because one income was increasingly difficult to maintain a family on and because of Japan's shift to a service economy, making such jobs increasingly available and desirable for women who sought them (Iwakami 2010, 102–103).

However, although increasing numbers of wives went to work in the 1980s and 1990s, the idea that "husbands should work, and wives should take care of the home" remained dominant. According to one set of surveys, in 1979, 72.6 percent of Japanese male and female respondents supported this view, and in 1992, 60.1 percent did; only by 2002 did a plurality forsake this ideal, with 46.9 percent of respondents agreeing and 47 percent disagreeing (Yamada 2004, 128). Not surprisingly, men more than women have supported this view: in the 2002 survey, for example, 51.3 percent of men supported it, whereas 43.3 percent of women did. Nonetheless, many women throughout those years did indeed desire to be full-time housewives, who enjoyed significant social respect and who also often felt that their lives were better than those of their husbands, who were chained to their companies (Mathews 1996, 98–103). They benefited from a wider set of social relationships and activities that supported them through various stages of their lives. As one social critic of the early 1990s wrote, "Men's lives in Japan today are confined and regimented by their jobs to an extreme. . . . Today, it is, in a sense, the husbands who are being controlled and the ones to be pitied" (Iwao 1993, 15, 7).

That era is largely over. Lifetime employment has frayed in most Japanese companies. One consequence of employment becoming less secure for men is that they are no longer quite so tied to their companies as they once were, and Japanese working hours have gone down as compared to several decades ago (Rebick 2006, 89). At the same time, there is the still lagging but nonetheless increasing emergence of women in Japanese corporate life, as well as the somewhat diminishing gender gap between men's and women's average hourly earnings (Rebick 2006, 85–86). Just as women have come to play a slowly increasing role in the workplace, so too men are beginning to take a more positive attitude toward engaging in housework and child rearing, even if this is not much apparent in actual practice (Nagai 2009; Nakatani 2006, 97–99; North 2009).

The extent of this change should not be exaggerated; Japan remains a more gender-segregated society ("husband at work, wife at home") than most other developed societies today. Nonetheless, it seems clear that the gender role division of twenty, thirty, and forty years ago is not as accepted today as it once was. The earlier gender ideology of husbands at work, wives at home seems to be giving way to an era of greater personal variation and a greater possibility of husbands and wives being equally involved in work and at home. Among the people I interviewed, this has led to a significant shift in attitudes toward married life and in ideas of what a husband and a wife should be. Even those I interviewed who resisted these new ideas were nonetheless influenced by them, simply because these ideas were around them in the attitudes expressed by family members, co-workers, and the mass media, as well as in government pronouncements and policy toward families (Roberts 2002; Takeda 2011).

It might be assumed that this shift is an unambiguously good thing: because women and men, wives and husbands, are increasingly freed from having to live in the separate realms of family and work, they can become more equal and can more fully share their lives together. This may be largely true, but among the people I interviewed, those who married under the earlier paradigm of "husband at work, wife at home" and have now been asked to shift the basis of their marriages, the personal and interpersonal strains created by the disconnect between the old expectations and the new ideology have generally not made their marriages happier. This is not simply because the men I interviewed felt resentment toward their more empowered wives. More, it is because these men have found themselves in a new familial world in which playing their stereotypical gender role of breadwinner is no longer enough. The earlier model of being a man has passed them by, and the new model they, and their wives as well, cannot fully grasp.

From Breadwinner to Communicator

Twenty years ago, a salaryman I interviewed said, "As for my marriage . . . I guess for each of us the other is like air"—that is, necessary but easy to take for granted (Mathews 1996, 59). Several of the wives I interviewed only half jokingly referred to the saying *Teishu wa jōbu de rusu ga ii* (It's good when the husband is healthy and absent). In these marriages, the separate roles of husband and wife were paramount: if the husband was off at work and reliably bringing home his paycheck to support his family, that was quite sufficient.

There are still marriages like this, but typically now more is required of a husband—not just his financial contribution to the family and marriage but an emotional contribution. A housewife in her seventies who jokingly but approvingly uttered the above saying to me twenty years ago today had a more critical attitude toward her retired husband: "He recently asked me whether if there were reincarnation, I would want to be with him again; I told him no. The way he treated me in our marriage was just too inconsiderate [omoiyari ga nakatta]. When his parents moved in with us, he didn't even ask me if it was OK; we never discussed it. No, I wouldn't want to be reborn with him."[3] Her husband could only joke about his wife's discontent and didn't fully seem to understand it. All his working life as a teacher, his family life was secondary to his career, a priority that he took for granted as how a man was supposed to live in supporting his family (see Hidaka 2011). As he told me in 1989, "In my house, my wife was like a widow; I was busy, even on Sundays, with my school clubs. So now, if I'm not home, everyone feels more relaxed" (Mathews 2003, 111). Since his career ended, he has apparently paid the price for this earlier emotional neglect toward his family in his wife's attitude toward him. Their relationship is better than in the past, she told me, but she cannot forgive him for his past mistreatment.

Twenty years ago, I interviewed a young woman of twenty-two who had dreams of traveling the world and becoming a novelist and poet (although even then she knew that those dreams would probably never be realized). She said then, in response to my question, "If I married a fairly good man and had two kids, working at the same government job I have now, would I be disappointed? Yes, I'd be disappointed!" Today this is exactly the situation in which she finds herself. "My life is good—I'm 90 percent satisfied—but I'm not completely happy." She makes more money than her husband. Her husband, a computer programmer whom she married in 2003, does fully half of the housework and child care, they both agreed when I asked them. Her husband joined the interview halfway through, having listened in from another room, and said to his wife, "So you wonder how we got here, in an ordinary family with two children, and why you're not completely happy? Sometimes I wonder too how I've gotten here and why I'm not completely happy." His wife looked at him in amazement and said, "You've never told me that before!" It took my presence to finally get them to talk, she told me later. His sense of being a man, he said, was very much linked to the success of his marriage and family, but communication with his wife seemed, given all the complications and harassments of everyday life, to be difficult. Unlike the older couple described above, this man and his wife never held to the idea of "husband at work, wife at home"; rather, both of them had aspired to a different kind of life than the conventional middle-class life they were now leading. Their difficulties lay in their inability to communicate about these aspirations and other matters deep in their hearts. But this difficulty too was related to changing conceptions of marriage and of what a man should be: if marriage has become based on communication, then a failure in communication may be seen as a failure of marriage. My interviewee, in her claim to be only 90 percent satisfied, seems a far cry from some Japanese women of earlier generations, for whom long-term endurance over decades of marriage was often called for (see the Japanese women depicted by Plath 1980). This difference marks how much marriage may have changed in Japan.

A corporate executive in her fifties said, "I don't know anyone who is happily married." She herself was newly married when I interviewed her twenty years ago, although she spoke little about her husband in our interviews. Now she has been divorced for twelve years from a husband she says didn't understand her (and who also made less money than she did). But why are the marriages I saw so often unhappy? This factor may be partly the result of my interview sample. The people who wanted to talk about their lives in such depth twenty years ago may have been more reflective and more prone to discontent than many of their fellow Japanese; that so many have been divorced or have less than satisfactory marriages twenty years later may reflect this fact. However, the unhappiness of many of my interviewees may also be due to greater demands on what marriage should be today as opposed to decades ago: playing a role is no longer enough. This apparent shift in the meanings of marriage has made the relationships of those who married with different expectations less fulfilling.

As one older salaryman I interviewed exclaimed, "[Now] you can't only make money for your wife and kids. You have to communicate too!" This echoes Yamada's key point (2001, 194): whereas in marriages of an earlier era, playing one's assigned role of breadwinner or homemaker was sufficient, in recent years more has become required—communication and emotional intimacy.[4] As Nakano puts it, there has been "a shift in understandings of marriage, from the idea that marriage involves social duty and the fulfillment of social roles, to the companionate model in which love, individual choice, and companionship form the basis of marriage" (2011, 135). As long as the basis for marital harmony was the husband's bringing home a secure income and no more than that, then Japanese familial stability was largely assured since this was a straightforward task to fulfill. Husband and wife had their separate spheres in life; heart-to-heart communication was largely beside the point. However, once these separate roles broke down—once "husband at work, wife at home" lost its ideological centrality—then the basis for marriage could no longer be practical but instead became emotional. Once women had opportunities to make almost as much money as men could, there was no longer any reason for them to remain in a marriage that was not emotionally fulfilling. However, for men raised in an earlier, breadwinner-oriented era of masculinity, the new demands for housework, communication, and emotional support may seem impossible to fulfill.

Value Conflicts over Children

A significant source of conflict in marriage among the people I interviewed is that of how children should be raised; a major source of parental pride, and many men's masculine pride, is having children turn out well. One man, who twenty years ago was a corporate worker with young children for whom he had high hopes, now feels upset when at a business meeting a customer or colleague mentions how his children are at top universities or companies when his own children have never been able to find career-track jobs. Two of my best Japanese friends for decades are now not talking to each other, evidently partly because while one of them has had a mediocre career and has retired, his two sons are both successful and have secure jobs and marriages that have produced grandchildren. The other, although still working as a corporate executive, has sons who are not working or married. When I meet these two men (separately), they refer obliquely to the other, asking, in particular, how the other's children are doing. This alienation is tragic, but given how these men define their sense of being a man, it is perhaps inevitable.

I interviewed a young man of twenty-five twenty years ago who worked for Takugin, Hokkaido's leading bank. At that time he chafed at the bank's restrictions on his life, such as requiring him to live in the company dormitory, but he accepted as a matter of course and with considerable pride that his entire career would be spent at the bank. In 1997 Takugin went bankrupt, as he learned from the news on television one morning at breakfast. After much initial shock, he recovered nicely, going to work for another bank and then changing jobs to work at a related company at a high salary. However, he remains haunted by how fragile such employment is; he quietly acquires rental properties in case his job again vanishes. His wife wants their daughter and son, aged twelve and ten, to go to good universities and enter top-ranked companies, but he is opposed: "My children need to be able to make their own paths in life, and have skills apart from their companies, because companies can go bankrupt. I know this from my own life." Because of his own career experiences, he, unlike his wife, does not trust conventional expectations of career success for his children.

This interviewee has a miserable relationship with his wife, a full-time housewife. He told me that he would like her to work, but she won't. She is completely uninteresting to talk to, he says, and they have nothing in common; when he makes breakfast once a week for his family, his wife is unhappy, he claims, since he is stealing her role. He and she remain as a couple for the sake of their children, he said. "Why did you ever marry her?" I asked him. "Well, I didn't know that marriage was going to be like this," he said. Twenty years earlier, I remember his girlfriend—not the woman he later married—as being beautiful but with nothing to say (although she may have been particularly shy in front of me); finding a person with whom he could communicate through thick or thin didn't seem to be on his mind then, and perhaps not later as well. In any case, it seems that the shock of his firm's collapse that has shaped his life and view of the world is one that his wife has never recognized, as is apparent in their different hopes for their children; he told me that they had never really talked about it.

Part of the problem in their relationship may lie in the changing nature of Japanese marriages, where the ideal of communication has only recently emerged; possibly, if he were a young man today, he would not embark on such a marriage. But part of the problem may also lie in the nature of marriage itself throughout the developed world, based as it is on romantic passion, which inevitably to some extent fades. Proponents of *miai kekkon*—marriages arranged by families (rather than through the individual choice of the partners), the dominant form of marriage in Japan up until the late 1960s (Edwards 1989, 53–76; Yamada 2004, 124)—have sometimes maintained that arranged marriages are superior to love marriages. In the latter, they say, love fades after marriage, whereas in the former, love—not necessarily romantic passion but deep friendship—grows. Looking at the marriages described by my interviewees, I wonder if this might not be to some extent true—although arranged marriage reflects an earlier Japanese era, never to return.

Another corporate employee I first interviewed in his mid-forties, now in his mid-sixties, has a similar story of marital disharmony, although opposite in its particulars. He has a son who has been *hikikomori*, or socially withdrawn, and another who quit his career-track job—two unemployed children in their late twenties living at home.[5] He has long tormented himself over how such a thing could have happened; today, in retrospect, he blames himself: "I wanted them to go to top universities and enter top companies, but I see now that I was putting too much pressure on them. I never should have done that."

His wife and sons sided against him for several years, and his family was an emotional battleground, as I saw when I visited them. His wife felt that he should simply let his sons make their own paths, rather than inflict on them his own high expectations, and she seems to have taken it out on him through emotional distancing. Finally, he came to see the error of his ways, he told me, and came to fully understand that his sons must be let go: "It's their own lives at this point. They need to make their own way." But at their age, can they? He believes that in Japan today, financial doldrums have created new opportunities for more diverse ways of life than in the recent past; one of his sons is studying to be a craftsman, while the other, in the privacy of his room, studies investing. He and his wife, after years of difficulties, seemed happy together when I last visited them, almost as they were twenty years ago.

The two men interviewed above have found their senses of being men not just in working hard to make a good living for their families, but also in trying to make families that are happy; one eventually succeeded, it seems, while the other seems likely to fail. Both these men fit the standard role of an earlier era: well-paid corporate employees with stay-at-home wives. However, it is not enough; value differences over their children have plagued their relations with their spouses, with one man blaming his spouse for her conventionality, and the other blaming himself for his own conventionality. Such conflicts could happen in any era but are more likely in today's Japan, where "bringing home the bacon" is not enough for a man to be a man and where society's once taken-for-granted paths for men and women have been called into question. What a man should be, and what a woman should be, were more settled in the Japan of thirty and forty years ago, but today the criteria are up for grabs.

Value Conflicts and Religion

Children were one major source of value conflicts among the men I interviewed, but there were others as well, with another source of conflict being religion. Two of the men I interviewed were profoundly religious, with their senses of being men linked to their religious beliefs.

One man was a doctor in his thirties and a staunch believer in the new Japanese religion Mahikari when I interviewed him in 1990. He spoke of sometimes trying to relieve his patients of their pain through a treatment called *tekazashi,* the raising of the palm of his hand to emit spiritual light. He was married to a woman who wholly shared his faith, and they had two small children. When I interviewed him again after two decades, he told me that he had lost interest in Mahikari a number of years ago because of "human relations problems" with others of its members, as well as a degree of new skepticism as to Mahikari's claims. His wife and children remained adherents, but he turned away, never actively renouncing the religion but not attending its meetings. His wife never directly confronted him about his lack of belief, he told me, but patiently awaited his return, gently asking him if he would attend a meeting, a request that he generally refused.

Then, in 2005, his daughter, in her early twenties, returned home from study overseas and began losing weight rapidly, eating and then purging; she apparently had bulimia. He took her to specialists, who announced that the cause of her eating disorder was the family situation, telling him that he was neurotic and needed counseling. Outraged, he took her to Mahikari therapy sessions—similar to exorcisms, as he described them—and over several months she became better; he subsequently returned to Mahikari and to the religious fold of his family. Now his daughter, as well as his son, works together with him in his medical practice, and all are fervent adherents of Mahikari. He told me that without Mahikari, his life would make no sense; his life now is preparation for a longer journey from lifetime to lifetime, where gender and individuality are transcended. He also told me that through his religious faith his relationship with his family, and particularly with his wife, was now healed since they all had a faith in common. His ongoing religious faith has enabled him to become rejuvenated as a man, he claimed.

I interviewed a corporate employee who subsequently became a Buddhist priest. He had had a European wife, whom he married in 1981, and had two children with her, but after ten years of marriage, she left him and returned to Europe with their children. His response to their departure and to other setbacks in his life was to become a priest, going on yearly meditation retreats in the mountains—not like other Buddhist priests in the "funeral business," he maintained, but as a spiritual path, to pursue the meaning of his existence over the course of many lifetimes. He became a priest while still a salaryman and was met with disdain by his various bosses, one of whom said, "Why are you spending time doing these things? You should spend your time on the company's work!" He finally managed to quit his corporate position in his early fifties to devote himself fully to his spiritual path; he has a temple in his house and meets with his small congregation of six or so people three times a month. As for his marriage and family, he says of his former wife, "If she would have me, I'd get together with her again."[6] She did not leave him because of his spiritual path, it seems, but because of a reluctance to raise her children in Japan.

These two men, one in a family and one outside family, have both made their spiritual paths the essence of their lives as human beings. Both these men see themselves as men only within this temporary setting of a lifetime; in a larger sense, their spiritual path transcends any gender identity, they maintain. Unlike the other men I have discussed, their lives have not been solely centered on work and family but rather on a search for larger meaning. Nonetheless, in this life, for one man a spiritual path brought him back to his family, while for the other, it was an alternative to a family he had lost. These men's spiritual paths can't be separated from their families, regained or lost in their lives.

Men Forced from the Family

Other men I interviewed found their senses of being men in pursuing their own artistic or career dreams as well as in having families, but these different goals may be incompatible. In the cases of the two men I describe below, their wives had no use for their dreams, and once these men's incomes shrank, their wives divorced them.

I interviewed a man of thirty in 1990, when he was on the cusp of getting married to a woman who disapproved of his unrealizable dream of becoming a doctor; they had two children within several years, and he abandoned that dream. In 1992, he found a job in a company doing marketing reports; he worked there for twelve years and was paid quite well. But he tired of it and quit to start a coffee shop—one more of his dreams and one that brought home far less money than his earlier job. His wife, a full-time housewife, accused him of abandoning the family by not earning enough money. "I wasn't her husband anymore because I wasn't supporting the family; that's what she told me," he said. "She didn't want to lose the high standard of living she had when I was working for a company. That, finally, is why we divorced. . . . She really didn't understand the kind of person I was, what I was looking for in my life. . . . Yes, my salary was really high when I worked for the company—it's really fallen! But we could have gotten by!" His wife eventually found a job, he told me, but one that brought in even less money than he was making; a court deemed that, other than a few remaining years of child support, he owed his wife nothing. He never sees his children now—his wife won't allow him to—but claims that he does not miss them too much. Now he lives alone and dreams of becoming a novelist. Just as he has for all of his adult life, he lives for his dreams, but now they are dreams he holds bereft of his family.

Another man I interviewed twenty years ago was a self-employed designer who had recently gotten married and had a son; he saw himself as an artist and felt considerable frustration at the gap between his artistic dreams and the requirements of his new family. His wife insisted that he devote himself to his family, he told me, and worried about whether he could make enough money to support his family. By the time I interviewed him twenty years later, he had lost his design company—it folded in 2000 in Japan's ongoing economic downturn—and had become a taxi driver, taking the night shift, which he has been doing for over a decade. Four years ago his wife divorced him while he was in the hospital suffering from stomach cancer. The divorce happened because of a specific incident: his son had a car accident for which my interviewee was indirectly to blame, and after a heated argument his wife served him with divorce papers. But underlying this discord is the lack of money. His income has consistently been low, and his wife, who also worked and brought home over half the family income, had grown increasingly weary of his lack of contribution to the family. He did half of the cleaning and cooking and child rearing, he claimed, but admitted that if he had had more money, the divorce might never have happened. His *ikigai,* the center of his life, he said, was half his children, whom his wife allows him to see once a month, and half the book he is writing about his experiences as a night taxi driver.

In both these cases, these men's wives seem to have felt that if their husbands weren't making enough money, then they weren't properly playing their roles as husbands. These men's dreams, so important to their own senses of themselves, were dreams that their wives seemed to consider no more than hobbies or pastimes, to be tolerated only if the husbands' income was sufficient. Their wives may have put up with them in the past for the sake of the money, but if they weren't bringing in money, why bother? One can hardly blame these wives. If they had married within the earlier assumption of a gender role division, then their husbands had shirked their responsibility by not adequately supporting their families. If they had married within the emerging new assumption, expecting communication and commitment from their husbands, then their husbands, in putting their own dreams first, had rejected such commitment. Or perhaps these wives expected both their husbands' high incomes and deep emotional commitment, a double expectation that may be impossibly hard to fulfill. We cannot know; we hear only from their husbands, who claim, one vociferously and the other more implicitly, that their wives failed to understand the dreams that they felt defined them.

Wives' satisfaction in marriage is consistently lower than that of husbands in Japan, by statistical measures (Inaba 2009, 122–130); this dissatisfaction is a major reason for rising Japanese divorce rates, which tripled between the mid-1960s and the early 2000s (Ogawa, Retherford, and Matsukura 2006, 27; Tsuya and Bumpass 2004, 7), with over 30 percent of marriages today destined for divorce (Alexy 2011, 238). Divorce has been increasing largely because with women's greater ability to earn a good income (as is the case for one of the wives discussed above, if not the other), they need not stay in a marriage only for the sake of their husbands' incomes if the marriage is not personally fulfilling to them (Yamada 2001, 196). Japanese divorce laws are, however, still rooted in an earlier era of gender role division, allowing only for single-parent custody, typically the mother's (Alexy 2011, 239; "Child-Snatchers" 2012; Kumagai 2008, 63–64). Thus divorced men can see their children only on their wives' forbearance. The two men discussed above both insisted on following their dreams and had sought to maintain families while more or less following those dreams. At this point, having been expelled from their families, these men had nothing to live for but their dreams.

Men Disabled and Loved

Among the women I reinterviewed, in at least two cases the men for whom they lived had died or become disabled. In 1990 I interviewed a mother of three small children. She had had problems in her marriage, but she said that even though the relationship still had its strains, "Our children now bind us." Subsequently her husband, a computer specialist, started his own business and was remarkably successful, but in 1999 he was diagnosed with brain cancer and then subsequently had a stroke, robbing him of the ability to speak, read, and walk. For seven years she took care of him, living at the hospital and nursing him at home, devoting herself wholly to this task and to defending her husband's pride—*puraido o mamoru,* his pride as a man. She is well aware that everything she has—her children and her financial well-being—came from him. He died in 2006. She is studying for a graduate degree at present but says that it really doesn't matter much to her; what's really important is the memory of her husband—a man who seemed to have played an emotionally more important role in her life when he was helpless than when he was able-bodied and able-minded, judging from all she told me.

I interviewed a couple in their fifties in 1990, who, two years after our interview, suffered a family catastrophe. Their daughter gave birth to a son who was severely brain-damaged; shortly thereafter, the daughter's husband died. The daughter then moved back to live with her parents; she works for a management company by day, and the three of them devote themselves to caring for this child-becoming-a-man of sixteen, a very sweet-natured being who can neither talk nor walk. The elderly couple told me that without their grandchild with disabilities, they really wouldn't have anything to live for. But as I observed them, it seemed clear that grandmother and mother were totally devoted to this child with disabilities, leaving grandfather out. He gets angry and does not know how to respond to their grandson's epileptic fits, he admitted to me. When I interviewed him and his wife twenty years ago, he was the patriarch, the center of the household, but now he is at its fringes. What we thus see is that a man who had supported his family for forty years was now displaced as the center of the household by his daughter's child with disabilities. This displacement no doubt has much to do with the role of caregiver in a Japanese context (Long 1996), in which caregiving, whether for a frail parent, a spouse, or an ailing child, may eclipse all other relationships. But in this case, it also seems to represent the wife's response to a less-than-fulfilling marriage over many decades; rather than care for an ailing husband, she chooses to devote herself wholly to her grandchild with disabilities.

Borovoy, in discussing the wives of alcoholics in Japan, notes the difficulties these women face in breaking free of their culturally imbued solicitousness toward their husbands; for these women, "the work of caregiving was their central source of validation" (2005, 101). This culturally imbued solicitousness seems apparent in the women I have here described. Caregiving may sometimes transcend gender: a husband may devote himself wholeheartedly to a stricken wife, for example, in return for all the care that she has given him over the years. But both the cases described above imply a rejection of men and masculinity, in that love toward thinking, responding men is problematic, while men who are unable to think, walk, and talk are loved unconditionally, or at least cared for wholeheartedly. These cases imply that it may be easier for a woman to love a man who does not wield any power over her.

Men and Retirement

A number of the men I earlier interviewed had in the intervening years retired; their senses of being men had shifted and diminished as compared to what they had been twenty years earlier, and their family relations had also changed. As one woman, now in her seventies, said about her husband, "Over the years, I began to understand how at heart he really was kind. Now I can be more relaxed with him and have a warmer feeling; that wasn't the case until recently, after he stopped being so busy at work. It's no longer a matter of man and woman but a human feeling that's most important in our relationship." Moore, in her study of men's extramarital affairs, found that after retirement, men had far fewer affairs (2010), in that they no longer lived in a separate realm from their wives and became more dependent upon them—or more aware that they were dependent. White (2002, 166) mentions how one older Japanese woman she interviewed described retirement with her husband as being "like heaven," in all the travel and fun within an equal relationship that they could now have. It may well be that for some fortunate couples, the husband's retirement is indeed joyful because it signifies that the gender role division of work and home has to some extent given way, and husband and wife can be together in the remaining decades of their lives. However, more frequently after men retire, they expect their wives to play the same homemaking role they played while the men were working, to their wives' frustration.

Indeed, many men are lost after leaving behind their careers, not knowing what to do with themselves. One scholar writes of how older Japanese men may become alcoholic in their retirement: they may have no friends or activities but only drink and watch TV (Takenaka 2000, 44, 47). Another remarks that these newly retired men "have wholly devoted themselves to work, and now they have no idea what to do with their lives. . . . This is especially true for corporate employees during the high growth era. . . . Losing their purpose in life in work, they may quickly grow old" (Kanemaru 1999, 10). Such responses may become less prevalent in years to come, as a new generation of men who have not wholly surrendered themselves to work enters retirement, but are still widespread today.

I interviewed one husband and wife twenty years ago who were then having a difficult time both because of the husband's depression, endangering his job as a corporate worker, and because of their worry about their children. Today, the husband has finished his career and retired at age sixty-two while their children are living conventionally successful lives, but both husband and wife continue to suffer from depression. As she told me, the problem is that although she has a reasonably comfortable life, without great money worries, there's nothing that she wants to do—nothing seems worth doing. She indicated that partly her condition was due to the influence of her husband, who, still under daily medication, does little all day but sleep and eat. However, since her husband retired, she has insisted that he do half the housework and cooking. She worries that if she dies, he won't know what to do; sharing the housework is a way of overcoming this worry.[7] Meanwhile, though, their life seems joyless, bereft of interests or of curiosity. It is as if he, having completed his forty-year role as a corporate worker, and she, having completed her role as a mother raising her children to adulthood, are empty. In terms of masculinity, having completed his masculine breadwinner role, there is nothing left for him to do but eat, sleep, and eventually die.

I interviewed another man with a wholly different approach toward life. He had been an ordinary corporate worker in the thick of his work twenty years earlier, with a wife and young children. Now, with his children grown up and his company role close to being finished, he could not wait to retire—indeed, when he was asked to be the branch head of his company, he refused, opting to leave instead. As he told me, "I don't yet know what exactly I will do—it's a year away—but I want to read all the history books I've wanted to read and then travel to those places, all over the world. My wife doesn't want to go—she doesn't speak any English—so I'll go alone. I can do it!" He told me that unlike twenty years ago, he has learned to enjoy life more, especially in the retirement he so looks forward to.

Whether the retirement he actually lives will be as fulfilling as he imagines it will be is an open question, and whether he can live it without becoming estranged from his wife also remains to be seen. The key issue here is this: why is one man, finished with his corporate role, essentially finished with life, while another man is able to dream and live beyond the role that he has played for all his adulthood? What accounts for this difference in personal flexibility? To some extent, this seems to be a medical issue, one of clinical depression and its ravages; clinical depression is apparently a significant factor in one couple's joylessness. However, in a more general sense, a key to being happy as a man is to be able to fully live life for all of one's years. From the literature, living life fully seems to be an enormous challenge facing retiring men of the postwar Japanese baby boom (see Yanagisawa 2007 for one example of all the exhortatory literature on how the elderly can find a new purpose in life). Being a man today requires more than merely playing a role in work and family, but for some retired corporate workers, this exhortation may be too late.

Conclusion: Being a Man in the New Japan

Twenty years ago, I found that most of the men I interviewed were forced to live for work, given the massive amount of time it took up in their lives and the limited role they were expected to play in their families. Today, however, the gendered division of labor of earlier years has partially given way: many women seek more from their marriages than a husband's salary; they desire affection and communication as well.

If a man has a family, I found from my reinterviews, then he typically cannot live for work alone, nor for his dreams alone; if he does, he may be ignored in the family or be divorced. Twenty years ago, I found that the men I interviewed couldn't easily live for their families. Today, I found that a man *must* live for his family if he wants to preserve that family in its harmony. Partly this shift is due to life course—the men I interviewed are twenty years older and either retired or over halfway to retirement, which is in effect expulsion from the world of work. But more, it is due to history: Japan has changed, with women's increasing role in the workplace and wives' increasing desire for their husband's emotional commitment and communication as well as paycheck. For the men I interviewed, this seems to have made marriage more difficult than in an earlier era, and it has made being a man more problematic.

One may rightfully ask whether the small sample of men I have discussed here is skewed. I have reported on every man I interviewed twenty-odd years ago and subsequently was able to reinterview. But is this small number of men representative of older Japanese men as a whole? I am acutely aware of the unhappiness of many of the people with whom I spoke, and I can only hope that they are not fully representative. But aside from issues of happiness, the difficulties these men (as well as women) face in their marriages are not unique to them, judging from the literature, but are more or less apparent in Japan at large.

The dominant ideal of being a man in Japan today is for a man to be devoted to his family, but as we have seen, such devotion may be difficult. It is not simply that men won't do their share of child care and housework—many men I interviewed indeed did, they said, although how much they actually did remains an open question. Rather, it appears to be more about their inability to fully communicate with their wives; if they tried to communicate, they often found that their values significantly differed from those of their wives. In some cases, if they didn't make enough money, their wives found these value differences intolerable and divorced them; in an era in which wives can go back to work, they might not tolerate differences in values that they might have in an earlier era. In other cases, if the men did support their families, these value differences led only to unhappy marriages. These differences in values were reflected in conflicts between spouses over how to raise children in a Japan where the standard life path of earlier eras was no longer assured as a route to success; they were also reflected, for some men, in conflicts with their spouses over religious paths. In some cases these conflicts led to situations where the male center of the household was not a man in full but disabled and in need of constant care and the focus of feminine love in the family, perhaps in part because such men couldn't play the often overbearing roles that older men still conventionally play in Japan. Finally, transcending family, there is the crucial matter of what a man is to do once his work role is done: how can he find the inner resources to lead a fulfilling life, whether within or beyond his family?

So is it any easier being a man today in Japan than it was twenty years ago? In one sense yes—it probably is easier for a man to live for his family because work is not quite so expected to be the center of a man's life. But in another sense it has gotten far harder because of the necessity for communication. As long as a man could contribute his paycheck alone to his family, then it was relatively easy to live for family, in at least a superficial sense. But that era seems over in a Japan with rising divorce rates and greater female expectations of what a marriage and family should be. Being a man in a changing Japan is harder than ever, it seems. Nonetheless, with greater diversity and acceptance of different life paths, the possibility of finding one's own happiness as a man has probably grown—if only a man can be smart enough and lucky enough to find his life path within or perhaps apart from family, as a few of the different examples I have discussed in this chapter have shown.

Notes

1. An initial reader of this chapter asked whether Sapporo, the site of my research, might be considered an "outlier" since it is a relatively newly settled city on the northern island of Hokkaido, rather than one of the more traditionally studied cities in research on Japan such as Tokyo or Osaka. It probably is the case, as several of my informants have told me, that the stress of work is somewhat lower in Sapporo than in Tokyo, not least because of shorter commutes. However, as the fifth largest city in Japan, it probably should not be considered an outlier, any more than, for example, Houston or Phoenix should be considered American outliers because they are relatively recently populated.
2. Hidaka (2011) compares concepts of masculinity among Japanese salarymen, with findings broadly similar to my own. She looks at three generations of men at one point in time, rather than looking at how men change in their senses of being men over time, as I do.
3. Japanese husbands and wives tend to be modest, even harshly critical, in describing one another to outsiders, particularly in front of one another; criticisms are more culturally acceptable than praise in this context. But in this case, the wife earnestly told me this when her husband had left the room; her words were not simply a product of modesty.
4. Yamada dates this change from 1980 onward, long before I saw it in my interviews.
5. *Hikikomori* refers to young people who withdraw from social life—school or

work—and sometimes remain in their rooms for years on end. This is a major Japanese social issue today (see Horiguchi 2011).

6. Japanese Buddhist priests, unlike Catholic priests, are not required to be celibate; most are married.

7. The problem of elderly husbands newly living alone has become the subject of a number of recent books—see, for example, Nakazawa (2010)—advising these men on such basics as what they should eat, how they should make friends, and what they should do with their time.

References Cited

Alexy, Allison. 2011. "The Door My Wife Closed: Houses, Families, and Divorce in Contemporary Japan." In Ronald and Alexy, *Home and Family in Japan*, 236–253.

Borovoy, Amy. 2005. *The Too-Good Wife: Alcohol, Codependency, and the Politics of Nurturance in Postwar Japan.* Berkeley: University of California Press.

"Child-Snatchers: Parental Abduction in Japan." 2012. *The Economist,* January 21–27, 32.

Edwards, Walter. 1989. *Modern Japan through Its Weddings: Gender, Person, and Society in Ritual Portrayal.* Stanford, CA: Stanford University Press.

Hidaka, Tomoko. 2011. "Masculinity and the Family System: The Ideology of the 'Salaryman' across Three Generations." In Ronald and Alexy, *Home and Family in Japan,* 112–130.

Horiguchi, Sachiko. 2011. "Coping with Hikikomori: Socially Withdrawn Youth and the Japanese Family." In Ronald and Alexy, *Home and Family in Japan,* 216–235.

Inaba, Akihide. 2009. "Fūfu kankei no hyōka" (Assessing the relationship between husband and wife). In *Gendai Nihon no kazoku* (Family patterns in contemporary Japan), ed. Fujimi Sumiko and Nishino Michiko, 122–130. Tokyo: Yūhikaku.

Iwakami, Mami. 2010. "Kōrei shakai o ikiru gihō" (Techniques for living in an aging society). In *Ima, kono Nihon no kazoku* (Families in today's Japan), ed. Iwakami Mami, Suzuki Iwayumi, Mori Kenji, and Watanabe Hideki, 90–131. Tokyo: Kōbundō.

Iwao, Sumiko. 1993. *The Japanese Woman: Traditional Image and Changing Reality.* New York: Free Press.

Kanemaru, Hiromi. 1999. *Jibun no tame no ikigai zukuri: Nakama ga iru to konna ni chigau gojūdai kara no ikikata* (Creating ikigai for yourself: Life after fifty will be very different when you have friends). Tokyo: Ichimansha.

Kumagai, Fumie. 2008. *Families in Japan: Changes, Continuities, and Regional Variations.* Lanham, MD: University Press of America.

Long, Susan. 1996. "Nurturing and Femininity: The Impact of the Ideal of Caregiving in Postwar Japan." In *Re-imaging Japanese Women,* ed. Anne Imamura, 156–176. Berkeley: University of California Press.

Mathews, Gordon. 1996. *What Makes Life Worth Living? How Japanese and Americans Make Sense of Their Worlds.* Berkeley: University of California Press.

———. 2003. "Can 'a Real Man' Live for His Family? *Ikigai* and Masculinity in Today's Japan." In *Men and Masculinities in Contemporary Japan: Dislocating the Salaryman Doxa,* ed. James E, Roberson and Nobue Suzuki, 109–125. London: RoutledgeCurzon.

Moore, Katrina. 2010. "Marital Infidelity of Older Japanese Men: Interpretations and Conjectures." *Asian Anthropology* 9:57–76.

Nagai, Akiko. 2009. "Otto no kaji sanka" (Husbands' participation in housework). In *Gendai Nihon no kazoku* (Family patterns in contemporary Japan), ed. Fujimi Sumiko and Nishino Michiko, 115–121. Tokyo: Yūhikaku.

Nakano, Lynne Y. 2011. "Working and Waiting for an 'Appropriate Person': How Single Women Support and Resist Family in Japan." In Ronald and Alexy, *Home and Family in Japan*, 131–151.

Nakatani, Ayami. 2006. "The Emergence of 'Nurturing Fathers': Discourses and Practices of Fatherhood in Contemporary Japan." In Rebick and Takenaka, *The Changing Japanese Family*, 94–108.

Nakazawa, Mayumi. 2010. *Otoko ohitorisama jyutsu* (For men: How to live if you're alone). Tokyo: Hōken.

North, Scott. 2009. "Negotiating What's Natural: Persistent Domestic Gender Role Inequality in Japan." *Social Science Japan Journal* 12, no. 1:23–44.

Ogawa, Naohiro, Robert D. Retherford, and Rikiya Matsukura. 2006. "Demographics of the Japanese Family: Entering Uncharted Territory." In Rebick and Takenaka, *The Changing Japanese Family*, 19–38.

Plath, David W. 1980. *Long Engagements: Maturity in Modern Japan*. Stanford, CA: Stanford University Press.

Rebick, Marcus. 2006. "Changes in the Workplace and Their Impact on the Family." In Rebick and Takenaka, *The Changing Japanese Family*, 75–93.

Rebick, Marcus, and Ayumi Takenaka, eds. 2006. *The Changing Japanese Family*. New York: Routledge.

Roberts, Glenda. 2002. "Pinning Hopes on Angels: Reflections from an Aging Japan's Urban Landscape." In *Family and Social Policy in Japan*, ed. Roger Goodman, 54–91. Cambridge: Cambridge University Press.

Ronald, Richard, and Allison Alexy, eds. 2011. *Home and Family in Japan: Continuity and Transformation*. New York: Routledge.

Takeda, Hiroko. 2011. "Reforming Families in Japan: Family Policy in the Era of Structural Reform." In Ronald and Alexy, *Home and Family in Japan*, 46–64.

Takenaka, Hoshirō. 2000. *Kōreisha no koritsu to yutakasa* (Old people's isolation and affluence). Tokyo: NHK Books.

Tsuya, Noriko O., and Larry L. Bumpass. 2004. *Marriage, Work, and Family Life in Comparative Perspective: Japan, South Korea, and the United States*. Honolulu: University of Hawai'i Press.

White, Merry Isaacs. 2002. *Perfectly Japanese: Making Families in an Era of Upheaval*. Berkeley: University of California Press.

Yamada, Masahiro. 2001. *Kazoku to iu risuku* (The risk called family). Tokyo: Keisō Shobō.

———. 2004. "Pātonā erabi to kekkon senryaku" (Choosing one's partner and using marriage strategies). In *Kazoku kakumei* (Family revolution), ed. Shimizu Hiroaki, Mori Kanji, Iwakami Mami, and Yamada Masahiro, 121–126. Tokyo: Kōbundō.

Yanagisawa, Isamu. 2007. *Ikigai aru jinsei kōhan o dezain suru* (Designing the second half of your life to be a life with purpose). Tokyo: Hōzuki Shoseki.

Work Conditions and Experiences

In part II contributors address work experiences and conditions during the 2000s. Sawa Kurotani (chapter 3) explores the lives of female full-time workers of the bubble generation, in their forties and fifties, who have never left their workplace for marriage or child rearing, as did most of their peers. Despite the Equal Employment Opportunity Law (EEOL), introduced in 1986, which officially opened the doors to career-track positions for women in the corporate world, the society continues to pressure married women to quit their jobs when they have children, and Kurotani's chapter sheds light upon the ways the long-term female workers have developed and coped with the persistent male dominance in the corporate world.

Nancy Rosenberger (chapter 4) tells us the story of a young woman, Kana, who has given up a middle-class lifestyle for an alternative life based upon organic farming. Following the ideals of environmental responsibility and food sufficiency, she strives to provide the safest vegetables that she can to her customers and spread her ideals among them through newsletters and face-to-face interaction. Her life path is at odds with the mainstream one, which depends on a corporate worker/husband in the capitalist economic system based upon mass production and consumption. Rosenberger delineates Kana's resistance to the status quo in contemporary Japan and its consequences, filled with contradictions and compromises.

Gavin Hamilton Whitelaw (chapter 5) draws readers' attention to the small-scale business families who own convenience stores in Tokyo. He reveals the storeowners' struggles to meet the demands of fussy urban consumers, make a profit, and grapple with everyday losses. Bound by franchise contracts set by headquarters to maximize corporate profits, storeowners are forced to pay "loss charges" on unsold food items. In the recessionary economy during the 2000s, it has become much more difficult to establish a thriving convenience store in Tokyo.

CHAPTER 3

Working Women of the Bubble Generation

SAWA KUROTANI

THIS CHAPTER IS an ethnographic study of professional Japanese women of the bubble generation *(baburu sedai)* who entered the full-time workforce in the 1980s and early '90s, at the height of Japan's postwar economic miracle. During the economic boom, Japan's strong economy and the Equal Employment Opportunity Law (EEOL) suddenly opened up professional opportunities for Japanese women, who had been marginalized for decades in the Japanese corporate world. Then, in the 1990s, they experienced a drastic change as the bloated economy collapsed and a decade-long recession put into doubt the efficacy of Japan's postwar economic regime in an increasingly globalized world. This chapter focuses in particular on three professional women, how they understand the effects of macrostructural forces in their lives, and how they have negotiated their professional and personal paths through these decades of socioeconomic turmoil.

Women of the Bubble Generation

The "bubble generation" commonly refers to the cohort of Japanese who were born in the mid- to late 1960s and started full-time employment during

83

the bubble era (1986–1991). A somewhat broader definition of the term—prevalent in Japanese popular culture—includes those who "came of age" in the late 1980s, formed their worldview at the time of economic effervescence, and are known for their taste for high-end consumer products and services. They are the children of the frugal and hard-working *yakeato sedai,* or the "burnt ruins" generation, who spent their formative years in the aftermath of World War II. If the childhoods of the "burnt ruins" generation were made difficult with loss and poverty, their adulthood was characterized by ever-improving standards of living and boundless optimism for the future. Already in the middle to advanced stages of their lives by the recession of the 1990s, they had amassed the world's highest rate of personal savings for secure retirement. Their children grew up in an increasingly affluent society. Unlike their frugal and conservative parents or their politically oriented big sisters and brothers of the *dankai no sedai* (the cohort born roughly between 1946 and 1954), those of the bubble generation learned to enjoy material comforts at an early age, drove the surge of conspicuous consumption during the 1980s, and came to expect a long, prosperous life as their birthright.

As Japan entered an extended period of economic stagnation following the collapse of the bubble economy, the bubble generation faced radical changes in corporate structure and workplace culture, as the corporate largesse of the bubble era disappeared and the promise of lifelong employment—a staple of postwar Japanese human resource management—quickly became a tale of the past. However, for them, falling into *makegumi,* or the loser's team (A. Miura 2005), was not an option. They worked harder—at times to the point of self-destruction. In the latter half of the 1990s, the wave of corporate restructuring ended the assumption of lifelong employment. When increased stress and anxiety over an uncertain future drove up the suicide rates among working adults, it was the bubble generation, men and women in their thirties and forties, who were hit the hardest.

While the bubble generation shares a significant historical experience that unites its members as a cohort, gender puts a distinct spin on the generational experience. Work is one of the most important factors of gender differentiation in the vast majority of human societies, and it is certainly the case in postwar Japan, where the strict division of labor between men and women was reinforced throughout much of the twentieth century (Rosenberger 2001). Even after World War II, the gender division of labor persisted, and Japanese workplaces remained male-dominated (Brinton 1993; Ogasawara 1998). Most women, whose labor participation increased gradually in the late twentieth century, continued to regard paid labor as a temporary engagement before they got married and had children; in turn, most Japanese employers relegated women to non-professional clerical positions and considered that their contribution to long-term corporate productivity would be limited (Kurotani 2005; Roberts 2007).

Major shifts occurred, however, as the bubble generation completed education and began to enter the workforce. The EEOL originally came into effect in 1986; it was intended to encourage gradual change in the male-dominated workplace and mandated some basic changes in employment practices, with no provisions to punish offending employers. The major change as a result of the EEOL was the prohibition of gendered career tracks. Prior to 1986, it was a widespread practice for employers to advertise for "male" positions in sales and technical fields, with opportunities for advancement, or "female" positions, mostly clerical work to support male workers and with no or few opportunities for advancement. In response to the EEOL, these gendered tracks were renamed *sōgōshoku* (professional career track) and *ippanshoku* (general, clerical track).

However, much gender differentiation in employment persisted, and female workers, while entitled to "equal opportunity" in theory, found it hard to break through the glass ceiling (Asakura 1999; Hamaguchi 2009). Takenobu Mieko's 1994 study of professional women reveals that despite the formal structural change, male-centered workplace culture and assumptions about women's domestic responsibility persisted, and these assumptions in turn became the biggest obstacles for female workers on the professional track. Many of them found it simply impossible to be female and have a career-track job, and they quit their coveted positions within a few years.

The economic downturn that struck Japan in the early 1990s also affected the fortunes of the bubble generation women with professional aspirations. The job market suddenly tightened in 1993 and brought on the *shūshoku hyōgaki* (job placement ice age), which lasted until 2000. While everyone struggled to find full-time employment, job opportunities for female college graduates all but disappeared, as the few available positions were given to men first.

Work and Lives of Three Bubble Generation Women

On one hand, the macrostructural changes discussed above define the professional lives of bubble generation women generally; on the other hand, individual women experience, understand, and respond to such changes differently because of their varying *habitus* (Bourdieu 1977). *Habitus* is a system of durable dispositions specific to class or other social groups that share the same material and social conditions. Inculcated early in an individual's life, it continues to affect one's relationship to the macrostructural forces throughout one's life. It is "durable" because once acquired, a class-specific system of dispositions strongly influences the ways in which a social actor responds to and interacts with the preexisting structure of power, in such a way that he/she remains in the same structural position—the very mechanism that keeps working-class "lads" on working-class jobs (Willis 1977).

We need to carefully consider, however, the cultural and historical context of postwar Japan to productively apply the concept of *habitus* in this analysis. The effects of class-specific *habitus* were obscured during Japan's postwar economic miracle, which continuously expanded opportunities for ordinary working Japanese for nearly a half century and created a collective illusion of an *ichioku sōchūryū shakai,* or "a 100 million all-middle-class" society. At the same time, the gender differentiation of the *habitus* was naturalized to the point that it molded the life courses of men and women without ever being scrutinized. In the latter half of the 1990s, however, class disparity became the new norm in post-bubble Japan, and gradual changes in gender role expectations began to take root. Throughout the 1990s and 2000s, individual social actors, in turn, adjusted their expectations and began to make novel choices in response to the new social reality.

In the following narratives of bubble generation women, we will see the dynamic interplay between their class- *and* gender-specific *habitus* and the concrete social conditions they encounter in their professional and personal lives. Yumiko, Maya, and Seiko (all pseudonyms) were all born in 1963 and grew up in the suburbs of Kanagawa Prefecture, south of Tokyo. They graduated from high school in 1982, went on to receive a post-secondary education, and began working full time between 1984 and 1986. Their life histories leading up to full-time corporate employment and the articulation of their individual choices and the macrostructural forces affecting them are of particular interest to me. The similarities and differences among them give us important clues toward understanding the lives and work experiences of bubble generation women.

Yumiko: The Clerical Track for Life

At the time of the interview, Yumiko had been working as an *ippanshoku,* or clerical-track employee of a small company. When I asked her what kind of ideas or dreams she had about her future career when she was in high school, she chuckled a little but did not say anything right away. I too chuckled and asked, "Or did you have one?" To that, she replied, "No, not really. I didn't know anything [about career planning]!"

Yumiko grew up in a coastal town in Kanagawa Prefecture, where her parents owned a liquor store. The youngest of three children (she has an older brother and sister), her childhood was relatively eventless and carefree. She remembers that summer was a particularly busy time for them, when the beaches attracted many tourists and everyone wanted liquor and food delivered all the time. "We never went on a vacation in summer," she recalls. "There was no way [my parents] could close the store for days during the summer. That's what happens when your family owns a shop. It's not like with other [kids] whose parents are salarymen." In her childhood and teenage years, she was surrounded by those "others," whose parents—fathers, really—had corporate employment. Moreover, knowing the drawbacks of owning a family business, her parents did not expect their children to carry it on. Both her older siblings took corporate employment and had left home by the time Yumiko was in high school. When I asked her if she had ever considered taking over the shop, she immediately said no. "My parents never wanted us to, and I really didn't think about it."

Yumiko went on to a local high school that was, in the strict ranking of public high schools in the district, considered decent but not top level. While only a handful of students were accepted to the best universities, most of her school's graduates went on to a post-secondary education of some sort. In her senior year class of forty students, all but a couple of girls went to a technical school, junior college, or four-year university. Yumiko herself opted for a technical school to learn computer programming. Was she interested in computers? "No, not really. I just thought it'd get me a decent job." Nor did she consider applying for college. She was not into academics, and all she wanted was to get a job so she could support herself.

Yumiko finished a two-year program at a large technical school in 1984 and found a job as an entry-level programmer—a decent one, as she had planned—in a small subsidiary of a large electronics company in Tokyo. She quit the job after a few years, however, because she found that she "wasn't really [cut out] for that type of work." She went back to school to learn basic accounting and found a job in the clerical staff of a mid-sized company in Tokyo. After five years, she found another job in a small trading company, where she works today. "That job [in Tokyo] was okay, but the commute was getting really tiring," she explained. "It used to take like an hour and a half to get to work; now it's about forty-five minutes door to door."

I found it difficult during the interview to get Yumiko to say much about the nature of her work, past or present. "My work? I'm just doing *jimu* [general clerical work], preparing documents, keeping books, helping the guys in sales, you know? All the routine stuff, that's about it." And her feelings about such "routine" work? She hesitated a little before responding. "It's okay. I have to work; everyone has to work, so I work! I mean, sometimes, I get tired of it. Oh, and the stuff that goes on with the other girls. . . ." Yumiko realizes that at her age finding a new job would be difficult. She has never been married and has no plan to do so. She is resigned to the idea that she will be single for the rest of her life. The notion does not seem to bother her in itself, but she notes that it means that she will need to work for twenty more years or so to support herself. That thought seemed to distress her a bit.

Yumiko characterizes her workplace as "very traditional" and having a clear division of labor between men, who are in sales and management, and women, who provide clerical support for them. In other words, top-level professional and clerical or low-level professional *(ippanshoku)* work is strictly divided along gender lines. As a gesture toward equal opportunity, however, the company assigns a couple of women in low-level management positions as "team leaders." Some women become very competitive and cliquish over these assignments, Yumiko explains. They try to get on the "good side" of their male supervisors, while handpicking their female allies, to increase their chances at the limited opportunities for advancement. Yumiko feels she is in an ambivalent position. She is, along with one other female worker, much older than the rest of the women, who are in their twenties and thirties. In a seniority-driven workplace, she would be a natural candidate for team leader. However, she entered the company late, and she also does not feel capable of taking on a leadership position. For the team leader who is younger than her, Yumiko is a potential threat to her authority. So she treats Yumiko with contempt at every opportunity, as though to demonstrate her superior position.

If the EEOL did not affect Yumiko's work experience much, how about the bubble economy and its collapse? Yumiko tilts her head slightly—a habit of hers when she wants to take a moment to consider the question—and makes a noncommittal "hmmm" sound. "I never thought about it much. I can say that I used to be busier before the economy went under. My company is struggling to keep our clients, and the business is much slower these days. So there isn't as much for us [clerical workers] to do."

Toward the end of our conversation, I asked Yumiko what she would like to do for a living if she had complete freedom to choose. She thought about it a little while and said that she would like to work at an *amamidokoro,* or a Japanese-style teahouse, where traditional sweets are served along with Japanese tea. "It seems like a nice, relaxed environment to work in," she explained. "Nothing strenuous or stressful. I could just serve tea and sweets to customers who are a little bit older and want a quiet place to relax." I asked her if maybe someday she would want to open her own teahouse. Yumiko laughed at my outrageous idea. "Oh, I don't know. Maybe, but I don't think so."

Throughout our conversation, Yumiko remained ambivalent about her life trajectory and career choices. She did not present herself as someone making active choices about her life and work. She chose computer programming not because of her own interest, but because of job prospects; then she dropped out of her technical career, not because there was something else she would rather have done, but because she did not like programming. She never married, but it was just because an opportunity had not presented itself. There may be a kind of work she would enjoy more than that of a clerical worker, but she is resigned to the reality that she will most likely retire from her current job, to which she has no particular attachment. Nor does Yumiko reflect upon her life course and the external forces that have been at work. For example, even when she is asked explicitly, it takes her a while to remember any changes in her work routine that occurred at the time of the economic change. One gets the impression that her life is left out of a historical context all together, placidly floating in a pond of water for eternity.

A closer consideration of her stories, however, quickly reveals that these impressions are not correct. The macrostructural framework of her life and work is evident in many parts of her interview. To begin with, Yumiko's family history places her at the margin of Japan's postwar economic development, which pushed "salarymen," or core corporate workers who worked on a salary basis (as opposed to hourly employees), to the forefront. Her older siblings responded to this marginalization by getting out of the family business, and Yumiko followed suit. Yet it was as though Yumiko lacked a viable alternative or a role model from whom to draw inspiration. Her parents, who encouraged their children to seek corporate employment and supported their educational preparations, themselves lacked a realistic understanding of the corporate world and thus were unable to help Yumiko navigate a path into that world.

Merchants did exist as a distinct class or caste in premodern Tokugawa Japan; more important, merchant families, until very recently, played an important role in the modern Japanese economy and in local communities

(Bestor 1989; Kondo 1990). Much has changed in post-bubble Japan, however, and the "burnt ruins" generation of merchant-class families was perhaps the last one for whom taking over the family business was not a choice but a fact of life. The following generations tended to frown upon family businesses as old-fashioned and burdensome; to them, "owning a business" did not signal entrepreneurship; it signified the outdated notion of *ie* (house or family), which stifled individual choice. At the end of the interview, I asked if Yumiko could possibly convert her family store into a teahouse. Her immediate rejection of the idea reflects the close, and often negative, association between small business ownership and *ie* entanglement, closing off, rather than opening up, an alternative path for an entrepreneur.

Yet Yumiko's attempt to leave the merchant class remains incomplete. Bourdieu points out that one of the effects of *habitus* is to exclude unlikely possibilities from one's worldview (1977, 77). In the case of Yumiko, who grew up in a supposedly "all-middle-class" society, class reproduction did not take place in a classical sense, as it did for Paul Willis' working-class lads. Instead, she works at the margins of the white-collar corporate world, locked into a routine clerical track, doing work not unlike the tedious bookkeeping that her mother did at their family store. Gender has also seemed to play a significant role here, as her brother did make it to the white-collar professional ranks, while Yumiko and her sister did not.

Finally, Yumiko's reference to a teahouse as a desirable place to work tells us a great deal about her sense of self at this stage in her life. Bubble generation women grew up hanging out at coffee shops and McDonald's, and now, in their forties and fifties, they often relate to things "traditional" as a novel and exotic cultural form, rather than their cultural roots. During the consumption frenzy of the 1980s, pieces of "traditional Japan," from Kabuki theater to *kaiseki* cuisine to hot springs spas, were repackaged as attractive consumer goods to be "discovered" again by younger generations of Japanese. Some Japanese confectionaries have become coveted brand names, featured on glossy pages of magazines targeted at younger women, and their beautifully appointed tearooms, often located in busy shopping districts or department stores, are depicted as quiet refuges where customers can take a momentary break from their fast-paced modern life. The meaning Yumiko attaches to working in a teahouse reflects such popular cultural clichés—a quiet, stress-free place where interactions are muted and work is light and clean. She is a reasonably friendly woman, but she does not consider herself an assertive or outgoing person. She does not crave mental or physical challenge and has no objection to simple work. The type of work required of a server in a Japanese-style teahouse fits perfectly with her perception of herself.

Maya: At the Lower End of Professional Work

Maya was Yumiko's high school friend. They went to the same technical school afterward and remained close friends after they graduated. While some aspects of their lives overlap, there are many key differences in their life histories. For one thing, Maya's father was a salaryman who worked for a major company that once dominated Japan's telecommunications market. "I don't know what he did. He was just a salaryman," Maya says. He left home early in the morning, came home late in the evening, and mostly slept on Sundays. Maya's home life centered on her mother, who worked at home as a seamstress. In high school, Maya had decent grades, particularly in math and sciences, but was not interested in going to school for four more years, so going to a technical school and becoming a programmer made sense to her. She never considered following in her mother's footsteps, as sewing, she said, "didn't interest me at all." She did not necessarily think about following in her father's footsteps either. "Working for a company" seemed to be the only occupational goal she had in her youth.

Maya found a job with a subsidiary of a major electronics company (a competitor of Yumiko's former employer) and was thrown immediately into projects. It was 1984, and the Japanese economy was going strong; Japanese corporations were just starting to computerize their operations, and there was a huge demand for programmers. Maya's primary job was to go to a client company with a team of programmers and set up or upgrade the company's computer systems. The team often worked under the pressure of tight deadlines and demanding clients. For many years, Maya routinely took the last train home and collapsed into bed at 1 a.m., only to get up five hours later to start all over again. She also worked all day on Saturdays on a regular basis, leaving Sunday to catch up with sleep and recuperate for the coming week. "Yeah, I used to work a *lot*. I'm amazed I lasted!"

Maya is slightly built and says she is not very sturdy. When asked how she managed such a heavy workload, Maya wiped a smile off her face and answered very seriously, almost angrily, "I just did it because I had to." Maya's company does not control its own work flow, as it receives work orders through its parent company. Salespeople from the parent company—who never even meet the technicians from the subsidiary—often make unrealistic promises in order to secure a contract, with little regard to those who have to go out and do the job. "We got so angry a few times and tried to complain to the parent company," she recalled. "But it was no use. They kept sending us contracts and demanded that we do them on time. They didn't care because they never had to deal with the clients. Even our own management didn't care. It was we, the programmers, who had to apologize to angry clients and bend over backward to appease them."

Maya stayed with the company despite many difficulties, and she became a team leader, trusted with large projects for important clients. She seemed reluctant to admit that it was an accomplishment to stay with the same company and advance to her current position. "I've been doing this for a long time. I didn't try to become a team leader, but before I knew it, I was one of the older programmers with the company who knew how to get the job done." I teasingly asked her if she was considered a so-called *otsubone-sama,* a long-term female employee who rules over younger women just as a shogun's concubines used to rule over attending ladies. "Yes, I suppose so," Maya laughed. "I'm definitely older than everyone else I work with!"

Maya's response to my question about the bubble's collapse was immediate and lengthy. "Yes, I definitely felt it [the difference between bubble and post-bubble times]," she said. "When the bubble collapsed, our work slowed down a bit. We didn't have as many projects, and I could usually go home by ten or eleven and didn't work on Saturdays, which was a lot better [than during the bubble era]." Still, she worked until ten on a regular basis. "Well, that's pretty normal in my industry," said Maya with a wry smile. "That just can't be helped."

The period of a more manageable workload did not last long. Things got tougher again as the economic recession dragged on. Desperate to keep business coming in, Maya's parent company started taking on projects at reduced fees under ever-tighter conditions. "In the end, all the forced effort *[muri]* came back to us at the job site. We got caught between the parent company, who wanted us to get the job done quickly with minimal staff to bring the costs down, and the clients, who were not happy to see that we weren't flexible [enough to accommodate their needs]." As a team leader, Maya constantly found herself between a rock and a hard place among her own supervisor, the clients, and her own team members. Then, a reduction in the workforce, through layoffs and a stoppage of new hires, began to affect them. "Sure, we have less work, but now we have fewer people to do it, too. So the pressure is up again."

Through the ups and downs of the economy and changing responsibility at work, Maya also had to take on family responsibility. Her older brother got married and left home when she was in her late twenties, while she never married and has remained in her parents' home all these years. Around 2000, her father's health began to decline markedly, and for the following several years, she shared the responsibility of caring for him with her aging mother. Every Saturday, she would drive her mother to visit with her father in the hospital. In the not-so-distant future the care of her mother will most likely fall on Maya's shoulders as well. "My mom's getting old. Eventually, she'll need somebody to care for her, and I suppose that'll be me. My brother? He's been gone for many years, and he has his own family, a wife and two children. He won't move back with us—ever. So that leaves me." Fortunately, she added, her mother was still in good health at the moment. Maya and her mother seemed to get along well, and as she put it, "Things are simple" with just two women living together. The house is paid for, and with Maya's salary, her father's pension, and her mother's savings from her sewing work, they were financially well off. While work continued to be demanding, this was a relatively calm period in Maya's life, and she hoped it would last for a while.

Maya had two different role models—her salaryman father and her mother, who worked at home while taking care of the family—but in her mind, the path of wife/mother did not seem to have much meaning. She realized that if she was going to be self-sufficient, corporate wage labor was the only option.

After she graduated from a decent—but not top-notch—high school and a trade school for computer programming, Maya's work life began in a small subsidiary at the bottom of the corporate pecking order. Often called *kogaisha,* or "child companies," subsidiaries live in the shadow of their powerful "parents"—usually world-class corporations with highly recognizable brand names and part of a gigantic assembly of corporations known as *keiretsu.* Along with subcontractors, subsidiaries serve the parent company by providing cheaper, more flexible labor. It is customary for subsidiary employees to be paid significantly lower wages, given fewer benefits, and subjected to harsher working conditions than the employees of the parent companies. Many of the difficulties that Maya has experienced are the results of her position within this elaborate tier structure of the Japanese corporate world.

Working in the information technology (IT) industry has its own trappings as well. The industry is known for high incidents of depression, nervous breakdown, and suicide, due to the highly competitive atmosphere and the isolating nature of programming work. IT technicians and managers in small subsidiary companies must deal with even harder conditions and added stress for less compensation than their counterparts get in the parent companies. At the same time, the IT industry tends to be more gender egalitarian than many other sectors of the Japanese economy, and female workers are often able to enter into professional and *senmonshoku* (specialist) positions. Such was certainly the case for Maya, who, despite her limited educational capital, managed to advance to a supervisory position in a highly competitive work environment. It was both because she had an aptitude for this type of technical work and also apparently because of her position as a team leader that she acquired management and leadership skills over the years. However, her current position at the lower end of the professional spectrum is most likely where she will end her career.

Maya's role as a senior female technician with management responsibility adds stress to her already complicated position at work. She does not see herself as a particularly good manager and emphasizes that she was made a manager merely because of her seniority. She clearly does not enjoy "standing above other people" *(hito no ue ni tatsu)*. While she would not have been able to stay in the position unless she was capable of managing her team, Maya's take on her managerial status remains ironic and self-deprecating.

Another key component in Maya's story is her family obligations. She has never been married and has no plans for marriage in the future. While Yumiko seems to have had a desire to marry when she was younger and perhaps dated a few men, Maya seems to have never considered marriage as a choice. They are part of the growing trend among bubble generation women who are more likely than previous generations to postpone or entirely forgo marriage and reproduction. Many of them are employed full time and live with their parents, allowing them a great deal of personal and financial freedom well into their thirties and even beyond. While marriage and reproduction are not entirely out of the picture for most of them, they often represent a more constraining, less attractive choice than they once did (Inoue and Ebara 2004; S. Miura 2009). Having stayed with her parents through her adult life, Maya has taken on the responsibility of caring for her parents in their old age, while her brother has remained largely hands-off. This is also an emerging pattern among contemporary Japanese families: unmarried daughters, instead of the oldest son and his wife, are becoming the primary caregivers for their elderly parents. This arrangement has certain advantages for both the parents, who find it easier to rely on their own daughters than on in-laws, and the daughters, who would rather prolong their carefree single lives than get married and become housewives and mothers (White 2002).

Maya's current situation is a relatively fortunate one. While she brings in an income to the household, her mother takes care of the domestic tasks. However, the situation can change at a moment's notice, depending on her mother's health. In the last few decades, the Japanese government has opted for home-based care of the elderly, touting the benefits of keeping the elderly with family members instead of increasing elder-care facilities, and it has established a long-term-care insurance system. While the system provides a degree of financial relief for families who care for their disabled elderly, it presumes the availability of a family member to serve as primary caregiver, usually a woman. At some point in the future, Maya will have to make some tough decisions between wage work and caretaking work, as many other working Japanese women are doing today (Roberts 2011).

Maya's case also brings to the foreground the significance of educational capital in professional career development in Japanese society, where such capital goes a long way—more so than in Bourdieu's study based in France (1984)—to compensate for a shortage of cultural capital that comes with one's class origin. However, Maya's hands-off father and stay-at-home mother did not push their children toward higher educational attainment, particularly not Maya, whose gender deemed it unnecessary at best and even harmful, as men have tended to view women of higher educational capital as unattractive marriage candidates.

Seiko: The EEOL's Poster Child

Seiko came running to the front entrance of the Mitsukoshi Department Store in the Ginza, a few minutes past our meeting time. "Sorry, sorry. I got held up at work!" Once we settled at a corner table in a small sushi place, she began to talk. She first asked about my work, then started talking about her own. We spent nearly four hours together that afternoon, and I had to provide only a few prompts to keep her going.

Seiko was born in Hokkaido in 1963. Her family moved to Yokohama, the largest city in Kanagawa Prefecture, when she was in the first grade, as her father, who worked for a well-known logistics company, was transferred to its main office in Tokyo. She graduated from a top-ranked high school in the district and entered one of the most prestigious private universities in Japan to study Russian, a choice she attributed to her family's origins in Hokkaido.

"In Hokkaido, Russia seemed much closer. Also, I wanted to do something different, [a field] not too many other people went into."

In her senior year of college, Seiko began to look into jobs. It was 1985, when the economy was very strong and the job market favorable for soon-to-be graduates. The EEOL was also coming into effect in the following year, and corporate employers were trying to recruit female graduates with bells and whistles. She quickly received *naitei* (preliminary offers) from two top-level corporations (both presented here in pseudonyms): TTEC, an electronics firm, and Quick News, a media conglomerate. The TTEC recruiters told her that they needed Russian-speaking personnel, as they were expanding their business into the USSR. Seiko had a favorable impression of the company but hesitated because she might be transferred to the USSR for a long time.

With Quick News, her primary interest was in the cultural projects division, where a wide range of cultural and educational programs were being planned for a lay audience. However, during the recruitment process she was told to change her area of interest to news reporting. "They really wanted female recruits [as reporters]," Seiko explains. "The EEOL was just kicking in, and big companies were eager to show that they were actively hiring women. It was as though we were *kyakuyose panda* [panda bears featured to gather a crowd]. Naturally, some female hires were selected primarily based on their appearance, to be used in the company's PR. But they also wanted to hire some tough ones who would stay on the job. I always tell people that I was a typical case of the former!" She laughs heartily and continues. "It's super male-dominant *[chō meeru dominanto]* in the world of news reporting. At that time, there were very, very few women working in any of those hard-core fields, like the economy, politics, and international affairs."

In the end, Seiko chose Quick News, despite the fact she was never interested in the news business. "I didn't think they would hire me unless I agreed to change my application. I figured it'd be all right [to work as a reporter] for the time being." Once on the job, she discovered that her male colleagues and supervisors were not ready for a female reporter among them. "[Male] reporters work day and night. They follow important politicians around, hang out at the police precinct, and so on, so they won't miss a scoop. But they wouldn't let me work overnight, so male colleagues would have to take over [after certain hours]." She felt that she was treated as not quite a full adult *(hanninmae)*. "I was like some sort of exotic animal. I was stationed in a small town up north for a while, and they [local reporters] would come to interview me as the 'first woman reporter from Tokyo'! I hated it so much! It was a major source of stress for me for years." After Seiko had spent several years at a desk job (as opposed to a field job)—an unusually long period compared to her male counterparts—her supervisor approached her and asked her where she intended to take her career. "I was appalled. It wasn't up to me to choose my job; it was *he* who put me on the desk and kept me there."

Seiko was eventually sent on a couple of long-term assignments abroad, and she carved out a niche as a reporter in her own right. She also married in her late thirties and became a mother of two. How has she juggled all that? For one thing, her husband was open to sharing domestic responsibility; his work schedule was more flexible than hers. Nonetheless, she gave up opportunities for career advancement that would have sent her far away from Tokyo. When she had her second child, it was clear that the lack of mobility would keep her off the fast track for the rest of her professional career: "With just one child, I thought maybe I would still have a chance [to take an assignment away from home and advance in her career]. But after the second one, I knew that was it; I couldn't do it anymore."

Seiko also blamed her own stubbornness for not doing all the "right things" to advance in the corporate organization. "Some people—good people who cared about my future in the company—told me that I needed to develop better relationships with my superiors. One of them said, 'It's not a big deal. If someone pushes you for a position that can benefit your career, go to him and pay your respects [aisatsu]. That's all.' But I just couldn't bring myself to do those things." What does it mean to "pay respects" in this context? "Oh, just pay a visit and say something like, 'Thank you for recommending me for the position. I appreciate your trust in me, and I'll do my best not to disappoint you.' I know a lot of people [colleagues] who are very good about doing such things, and I suppose it really works. But I was never into doing that." She thinks that she inherited this stubborn streak from her father, who worked in a large company but never took part in the customary paying of respects or *tsuketodoke* (giving of gifts to curry favor of those in power).

When I asked her what work meant for her, Seiko replied that it was the foundation of her adult life, and she could not imagine herself not working. In fact, she confided, she once considered marrying a man who would have liked her to quit her job and become a stay-at-home wife. She was thirty years old and was about to go on a long-term training program in the USSR. "We never officially got engaged, but it was in the air. I sensed that he didn't want me to go to the USSR but didn't want to say anything, fearing that he might appear too old-fashioned and controlling." In the end, they broke up and she went to the USSR. In retrospect, she characterized men of her generation as being caught between the old and the new: "They had to meet the expectations of their families, to marry a nice girl, have children, and carry on the family name. Yet women of their own age group were more career-oriented and not content with domestic life."

Seiko spoke about her career choices with a strong sense of control. While she downplayed it throughout the interview, she had had the ambition to go into a profession that had previously been male-dominated, and she was willing to endure everyday gender-based discrimination and even occasional sexual harassment to establish herself in the field. She was highly conscious of her historical positioning in the first generation of women with equal opportunity, and she articulated the effects of macrostructural forces that worked in her favor. To her corporate employer, she was a rare find too, with her excellent and unique academic background, outgoing and energetic personality, and the toughness that was essential to survive in a male-dominant workplace. Seiko has stuck with her job for over twenty-five years and now works as a reporter out of Quick News' Tokyo office, using her foreign language skills. In many ways, she has met the expectations of her company as a poster child of its progressive response to the EEOL.

At the same time, Seiko's work experience suggests many effects of an enduring male-centered workplace culture. While the EEOL officially made the equal treatment of male and female workers possible, her male colleagues and supervisors were not prepared to accept women as their equals. On one hand, they continued to treat women as a burden, co-workers who would never have the same commitment to the profession as they themselves. One senior colleague even told her (when he was drunk) that he disliked having to work with women, period. On the other hand, some men got "overly excited" (in Seiko's words) about their responsibility to help women make it in the professional world, and such a response often led to excessive paternalism toward female employees and misguided interference in their personal lives. Her superiors also had a difficult time placing her on the prescribed career track because she was a woman, yet, the customary *nenkō joretsu,* or seniority-based advancement system, required that they keep her on the same advancement schedule as her cohort. They would have to send her on field assignments—a key to advancement for those in the news business—yet they could not send a woman just anywhere, so they dragged their feet and kept her around doing a desk job for much longer than they ought to have. It seems as though her superiors, working under the corporate mandate to train female reporters, did not really know what to do with her because she was not just a support worker but was not exactly one of the guys either.

Seiko's decisions about marriage and motherhood tell us a great deal about her perceptions of her professional self. At age thirty, she had to choose between her first major assignment away from home and an engagement to a man with traditional expectations. She chose the former, a necessary step for her professional development as a reporter. Yet the glass ceiling was ever-present in her career path. Even if she was willing, she would never be allowed to do what male reporters did, and thus her career would never go as far as those of her male counterparts. Seiko did not explicitly comment on the connection among her career, marriage, and children, yet I have a sense that the timing was not purely coincidental. Once she started having children, it simply became less and less likely that she was going to advance in her career as a reporter.

Seiko seemed reasonably happy with her current job. It would perhaps be considered a dead-end job by an ambitious mid-career reporter, yet there were many things about her current position to be thankful for: the office location in central Tokyo, which is convenient for commuting; decent pay and benefits; a stable work schedule; and a relatively relaxed atmosphere. Seiko was clearly a very involved mother to her two young children and became visibly animated as she told me some funny stories about them. She did not say much about her husband, but I detected genuine affection every time she referred to him.

In Seiko's case we find how cultural capital (born and raised in a household of a white-collar salaryman) and educational capital (a graduate of a prestigious university with strong foreign language skills) converge to mold a sōgōshoku career in one of Japan's premier corporations. Her story is, however, fraught with the tension between her privileged professional position and her gender at every turn, and her career success is conditional—"for a woman"—at best. Here, gender appears to transcend both her class origin and educational capital, and steer her career trajectory away from what is considered ideal in the Japanese corporate world of work whose dominant ideology remains masculinist deep down.

Conclusion

As I consider the stories of the bubble generation women, some patterns begin to emerge. First and foremost, the mid-1980s were a major turning point in

Japan's labor history, when the booming economy and legal changes coincided to open up the job market to women with a post-secondary education and gave them a realistic chance at developing a lifelong professional career in the corporate world. Seiko was obviously the most conscious of her "luck" in being a woman of this generation, but even Yumiko, who did not see much of a tangible connection between macro-level changes and her own work experience, definitely benefited from them. A woman of her educational capital who was ten years older or younger than she would not have been able to find and switch jobs as she did in the late 1980s and early '90s.

Major Japanese corporations, including TTEC and Quick News (which wooed Seiko), were eager to recruit qualified female candidates, in part to maintain a positive public image in the advent of the EEOL, but also to secure high-quality workers in a seller's market. Moreover, since the late 1990s the Japanese government has been eager to recognize and reward "family-friendly" companies (Roberts 2004). By contrast, small and mid-sized companies—including Yumiko's current employer—have less to gain from a progressive image, as their recruitment patterns were much less a public affair than those of the major corporations; they also lacked the financial resources to invest in female employees, whom they continued to perceive as high risk. Twenty-five years after the EEOL, it seems, equal employment opportunity is far from common in the Japanese corporate world.

Most significant, the bubble generation women's stories indicate that formal changes in employment policies are rarely supported by the informal workplace culture, even in the top-tier corporations. Seiko has experienced the duplicity between the *tatemae* (public behavior) toward gender tolerance and the widely shared *honne* (honest inner feelings) among male workers and managers, who believe that women can never measure up to the demands of a professional career. Not all men intentionally try to marginalize professional women, as is evident in Seiko's narrative. Yet their well-meaning assistance has only reaffirmed that she is different—female—and cannot be treated the same way as a man. In Takenobu's analysis (1994), too, such duplicity is identified as the root of professional women's discontent and the primary reason why many of them give up on their careers after a few years. Some women, including Maya and Seiko, have persisted, but they may indeed be among a particularly resilient few (cf. Roberts 2011).

As we turn our attention from the macrostructural forces to the experiences of individual women, the single most striking difference in Yumiko's, Maya's, and Seiko's narratives is the notion of choice—or lack thereof. Yumiko gave the distinct impression that she had no career direction and had drifted from one job to another to make her life easier; Maya often downplayed her individual agency, particularly in reference to the structural constraints of her workplace. Seiko, by contrast, emphasized her conscious decisions at every turn of her career path, from her job search process to her reluctance to do what it took to advance in the corporate organization. The women's discussion of family life shows exactly the same pattern. Yumiko and Maya explained their passivity and lack of opportunity as the reasons why they had remained single. Taking on the responsibility of caring for aging parents (as Maya has done) is also presented as a default move. Seiko, on the other hand, represents herself as a conscious agent in her choice to leave her boyfriend to take a long-term assignment in the USSR, to later marry a man who was willing to share domestic responsibilities, and finally to have two children despite the negative effects of such a decision on her career.

Other aspects of the women's narratives suggest another, quite different reading of their stories, however. Yumiko's comments about female team leaders and the cliquishness of her female colleagues suggest a critical consciousness about the complexity of office dynamics, in which women are pitted against each other to take advantage of scarce opportunities (cf. Ogasawara 1998). Nor did Maya take it sitting down every time her superiors put her team in a seemingly impossible situation. She got angry and tried to negotiate, on behalf of her team, to improve working conditions. On the other hand, Seiko admitted that she could have made different choices during her job search and at the key turning points in her career, but she just simply did not make enough of an effort. While presenting her marriage and motherhood as a choice, she also recognizes that she was lucky that her circumstances allowed her to have both a full-time job and a thriving family.

The women's self-construction is, then, at once agential and relational, the dual aspects of being a woman who is able to recognize and act upon her needs and desires but is also mindful of her interdependence with others, her corporate affiliation and its consequences, and the contextual nature of decisions she may make at various junctures in her life. Their varied emphasis on agency and relationality is also a reflection of their respective positions in the highly stratified social reality of corporate Japan. As Japanese women attain more education and advance into the professional world of work, they are exposed to the same structural constraints as men; one of these is the central significance of *gakureki,* or educational pedigree, in career development. For women, the effects of this positioning are not limited to the professional sphere but extend into their personal choices as well. Seiko gets to hold down a full-time job while being the mother of two at least in part because she was able to convert her educational capital into a good job with a major corporation that has the resources to support its employees' personal choices.

The last important point to take away from the stories of Yumiko, Maya, and Seiko, then, is that a widening disparity is emerging among working women, or *jojo kakusa* (female-female disparity), as opposed to the traditional *danjo kakusa* (male-female disparity) of previous eras (Tachibanaki 2009). In theory, educational pedigree allows those who accumulate greater educational capital to advance beyond their class origins, and it thus acts as a sort of equalizer. In reality, however, the emphasis on educational capital often encourages class reproduction, particularly for women. Japanese families have tended to prioritize education for male children over female children, and while parents are often willing to invest significant financial resources to provide the best education possible for their sons, they are less likely to do so for their daughters. Thus girls who are given equal educational opportunities as boys are primarily from families with considerable financial means, where they do not have to compete against male siblings for family support. Once women were largely dependent on their fathers and husbands for their cultural and social capital; now a new form of differentiation is emerging among girls and women in contemporary Japan based on the availability of familial educational support (Tachibanaki 2009, chapter 3).

Furthermore, the stratification among female workers has created a new source of stress. Once every woman in a corporate workplace was an "office lady," making photocopies and serving tea; now professional women and clerical women work side by side, not as equals, but as managers and managerial candidates, on one hand, and support staff on the other. While clerical women accept their supportive role vis-à-vis male professional workers, they often resent having to serve female professional workers. In turn, many professional women hesitate to "give orders" to clerical women, as their male counterparts would. A similar conflict is suggested in Yumiko's story, in which she characterizes some of the more ambitious female workers in negative terms. Such a characterization suggests that the deeply entrenched gender division of labor remains not only in the minds of male workers and managers, but also in the worldview of female workers themselves.

Japanese women's work experience today is diverse and complex. While some of the earlier disparities between men and women have been remedied to an extent, new forms of difference are emerging. In the ever-changing social environment of contemporary Japan, individual women respond to the effects of macrostructural forces the best way they can within the range of choices available to them. While the power of *habitus* is undeniable in the stories of the three women in this chapter, it is also important to recognize how they formulate and find meaning in their work and lives, no matter how trivial or unremarkable they may be from an outsider's point of view.

References Cited

Asakura, Mutsuko. 1999. *Kintōhō no shinsekai* (The new world of EEOL). Tokyo: Yūhikaku.

Bestor, Theodore. 1989. *Neighborhood Tokyo.* Stanford, CA: Stanford University Press.

Bourdieu, Pierre. 1977. *Outline of a Theory of Practice.* Cambridge: Cambridge University Press.

———. 1984. *Distinctions: A Social Critique of a Judgment of Taste.* Trans. Richard Nice. Cambridge, MA: Harvard University Press.

Brinton, Mary. 1993. *Women and the Economic Miracle: Gender and Work in Postwar Japan.* Berkeley: University of California Press.

Hamaguchi, Keiichirō. 2009. *Atarashii rōdōshakai* (New labor society). Tokyo: Iwanami.

Inoue, Teruko, and Yumiko Ebara. 2004. *Josei no dēta bukku* (Women's data book), 4th ed. Tokyo: Yūhikaku.

Kondo, Dorinne. 1990. *Crafting Selves.* Chicago: University of Chicago Press.

Kurotani, Sawa. 2005. *Home Away from Home: Japanese Corporate Wives in the United States.* Durham, NC: Duke University Press.

Miura, Atsushi. 2005. *Karyū shakai* (Lower-class society). Tokyo: Kōbunsha.

Miura, Seiichirō. 2009. *"Kawatteshimatta onna" to "kawaritakunai otoko"* ("Women who have changed" and "men who refuse to change"). Tokyo: Gakubunsha.

Ogasawara, Yūko. 1998. *Office Ladies and Salaried Men: Power, Gender, and Work in Japanese Companies.* Berkeley: University of California Press.

Roberts, Glenda. 2004. "Globalization and Work/Life Balance: Gendered Implications of New Initiatives at a U.S. Multinational in Japan." In *Equity in the Workplace: Gendering Workplace Policy Analysis,* ed. Heidi Gottfried and Laura Reese, 305–321. Lanham, MD: Lexington Books.

———. 2007. "Similar Outcomes, Different Paths: The Cross-National Transfer of Gendered Regulations of Employment." In *Gendering the Knowledge Economy: Comparative Perspectives,* ed. Sylvia Walby, Heidi Gottfried, Karen Gottschall, and Mari Osawa, 141–161. London: Palgrave.

———. 2011. "Salary Women and Family Well-Being in Urban Japan." *Marriage and Family Review* 47, no. 8:571–589.

Rosenberger, Nancy. 2001. *Gambling with Virtue: Japanese Women and the Search for Self in a Changing Nation.* Honolulu: University of Hawai'i Press.

Tachibanaki, Toshinori. 2008. *Jojo kakusa* (Female-female stratification). Tokyo: Tōyō Keizai Shinpō.

Takenōbu, Mieko. 1994. *Nihon kabushikigaisha no onnatachi* (Women of Japan, Inc.). Tokyo: Asahi Shinbunsha.

White, Merry Isaacs. 2002. *Perfectly Japanese: Making Families in an Era of Upheaval.* Berkeley: University of California Press.

Willis, Paul. 1981. *Learning to Labor: How Working Class Lads Get Working Class Jobs.* New York: Columbia University Press.

CHAPTER 4

"Making an Ant's Forehead of Difference"

Organic Agriculture as an Alternative Lifestyle in Japan

NANCY ROSENBERGER

MY FIRST GLIMPSE of Kana was at a discussion of organic agriculture techniques in Tokyo. In a roomful of male panelists and mostly male audience, she was the only woman who offered a technical suggestion. Standing against the wall, her long hair pulled back from her narrow face, she said, "My friends and I are doing a rice paddy on a hill, and we thought that the water coming from the hills above was polluted from fertilizers. We built a filter of stones and some purifying plants that the water has to flow through before it gets to our paddies." People nodded in the hot, stuffy room, but no one responded.

I was beginning a study of farmers connected with the Japan Organic Agricultural Association (JOAA) and cornered Kana in the lobby afterward. Hesitant at first, she broke into a smile when we found that friends of mine, a young couple who are organic farmers in northeast Japan, are also good friends of hers. Yes, it would be fine to visit her farm several hours south of Tokyo.

On a cool but sunny December morning in 2008, I climbed off of a lumbering bus to find her and her father drinking tea outside the barn, nestled in a small valley among the Hakone Hills not far from Mt. Fuji in Kanagawa Prefecture, south of Tokyo. Kana trilled a warm welcome and offered me an apple crate to sit on. "My father always says we have to take our tea breaks in the morning, even though I want to keep on working. I'm not really a farmer because I like to stay up late and don't get started until later!" she laughed. She introduced her father as her helper, and he agreed, "This is my second career after being a salaryman. She's the one who knows about organic agriculture, but doing farming is a lot easier with two people."

Our trip to the outhouse gave Kana and me a chance to talk a bit more. "You're strange for an American. You're thin," she commented. She said that she had spent a year abroad in the United States and had been an English major at a national university near Tokyo. Not a word of English passed her lips, however. Rather, at thirty-three, her memories of the United States were of obese people, of people who did not care about Japan, and of wasteful habits like central heating in big houses—the last of which of course I was completely guilty.

Kana's American experience motivated her odyssey to live her life differently from both Americans and Japanese. "After I graduated from college, I looked for jobs in Japan, and I was attacked by doubts [about what to do in the future] because of the way Americans, Japanese, and the Japanese economy have ended up sacrificing nature. I took a job crunching data at the Asian Rural Institute (Asia Gakuin)." There Kana met people from Asia and Africa who were learning organic agriculture in order to allow their countries to gain some measure of food self-sufficiency, growing their own food rather than importing most of it. "Mornings and evenings I was out in the fields learning about the cycle of land and plants and animals, of how you could live in one place and be self-sufficient. These people were helping their own countries to be self-sufficient, and I realized that Japan also needs to be self-sufficient! The most important thing about organic agriculture is that it lets Japan be independent," she said with an emphatic wave of her hand.

I nodded my understanding as we made our way along the narrow path between rice fields. Japan is less self-sufficient in food than any other developed nation—39 percent in 2010 ("Food Self-Sufficiency Rate Fell below 40% in 2010" 2011). The country imports almost all of the wheat for bread and noodles, soybeans for soy sauce and *miso,* corn for livestock, and oil for fertilizer and farm machinery. Such low self-sufficiency is the result not only of Japan's lack of natural resources and limited agricultural land, but also of the country's postwar economic policy, encouraged by the United States, which invested highly in industrial growth for export but did not support diverse agriculture (Mulgan 2006). Rather, Japan has imported U.S. agricultural goods at the behest of the U.S. government.[1]

But this dissatisfaction with the status quo was not the only factor that motivated Kana to become an organic farmer. Environmental concerns were also on her mind. As we jumped into her small truck to ride up the hill to her fields, she said, "I'm showing a film next week about Rokkasho-*mura*, where they want to build a factory that makes plutonium out of reused nuclear fuel. Rokkasho is up in the very north of Honshu, and if it ever leaks, radioactivity will be carried right down the coast. I'll put an announcement about it in my newsletter this week when I deliver my food to my consumers." She was already part of a protest movement against nuclear power that supplies about a third of Japan's electricity needs. She knew that not all of her consumers agreed with her anti-nuclear beliefs, and indeed the movie itself revealed a debate among the Rokkasho villagers about whether to support the nuclear power plant; some of them wanted jobs in the nuclear industry, and some feared the threat of radiation.[2]

Little did Kana know at the time how prescient her concern was for radioactivity pollution in Japan, for the tragedies of the earthquake, tsunami, and explosion at the Fukushima nuclear energy plant were still to come. When I interviewed her again in 2012, however, she was dealing with the direct effects of the radioactive fallout, as we will see below. In 2008 it was a hard sell to stir up consumers' interests in radioactivity, but by 2012 she said that at least her consumers "realized the dangers," though they were not ready to accompany her to anti-nuclear demonstrations.

In my field notes after this first visit to Kana's farm, I described Kana as "clear-thinking, warm, passionate about her ideals and easy to get along with but at the same time firm about certain things that need to happen." My subsequent dealings with her bore out these words. Kana was also an independent thinker, having taken up organic farming against the wishes of her parents and her employers at a shop where she worked.

Resistance and Identity

In tracing alternative ways of living in Japan in the 2000s, I center my exploration of this young organic farmer around two key concepts: resistance and identity.

Resistance is the active, intentional efforts made by groups and individuals to change or live differently than the dominant status quo. In Japan in the 2000s resistance means living according to values, roles, and actions that are alternative to those favored in postwar mainstream life, which was centered on rapid industrial, export-centered economic growth—an economic situation that has now faded. Resistance is never completely outside of the generally accepted truths and power dynamics of the times but is always present in a society (Foucault 1980). Resistance can be more alternative, suggesting gradual changes within the system, or more oppositional, pushing toward radical change in the system (Allen 2004). When groups or individuals resist in a certain time and place, they draw on both "residual" beliefs and practices from the cultural-historical past and "emergent" beliefs and practices that are being developed anew (Williams 1994). Resistance of a long-term nature is tense and ambivalent with ambiguities and contradictions (Rosenberger forthcoming).

Identity is the psycho-social sense of who one is in one's various social groups. It often implies accepting a certain societal role offered by the social group, like salaryman or housewife or career woman in Japan (Hall 1996). But it can also be a process of enacting various identities in different social groups (like worker by day and musician by night) or of creating a relatively new role (in this case, young woman organic farmer) (Ueno 2005). Family and school train people to play the game of their social group and class as they grow up; their habits are formed and effective in negotiating for power on this 3-D gameboard (Bourdieu 1989). But if people try to take on new identities, they have to learn new ways of thinking, acting, and interacting so they can play the new games that they meet. Newly created identities are a kind of resistance to the status quo (Melucci 1989). When identity and resistance meet in an individual, inevitably contradictions and ambivalences emerge because the person is always between the old and the new ways of being in his or her life (Gunewardena 2007; Ortner 2006).

In this chapter, my main aim is to illustrate a particular way of resisting the status quo in Japan in the 2000s through organic farming and to explore what kind of resistance is possible in the contemporary Japanese context (Honda 2006; Lunsing 2006; Mathews 2003; Rosenberger 2001). I also examine the nuances of the social identity that Kana works to create in relation to the historical-cultural context of her life and the innovative future that she and the organic movement envision. Second, I touch on two larger questions: (1) What is the nature of resistance here, and what does this teach us about resistance? (2) What can we learn about the process of creating a new social identity?

Facing the Nitty-Gritty of Organic Farming

Kana took a risk and returned home in her late twenties to learn organic farming, going several times a week to work with a nearby organic farmer for the first year and appealing to him for advice as she started up. She acquired five different pieces of land for vegetables. One large piece crowned the hill behind and above her house and had a great view, spoiled only by a smudge of brown pollution in the direction of Tokyo. We picked small stalks of broccoli with leaves, *matsuna* greens, and large turnips. Another small field was nearby on the side of the hill. It was a fifteen-minute drive to three other pieces of land in the next village, all located at various spots on a hillside going up the side of a valley. The lower land could support carrots and onions, but the higher land got less sun and was mainly for daikon (long white radishes).

As we came to the top of the slope of the hill above her house, she pointed to a hilltop where a cell tower was located. "I tried to get farmers together in this area to protest that cell tower. Concentrated electromagnetic waves are not good for the crops. But they didn't respond at all. I had to quit because I need their goodwill. They don't understand." Her forehead wrinkled in exasperation.

Kana brightened, however, as she showed me a pile of compost that she

FIGURE 4.1

Kana

was making. Taking off on a Japanese proverb, she said, "I can't do much. I can't even make a cat's forehead of difference. I'm just making an ant's forehead of difference." She shot a grin at me. "But I make the safest and most delicious vegetables that I can to give to my consumers. It's the cycle with the land that is important. To make compost, I get rice bran *[nuka]* and mix that with about 10 percent chicken droppings from a farmer nearby who uses good feed and no antibiotics. Then I layer them, add water gradually, stamp them down, and mix them about five times. They ferment and bake and become this wonderful compost for my fields." She ran her hands through the soft soil in the most mature pile and gave some to a nearby onion that was growing through the relatively warm winter in her area. However, as we will see, the earthquake and tsunami of 2012 would challenge her use of natural materials close at hand to make nourishing compost.

The JOAA and Japanese Agriculture

Kana illustrates one choice that young Japanese are making in the 2000s. She comes from the mobile middle class of the 1960s and '70s; her father, a second son in a farming family, became a local government worker. Kana grew up in a small house on the family's land, but the salary of her father and the part-time wages of her mother sent her to a mid-level university and enabled her to study abroad. In becoming an organic farmer, Kana chose to be poor but true to her values. Kana has turned to living locally in an environmentally responsible way by raising and distributing organic vegetables. She has rerooted herself in the land where she and her ancestors were raised, dedicated to revitalizing the natural farming methods of the past and using them as a beacon of hope in the present.

Through the Asian Rural Institute, Kana found a group of like-minded people in the JOAA, an association founded in 1971 by people who were concerned about the health and safety of their food as Japan surged toward massive industrialization (JOAA 2011). In the late 1960s, women consumers wanted food that was not laced with chemical fertilizers and herbicides. In Tokyo, a group of women asked a group of farmers out in Chiba, several hours away, to grow organic vegetables for them. At first the farmers did it mainly for economic advantage, as the *mikan* (tangerines) in which the government had told them to specialize had failed to bring profit. But they delivered organic vegetables to the Tokyo women, who brought their children out to help on the farms in the summers (Moen 1997).

Under the leadership of "pioneer" organic farmers, who are now in their sixties and seventies, the JOAA laid down three main tenets by which their members should try to live: *teikei,* or consumer groups with face-to-face, non-market relationships with particular farmers, similar to community-supported agriculture (CSA) in the United States; *jikyū,* or self-sufficiency for the farmer's household; and *junkan,* or a local cycle of farming on the land, using plant and animal waste for compost (JOAA 2011). The JOAA and its members—both farmers and consumers—have established a resistance that is oppositional to the capitalist market and economic growth. The aim is to take food out of the commodity market and put it squarely within a relationship with the land, the local climate, and the people producing and eating it.

Thus the inheritance of Kana and other young organic farmers is an organic food movement that in the face of poisoning from industrial and agricultural pollution has stood against the use of any agricultural chemicals. The pioneers refused to buy the agricultural chemicals and fertilizers sold by the powerful agricultural cooperatives *(nōkyō),* which operationalized the government's agricultural policies. The pioneers also rebelled against the government's policies to control farmers' use of the land and its products—such policies as rice mono-cropping; government payments to let certain land lie fallow; and the sale of rice to the government with controlled prices. Furthermore, they objected to the hollowing out of agricultural villages as the government encouraged mechanized, part-time farming and the migration of farm household members to the cities to work in industry. All such measures supported rapid economic growth, the main aim of the postwar government that was supported by the United States. The result was that Japanese agricultural policy allowed small farmers with an average of about five acres or two hectares to survive, but it has not allowed agriculture to flourish (Mulgan 2006).

Two examples of organic farmer pioneers illustrate the experiences of that generation of organic farmers. One man in his late fifties had been motivated to go into organic agriculture by his anger over Minamata disease—an illness caused by mercury dumped into a bay in southern Japan by the Chisso chemical company; the government took years to admit to it and decades to compensate the victims. A group of consumers in Tokyo set this pioneer and his friends up in farming in the seventies several hours north of Tokyo, but after several conflicts, the farmer and his wife went independent and set up a group of consumers to whom they still deliver food in Tokyo. Unlike other postwar educated people, they were satisfied to educate their four children in rural schools and on the land. Now they farm with their eldest son while educating others, helping to run an urban organic garden in a park in Tokyo and an organic garden beside a tourist restaurant near their home.

In the second case, a man who grew up on a farm in northeastern Japan was convinced that his mother had become sick because of agricultural chemicals used in his father's apple orchards. He did not want the same fate for his wife and child, so they took a pilgrimage to see a Dr. Yanase in western Japan. They had heard that by growing and using organic vegetables as medicine, the doctor had healed his rural patients who were suffering from the effects of agricultural chemicals and had symptoms much like his own mother's. They became believers. His mother soon died, but his father never gave his permission to switch the farm to organic. This man and his wife did what they could, buying land in another village while helping his father on his farm. They continue to deliver a weekly box of vegetables, fruit, and rice to consumers who have become old friends in the nearby regional city and manage many aspects of their consumer group. Now their son farms the grandfather's farm while their daughter and her family live with the parents and help with vegetable production.

Organic farmers like Kana face a somewhat different set of policies than these pioneers did, but the emphasis on industrial growth and an anemic agricultural sector have not changed. In the 1990s and 2000s, the World Trade Organization brought increasing pressure on Japan to open its markets, even to rice, and in response Japanese agricultural policy has required farmers to integrate their lands, using local growing cooperatives or group contracting in order for them to get government subsidies. The government also now rewards farmers who diversify their crops. Although the average age of farmers in Japan was sixty-six in 2010 ("Japan Aims at Bigger Farms to Boost Competitiveness" 2011) and usually younger people do not opt to continue farming, families do not want to give up their land and fear corporate incursion. Both conventional and organic farmers are up in arms because in the beginning of 2012, the government announced that it would pursue membership in the Trans-Pacific Partnership, a free trade organization that would open Japanese markets further to cheap, imported foods. This situation has put the JOAA organic farmers into an uneasy alliance with conventional farmers.

As an organic farmer in the 2000s, Kana is part of a minority of farmers in Japan, although their numbers are slowly but steadily growing (Kubota and Yoshino 2011). In 2011, there were twelve thousand organic farming households, only .47 percent of the farming households of Japan, farming only .36 percent of the agricultural land, and delivering .35 percent of the food. The average age of organic farmers, however, is lower than that of conventional farmers (whose average age is fifty-nine), with 9 percent below forty and 38 percent between forty and sixty, figures that reflect the appeal of organic farming to younger people like Kana, who want to live life differently ("Yūkinōgyō 12,000 ko: Heikinnenrei wa 59 sai" 2011).[3] JOAA farmers worry about the cheaper prices of imported organics because by official statistics more imported organic products than domestic are sold in Japan (Kumasawa 2009).

Compared to the unfriendly context within which the pioneer organic farmers worked in the seventies, organic farmers in the 2000s practice in a policy environment that gives them some support. The government has passed two laws, one in 2001 that set standards for organic products through the Organic JAS Inspection and Certification System and another in 2006 that promotes organic farming with some monetary benefits attached. The JOAA fought to pass both laws, but many organic farmers find organic certification expensive and unnecessary because they find their standards to be actually above the government's standards. Kana, for example, does not have certification. Even the promotion of organic farming law has pitted the JOAA against large companies (started in the 1980s and '90s) that contract with farmers and distribute organic food along with foods grown with "low" agrochemicals right to consumers' doors.

These large distribution companies, such as Daichi or Radish Bōya, are quite popular with working mothers and aging women, who find the purely organic food from farmers like Kana expensive and less convenient (Moen 2000). The price of organics is about 1.65 times the price of conventional food ("Domestic Market of Organic Products" 2006). Typical Japanese consumers demand safe, healthy food; enjoy seasonal food; and are very concerned about the food's place of origin; they are less concerned for the environment and demand perfect products, convenience, and reasonable pricing (Hasegawa 2008). Consumers who belong to consumer groups do so first to get safe food; second, to support the farmers; third, to get healthy food; and last, to increase national self-sufficiency in food. About a third of consumers who frequently buy organic food belong to consumer groups, whereas two-thirds of occasional consumers buy organics at supermarkets—an option that is increasing in the 2000s but did not exist in the seventies (Kubota and Yoshino 2011). In short, as a young organic farmer in the 2000s, Kana faces a lot of competition from other sources of organic food and even more from sources of sustainable products that use lower quantities of agrochemicals and guarantee no genetically modified food, just like organic produce.

By 2008 organic food was accepted in part because it appealed to fears that Japanese hold about the risks harbored by foods imported from other countries and even some Japanese foods. Postwar Japan had seen many problems with foods because of pollutants. In the 2000s incidents of tainted beef in Japan and poisoned pot stickers from China reinforced the sense that food was risky and that mothers needed to take great care to protect their children (Rosenberger 2009). Many people have feared American imported food because of overuse of chemical fertilizers and genetic modification of plant DNA. Thus organic consumption was one way for mothers to deal with the uncertainties of raising children in a global food system with risks that they themselves could not trace and that even their government could not fully monitor.

The radioactive contamination of parts of Japan after March 11, 2011, changed the scenario, making some Japanese food unsafe and all Japanese food potentially unsafe. Suddenly imported foods like Australian beef and American soybeans seemed appealing. Kana and others had cherished the ideal that organic food was "safe" and gave a feeling of calm and security *(anzen, anshin)* for themselves and their consumers, but now they could no longer necessarily make such a claim. The fact that the government pointed to the dangers of using natural compost, implying that imported, man-made fertilizers were better, did not help the organic farmers. But more on that below.

Consumer Groups: Links between Producers and Consumers

Kana does not worry about growing market competition but follows her ideals to resist the rule of market relationships. In fact, she refused the offer of a local restaurant to buy her vegetables because it demanded a certain amount at certain times and was not willing to respect what the farmer, the land, and the climate could produce. Likewise she does not sell in government-built and farmer-run direct-sale stores *(chokubaisho)* because the produce is mostly conventional and cheap. She looks down her nose at "eco-farmers" who have promised the government that they would halve the amount of agrochemicals that they use and who often sell in supermarkets.

Kana prefers the consumer groups *(teikei)*, with their ideal of face-to-face relationships based on trust and has developed such a group with people who live in the towns near her farm. Her consumers promise to buy a "set box" of vegetables every week throughout the year for ¥2,000 per box ($20 or so, depending on the exchange rate). They agree to accept the vegetables that Kana can produce in cooperation with the local land and weather, instead of eating and cooking according to their own desires via global food bought at the grocery stores. Ideally the consumers pay the farmer at the beginning of the season, but in Kana's case, this effort has not succeeded, and she has to collect money by the month.

Kana bewailed the fact that the consumers in her group were mainly in it for food safety and security *(anzen, antei)*. Women make up most of the consumers now and in the past, but younger women are less willing to be active members. In contrast, older consumers of the group who have long bought food from the northeastern couple mentioned above have held study meetings where they consider Japan's agricultural policies, health effects of pollution, and Japan's military and trade relationships with the United States. Consumers have helped the farmers by meeting and dividing the produce into boxes at a consumer's home. Now young women are not so interested in these broader political considerations, and they are too busy to do anything but receive the box sets at their doors.

When I went with Kana on her deliveries one Friday evening, she could not talk to about half of her consumers because many were either not home or did not come to the door. At those houses, she just left the box (filled with veggies such as Chinese cabbage, pumpkin quarters, and broccoli) on the dark porch. Sometimes she slid the box into the front hall with a shout into the house and got an answering "Thank you." When women did come to the door, Kana talked about the vegetables, the weather, and the children of the household and only then ventured into her political concerns about nuclear energy.

Going down the front steps of a consumer's house, she said, "I can learn about child rearing from my customers, and they can learn from me." She laughed merrily. "My parents want grandchildren, especially my father. My mother doesn't want to be a grandmother so much. But my sister lives close and she is married. No children yet!" After she started up the truck, she commented more seriously, "I am in no hurry to marry. It would have to be the right one who liked this kind of life."

Kana said that the women in her group were mostly concerned about the health of their children. At one house Kana talked for fifteen minutes across the threshold to a woman in her forties who had asked her to speak to a group of mothers on *shokuiku,* or (literally) food education. This topic included not only ideas about healthy food but also historical ethical notions about how children would grow up more grateful, empathetic, and cooperative if they have a deeper relationship with their food. Kana was more than glad to oblige.

It was not where she had started on her personal search for an alternative to wasteful consumption and production, but she wanted children to know about how their vegetables grew and how delicious they could be if grown organically and eaten fresh. She told of the delight of one mother among her consumers who said that even her high-school-age son had noticed the delicious taste of Kana's vegetables. "The vegetables speak for themselves," said Kana with a satisfied smile.

"I have realized that my consumers have to become my fans and the fans of my vegetables. I wish they would develop a feeling of affectionate attachment [aichaku] with the land where these vegetables are growing and come help, but most are too busy." However, that Friday evening one particularly devoted middle-aged woman invited us to sit on the step in her front hall and brought out a notebook containing all the newsletters Kana had ever written to show to me!

Organic farmers with whom I talked developed consumer groups in a variety of ways: from friends, past co-workers, relatives and their contacts, mothers at a kindergarten, church members, children of older members, and people concerned about health. The ideal is that members are local, but nearby rural people supply their own food and do not want to join, so organic farmers need to find people in cities or towns. In several cases, farmers drove their vegetable boxes several hours to consumers in Tokyo or sent boxes half the length of Honshu. In this case, emphasis is on "organic," and "local" expands to mean Japanese as opposed to imported food.

An organic farmer in Nagano, the central mountainous part of Japan, expanded the notion of building links through her consumer group, trying to build the value of human relations over market relations in Japan. Though she lived three hours from Tokyo, she had traveled there for over ten years every other week to deliver her boxes to her consumers, sending the boxes by refrigerated overnight delivery the other weeks. In addition to her Tokyo consumers, she was devoted to developing links (tsunagari) with a broad range of folks who visited her big farmhouse throughout the year: a disabled group from Tokyo, university students on field trips, high school students, and year-long interns who boarded with her as they learned organic farming. A former teacher, her mission was to improve the values of selfish, materialistic Japanese and engender values of gratefulness and empathy through contact with the land, the food the visitors had helped to produce, and the people with whom they worked.

An organic farmer on the outskirts of a regional city in the northeast combined contemporary globalized interests with his consumer group, building common interests more than deep relationships. Finding little meaning in his job as a salaryman in a large city and following his interests in hiking and gardening, he had left his company job and moved to his wife's natal home. He appealed to his consumers with weekly recipes and beautiful pictures of the Italian, Chinese, and Thai dishes that he made with the vegetables that he grew and delivered to them, and he even opened a small reservations-only restaurant to share his cleverly cooked vegetables. He got together with his consumers to make *miso* (fermented soybean paste) or *nattō* (fermented soybeans) in the spirit of Japanese cuisine as one more exotic world cuisine. Thus he combined a turn to an older way of farming with contemporary interests in globalized cuisine.

Past and Present: Residual and Emergent Resistance

The resistance that Kana and other organic farmers associated with the JOAA practice in Japan is an interesting example of resistance that is dynamic and contradictory. On the one hand, this resistance builds on residual beliefs and practices derived from the historical past in Japan—older agricultural and processing techniques combined with the ideal relations imagined in Japanese agricultural villages of the past. On the other hand, this resistance is very much of the present and employs emergent beliefs and practices—those that are developing in the margins out of a new set of social interactions that challenge the dominant way of life (Williams 1994). In the rest of this chapter, various examples will show the ways in which Kana wends her way carefully between older ways and relationships and newer lifestyles and meanings. In the following vignette, we see Kana learning old food techniques while defending her independence and alternative lifestyle.

One cloudy Saturday morning in December, Kana had a *mochi*-pounding party at her barn; *mochi* is pounded sticky rice that becomes smooth and is eaten in soups with sauces or shaped into confectionaries. (Kana used brown rice, which is unusual.) She invited all of her customers and volunteers who had helped her during the year. Her mother and father, as well as one of her father's former colleagues, were also there. She was disappointed that none of her consumers came. Two young women who had volunteered on the farm in return for vegetables came from Tokyo. They were both artists who were working part time in Tokyo and saw organic farming as one avenue where they could express their wish for an alternative lifestyle within Japan.

Borrowing the equipment to steam the rice from the local community hall, Kana worked with some help from her parents to prepare the *mochi*. As her father and his colleague wielded a large wooden hammer, she reached her hand into the large wooden bowl with the rice and turned it between hits. "She is getting quite good at that," her mother commented to me. Then Kana laid the sticky rice out on a table, putting it into a shallow frame so that she could roll it out with a long rolling pin that pushed it to the even depth of the frame. Her mother advised her through this process, but Kana was insistent on doing it and not shy to tell her mother that she knew what she was doing and did not need help. She folded the edges in and then picked out the round globs that would be put into the soup that had been boiling in the big vat on an outdoor stove. When everyone was finally gathered around the long table in the area outside the barn, there was a huge *itadakimasu* (I receive), and everyone took up soup bowls and chopsticks and fished out the *mochi* to eat. Kana's face was radiant as she took her first bite. This was the first time that she had eaten *mochi* made from the rice grown with her own hands.

Kana's bid to live her life differently through organic agriculture linked with visions of Japan's past in order to change the present and envision a different future. Growing the rice for and making her own *mochi*—still a ritually significant food to eat at New Year's for strength and prosperity in the year to come—is a good example of this revival of Japanese actions from the past so as to model an alternative relationship with land and food for modern consumers. The farming methods used by farmers in the JOAA take advantage of the knowledge of older farmers and of farming practices from three hundred years ago. As one of Kana's friends, a young male organic farmer in northeastern Japan, said, "I want to use farming methods like they used in the Tokugawa era. Then they really used everything they had locally." Another of her friends, a young female organic farmer several hours on the other side of Tokyo, said, "I try to have conversations with the really old people around here, like in my grandparents' generation. They remember farming before all the modern conveniences. The ones in my parents' generation believe strongly in using chemical fertilizers, and they can't imagine why we would want to give up the increased productivity from fertilizers for organic farming."

The organic methods that Kana is using are a complex combination of new and old—some methods that have been passed down from long ago, some methods learned from European and American experiments in organic farming in the twentieth century, and others that have been developed by pioneering organic farmers in the last several decades. She fretted over exactly what methods to follow. For example, a "natural" or do-nothing method of farming was started by Fukuoka Masanobu, an internationally famous Japanese organic farmer–philosopher of the twentieth century who argued that seeds could just be sown among the grasses. This is a method without weeding, tilling, or fertilizer that claimed to sustain the natural balance of micro-organisms in the soil and thus sustain fertility in the long run. However, the yields are lower than in other forms of organic agriculture. As we walked around her fields out in the hills, she said thoughtfully, "Sometimes I do part of the field of daikon without tilling and weeding and the other part with tilling and weeding." Finding an alternative farming style that preserved the environment had to be weighed against the need to survive.

A Path for Challenging the Status Quo— with Compromises and Contradictions

Through organic farming, Kana has found a way to exist according to her ideals and receive respect yet live in a way that is extremely oppositional to the status quo in Japan. The beliefs and practices of the JOAA by which Kana has tried to live are quite radical and, if followed, would disrupt international trade. The organic ideals spurn the capitalist industrialized market system on which modern Japan is based and harken back to a person-to-person local economy of self-sufficiency lived in concert with the land. JOAA ideas argue against assumptions of distant trade within the global food system and even the import of foreign organics into Japan. Indeed, if taken to their limits, the JOAA ideals refuse high technology, industrialization, and consumer culture.

The JOAA ideals give opportunities to people like Kana to live according to their beliefs and to establish an alternative identity within Japan, but these ideals are also extremely challenging to live by. The JOAA urges member-farmers not only to grow food without agricultural chemicals, but also to raise chickens or cows whose manure could furnish the basis for compost fertilizer. They should live off of their land—that is, be self-sufficient through the food that they grow and through money they receive through the consumer organizations.

Kana believes in these ideals and tries to live up to them because she is dedicated to improving the environment, making healthy and safe vegetables, and helping to make Japan self-sufficient in food. Unlike most Japanese women her age, she is totally uninterested in consumer luxuries that make her life easier or enhance her appearance (Rosenberger 2001). She is not interested in accruing wealth. She uses an older computer and printer to do her newsletters, but she does not buy the latest electronics, wear makeup, and worry about fashion (she usually buys used clothing).

Nonetheless, Kana realizes that she is not able to live up to all of the JOAA ideals for organic farmers and finds her identity as an organic farmer filled with compromises and contradictions. Her living situation has been one of these. In 2008 she was living with her parents, as this is the area in which she has the best chance of renting land because her father's family is an old farming family in the area. Her father did not inherit any property, only a house (the elder son inherited the property), but he remained in the community working in the local agricultural cooperative. It was very difficult for Kana to give up her wish in her late twenties to live by herself, independent from her parents. "For a while, I wanted to move out from my parents' house in the worst way!" She grimaced. But at thirty-three she said, "I realized it was better to live together. We save on energy for the environment by using the same refrigerator and stove." She had a room of her own on one end of the small house, built in the early sixties, with a squat, non-flush toilet and older, wood-frame sliding windows that leave cracks for the cold to enter. Jokingly she called herself a "parasite single," the label for single people who live with and sponge off of their parents, but in fact she was supplying the house with its vegetables and part of its rice.

Despite her wish to live her life differently, Kana was unable to live entirely according to the ideal of self-sufficiency outside of the market economy. For one thing, she had to compromise because she lives with her parents, who have certain preferences for what they want to eat. They bought meat, for example, which she shared, and they purchased white rice, while she liked her own brown, unpolished rice *(genmai)*. Kana showed me the big ceramic pot of rice bran that sat in their kitchen and that builds up over the years. Fresh vegetables like cucumbers and eggplants are put in there, fermented a bit, and then eaten. She said that some people, implying even her mother, do not like the smell much, but it is a good traditional way to extend the life of vegetables.

Furthermore, Kana realizes that her parents were furnishing the roof over her head, and their support had enabled her to start her farm and consumer organization gradually and still survive. At first she had only twelve members and was barely making it. When I interviewed her, she was up to thirty-five and claimed she was making a small profit, although she was still dependent on her parents and lacking benefits. It was not until the second day on her farm that she told me about a prize from a food-buying club concentrating in organics (Seikatsu Club) that she had received in 2006. Her mother had come home from her part-time job and we were having green tea and rice crackers at the low table in their small living room. Her mother urged her to show me the newspaper report that showed Kana receiving the prize and that gave some publicity to her work and philosophy. She smiled shyly, though with pride, as she handed it to me. This prize had made her locally famous and she had almost doubled the membership in her consumer group.

By early 2012, Kana had in fact just moved out of her parents' house and moved to a small, rather cold, two-room house just on the other side of the barn that she and her father used. Before the earthquake, her consumer group membership had increased to forty-five, making the move economically feasible. "It was a very important move for me psychologically too," she said. She now could eat just as she wished and move entirely at her own pace.

Finding local friends with whom she can talk about her challenges as an organic farmer is one of the difficulties in the unique and sometimes lonely path that Kana has chosen. Although she has friends among the young mothers in the consumer group and the volunteers from Tokyo, no one locally shares her particular challenges. Kana is active in the young people's section of the JOAA. It is to these other young farmers that she turns for social and moral support as they all struggle to live up to the JOAA ideals and interpret them within the Japan of the 2000s. "I could really talk sincerely with them in the second party (*nijikai*, or going out drinking) after our meeting," she says. Kana's best friends are other JOAA women farmers struggling toward the same goals as she is. In our various talks, she often referred to two women in particular with whom she was close. I became aware of them because she received rice from one of them to augment her rice for a party described above. As she worked her fingers through the rice, rinsing it with cold water from the outside faucet, she said, "I love getting together with them. We are close philosophically on how we want to do organic agriculture. We just had a harvest party not long ago at the house of the one in Chiba, and we all brought food to share. After New Year's I go up to the farm of the other one in Nagano and spend several days. That is the only week that I take off from delivering a box. We laugh and cry together."

Gender and Organic Farming

Kana and other organic farmers meet with various ambiguities and challenges as they create alternative identities in the midst of Japanese life, especially because organic farming combines residual and emergent forms of resistance. Nowhere is this clearer than in gender relations, an issue that has remained tangential to the main goals of JOAA organic farming but is important to many of the members, especially younger ones. Kana's relationship with her father-assistant is a case in point.

If the household is taken as the unit of self-sufficiency in the ideal of JOAA organic agriculture, Kana's father's help fits the ideal lifestyle of organic farming. Originally the aim of the JOAA was to reinvigorate the ideal of the multi-generational farm household, which in the 1960s and '70s was fragmenting as people were encouraged by economic circumstances and the government to leave rural households and work in the cities—or to farm part time and get another job near the farm. The JOAA leaders were firmly against these trends, wishing to maintain strong, full-time farming households that they believed would sustain values of group cooperation, empathy, and respect, as well as people's personal care for the land in an environmentally sustainable way over generations. Indeed, their ideas fit with mainstream ideals in postwar Japan around selected values of agricultural households, which were often envisioned as the backbone of the Japanese value system. In this sense, Kana and other organic farmers were delving back into Japan's traditional past in order to reshape and revitalize the values of the present so that they would be more focused on personal rather than economic relationships (Block 1990). They felt they were providing a path back to core agrarian values, which were still taught in schools and which shored up Japan's vision of itself as psychologically and socially unique even if the nation had been badly tarnished during World War II (Allen 2004; Befu 2001). Thus, from this point of view, strong kinship ties between father and daughter that function to support a household economically (as in Japan's history) are not out of line with JOAA goals and endear these goals to mainstream Japanese.

But the relationship between Kana and her father was tricky and shed an interesting light on the delicate balance between residual and emergent values in this alternative lifestyle. Kana and others in this movement were looking back toward an idealized picture of the agricultural household, but that picture did not necessarily take into account male-female and age hierarchies. In the past, young women obeyed their fathers. In taking on her father as her assistant, Kana drew on past kinship traditions but simultaneously challenged them: her father was an older male whose experience and knowledge should be respected by his daughter, although his retirement signaled a gradual shift in power relations.

In 2008, I watched the relationship of the two of them with interest. At one point, they had a disagreement about whether the compost pile that was ripening in a wood-lined cage against the barn needed to be turned or not. He said, "It'll be okay; just leave it." The turning required the cooperation of the two of them to take down the wooden walls. Kana replied, "Definitely not," and started to take down the walls by herself. The father said nothing, silently pitching in and helped her dismantle the wood, corrugated metal sheets, and tarp, later wielding the hoe to loosen the compost while she turned it with a shovel. Even I could see that the texture was changing as she stirred it. The tension was eased when he commented, "Ah, this turned out well." Later, the father said to me, "She knows about organic agriculture. There has to be a leader or there is no production. I give guidance, but 80–90 percent of the time, she is right, so I back off." Kana also said of her father and her, "We get along well. He knows about farming because he grew up on a farm." She was willing to give him credit for being better than she at estimating the weight of a bunch of vegetables, for all vegetables had to be weighed so each person's box was given an equal amount. He would pick up a bunch and say "300 grams" and be very close. If they misjudged by too much when picking, vegetables would go to waste.

In short, Kana and her father were working out a new style in their father-daughter relationship that actively denied the traditional hierarchical relationship and put her in the driver's seat of her organic agriculture business yet gave him respect as well. In this sense, this alternative lifestyle was using old ways to forge new ways that fit the ethos of the contemporary era. It satisfied her wish to actively change Japan and his wish to have an active retirement.

Part of the ambiguity of both resistance and identity in this alternative lifestyle is that the expressed goals of the organic movement are not clear about gender relationships. The goals are explicit only in terms of the producer-consumer relationships, which should be non-market and personal. That said, people who have come into this movement over the years have carried with them the ideas of other movements for social change, including that of more equality between men and women. The couple in northeast Japan who were mutual friends of Kana's and mine wanted to change the gender system as well as the food system. They could not marry if they maintained separate names in protest of the law, which does not allow married people to be on the same household register unless they both have the same name. At forty, they have had three children and are still not legally married. Their neighbors in rural Iwate Prefecture do not like this arrangement, but they ignore it because they like them and value having younger farmers in the neighborhood. "We thought the law would change long before this and it is still under discussion, but . . . sometimes it gets difficult for us," they said. They get implicit support from their JOAA friends. What is hard for them now is to maintain their ideal of equality between man and woman while the woman births and breast-feeds children. Although they try to make decisions together, he tends to spend more time in the fields.

The modern gender relations sought by another of Kana's friends, Emi, a woman in her mid-thirties, are also a contradictory combination of new and old ways. Emi interned for a year with a Tokyo organic farmer, then married a fellow JOAA member who was already farming in Chiba. Taking advantage of inheritance customs in order to own farmland in the area, he had arranged to be adopted into the family register of a farmer's widow who would soon die. He would get the house and land and in return would carry on that family's name in the village and care for the family's ancestors, graves, and neighborhood relationships. Thus when Emi got married, she took on the name of this family rather than that of her husband. Emi said, "It's a bit strange having this last name that doesn't even belong to my husband, but I am adjusting to it." Because of their responsibilities, they were expected to enact the gender relations customary to the village; Emi's husband was assumed to be the household head who represented the household in village and shrine organizations. Although Emi had her own independent consumer group, he was viewed as the farmer, and they had to actively resist this external prejudice within their own relationship.

Kana was struggling with her own decisions about how to negotiate a marriage relationship in 2012 because she was determined to stick to her oppositional ideals to the extent possible in terms of gender and organic farming. After we had settled into her *kotatsu* (low warming table with heater underneath and blanket under the tabletop to keep in the warmth) in her small house, she surprised me with the news that she herself was going to be married. Now thirty-eight, she had indeed surprised herself by agreeing to marry a local man who was a salaryman, not a farmer, to whom she had been introduced and had grown quite fond of. "I didn't want to marry a salaryman—someone who didn't really like his work. And I don't want to quit farming. But I realized he was honest and good and didn't mind that I don't like to decorate myself or my house much." They had talked at length and come to various agreements. She would continue to farm, and they would live in this village near her barn and biggest field, though in a bigger house. They would each keep their own bank accounts and share tasks at home.

Her biggest decision was whether to have children or not, but she was finally convinced to do so by the words of one of her organic farmer friends who said, "I understand not wanting children, but people who don't want to have children want to remain as a child. They want to be treated as a child." Kana said, "That hit me hard," as she punched her fist into her forehead. "In thirty minutes I decided to have children." Her husband-to-be was glad, as he wanted children, but she requested that he take time off from his company for child leave—guaranteed for men by law. He asked and his company would give only six months rather than a year, but she was satisfied with that.

Kana is now looking at models of other women farmers who farm at a lower level and sell their goods mainly at special events rather than through a weekly consumer group. Her future husband has not yet offered to help her in the fields, but she realizes that her father's strength is an important part of her operation, and she hopes she will get some weekend help from her husband-to-be if and when needed. Her organic friends wager that in the long run, he will become interested and help her.

Dealing with the Local Farming Community

One of the original ideals of the JOAA movement according to the philosophy of its main founder, Ichiraku Teruo, was to restore the ideals of the traditional agrarian Japanese village, even though everyday practices and kinship relationships varied throughout Japan. Ichiraku imagined a utopian restoration of the mutual help and cooperation among households and the ability of the agricultural village to have a diverse local agriculture that could be independent from the state and its requirements (rather than part-time farming or intensive rice farming without soybean production, for example).

It soon became clear to organic farmers in the seventies, however, that their ideas, such as not using chemical fertilizer and operating outside of the rules issued and privileges given by the agricultural cooperatives, were not popular in farming communities. Young people like Kana, going into organic farming to express their beliefs and live an alternative lifestyle in the 2000s, were under no illusions that they would receive the enthusiastic cooperation of other local farmers unless there were a community of like-minded organic farmers around. Even though farmers are aging and farming their land less, obtaining land for young farmers is difficult at first. In Kana's case, she was viewed with suspicion because she was a young woman farming and doing it organically at that. However, it was ultimately the long-term trust among local families, concerned with their private lands, that earned her the access to farming land.

It was a dilemma that seemed to blend with the darkening night sky as Kana and I drove from her rice fields into a nearby town where I could catch a train back to Tokyo. She told me the story of renting several small rice paddies (located in a near yet different village from that of her other fields) that she cultivated with another woman farmer. Several years ago, they had seen the fallow rice fields on a hillside and asked a woman passing by who owned them. Boldly, they called on the owner and said they would like to rent these fields. They heard nothing for several months, but finally the owner gave his okay. He was a local government representative who knew their neighbor (also a government representative), who probably vouched for them as being members of an old family. "People don't trust outsiders," she informed me.

Steering along the windy, narrow country roads, Kana reflected, "The owner is a nice person. It is hard to get the land, but then when you do, it is good. People don't trust outsiders because if you produce well, then there is the feeling that the land should belong to the cultivator rather than the owner. If the government notices and you [the renter-cultivator] have produced well for ten years, the government will say that it belongs to you, the cultivator. Since the land reform of 1947, it is the cultivator who is actually working the land who should get ownership. But for the owner, it is a matter of taking responsibility for the land, for the ancestors. It's the household's inheritance (zaisan). So often the [landowners] just till it and weed it so they can keep it zoned as agricultural and pay lower taxes on it."

I noticed that Kana hadn't been saying "rent the land," so I asked, "So are you really renting this land or just using it?"

"Actually I am just using it. They don't want to rent it." She hesitated because this got into delicate ground with the tax authorities, but the cover of night seemed to give her permission to talk freely.

"I am able to use all of my fields without money."

"That's convenient," I quipped.

"Yes, but the bad part is there is no contract and so no guarantee of being able to use it over a long period of time. Do you remember that big sunny field up above my house? I am supposed to just say that I am helping the owner. Even the tax guy says it is okay to do it that way. But if government people looked at my production and profits, they would know. They'd ask, 'Where are you doing your farming?' and I could get into trouble."

Kana wanted to live an alternative lifestyle outside of the capitalist bureaucratic system of the modern nation, but that was impossible. She was both endangered by the laws and trapped by them. As we bumped along the country roads, she expressed her main worry: "I am developing these organic fields and building up the quality of the soil with compost, but I have no legal right to them. The owners could take them back from me whenever they want." In short, in the final instance, this was a system of private property, and no amount of talk about cooperation and mutual help among households in agricultural villages could change this. "The younger people around here now," Kana said in a tone that was uncharacteristically bitter for her, "they aren't farming, and they just want the land for the money it will bring."

Thus the JOAA ideal of cooperative relationships in farming communities devoted to local self-sufficiency, care of the land, and production of food was difficult to attain in practice. In a sense Kana was able to avoid the land market and embed her use of the land in personal relationships, but the motivation for the people renting the land was tied up with concerns for private property, family sentiments, ultimate profit from the land, and loopholes in the law. Herein lies a sense of alienation from the land that forced Kana to live in cooperation with others in her farming community but in a way that was alien to her ideals.

Effects of the 3/11 Disaster

In Japan, people refer to the triple tragedy of the earthquake, the tsunami, and the Fukushima nuclear plant explosions in northeastern Japan as "3/11"— their version of 9/11 in the United States. I met with Kana in January 2012, ten months after the quake. She was fortunate in many ways because she lives south of Tokyo in an area to which the wind did carry some radioactivity but much less than in other affected areas. Unlike farmers in Fukushima Prefecture, home of the nuclear plant that exploded, she can still farm, and her goods are not tainted by the very geographical name of her area.

Nonetheless, Kana has problems. The number of members in her consumer group declined to thirty-five because mothers of young children were worried about radiation levels of Japanese food. Many started buying imported food or at least food from only the very south or the very north of Japan— areas that were not affected in any tangible way by radioactivity. The spread of the radioactivity, mainly of cesium (some of which has a half-life of thirty years), depended on the wind and the rain. Ironically, the wind had blown northwest for a while but then headed out to sea and back in over Japan to affect places far south of the exploding nuclear plant, including Tokyo and Kana's area of Kanagawa.

In 2012, organic farmers assiduously measured the level of becquerels of cesium in a sample of each of their crops or compost ingredients to see if they contained radioactivity.[4] Measuring each item is expensive—from $70 to $150 per item—but Kana got in on a research study through which she received measurement for free. She breathes a sigh of relief that her vegetables came back "ND"—no detected level of radioactivity. That does not mean zero, but it means that the machine cannot detect any. However, out on the same hilltop field as before, as she pulled the long white daikon by their green leaves from the loose, black soil, she said, "The problem is the compost I make. I have always used a lot of rice bran, but now we find that the rice bran around here measures positive for radioactivity. It seems to absorb the radioactivity more than the rice kernel, and my rice actually showed a low level of radioactivity. So now what shall I use?"

Last summer Kana had bought organic fertilizer because the government said not to use natural, local items, but on economic grounds she could not continue doing this. Like other organic farmers, she thought of using fallen leaves or the chips from the fallen trees used to grow mushrooms, but all of these resources from the mountains had absorbed radioactivity. Kana said, "I realize that what I have to do is to plant other plants [rokuhi] that I can use as compost. That means there won't be as much land for the vegetables I sell, but. . . ."

I ventured to say, "But if you marry, perhaps you won't have to make so many vegetables."

She laughed and bent her head with some embarrassment, not yet used to the idea of depending on her husband. "I have thought of that. I can maybe make fewer, higher-quality vegetables for fewer customers."

The big earthquake of 2011 was a huge turning point for many Japanese and was rumored to have encouraged people to think more seriously about marriage and family, but for Kana, the contribution of organic farming was less clear. She felt a strong responsibility to make her vegetables in a way that would maintain the safety of her consumers. Her alternative lifestyle had centered on creating a local economy that would improve the environment, but now she said, "Local production and local consumption [chisanchishō] are in a hard place with the radiation. Maybe it will all fall apart."

Soon Kana's old self-confidence and passion revived, however, as she declared, "People eat food with agrochemicals as if it is nothing, but they won't eat food with radioactivity. People say it is because you can't chose when it comes to radioactivity. But I wonder if it is only radioactivity we have to worry about. Society has various problems—not just radioactivity or electric power. The goal of economic growth itself is a problem."

Conclusion

Kana has found a way to buck the system and to forge a path with values that are the opposite of the consumer-centered, competitive values followed by the mainstream in Japan. She has found a way to model and bring others into a different relationship with the local land and the land of Japan.

Kana's life as an organic farmer illustrates one viable way for young Japanese in the 2000s to resist the postwar status quo of living as mainstream housewives or company workers, dependent on the Japanese economy. As a young adult, she has refused those identities because they are inextricably linked with the degradation of the earth. Her path is not easy because, raised to play the game of a typical Japanese adult throughout school, she was trained to plan for a career that would then give way to marriage, motherhood, and a home that would require a husband's income. Her difficulty in now agreeing to be tangentially part of this system through marriage shows the distance that she has come in her thinking. She has played a different game with different rules and has forged a new identity as a young, woman farmer, for which there has been no easy script.

Kana's chosen lifestyle is full of contradictions because she must practice it within a system that espouses and operates by the very capitalistic, competitive principles to which her life is designed to provide an alternative. At every turn—ecologically, economically, socially, politically—she confronts institutions and people who disagree with her. Her organic practice is a voice in the global consumer wilderness that continually must compromise and negotiate with contemporary Japanese ways. Her resistance requires a strong inner spirit shored up by firm relationships with distant JOAA friends and the JOAA as an organization. She is not a stranger to psychological stress, she admits, particularly in the creation of her own farm and development of her own consumer group. Although part of a larger movement, she must build her own structure and spirit of resistance in her local setting, testing how far she can go at any one time.

Furthermore, Kana holds within her the habitual ways of thinking and acting of her upbringing, as well as those she has developed through organic farming. Her identity is fragmented and mixed—to some extent, a result of the coincidences, contradictions, and ambivalences that exist between these two games of life in which she plays, the slowly changing dominant ways of postwar Japan and the alternative world of organic farming (Ortner 2006). Marriage and children, as well as owning private property, are hopes of hers even as she is committed to the calling of an organic woman farmer living and working with the land outside of the market system. She is like her generation in her wish for a man who will respect and honor her opinion, but because the resistant nature of her career infuses her lifestyle, she has brought strong de- mands to her impending marriage. She is willing to compromise up to a point in that she is marrying a salaryman whose company is embedded in the fate of Japan's market system, but she must be able to continue her anti-market, agricultural-based activities.

Resistant as her life is, several situations have made Kana's path easier. First, the dissatisfactions of her generation with their parents' lifestyles and the difficulties in getting jobs in recessionary Japan have infused the air along her journey. Her choices are not completely strange within her generation. Many of her generation have reacted by refusing to take on adult identities— working part time, continuing a dependence on parents, and taking on child- like manners. Others have quietly opted for different identities than they were trained to fulfill—women opting for careers and avoiding marriage; men working part time and investing in full-time hobbies. Kana is part of a group of people who have demanded a more complete independence that is free from both economic dependence on markets and companies and psycholog- ical dependence on others. Indeed it is a higher level of independence and maturity that allows her to accept the idea of having children.

Second, the path of organic agriculture offers a lifestyle and identity that link with certain residual virtues that Japanese value from their agrarian past (Kelly 2006). For example, Japanese idealize the cooperation, compassion, and sense of gratitude that supposedly flourished in traditional agricultural village life; they cling to ideas of living according to the seasons and appreciating parts of nature as a way of attaining purity or sincerity. These values echo in the postwar morality taught in the schools and in the contemporary morali- ty taught through food education. Thus Kana's emergent, innovative form of farming and distribution resonates with idealizations of Japanese history and culture that are thought to contribute to the goodness of Japan today. This connection facilitates her ability to bridge her own upbringing in a rural area with her alternative lifestyle today and to overcome some of the contradictions that exist between her newly chosen and given identities. Old habits can be used and adapted to new ways.

Third, until the 3/11 earthquake, tsunami, and nuclear explosions, Kana's production of local, fresh, healthy food responded directly to certain anxieties of Japanese people about risks in the current global world. People are worried about their ability to protect their health, particularly the health of children, in a globalized age when foodways are industrialized and globalized and thus beyond their control. The appeal of local, organic food is that it can reduce the risk that each person, particularly mothers, is now responsible for handling. Whether Kana's food, grown in a comparatively but not completely safe area, will still be able to reduce that risk is a worry for Kana. But the trust that she has established with the majority of her customers has survived; they believe that she will be honest in her measurements and give them safe food. In short, Kana has found allies even among people living a mainstream life.

What have we learned about the process of creating a new social identity and the nature of resistance by delving into the life of an organic farmer in Japan? On both counts, Kana's experience tells us that these processes are partial. The process of identity harbors some ambivalence, and the nature of resistance, some ambiguity. For an organic farmer to be successful, compromises with the economy, the bureaucracy, the community, family, and so on are necessary even as one lives by resistant principles and pursues a new identity that fits these principles. While more complete resistance is possible at the level of organizational ideals, in everyday life, flexibility is necessary to survive. Nonetheless, psychological stress, social conflict, and compromise are almost inevitable, and thus personal and institutional alliances for support are paramount.

Finally, the context surrounding the practice of resistance and the creation of a new identity is of extreme importance. These will be much easier if debate is already going on throughout society on the pertinent issues. Japanese society is experiencing upheavals economically, politically, socially, and culturally. A sense of risk and an ensuing search for new ways to live life and solve problems have captured the imagination of the young people in the nation. With the 3/11 tragedy, older people have also realized that the postwar way of life that they established requires huge energy inputs and has caused radiation problems for future generations. Still the government argues that nuclear energy plants are necessary for adequate electricity to support economic growth. The debate is quiet but strong.

Kana can live as an organic farmer who challenges and resists basic truths of the status quo because the atmosphere is full of debate about energy sources, the environment, healthy food, Japanese food self-sufficiency, economic stagnation versus growth, and family versus individual values. Her practice of local, organic agriculture, which emphasizes food embedded in social relationships and a relationship with the land outside of the market (Polanyi 1957), has presented an option that is enticing for the purity of its answer to current complicated pressures to participate in globalized, free trade. Few will actually take on the practice of organic agriculture as Kana has, but some can participate in it as consumers and others witness it as a resistant way of living that stretches the potentialities for engaging with the world in Japan in the 2000s.

Notes

1. Japan imports 25 percent of its agricultural products from the United States and 39 percent from the Association of Southeast Asian Nations (ASEAN), China, and the European Union (EU) together. Japan is the largest meat-importing country in the world, with much coming from Australia and New Zealand ("Trade" 2012).
2. The Rokkasho plant, which will process spent uranium and plutonium, is located north of Fukushima, where the 2011 tsunami and meltdown occurred. The Japanese government plans to continue to build Rokkasho in order to power its nuclear power plants, despite the fact that the extent to which Japan will continue to use its nuclear power plants is under debate ("Japan's Nuclear Future" 2012).
3. The survey from which these figures are taken included organic farmers with Japan Agricultural Standard certification and those who farm by organic methods without certification. The former farmed 9,000 hectares and delivered 57,000 tons of food, whereas the latter farmed 7,000 hectares and delivered 44,000 tons of food.
4. Kana's rice measured 50 becquerel; one becquerel is defined as the activity of a quantity of radioactive material in which one nucleus decays per second. The Japanese set the maximum acceptable safety figure at 500 becquerel for the first year after the explosion, but as of April 2012 it was decreased to 100 becquerel. This measure varies, however, by food item so that items like milk and water, which are consumed more often, are assigned lower figures.

References Cited

Allen, Patricia. 2004. *Together at the Table: Sustainability and Sustenance in the American Agrifood System.* University Park: Pennsylvania State University Press.
Befu, Harumi. 2001. *Hegemony of Homogeneity.* Melbourne: Trans-Pacific Press.
Block, Fred. 1990. *Postindustrial Possibilities: A Critique of Economic Discourse.* Berkeley: University of California Press.

Bourdieu, Pierre. 1989. *The Logic of Practice.* Cambridge: Polity Press.

"Domestic Market of Organic Products." 2006. Food and Agriculture Organization, June 30. Www.fao.org/organicag/display/work/display_2.asp ? country=JPN&lang=en&disp=summaries. Accessed January 13, 2012.

"Food Self-Sufficiency Rate Fell below 40% in 2010." 2011. *Japan Times,* August 12. Www.japantimes.co.jp/text/nn20110812a7.html. Accessed January 6, 2013.

Foucault, Michel. 1980. *The History of Sexuality.* New York: Vintage Books.

Gunewardena, Nandini. 2007. "Disrupting Subordination and Negotiating Belonging: Women Workers in the Transnational Production Sites of Sri Lanka." In *The Gender of Globalization: Women Navigating Cultural and Economic Marginalities,* ed. N. Gunewardena and A. Kingsolver, 35–60. Santa Fe: School for Advanced Research.

Hall, Stuart. 1996. "Introduction: Who Needs Identity?" In *Questions of Cultural Identity,* ed. S. Hall and P. duGay, 1–10. Thousand Oaks, CA: Sage.

Hasegawa, Hiroyo. 2008. "Government Initiatives to Support a Sustainable Agricultural Industry in Japan." *Japan for Sustainability Newsletter.* Japanfs.org/en/ mailmagazine/newsletter/ pages/o27845.html. Accessed January 13, 2012.

Honda, Yuki. 2006. "'Freeters': Young Atypical Workers in Japan." In *Perspectives on Work, Employment and Society in Japan,* ed. P. Matanle and W. Lunsing, 143–168. New York: Palgrave Macmillan.

"Japan Aims at Bigger Farms to Boost Competitiveness." 2011. Asiaone News, October 20. News/Latest%2BNews/Asia/Story/A1Story20111020–30632.html. Accessed July 17, 2012.

"Japan's Nuclear Future: Rokkasho and a Hard Place." 2012. *The Economist,* Asia edition, November 10. Www.economist.com/news/asia/21566018-governments-fudge-its-nuclear-future-remains-unconvincing-rokkasho-and-hard-place. Accessed January 6, 2013.

JOAA (Japan Organic Agriculture Association). 2011. JOAA website: www.joaa.net/ english/ teikei.htm. Accessed November 11, 2011.

Kelly, William W. 2006. "Rice Revolutions and Farm Families in Tohoku: Why Is Farming Culturally Central and Economically Marginal?" In *Wearing Cultural Styles in Japan: Concepts of Tradition and Modernity in Practice,* ed. C. Thompson and J. Traphagen, 76–95. Albany: State University of New York Press.

Kubota, Hiroko, and Keiko Yoshino. 2011. "The Present Situation of Organic Farming and Teikei Movement in Japan." Paper presented at the 17th IFOAM World Congress, Korea.

Kumasawa, Natsuko Iino. 2009. "Organic Agriculture in Japan." *Shokuhin to kurashi no anzen* (Safety of food and life). Tokyo: Japan Offspring Fund.

Lunsing, Wim. 2006. "Quitting Companies: Individual Responses to Changing Employment Patterns in Early 2000s Japan." In *Perspectives on Work, Employment and Society in Japan,* ed. P. Matanle and W. Lunsing, 168–186. New York: Palgrave Macmillan.

Mathews, Gordon. 2003. "Can 'a Real Man' Live for His Family?: *Ikigai* and Masculinity in Today's Japan." In *Men and Masculinities in Contemporary Japan: Dislocating the Salaryman Doxa,* ed. James E. Roberson and Nobue Suzuki, 109–125. London: RoutledgeCurzon.

Melucci, Alberto. 1989. *Nomads of the Present: Social Movements and Individual Needs in Contemporary Society.* Philadelphia: Temple University Press.

Moen, Darrell Gene. 1997. "The Japanese Organic Farming Movement: Consumers and Farmers United." *Bulletin of Concerned Asian Scholars* 29, no. 4.

———. 2000. "Grassroots-Based Organic Foods Distributors, Retailers, and Consumer Cooperatives in Japan: Broadening the Organic Farming Movement." *Hitotsubashi Journal of Social Studies* 32:55–76.

Mulgan, Aurelia. 2006. *Japan's Agricultural Policy Regime.* New York: Routledge.

Ortner, Sherry. 2006. *Anthropology and Social Theory.* Durham, NC: Duke University Press.

Polanyi, Karl. 1957 [1944]. *The Great Transformation.* Boston: Beacon Press.

Rosenberger, Nancy. 2001. *Gambling with Virtue: Japanese Women and the Search for Self in a Changing Nation.* Honolulu: University of Hawai'i Press.

———. 2009. "Global Food Terror in Japan: Risk Perception in Media, Nation and Women." *Ecology of Nutrition and Food* 48, no. 4 (July–August): 237–262. doi: 10.1080/03670240903001100.

———. Forthcoming. *Dilemmas of Adulthood: Japanese Women and the Nuances of Long-Term Resistance.* Honolulu: University of Hawai'i Press.

"Trade." 2012. USDA Economic Research Service, updated November 15. Www.ers. usda.gov/ topics/international-markets-trade/countries-regions-japan/trade.aspx. Accessed January 6, 2013.

Ueno, Chizuko. 2005. "Datsu aidentitī" (Beyond identity). In *Datsu aidentitī no riron* (Theory of beyond identity), ed. C. Ueno, 1–42. Tokyo: Keisō Shobō.

Williams, Raymond. 1994. "Selections from Marxism and Literature." In *Culture, Power, History,* ed. N. Dirks, G. Eley, and S. Ortner, 585–608. Princeton, NJ: Princeton University Press.

"Yūkinōgyō 12,000 ko: Heikinnenrei wa 59 sai" (Organic farm households 12,000: Average age 59). 2011. *Nihon nōgyō shinbun* (Japan agricultural newspaper), July 14, 1.

CHAPTER 5

Shelf Lives and the Labors of Loss

Food, Livelihoods, and Japan's Convenience Stores

GAVIN HAMILTON WHITELAW

A Vignette: The Evening Shift

AT 8 P.M. in Daily, a *konbini* (convenience store) in central Tokyo, a young clerk places a shopping basket at his feet and begins examining the prepared foods arranged inside the store's open refrigerated cases (see figure 5.1).[1] His task is to comb the shelves and remove all "loss" *(rosu)*—food products nearing expiration. The clerk starts with the packaged rice balls *(onigiri)*. He turns the first item over and scrutinizes the consume-by date *(shōhikigen)* printed in bold on the white label stuck to the back of the package. Methodically but with considerable speed, he works his way through shelf after shelf of sandwiches, *obentō* (rice- and noodle-based lunch boxes), single-serve salads, and chilled desserts. Each item gets inspected. Most items remain on the shelves, but some do not. When the clerk's mission concludes at a heat-lamp-warmed case incubating deep-fried snacks, there are two shopping baskets filled with nearly ¥8,000 ($88) in perishable food products resting at his side.[2] Combined, the baskets are worth about as much as his take-home pay for a double shift. Gripping one basket in each hand, the clerk staggers behind the counter and into the back room, or backyard *(bakkuyādo)*, of the store, where Wakamatsu,

Daily's senior manager (senmu), sits at a desk in front of the store's computer. The clerk deposits the baskets on the floor beside Wakamatsu and returns to the counter.

Wakamatsu is a heavyset, middle-aged man and the youngest son of a shop owner family. He is also a fifteen-year veteran of the convenience business. Reaching into the basket closer to him, he plucks a fried noodle (yakisoba) obentō out and presses a barcode reader to the label. Beep! The item appears on the monitor, and Wakamatsu strikes the "enter" key with his index finger, officially registering the unsold product as "food waste" (shokuhin haiki). Although on the computer screen the yakisoba lunch box moves with digital seamlessness from the world of commodities into the realm of trash, the product itself does not go directly into the garbage. Wakamatsu places it into an empty basket on a chair to his right and grabs another product from the stack of food to be processed. The beeps of the scanner and the clicks of the keyboard are punctuated by short grunts as Wakamatsu bends in his chair to scoop up item after item. Upon recording the contents of the first basket, he pauses to stretch. After staring for a moment at the growing pile of decommissioned food, he reaches over and selects a fried pork cutlet sandwich. He tears the package open, takes a few bites, swallows, and then turns back to face the next basket of loss waiting at his feet.

Scenes such as this are commonplace among Japan's forty-seven thousand convenience stores, or konbini, as these shops are popularly known. Japan's major chains are concerned about freshness and food safety and stipulate that store franchisees must adhere to a strict policy of collecting, recording, and disposing of unsold food products on or nearing their consume-by date. Such practices contribute to staggering statistics about Japan's annual food waste. According to a 2013 newspaper editorial, Japan discards between 17 million and 23 million tons of food each year; 23 million tons of food is worth ¥11 trillion, equivalent in yen to Japan's total annual agricultural output ("An Appalling Waste of Food" 2013). In just a single twenty-four-hour period, Tokyo alone generates six thousand tons of food waste (ibid.). This is enough food to sustain approximately one-third of the city's own population for an entire day. Household food waste and loss resulting from the production and distribution process are also included in these statistics. The convenience store is readily singled out, however, for the role it plays. In 2003, Japan's Ministry of Agriculture reported that six hundred thousand tons of Japan's food waste were "loss" recorded by convenience stores and supermarkets. The amount of food waste generated annually by this segment of the retail industry alone can feed a city

FIGURE 5.1

Gavin Whitelaw arranging and checking store lunch box selections

of 3 million people for a year at the minimum daily nutritional requirement levels set by the World Health Organization (WHO) (Ōsako 2005, 1).

Sobering data on unsold products and food waste expose the darker side of convenience culture and are a sharp counterpoint to media-driven depictions of convenience stores as rationalized retail cornucopias. But while these stores may epitomize "disposable society" *(tsukaisute shakai)* in Japan, a significant portion of unsold convenience store food does not wind up in the garbage. Many store owners and workers take issue with the rules regulating how food products are to be treated in their post-shelf lives. Franchise operators, like Wakamatsu, are disturbed by the sheer wastefulness of throwing out perfectly edible products that they are essentially buying from the chain headquarters. They ignore corporate directives and turn to eating their losses— literally. Although recorded as waste, a wide range of prepared and packaged convenience foods—rice balls, *obentō,* sandwiches, salads, *oden* (hot stews), desserts, bread products, milk—actually make their way into the mouths of owners, their families, their staff, and others. In this chapter, I explore food—unsold yet edible food—as a site of uncertainty, discomfort, and even negotiation for those running one of the most rationalized and efficient retail systems on the planet. Digging deeper into issues of disposability that are so readily associated with the convenience store, I examine post-commodity consumption practices and behind-the-counter gleaning to understand how store owners and staff struggle with and informalize a highly formal retail system.

Convenience Stores, Shelf Life, and the Logistics behind Loss

Convenience stores are a ubiquitous component of Japan's neighborhood commercial landscape. Based on an American convenience store franchise model introduced to Japan in the late 1960s and early 1970s, these stores have transformed Japan's distribution system and modernized its small shop sector by turning aging mom-and-pops into state of the art minimarts—late modern iterations of the general store *(yorozuya)* that offer an ever-evolving array of products and services meticulously tuned to the changing needs of consumers. But unlike the rural general store, convenience stores are a formidable commercial force. Currently, the industry generates ¥9 trillion ($96 billion) in sales annually (JFA 2012), outranking Japan's department store sector in terms of profitability. From only a few chains and a small number of stores in the 1970s, Japan has reached convenience store super-saturation *(hōwa jōtai)*. According to 2007 statistics from the Japanese Ministry of Economy, Trade, and Industry (METI), Tokyo is one of the most *convenienced* landscapes in Japan, with one store for every 2,300 people. Nara Prefecture, on the other hand, is near the bottom of the list, where there is still only one store for every 4,000 residents.

In the 2000s, industry analysts labeled the intense domestic competition among chains as the beginning of Japan's "convenience store war era" *(konbini no sengokujidai).* Battle lines still smolder on urban street corners and suburban neighborhoods where chains struggle for dominance by opening multiple stores within a short distance of one another to drive out or ward off competition. Wakamatsu's store was situated in the midst of one Tokyo convenience store battleground. In the spring of 2005, over ten stores competed for customers within a five-hundred-meter radius of Daily's front door. Analysts have a name for this kind of commercial situation as well: *konbini jigoku,* or convenience store hell (Fukunaga 1999, 5).[3]

In the age of cutthroat street corner competition, food remains a critical weapon. Three-quarters of all convenience store sales are either food or drink, with prepared and packaged foods, such as rice balls, *obentō*, and sandwiches, consuming the largest share and offering one of the largest profit margins (Chiba et al. 2005, 11–12). In the case of *obentō*, for example, the stores stock an average of fifteen varieties each day and sell upward of 130 boxes in a twenty-four-hour period (2005, 16). Since the convenience store's humble beginnings in backwater industrial urban neighborhoods, prepared foods like rice balls (Whitelaw 2006) and *obentō* and their constant improvement and reinvention have given chains a means for attracting new customers and differentiating themselves from other stores in the industry.

Taste, freshness, safety, and seasonality are critical ingredients for selling food in Japan's highly competitive and fussy consumer market and convenience store companies pay considerable attention to product freshness and appearance. In compliance with government standards, all prepared foods sold in convenience stores are labeled with a production date and consume-by date and time *(shōhikigen)*. By the time many prepared foods reach the store, they often have less than twenty-four hours of shelf life remaining. In contrast, packaged foods, like instant coffee, *sembei* (rice crackers), and bottled water are stamped with a "best-before" date, or *shōmikigen*. Best-before dates are typically much longer—half a year or more in some cases—and the rules governing the handling and sale of expired products are less strict. Because of the small amounts of packaged products stocked at any one time and the high turnover rate in product sales, owners in the convenience stores where I did my research were typically less concerned about best-before dates. They did, however, keep careful watch over the consume-by dates on prepared foods, milk, and bread products.

The sales window for prepared foods is shortened further still by precautionary measures that particular convenience store chains impose upon themselves. Uncertain when a customer will eventually consume his or her purchases, some chains stipulate that all *obentō*, rice balls, and sandwiches be removed from the shelves two hours ahead of the expiration date printed on the package. Loaves of bread are pulled a day before the expiration date and milk four days before the expiration date. With new products being delivered morning, noon, and night, the task of inspecting expiration dates takes place as frequently as ten times per day.

The management of freshness *(shinsenkanri)* is an important component of and driving force behind the convenience store's highly integrated production and distribution system. The critical synapses and surveillance for the system are Point of Sales (POS) terminals, computerized cash registers connected to a store computer that allow retailers to keep track of sales and profits, manage stock, and gather critical customer marketing data with every transaction. Through product bar codes and the POS system, retail information can be exchanged in real time among stores, the chain headquarters, food manufacturers, and distribution centers. However, for store stock and profits to be accurately calculated, even items that are not sold must still be accounted for. As was seen in the case of Daily above, such products are removed from the shelves and recorded (see figure 5.2). Unlike damaged items that can be returned for credit, loss that results from stealing or products that cannot be sold because their shelf life has expired is the responsibility of the store owner and not reimbursable under the franchise contract. The store owner must bear the entire cost of the product as if he had purchased the item as a customer.

FIGURE 5.2

Convenience store worker decommissioning
unsold food in the store's backyard

Although in some stores shoplifting is a major problem, the most common source of loss is food products that have passed their consume-by date. According to one industry insider, most store owners can expect losses to total between 3 and 5 percent of their average daily sales—about ¥10,000–20,000 ($105–215). If a store has ¥400,000 ($4,300) in sales per day, then within a month-long period, approximately one entire day's worth of sales is *lost* to "loss" (Takada and Masumitsu 2009, 1). While owners may carry insurance to guard against devastating losses in the event of a flood, fire, or prolonged power failure, none can afford a policy to compensate for every expired rice ball.

The Real Pain of Loss

Convenience store owners accept loss as part of the risk they take in this line of work. Profit and loss are two sides of the same coin. Shelves must have products to attract customers, and freshly packaged foods offer one of the highest profit margins among convenience store commodities. While the store's computerized ordering and marketing system is designed to take much of the guesswork out of retail, often it is the owner's local knowledge, attention to factors such as weather, and willingness to take risks by ordering more or less of a given product that push a day's sales into the black.

Store owners get support and advice (known in the industry as "backup") when it comes to things like food ordering. Through the use of sales representatives (or SVs), store chain headquarters work with individual franchisees to analyze the buying habits of their customers and adjust product ordering to boost store sales and profits. SVs visit stores several times a week and are likely to encourage owners to order more product rather than less. The store's computerized ordering and sales system permits owners to know almost immediately if a product sells out before a new shipment arrives. The chain headquarters knows as well. The SV may then chide the owner for missing a valuable sales opportunity due to lack of stock, known as "chance loss." From the company's perspective, as competition among rival chains grows more fierce, empty shelves and missed sales opportunities are a greater threat to brand image and chain profit than unsold food. Under the chance loss logic, only by having some loss can the owner and the chain be certain that the store reached its potential of selling as much as it could of a particular product during a certain period of time. Despite the postindustrial efficiency of the just-in-time distribution system, loss is not simply unavoidable, but also desirable and, in fact, healthy for the bottom line. For the store owner, negotiating a balance between possible chance loss and the more visible loss due to product overstock is a daily struggle. For some franchisees, edible loss is the harsher of the two to swallow. Moral discomfort with food going to waste is part of the reason. But the unsold food is also a tangible sign of how little risk the chain headquarters will accept. The store owner pays for the unsold product and its disposal; the company still takes its portion of the profit.

Franchisees are willing to accept the responsibility for loss, but as store owners, they often harbor resentment concerning the policies that franchise headquarters take toward unsold products. One issue is with the way in which loss is calculated. Ambiguity in most contracts leaves the franchisee bearing the brunt of the cost for unsold food products. When a store owner pays for loss, he also pays the headquarters a royalty fee that is embedded in the selling price of the item. Critics of the convenience store system refer to this fee as a *rosu chāji* (literally "loss charge"). Ishii Itsurō, a Tokyo lawyer fighting the loss charge practice, argues that the system of embedded fees on food is "convenient for the corporation that desires to minimize its risks by charging the store owner for an item whether the product is sold or not" (Ishii 2006, 12). The corporations counter such a claim by pointing out that the fee—to their eyes a penalty—is necessary to keep owners mindful of their ordering practices and safeguard against owners selling merchandise under the counter for a profit. Similarly, chains also frown upon and in some cases forbid the practice of discounting product that is near its consume-by date, also called "time sale reduction" *(mikirihanbai)*. Large chains have been some of the most adamant opponents to this practice, which is common among independent shops and large supermarkets sometimes owned by the parent companies of these same chains. Corporate spokesmen claim that the practice is detrimental to store profits and undermines a guiding principle of the convenience store—customers' willingness to pay a small premium for the convenience of "twenty-four-hour, year-round" *(nenjūmukyū)* access to products and services. Slashing the price on food products would hurt store owners and the company alike by further stoking the flames of competition, altering customer expectations, disrupting established buying patterns, reducing food sales, and adding even more tasks to the workload of the convenience store management. Japan's largest convenience chain, 7-Eleven, told one group of questioning store owners that if all 7-Eleven stores nationwide (some 14,883 units in 2013) began practicing time sale reductions, the company "would go bankrupt" (Takada and Masumitsu 2009, 1).

Chains' rules that all unsold food should be thrown away further aggravate owners. Chains make efforts to ensure that food freshness standards are strictly maintained by all franchises. The store headquarters is concerned about the potentially damaging effects that a food poisoning case would have to the chain's brand image and individual store sales. To prevent old food from being sold and eaten, the chains maintain that the safest policy is for unsold food to be taken off the shelves, removed from its packaging, and disposed of in the trash. The rigorous multi-week owner-training courses that new franchisees must undergo reinforce the importance of properly discarding food. Course instructors will point out that an owner seen eating expired food or engaging in the practice of giving away loss to store employees risks setting a dangerous precedent among the store staff that may lead to workers taking food for themselves.

Owners are not blind to the fact that by "properly" disposing of all unsold food, they ensure that their workers will be more likely to become their customers and buy store food. Despite corporate appeals to consider brand protection, store liability, and the potential for profit, the sheer waste of throwing away thousands of yen in edible food a day weighs heavily on the consciences of many store owners. The term that owners most commonly used to sum up this feeling was *mottainai;* the term means "waste," but it also carries connotations of shame, even disgrace, for not giving a material object the proper respect it deserves. One book dedicated to the term framed *mottainai* thus: "Everything that exists is the result of someone's hard work and the time spent on it—it has a history. *Mottainai* embodies an appreciation of that history from those on the receiving end. That is why *mottainai* reflects a sense of guilt for the end-user when he/she lets things go to waste" (Planet Link 2005, 9). In 2005, the popularity of the term was further invigorated with the visit of the Kenyan activist and Nobel Prize laureate Wangari Maathai to Japan. On a speaking tour organized by the *Mainichi Shinbun,* a major national newspaper, Maathai embraced the phrase, saying that it captured in one term the "4Rs"—reduce, reuse, recycle, and repair—which have long been the focal point of grassroots initiatives to protect and restore the environment (Planet Link 2005, 5).

In the interactions and interviews I conducted in 2004 and 2005 with convenience store owners, I found *mottainai* was most prevalently used among those in their late forties to early sixties. Having grown up in Japan's immediate postwar period, when soaring food costs and scarcities of rice, meat, and vegetables were a fact of daily life, they or their parents would have known privation, and the sight of good food being thrown out would be something hard to bear.

An After-Shelf Life

As noted, in defiance of the manual and their training, owners—young and old alike—frequently take loss for their own consumption and offer it to the workers at their stores. The dozen owner-run convenience stores with which I had substantial contact during the course of my research threw away only a fraction of the products that had reached their consume-by date. In each store, staff members were allowed to glean their lunches, dinners, and snacks from the baskets of loss once the products had been recorded. In some of the stores, the owner or owner's spouse was responsible for processing the loss. Immediately after the recording process was complete, they helped themselves to the food that they wanted, placing it on a desk or sometimes in a plastic bag to take home. The remainder of the loss was then made available to the staff. In Daily, where I worked as a clerk, the staff established a pecking order. Veteran staff chose the food they wanted first, followed by junior staff, and finally the new recruits. It was commonly a junior staff member who explained the policy on loss gleaning to the new recruit, frequently adding a comment such as, "This is actually not supposed to be done, but. . ."

In my interviews with store clerks and observations of behind-the-counter activities, there was very little evidence to suggest that the consumption of loss by owners and store staff was detrimental to the work ethic. To the contrary, loss distribution may have helped strengthen bonds and employee loyalty by creating opportunities for backroom commensality. While eating a "loss" lunch during a shift break, one college student who worked several mornings a week at Daily explained how he privately calculated the free foods he received into his hourly wage. He joked that the only time he could afford a convenience store lunch *(konbini obentō)* was when he worked at the store and received the product for free.

In Tokyo, where convenience stores are plentiful and part-time job opportunities are, literally, just around the next corner, young people interested in clerking positions categorize stores according to owner attitudes toward food and gleaning. It is an owner's lenient approach to loss that may help strengthen part-time workers' tenuous commitments to a store. Free food came up when students and *furītā* (young, part-time workers not in school) talked about why they continued to work at a particular store. It even led several workers I interviewed to recommend clerking positions to their friends when the store was struggling to fill shifts. Such worker-initiated recruitment might be seen as a form of reciprocity for the free meals being given. Loss distribution practices revealed the kinds of personal networks that workers maintained. A Chinese exchange student who worked night shifts and on weekends at Daily regularly hauled home several bags worth of food and shared it with the other students he lived with in a rundown dormitory-style building a few blocks from the store. The student would sometimes jokingly refer to Daily as his "kitchen." When the store was short-staffed, the student took on additional shifts and began introducing his friends to Wakamatsu as potential recruits. At one point in my fieldwork, five workers out of Daily's twenty-one-member crew were "recommendees" of this one Chinese student.

For certain store owners and managers with family backgrounds in neighborhood commerce, a disposition toward recycling and eating unsold food was a part of the merchant lifestyle, a kind of shopkeeper *habitus* ingrained in the selling of perishable products. I talked to Wakamatsu about convenience foods and unsold product one night while we walked home to our respective apartments after the evening shift. Wakamatsu was on orders from his doctor to reduce his weight and get more exercise and had taken to commuting to and from the store on foot rather than by train. As we strolled along the empty city street, passing convenience stores on almost every block, he reminded me that he was the son of a sweetshop *(wagashiya)* owner. What gets made doesn't always sell, and consuming and giving away food was, for him, common practice. He recounted a story from the early days of his family's convenience store contract. There was a weekend summer fireworks festival planned not far from where the family had their new store. Tens of thousands of visitors were expected to surge through the neighborhood on their way to the event, and the Wakamatsu family adjusted the daily food orders accordingly. Weekends were typically slow times for the store, but because the fireworks would be on a Saturday night, Wakamatsu purposefully overordered "practically a month's worth" of prepared foods and bottled drinks. So much food was on hand, in fact, that it couldn't be put on the shelves when it arrived and instead had to be squirreled away in the store's walk-in cooler where drinks were stored and chilled. The family anticipated a very profitable weekend.

When Saturday arrived, however, the weather was overcast and thunderstorms were predicted by evening. By midday the rain had already started, and the fireworks festival was canceled by the city, leaving the Wakamatsu store with a mountain of perishable food and few customers until Monday. Wakamatsu and his family froze what food they could. "We ate nothing but *obentō* until October," he joked. What they couldn't freeze they gave away to neighbors and friends. It was an expensive lesson for Wakamatsu and one that even a few neighbors still recall.

Konbinization and the Wider World of Waste

"Observant participation" (Wacquant 2003, 2005) in the convenience store culture had its gustatory dimensions for me as an anthropologist. I was given and ate a lot of loss over nearly two years of ethnographic research. Following an interview with a family running a Lawson convenience store in Shizuoka early on in my study, the owner's wife, who was also the store's *tenchō* (manager), rushed out to the street as I was leaving and pressed a bag of expired rice balls and bread snacks into my hand, apologizing that there wasn't more to offer me but noting that these foods would keep me from getting hungry on the train. Only a half hour before, I had observed her decommissioning the food in the shop's backyard.

Halfway through my fieldwork when I was fully embedded as a store clerk (see Whitelaw 2008), the convenience store became my kitchen. This experience intensified my appreciation for the various roles that loss plays in the life of this institution. For one month I consciously lived out of these stores, using them not just for work but also as a place to find sustenance, socialize, and relax. I conducted most of my financial transactions there, posted all my mail in them, arranged to meet people at the stores, and made ample use of their bathrooms and trash receptacles. I referred to the experiment as "*konbini*zation."

My intentional embrace of convenience-store-as-life-support was not without precedent. Since the mid-1990s, Japanese authors have explored the possibilities of the convenience store diet (see *Kon'ya mo konbini ga yamerarenai!* 1994). Clerking at a store provided me, however, with an opportunity for far greater immersion. Another obvious influence on my methodological turn was the film *Supersize Me,* a "shockumentary" by director Morgan Spurlock in which he chronicles a month of him eating nothing but McDonald's food. However, my interest in *konbini*zation differed from the approach Spurlock took in his film. I was less interested in a gratuitous, belly-churning exposé on the legal, financial, and physical costs of Japan's convenience food hunger. Spurlock's investigative punch was in drastically altering his lifestyle to accentuate the habits of the average American. He limited his daily exercise and diet while increasing his visits to not one but three doctors for their professional opinions on how his health was faring as he ate his way through ninety-three consecutive McDonald's meals. The study I envisioned demand-ed a different set of parameters. I wanted to keep doing what I was already doing (studying convenience stores) but do it more intensively and conscious-ly than my initial methodological structure allowed. Also, restricting myself merely to food was too narrow a focus considering all the functions conve-nience stores fulfill in people's daily lives.

After two full weeks of *konbinizing*, my refrigerator flushed itself out and reached a steady state of near emptiness. All the food products fit on the top shelf. For the first time in my life, I knew exactly what my refrigerator con-tained. But by the end of the second week, I was also feeling a pinch. Not in the stomach but in the wallet. I ate mostly prepared foods, and my dai-ly consumption was costing me between ¥1,800 and ¥3,000 ($19–32). Such costs encouraged me to take on more shifts at Daily and accept more unsold food. I froze the food that I couldn't consume immediately, a technique I had gleaned from my conversation with Wakamatsu mentioned above. On oc-casion, I would give unsold food to my landlord. He was grateful and never refused my offers. Meeting a friend for dinner became harder a few weeks into my project, when acquaintances got sick of my warm invitations to dine at Family Mart or 7-Eleven, so I focused my convenience commensality on "loss" meals during my store breaks. I lingered after my shifts to nibble and chat. It felt nourishing not to be alone, even in the dim, cramped confines of the store's backyard.

During my month-long immersion in convenience life, I also took to throwing away much of my waste in store trash cans. In the course of just the first week of convenience living, I amassed twenty-eight plastic bags; six plas-tic straws; thirteen pairs of chopsticks; eleven plastic spoons of various sizes; a few plastic forks; and two ten-liter trash bags of plastic plates, covers, cello-phane wrapping, and PET bottles (recyclable plastic bottles). In Tokyo, almost all convenience chains take part in municipal recycling programs. Whereas in the United States one is lucky to find a recycling bin outside a store, in Japan there are several containers for different types of recyclables: non-com-bustibles (plastic products, Styrofoam material); combustibles (newspapers, magazines, food products); cans and glass bottles; and PET bottles. Whether a plastic bag is a combustible or non-combustible depends on the person who is doing the discarding, but I found that the non-combustible trash can was usually brimming with bags, and many of the bags were from different chains than the store whose trash can I was using.

On my daily visits to store waste bins, I also crossed paths with people, usually men, tugging small carts or suitcase dollies with cardboard boxes lashed to them. These people paid quick visits to the combustible trash cans and fished out magazines and comic books. They didn't dig or pull trash out. Like a bee collecting nectar, they hovered for a moment, popped one hand into the mouth of the receptacle, and then withdrew the item they wanted. In a blink of an eye, they were off down the sidewalk to the next convenience store. On one occasion, I followed a particular gleaner on his rounds starting at Daily. His pace wore me out, but thanks to him, I learned the location of half a dozen new stores. Japan's *rojōseikatsusha* (people living on the street) earn part of their living by gleaning and recycling from convenience store trash cans (see figure 5.3). In addition to magazines, the street people also collect cans that they redeem for money. Until 2006, one kilogram of cans earned the collector ¥116 (around $1 at that time), though the rate fluctuated (Sakaguchi 2007, 43). Can competition around convenience stores is fierce according to a street couple interviewed by architect and activist Sakaguchi Kyōhei. Tokyo convenience stores, including Daily, typically lock their large trash bins in order to guard against waste and recyclables being disturbed by humans and animals, including the city's sizable crow population (Kirby 2011). As a way around these measures, some street people establish private agreements with store owners to allow them access to cans and other "recyclables"—including unsold food.

Several studies have been conducted to examine the patterns of people living on the street. In 1995, the forced eviction of thousands of street people from major parks around Osaka prior to the Asia-Pacific Economic Cooperation Summit and a similar roundup before the 2002 World Cup Soccer Tournament prompted economists at Osaka University to study why street people congregate in certain urban areas. The project team members were surprised to find that convenience store density and access are statistically more important in street life settlement patterns than proximity to welfare offices or even public hospitals (Suzuki 2002). In 2005, members of the same team assisted with a survey of street people in Tokyo's Sumida Ward. Eight percent of the six hundred people surveyed in this study specifically reported eating expired convenience store food (Mizuta et al. 2005, 37). Much of this food may not have come from the trash but reached the street people through the backdoor beneficence of store owners and staff, an activity memorialized in the award-winning film *Nobody Knows (Dare mo shiranai)*. In the film, based on a true story, four abandoned children living in the Tokyo metropolitan area survive in their suburban neighborhood through the largesse of

FIGURE 5.3

Gleaning from a convenience store's trash can

sympathetic convenience store attendants who take pity and share what is presumably unsold food.

Loss and Affect

My *konbini*zation project brought me into more frequent contact with the workers and owners of convenience stores in my neighborhood. I visited the store around the corner from where I lived almost every day. I purchased mostly milk and rice balls at that store, and I made a lot of photocopies there as well, having found the quality of the photocopier to be the best in the area—even better than that in the convenience store next to the public library where I borrowed most of my books and magazines. In a month's time, the store become my "third place" (Oldenburg 1989), a point of regular social interaction outside of work and home. But not for long. Soon after my *konbini*zation experiment ended, the store owner, Aoki, whom I had come to know over the course of daily visits, offered me a job working at his store. He knew that I was doing research on convenience stores and didn't mind. The job offer came with an opportunity to study the management practices of yet another convenience store.

Convenience stores are standardized retail formats, and there was much that was familiar to me when I put on a new uniform and started working. But there were differences as well. Aoki's management style and approach to ordering food was one example. When ordering food, which Aoki did alongside his wife, the couple relied less on the store computer and the number of items that the store computer recommended they order and more on a handwritten log they kept in a three-ring binder. Maintaining an accurate record in this log book was important to the store, and the couple trained their staff on how the data were to be collected. Recording loss in the three-ring binder was part of the store's informal management.

Despite efforts to reduce the amount of unsold food, it was impossible for the Aokis to avoid loss. Unsold food was not discarded but taken for consumption. The redistribution of store loss took two forms. First, certain items were given strategically to particular customers. Such giveaways, known as *omake,* are long-standing merchant practices in Japan. They are a display of preferential service bestowed upon customers to both thank them for their patronage and encourage their continued loyalty. Although the convenience stores' emphasis on "dry" customer relations and a strict accounting system curbs this practice, owners like Aoki could and did use expired food products to add flavor and character to the standardized service provided by their store.

The deliveryman who received packages of pastry while purchasing lunch is a particularly interesting case. Several months prior to my starting my second clerking job, the chain to which Aoki belonged cut off contract relations with this deliveryman's company when the chain decided to become a vendor for a new package delivery system offered by Japan Post. All at once, the chain's several thousand stores nationwide ceased to accept package delivery orders from this company. But the bad blood between the chain headquarters and the package delivery firm did not prevent the deliveryman from occasionally dropping by Aoki's store to buy food and drink. On such occasions, Aoki would relieve me at the counter and slip an expired package of sweet rolls into the deliveryman's bag of purchases. Both men nodded their bows, but no words were exchanged.

The Aoki couple also consumed loss and shared it with their employees, yet they did so in a way that drew them together with the staff. Instead of their simply handing out unsold food to workers, the food was incorporated into home-cooked meals. (Preparing and sharing meals with employees is far from rare in the world of Japanese small business.) The couple would ferry unsold food items into their apartment, where Aoki's wife would transform rice balls into steaming plates of fried rice. Expired tofu went into freshly made miso soup or *mābōdofu,* a flavorful Chinese dish. *Obentō* were disassembled and recombined with other ingredients into full meals on proper porcelain plates. In the dozens of meals I shared with the Aokis and other workers, not once did disposable chopsticks appear on the table. If I had not seen the food leaving the store and the plastic packages and the evidence left by wrappers piled on the kitchen counter of the apartment, I would not have known that lunch was loss. Without children of their own, the Aokis found a certain satisfaction in eating with others. Aoki admitted that not everyone was appreciative of their approach, but the workers who remained as employees mentioned that being served a meal distinguished the Aoki's operations from establishments where they had worked, convenience stores included.

Living Out of the Trash

While some owners, like the Aokis, were able to transform loss into a convivial mode of survival, other families struggled. For the Ishiguros, loss became a metonym for personal dissolution and despair. Ishiguro Kazuhiko and his wife, Keiko, were approaching their sixties when they became convenience store franchisees for one of Japan's largest chains. Kazuhiko was nearing his retirement, and he started to ponder a fresh approach to the decades that lay ahead. He had worked as a salaryman for the same company for thirty years, was restless in his job, and yearned for a new challenge without a large amount of risk. Owning a convenience store came to mind. He and his wife looked into various chains, focusing on the more well-known store chains, which boasted considerable instruction and "backup" for their franchisees. "We didn't have any experience. We had no idea what we were getting ourselves into," Kazuhiko said in retrospect.

Kazuhiko admitted that the convenience business fit well with a larger hope he had for his family. Both of Kazuhiko's children were settled abroad. His son was working for an American company, and his daughter was about to begin graduate school. He and his wife hoped that some day one or both of their children would return to Japan and join them in running the business. A convenience store franchise was a business that he could offer his children.

Taking on a franchise was not an easy decision. Kazuhiko had no experience in the field of small retail. But buffering some of these concerns were resources and experiences that his family possessed. To start with, the Ishiguros had financial resources to draw on. They owned a home and were not in debt. Their children were independent, and by taking an early retirement, Kazuhiko would receive a "golden parachute," enough to cover the startup costs of the business. Keiko also possessed skills that would be helpful in running a store. She had previously held a job in insurance sales and was experienced in customer service. The chain they were courting recognized these assets. The chain's recruiters were looking for families who would make successful and reliable franchisees. Simply being a married couple is not enough; franchise chains use interviews as a way to get behind a couple's salaryman-housewife image to see how the pair might or might not work together in a store management situation. The interest of the wife is weighed more heavily than the enthusiasm of the husband.

Initially Keiko was not excited about the plan. Kazuhiko assured her that they would not be stocking shelves for the rest of their lives. He argued that it was a chance to own and grow a business that would sustain them into their elder years. He foresaw his son and daughter taking on positions in the store and the family expanding the business to two franchises within the first two years, then adding a third store by the fifth year of their contract. Kazuhiko's plan was exactly what many major chains currently outline to prospective owners. Owning multiple stores minimized risk and maximized profit. In the multiple franchise formulation, three stores represented the ideal; one store was likely to be a dud, but the profits of the other two would make up the difference. Kazuhiko felt he had the energy and management skills to build an enterprise. After five or six years he and Keiko could step back and enjoy more free time for themselves, supported by a steady income from their franchise holdings. The store chain's representatives encouraged the Ishiguros to think in this way. Like other chains, this company also faced challenges in finding "capable" new owners and in recent years had begun encouraging its prospective franchisees to have a long-term business plan that included license expansion.

Immediately after opening their store, the Ishiguros found that running a convenience store entailed far more than they had been trained for. For starters, they faced issues with schedules and staff. Kazuhiko summed the issues up in this way: "There is a lot of discussion about being more independent these days. The convenience store seemed to be an image of that; it seemed to make that possibility a reality. But [I] just didn't understand what running a twenty-four-hour business meant. The headquarters gives you these model schedules of work shifts, showing who is working when. . . . That is not easy to arrange. The headquarters didn't explain this reality. Cultivating a reliable workforce is difficult. It adds to the pressure and unease of the job." Troubles for the couple mounted. Store costs were much higher than they had anticipated. They had trouble with a worker whom they caught stealing from the store. His forced dismissal brought threats on their lives. Kazuhiko said, "The store was supposed to be our business, but increasingly we wondered for whom we were really working this hard and suffering this much." Kazuhiko recalled his task each night to throw away the store's unsold food. He wondered where the know-how was that the corporation was supposed to possess and share with the owners. He questioned why every day his family's store had to throw away so much food, and he would reach into the trash *(gomi)* and remove things to consume. "I thought, I am living a life in which I am eating trash," he said during an interview. "I hated this, too."

Kazuhiko spoke with the company service representative during the visits he made to the store several times each week. The man placated the family by saying that a lot of first-time owners faced such challenges and that with time and perseverance the store's situation would improve. He cajoled the couple into sticking it out. But within several weeks, the couple submitted a handwritten letter requesting a termination of their contract:

> Before we began business, we were told that from November onward the store would become profitable enough that we could begin to pay ourselves a salary, but as of November there is still no prospect of our earning any income; night shifts are filled with a sense of terror that we can no longer endure; various costs are higher than were estimated before we began business; estimated store sales were significantly lower than projected; the demand that both the owner and manager must each work for over fifteen hours a day makes it impossible to properly maintain our health.

After several months of hard work to lift store sales and a sizable fine, the couple was released from their contract.

Loss Battles and Hidden Costs

While part-time workers may see the opportunities to glean store loss as a bonus to low hourly wages, for owners like the Ishiguro and Aoki families, eating loss while on the job and bringing it home to feed the family can amount to more of a financial necessity. Since the latter half of the 1990s, the average daily sales figures of convenience stores have steadily declined as more stores have opened and competition from other parts of the retail sector, like supermarkets and drugstores, have increased. According to Takeuchi Minoru, an industry analyst, only a third of all Japanese convenience stores are turning a significant profit. The remaining stores are either in the red or just getting by. The work hours and eating habits of store owners tend to bear out these divisions. Unable to raise profits, store owners forsake hiring additional staff and assume the burden of more shifts, often the evening and late-night shifts because those are the positions that are most expensive to fill. Longer shifts at their stores increase opportunities for owners to consume unsold food. Certainly eating unsold food is not a recent phenomenon in the world of small-scale retail. For centuries, greengrocers, fishmongers, and butchers have engaged in the practice of consuming their merchandise when the need arose. But mass-produced convenience store foods tend to be high in sugar and salt. In addition, what an owner consumes is limited to what has not sold. While stores stock salads, fruit, and even tofu, owners may forgo the hassle and added expense of purchasing healthier foods in favor of simply taking the food they have already been forced to buy before it goes bad.

Suggestive of the potential negative impact that convenience store food, work, and lifestyles can have on the physical condition of store owners, at least five of the twelve owners with whom I maintained regular contact in my study reported health problems during the course of their store contracts. Three owners reported struggling with diabetes, one suffered a mental breakdown, and another had stomach ulcers. All were forced to take substantial time off of work in order to rest. They also had to alter their diets. Wakamatsu is a case in point. Upon returning to work following a brief stint in the hospital to bring his diabetes under control, Wakamatsu was under strict orders from his doctor not to eat any convenience store food. Each day he brought with him to work a thermos of tea and an *obentō* prepared for him at home. But it wasn't long before Wakamatsu began to slip back into his old habits. One evening, about a month after his return, I came into the store's back room to pick up the cleaning supplies. I found him seated at his desk and staring at the store's computer screen while snacking on a package of deep-fried chicken nuggets that I had pulled from the shelves a short time earlier. He looked up to see who was there, grinned somewhat guiltily, and silently offered me what was left.

Food remains central to the convenience store's dual affect—that of refining standards while at the same time creating differentiation. Customers expect to find a standard fare of edible options when they enter these establishments. Yet be it in the form of rice balls or Christmas cakes, prepared foods are also the flavorful field on which chains seek to differentiate themselves from their competition and encourage "healthy" competition among members of the same chain (Whitelaw 2006, 2008). Convenience store food contributes to what anthropologist Richard Wilk terms the "structure of common difference" (1995, 111). The stores and the food they provide organize diversity rather than simply replicate uniformity (119).

As this chapter illustrates, however, convenience store food should be followed further than the cash register to understand how this cultural form functions to differentiate the practices of owners and franchise chains within what is typically taken to be a highly uniform, undifferentiated retail system. Furthermore, food, particularly unsold food, is a metonym for the less visible dimensions of global consumer culture and convenience. The growing international prominence of Japan's convenience stores and their success on new soil has not altered the fact that in Japan, franchisees and workers are burdened with maintaining these twenty-four-hour hubs of sustenance and relief. For some owners, the expansion of chains overseas and growth in company profits only deepens uncertainties and anxiety about the future of the business they run.

In the era of the convenience store's (second) overseas expansion, unsold food has become a catalyst for action, both individual and collective. In 2005, a "food fight" broke out when a 7-Eleven franchisee filed a suit against the company for imposing royalty fees on unsold food product. 7-Eleven lost the case but appealed to the Tokyo High Court, where the lower court's decision was overturned. In 2009, the issue flared up again. This time 7-Eleven, the largest chain in Japan, was accused of violating the anti-monopoly laws by pressuring its franchisees not to discount and sell food close to its consume-by date. In open challenge to 7-Eleven's rules that food should not be sold at a discount, owners of a handful of stores banded together and discounted food that was nearing its expiration date. The court upheld the owners' challenge to 7-Eleven, and the company announced that it would create a compensation system for owners (Takeuchi 2009). This band of owners also founded a fledgling union of owners to push for further reforms to the practices that contributed to unnecessary food waste. In a report published by researchers at Chiba University (Anzai et al. 2009), a study of discounting food practices at Kanto area convenience stores showed that food loss was reduced by 50–80 percent with no or little impact to overall store sales. A 7-Eleven owner who started using time sale reductions in 2009 revealed that there was a 5 percent reduction in store sales compared with the month before price reductions began, but the store's overall profits increased by 30 percent because food was sold. The same owner said that store staff, particular female part-time workers, were pleased with the new discounting practices because they felt guilty having to throw food away (Takada and Masumitsu 2009, 1).

Concerns about food waste have spurred particular chains to experiment with other ways to reduce waste. Using information technologies and exclusive contracts, companies have reduced inefficiencies in ordering, delivery, and merchandise control (Ishikawa and Nejo 1998; Kawabe 2004). Chains have also improved production processes and packaging so that prepared foods have a longer shelf life. Since the early 2000s, corporations have experimented with recycling waste food. In one project carried out by Lawson, Japan's second-largest convenience store chain, unsold food from a group of stores in the Yokohama area was collected and given to a nongovernmental organization (NGO) to be "remade" into food for a soup kitchen. In another project by the same chain, unsold *obentō* and rice balls were collected and brought to a processing center where the food was separated from the plastic packaging and transformed into fertilizer and pig feed. Such initiatives, however, are still being piloted, and questions remain about the economic feasibility of carrying them out on a large scale.

Chain-led food waste management programs and nascent owner unions around the discounting of food are two forms that differentiation has taken, but perhaps the more meaningful differentiation that this study found was in the ways that individual owners dealt with unsold food in their own stores. When I followed expired rice balls and boxed lunches, the contours of changing lifestyles came into focus—not just consumer lifestyles, but also the working lives of small shop owner families who have been the bulwark of neighborhood politics and community identity in the postwar era. Within the policies and practices of the convenience store, franchisees still struggle as small proprietors seeking to sell products in an ever-changing retail landscape. Although all the owners may wear the same uniform, seasoned merchants with backgrounds in small business tended to be more adept at reinterpreting and informalizing the convenience stores' globalizing standards and seemingly rigid contractual agreements. People like Wakamatsu, with his appetite for distributing free food, and the Aoki couple, who reached into their recipe book to turn store losses into opportunities to personalize their workplace and cultivate loyalty, reveal that the convenience stores can be made, in small ways, more palatable. In the case of former white-collar, salaried employees, like the Ishiguro family, who enter a store contract without much prior knowledge, experience, or local support, the transition tends to be harsher. The new work regime of a twenty-four-hour franchise can quickly sour a couple's dream of "low-risk" independent store ownership. For such families, unsold food indexes just how sharp a turn their lives have taken.

By selling the first plastic-wrapped rice balls, Japan's small shop owners immeasurably contributed to localizing the convenience store franchise within Japan's neighborhoods. They have also played an important role in turning this reinvented general store into a new global template. One of the ways that Japanese industry leaders and government officials packaged the convenience store model was as a way to help struggling shopkeepers maintain neighborhood family businesses for the next generation. In 2013, the convenience store business model's "best-before" date seems to have passed, particularly for local merchant families. Shortly after I completed my fieldwork at Daily, Wakamatsu's family decided not to renew their franchise contract and turned over the keys of the operation to the chain headquarters. Wakamatsu's older brother, the actual owner of the franchise contract, threw a party at his "other business"—a restaurant—to thank Daily's staff for its dedication and service. While plates of steaming spaghetti, salad, and freshly baked bread were being delivered to the long table that seated some twenty-five staff and former part-time workers, the owner made a short speech. He commended his younger brother and wife for their diligence in running Daily and praised the workers for their efforts to successfully close the store. He also noted his brother's health condition and the intense competition from other chains. "A convenience store cannot survive unless the people who run it do," he concluded, raising his glass for a toast. "That is all I want to say. *Kampai* (cheers)."

Notes

A 2004–2005 Fulbright Doctoral Dissertation Research Fellowship supported the initial research for this chapter. A 2009–2011 Young Researchers Start-Up Grant from the Japan Ministry of Education, Culture, Sports, Science, and Technology (MEXT) contributed to follow-up research. I would also like to thank Jordan

Sand, Satsuki Kawano, Glenda Roberts, and Susan Long for their helpful comments and suggestions at critical stages of the drafting process.

1. Daily is one of three convenience stores where I conducted participant observation as a clerk between 2004 and 2005. In accordance with practices common to anthropology, the names of the actual individuals have been altered to protect informant identities. In addition, certain identifiable details of stores have been altered for the same reason.
2. At the time that this research was conducted the exchange rate was approximately ¥90 to $1.
3. In follow-up research conducted in 2012, the same area had only half the number of stores, upgrading the district in industry lingo from a "*konbini* hell" to a "*konbini* village" *(konbini mura)*. Daily was among the half-dozen convenience stores which had gone out of business or moved to a different location.

References Cited

"An Appalling Waste of Food." 2013. *Japan Times Weekly,* February 2, 18.

Anzai, Yōta, et al. 2009. "Konbiniensu sutoa ni okeru shokuhin mikiri hanbai no shakaiteki kekka." Paper presented at Nihon Seiksaku Gakusei Kaigi conference, "Seisaku Fōramu 2009."

Chiba, Tamotsu, et al. 2005. *Konbini bentō 16 man kiro no tabi: Tabemono ga sekai o kaeteiru.* Tokyo: Tarō Jirō-sha Editus.

Fukunaga, Kazuhiko. 1999. "Konbini: The Japanese Convenience Store." *Look Japan,* March, 4–8.

Ishii, Itsurō. 2006. "Konbini wa haikishōhin keigen e." *Mainichi Shinbun,* January 26, 12.

Ishikawa, Akira, and Tai Nejo. 1998. *The Success of 7-Eleven Japan: Discovering the Secrets of the World's Best-Run Convenience Store.* London: World Scientific.

JFA (Japan Franchise Association). 2012. *2011 nendo JFA furanchaizuchēn tōkei chōsa hōkoku.* Tokyo: Japan Franchise Association.

Kawabe, Nobuo. 2004. *Konbiniensu sutoā keieishi: Nihon ni okeru konbiniensu sutoā no 30 nen.* Tokyo: Waseda University.

Kirby, Peter W. 2011. *Troubled Natures: Waste, Environment, Japan.* Honolulu: University of Hawai'i Press.

Kon'ya mo konbini ga yamerarenai! 1994. Tokyo: NTV (Nihon Terebi) Publishers.

Mizuta, Megumi, et al. 2005. *Sumida-ku hōmuresu jittai chōsa.* Tokyo: Sumida-ku Hōmuresu Seisaku Kenkyūkai.

Oldenburg, Ray. 1989. *The Great Good Place: Cafés, Coffee Shops, Community Centers, Beauty Parlors, General Stores, Bars, Hangouts, and How They Get You through the Day,* 1st ed. New York: Paragon House.

Ōsako, Makiko. 2005. "Shoku no genba kara mottainai: Konbini, sūpā" (From food's scene mottainai: Konbini and supermarkets). *Mainichi Newspaper,* June 6, 1–2.

Planet Link. 2005. *Mottainai.* Tokyo: Magazine House.

Sakaguchi, Kyōhei. 2007. "0 en seikatsu no hōhō." *Aera,* February 26, 40–44.

Suzuki, Wataru. 2002. "Analysis of the Distribution of Homeless Using GPS." In *Research Seminar of the Japanese National Cabinet Office.* Osaka: Osaka University Graduate School.

Takada, Hide, and Yūichirō Masumitsu. 2009. "Konbini tenshu nebiki ni hataraku." *Asahi Shinbun*, May 6, 1.

Takeuchi, Wakeko. 2009. "Haiki dō eikyō?" *Yomiuri Shinbun*, June 24, 10.

Wacquant, Loïc. 2003. *Body and Soul: Notebooks of an Apprentice Boxer.* Oxford: Oxford University Press.

———. 2005. "Carnal Connections: On Embodiment, Apprenticeship, and Membership." *Qualitative Sociology* 28, no. 4:445–447.

Whitelaw, Gavin H. 2006. "Rice Ball Rivalries: Japanese Convenience Stores and the Appetite of Late Capitalism." In *Fast Food/Slow Food: The Cultural Economy of the Global Food System,* ed. Richard R. Wilk, 131–144. Lanham, MD: Altamira Press.

———. 2008. "Learning from Small Change: Clerkship and the Labors of Convenience." *Anthropology of Work Review* 29, no. 3:62–69.

Wilk, Richard R. 1995. "Learning to Be Local in Belize: Global Systems of Common Difference." In *Worlds Apart: Modernity through the Prism of the Local,* ed. Daniel Miller, 110–133. London: Routledge.

Exploring New Roles and Identities

Part III consists of three chapters that examine formerly uncharted or under-explored roles and identities. Nakano (chapter 6) analyzes single women and their perceptions of themselves during and after their marriageable years. In postwar Japan the life course was highly standardized, but with the growing number of singles in today's Japan, how are they scripting their lives? In a society that expects women to play the role of wife-mother and care for others, how do single women see themselves, and what meanings do they find in their lives? How do their experiences of pressure to marry change over time? Nakano illustrates that as they grow older, they are no longer pressured to marry but feel an intensified need to remain competitive in the employment market, qualify for pensions, and ensure their security in old age.

Long (chapter 7) explores the world of grandparents and great-grandparents, in particular their relationships to their grandchildren and great-grandchildren. Like the declining marriage rates that led to mass singlehood, increasing life expectancies have led to mass longevity. Many older persons now experience grandparenthood and sometimes even great-grandparenthood, but what are their roles in postindustrial Japan, where co-residence with grandchildren is increasingly unlikely? Despite the fact that grandchildren are no longer seen mainly as inheritors of family businesses perpetuating the family line, the frail elderly interviewed in Long's study still saw a sense of continuity in their grandchildren but also a sense of difference. Grandchildren remind them that times have changed.

Nakamura (chapter 8) shifts away from age status to sexual identity. People with disabilities were formerly seen as asexual, but recently there has been a move to reevaluate their sexual needs and access to emerging sexual services. Nakamura asks whether people with disabilities have the right to fulfill their sexual needs. If so, how? Is it acceptable for their attendants to take them to brothels? Whose sexuality is excluded from the current debates? By providing a culturally specific, historically informed account of prostitution and various sexual services in Japan, Nakamura examines the lively discussions surrounding what constitutes sexual needs and rights for people with disabilities.

CHAPTER 6

Single Women in Marriage and Employment Markets in Japan

LYNNE Y. NAKANO

SINGLE WOMEN ARE described in remarkably negative terms in the Japanese mass media. One such term, for example, "parasite singles" *(parasaito shinguru)* refers to adult single women who live with their parents. The term became popular following the publication of the book *The Age of Parasite Singles (Parasaito shinguru no jidai)* (1999) by the well-known sociologist Yamada Masahiro, who argued that single people were enjoying a comfortable life and consuming luxury products because they were living with their parents without paying rent or household bills. Although Yamada explained that both single women and men were parasites, the term has been used in the media largely to describe women. This view of single women as parasites is highly problematic because the decision for a single daughter to live with her parents is negotiated between the two generations; often a single daughter may be chosen among other siblings to care for her parents in their old age (Nakano 2010), and parents may prefer that their daughter live with them as a form of social security. Terms such as "parasite singles" reveal how some people in Japan view single women, but they do not tell us how single women actually live or how they see their lives. This chapter explores single women's perspectives based on research that involved extensive interviews with single women and participation in their daily lives.

The numbers of single women in Japan have increased significantly in recent decades. In 2010, 4.5 percent of women between the ages of thirty and thirty-four were single, compared to only 7.7 percent in 1975 (National Institute of Population and Social Security Research 2011).[1] The rise in the number of single women is related to the rise in the average age of first marriage for women. Between 1970 and 2011, women's mean age of first marriage rose by four years, from 24.2 to 29.0 (Ministry of Internal Affairs and Communications 2012), a rapid rise compared to Western societies, where the age of marriage has risen much more gradually. Women marry later in Japan than in most other societies, including the United States, where the age of first marriage was 26.1 in 2010 (U.S. Bureau of the Census 2011). Men's mean age of first marriage in Japan has also risen; between 1960 and 2011, the figure rose from 27.2 to 30.7 (Ministry of Internal Affairs and Communications 2012). My research focuses on women, however, because the contrast between marriage and singlehood is far more dramatic for women than for men. For men, both marriage and singlehood require continuous commitment to work. For women, in contrast, marriage generally involves a commitment to caring for children and a husband while singlehood brings continuous full-time employment.

The contrast between the lives of single women today and those of previous generations of women is also striking. In the 1970s and 1980s, marriage was seen as a natural part of a woman's life course (Creighton 1996; Hendry 1985; Lebra 1984). Women nearly universally married, and if family resources allowed, they withdrew from the workforce to care for their families while their children were young, even as many women later returned to part-time or full-time work when their children were of school age (see Iwao 1993). By 2010, however, nearly 30 percent of women in their thirties were single (Ministry of Internal Affairs and Communications 2012). The trend toward longer and perhaps permanent singlehood suggests a major shift in women's values and ways of thinking.

The rates of marriage are not the same across Japanese society. Women with fewer financial resources and lower levels of education may need to marry earlier as a means to support themselves (Ogura 2003, 31). Women with higher educational levels and good jobs may be able to wait indefinitely until they find an appropriate person. Women in rural areas tend to marry earlier than women in urban areas. My informants told me that the pressure to marry from friends, family, and neighbors is greater in smaller cities and towns than in Tokyo. Compared with other cities and towns in Japan, Tokyo offers women better education and employment opportunities and a social environment that is relatively more accepting of single people. Tokyo attracts women from around the country who wish to escape from pressures to marry early and start a family. The mean age of marriage for women in Tokyo is the highest in the nation and nearly one year later than for women in Japan as a whole.[2] This study focuses on women who were more likely to be single than other women in their age group; they were high school- and university-educated women who felt that they did not need to marry for financial reasons, and they were living in Tokyo at the time of the interviews.

This chapter explores how these single women view their lives. What challenges do they face, and what are their concerns and aspirations? Are they living for their work, are they hoping to marry and leave the workplace, or do they have altogether new dreams? I argue in this chapter that single women's experiences in the 2000s were shaped by two markets in which they were expected to compete and in which their value declined as they aged: the marriage and employment markets. Women could choose to avoid the marriage market if they decided not to marry, but for those who wished to marry—and the majority did—the marriage market had changed little from previous decades. It continued to emphasize youth, beauty, and women's willingness to provide services to family members. Women were staying longer in the employment market, but the changes occurring in the economy, such as the decline of the lifetime employment system and the growth of the part-time and temporary work sectors, disadvantaged older women. Employment markets in the 2000s privileged youth, higher education, and specialized skills. Single women who were already working in the 2000s saw that their opportunities for employment would decrease as they aged and they would need to acquire specialized skills to remain competitive. In other words, women could see that they would be marginalized from both the marriage and the employment markets. As a result of this realization, women began to articulate values that emphasized innovation, initiative, perseverance, hard work, and independence. These values, perhaps not surprisingly, underpin global capitalism at a moment when corporations are downsizing, shifting from manufacturing to service sectors, and demanding an ever more mobile workforce with shifting specialties that address rapidly changing markets.

Perceptions of Single Women in Japan

The increase in the numbers of single women has attracted enormous media attention in Japan. Single women in their thirties and forties have been the subject of TV dramas that focus on the attempts of successful career women to juggle romance and work.[3] Popular new vocabulary words, such as "parasite singles," mentioned above, have emerged to describe single women and their lives. Single women have been called "loser dogs" in the media following the publication of the book *The Distant Cry of Loser Dogs (Makeinu no tōboe)*, by Sakai Junko (2003). A single woman herself, Sakai used the term "loser dogs" with tongue-in-cheek irony to criticize the ways in which labels of "winners" and "losers" are used to categorize women based on marital status and whether or not they have had children. Sakai sympathetically described single women in their thirties as courageous achievers who pursue their interests rather than marry for money and security. In spite of Sakai's intention to draw attention to society's stereotyping of women, the term "loser dogs" has been widely used by the media to negatively label single women. Another new term, "spouse-hunting activities," or *konkatsu* (from *kekkon katsudō*), is a play on the Japanese term for "job-hunting activities" *(shūshoku katsudō)* and refers to the practice of some women to actively search for a spouse through participating in matchmaking and dating activities. The term "carnivorous women" *(nikushokukei joshi)* refers to women who actively pursue sex and marriage, and *sōshokukei danshi* (herbivorous men) refers to men who are not interested in sex and marriage. These stereotypes are highly problematic because they ignore the diversity of human personalities and the contexts that make behaviors meaningful. Instead, they reproduce stereotypes in which only two dichotomous personality types are possible—passive or aggressive—with the assumption that men should be aggressive and women should be passive.

The issue of the rising numbers of single women has attracted the attention of the government, media, and academics in Japan because singlehood is associated with the nation's declining birthrate and aging population. In 1975, the nation's total fertility rate fell below 2.0, the rate required to maintain the population, and it dropped to a low of 1.26 in 2005 before rising to 1.39 in 2011 (Ministry of Internal Affairs and Communications 2012). By 2020, Japan is expected to have one of the oldest populations in the world, with over 30 percent of its population over the age of sixty-five (Ministry of Internal Affairs and Communications 2012). Conservative politicians and commentators have urged single women to marry and have children as the solution to Japan's aging population problem. They target single women in part because very few births occur outside of marriage in Japan; in 2009, the figure was only 2.1 percent (Ministry of Health, Labor, and Welfare 2012). This approach, however, overlooks the fact that single men outnumber single women;[4] ignores the problems faced by both women and men in finding appropriate partners; and obscures other possible solutions to population decline, such as the implementation of policies that encourage foreign immigration to Japan and the provision of greater public assistance to single mothers and married women.

Academic research has tried to explain why women are marrying later (Ogura 2003; Tsuya 2000; Tsuya and Mason 1995; Yamada 1999). Many studies propose that marriage has become less attractive to women because rising levels of education and increased opportunities at work have given women more resources and the option to remain unmarried. At the same time, women are still expected to provide care for family members, and thus women view marriage as burdensome (Ōhashi 1993; Tsuya 2000; Tsuya and Mason 1995). Ochiai (1997) suggests that as divorce rates have risen and as male employment has become increasingly insecure, marriage no longer offers security for women and is thus less attractive. Yamada (1999) argues that the depressed economy of the 1990s lowered men's earning capacity, and thus women remained single because they were unable to find men capable of supporting their sought-after lifestyle of full-time housewives. Rosenbluth (2007) maintains that persistent gender discrimination at the workplace encourages women to struggle harder at work, thus delaying marriage and resulting in declining birthrates. These studies are useful in depicting the historical context in which women are marrying later in life in Japan.

The research for this project took place in Tokyo because this city, as mentioned, has the highest concentrations of single people in Japan. In 2010, for example, 17.37 percent of women in Tokyo had never been married, compared to 10.61 percent nationally (National Institute of Population and Social Security Research 2011). A research assistant and I interviewed thirty single women in Tokyo over a three-year period. We found informants through snowball sampling, and we used a variety of contacts to initiate our interview networks. About half of the informants described themselves as "regular staff" (seishain), or permanent employees who enjoyed a full package of company benefits. Two of the informants held MA degrees, about one-third had graduated from four-year universities, and the remainder were junior college or high school graduates. The women worked in a variety of industries such as banking, travel, pharmaceuticals, trade, and communications. Two worked in government-affiliated institutions. Others worked for Japanese, foreign, and multinational firms; they worked for large companies, medium-sized firms, and small family businesses. A few worked for themselves, including an entrepreneur and a freelance editor, and one woman was unemployed and looking for work. About half of the informants were Tokyo natives, and half had come to Tokyo from other parts of Japan as young adults for schooling or work. The study does not include women from the highest or the lowest strata of Japanese society; none of the women were disabled, single mothers, unable to work, or from impoverished backgrounds. Nonetheless, the women interviewed represent a large cross section of single women who work and live in Tokyo. In the next section, I explain the marriage and employment markets experienced by the single women we interviewed.

Marriage and Employment Markets

Marriage involved a market in the sense that women and men searched for partners according to particular criteria and values. In referring to marriage in this way, I do not mean that love and affection were not important to Japanese women. Nearly all women we interviewed wanted to find romantic love and thought that romantic love should accompany marriage. In a 2010 national survey, 88.1 percent of women who had married in the past five years reported that their marriages were "love marriages," relationships they had started through their own initiative and contacts, while only 5 percent were reported to be "arranged" by *omiai* (arranged meetings for the purpose of marriage) (National Institute of Population and Social Security Research 2011). My perspective, however, is that feelings such as romantic love and attraction are intertwined with social, economic, and practical considerations.[5]

Some women, particularly women over thirty-five, wanted to find romantic partners or lovers, and they were not interested in marrying. In this chapter, however, I will not discuss the market for lovers, boyfriends, or girlfriends. I focus on the marriage market because of its power to shape people's views of their choices and because most single women in my sample, like most women in Japan, wanted to marry. A 2010 national survey, for example, showed that 89.4 percent of single women ages 18–34 said that they wished to marry. Only 6.8 percent said that they had no intention to marry (National Institute of Population and Social Security Research 2011). Through interviews, I found that women's degree of interest in marriage varies greatly. A handful of women were extremely eager to marry; about half said that they wanted to marry if an appropriate person appeared, and about one-quarter expressed ambivalence about marriage. Only one woman in my sample, a lesbian, said that she did not want to marry—although even she had considered marrying at one point in her life.

What do women and men want from a marriage partner? In a national survey of over ten thousand unmarried women and men between the ages of eighteen and thirty-five, both women and men selected "personality" *(hitogara)* as the most important criterion in deciding on a spouse. The second most selected answer for both women and men was "a partner's ability to perform housework and take care of children" (National Institute of Population and Social Security Research 2011). These surveys tell us what kinds of issues are important to women and men, but they do not reflect how people actually make decisions about marriage partners. Sociologist Ogura Chikako has considered how women choose spouses. She writes the following: "Marriage is an exchange of resources between women and men. You have to locate your own resources, and even if you make a high standard of requirements of the other person, you may never meet your appropriate mate. According to a survey of university students, women most want 'economic ability' from men, and men want 'beauty' from women. Although they do not say this in so many words, this is what they persistently ask for. As a result, marriage is an exchange of *kao* [face] for *kane* [money]. Women offer their 'faces' and ask for 'money.' Men offer money and ask for beauty from women" (2003, 29).

Ogura interviewed fifty-two women and found that educational background was the primary factor that shaped women's views of marriage. According to Ogura, high school–educated women wanted to marry to financially survive *(seizon),* graduates of two-year colleges wanted to marry to depend on a man so that they could pursue their own interests *(izon),* and university-educated women wanted to marry while preserving their career choices *(hozon)* (2003, 31). Ogura believes that women's expectations for their potential marriage partners—for example, that they will find a man who will earn a high income and help with housework—are unrealistic, leading to later and lower rates of marriage. Recent popular phrases play upon women's expectations for marriage partners. In the past, the three "highs" women expected of men were said to be high education, high income, and height. Since the 1990s, however, it is often said to be the "three Cs," referring to "comfortable" (i.e., the husband brings in sufficient salary), "communicative" (he understands the woman's feelings), and "cooperative" (he will help with the housework) (Mathews 2003, 116; Ogura 2003, 36).

Although my informants told me that women today may choose not to marry, women who wish to marry face pressure to marry sooner rather than later because of the continued emphasis on beauty and youth in the marriage market. In the 1980s, women's value in this market was described by the analogy to the Christmas cake, which in Japan is customarily consumed on December 25. Like Christmas cakes, women were said to lose value after the age of twenty-five (see Brinton 1992; Creighton 1996). As the average age of marriage has risen, however, the Christmas cake analogy is no longer used. The once-popular phrase "appropriate age for marriage" *(tekireiki)* is also rarely heard. Nonetheless, my informants felt pressure to marry by age thirty, as this age represented a cutoff date after which women's value on the market declined more steeply. As men's value in marriage markets continues to be associated with income, men's ability to marry is less closely associated with age, and a man over forty may still marry a younger woman if he has money.

Employment markets for women in the 2000s were equally unforgiving. My research was conducted at a moment of change in the employment markets, as many companies had reduced costs by cutting "regular staff," who enjoyed corporate benefit packages and lifetime employment, and replaced them with cheaper part-time and temporary workers. Companies were cutting "office lady" jobs *(ippanshoku)*, clerical positions for women that generally offered corporate benefit packages and continuous employment contracts, and were hiring temporary staff *(haken shain)*, part-time workers on short-term contracts who received much lower wages and few if any corporate benefits. For some younger women with higher levels of education and specialized degrees, these changes in corporate culture afforded opportunities for advancement and allowed them to be recognized for their abilities. For the women I met who had entered the workforce in the 1980s and 1990s, however, the changes in the economy brought increased pressures to gain a specialized niche in the workforce and worries about whether they would be able to compete in the new economy. When these women first entered the workforce, most were able to find work as regular staff in either management or clerical positions, regardless of their educational levels. They worried that if they lost their current regular staff positions, they would not be able to find another job as regular staff, and they would be downgraded to part-time and temporary work. Companies routinely discriminated against both older women and men in hiring, but age limits were more severe for women than for men. Newspaper advertisements, for example, commonly stated that particular positions were open to women under thirty-five and to men under forty, and informants told me that they believed that they were not being considered for jobs because of their age. Age discrimination in Japan is endemic and goes hand in hand with Japanese companies' rigid internal labor systems, which operate by hiring junior staff directly from university, training them internally, and promoting staff according to seniority.

The remainder of the chapter introduces the stories and experiences of single women. I argue that younger women under thirty-five were caught between marriage and employment markets in which their value fell as they aged; after their early thirties, single women saw themselves moving further away from conventional life choices even as many continued to hope for some combination of romantic relationships, work, and hobbies. After forty, single women viewed their struggles and achievements at work with varying degrees of satisfaction and saw romantic relationships and hobbies as luxuries. The women I met viewed the changes in the economy in the 2000s with worry, as most were unable to benefit from the opening of opportunities that they saw had become available to better educated and younger women. At the same time, perhaps because of their disadvantaged positions in the employment and marriage markets, women began expressing a new set of values, as noted above.

Late Twenties to Early Thirties:
Conflict between Marriage and Employment Markets

Women under thirty-five faced pressure because most wished both to work and to marry, and they realized that their value in both employment and marriage markets declined as they aged due to discrimination against older women. Further, women felt that they could not simultaneously succeed at both markets. If they invested time and energy into their work, some feared that they would lose the opportunity to marry. But if they married earlier and made sacrifices in their career for children or family, they worried that they would lose opportunities in the employment market. Women thus were faced with the same problem encountered by previous generations of women of having to choose between marriage and career, but in an age in which one in four marriages ends in divorce, marriage is no longer a source of security. The women I met understood that in the event of an unsuccessful marriage, they would be thrown back into the job market with significantly lower employability and earning power than when they had left. They were worried but held on to hope that they would be able to succeed in the marriage and employment markets by developing their abilities and through perseverance and hard work.

Consider the example of Yūko, a twenty-nine-year-old woman who had been successful in her career and continued to be ambitious but worried about her ability to marry. Upon graduating from a mid-tier university in Tokyo, Yūko found a job at a TV station and eventually was allowed to film short documentaries while carrying the camera and writing the script herself. After suffering from a health crisis due to overwork, she decided to change career paths and through her connections in the media industry was hired by a major advertising company to promote advertisements through mobile phones. The department in which she worked was staffed primarily by women, many of them single and in their thirties and forties. While Yūko claimed to admire these women's independence, she did not want to follow in their path. Rather, she wanted to marry as soon as possible to start a family. The main obstacle to her marriage was her boyfriend. She said, "This contradicts what I just said [about the opportunities women have at work], but I want to get married! I've been seeing my boyfriend for three and a half years. . . . He's just changed companies again, and he's really busy now. Last year I asked him when we would marry, and he said next year. This year he says "next year" again. Now I'm wondering if he's really the best person for me."

Yūko lived with her parents at the time of the interview—she had returned to live with them after a few years of living alone in a rented apartment in To-kyo. Although she needed to commute a longer distance to work when living with her parents, she said that her parents preferred that she live with them so that they could ensure that she was eating properly and not working ex-cessively, as she had done when living alone. Her parents urged her to marry, reminding her with greater frequency as she approached thirty. Yūko agreed with her parents that she should have children by her early thirties. Surveys in Japan show that the most common reason for women's wish to marry is the desire to have children and a family; 47.7 percent of single women aged 18–34 in a 2010 national survey indicated that they wanted to marry for this reason (National Institute of Population and Social Security Research 2011).

Yūko was unusual among my informants in the strength of her ambition and devotion to the dual tasks of developing a career and finding a husband. She was not unusual, however, in expressing her anxiety about being able to achieve both career and family. Her narrative emphasized her achievements at work, attained through hard work and perseverance, but she found that these approaches were not successful when applied to securing a husband.

Not all women I interviewed wanted to continue to work. Mari, a thirty-one-year-old high school graduate, lived with her parents and said that she wanted to become a "full-time housewife." She was not as ambitious as Yūko, but she was also aware of the dual markets and wished to succeed in both.

While in her twenties, she had worked as a regular staff member for a record company and then quit to spend eighteen months studying English in New York, an experience paid for by her parents. When she returned to Tokyo, she found a job at a small perfume-importing company consisting of seven family members, she being the only non-family member on the staff. She found this situation to be difficult and stressful, however, and was searching for another job, also as a regular staff. She said, "After taking one more job as a regular staff person [after this job], I want to marry and work as a temporary staff and take it easy. At least, that's the plan. [Laughs.] I want to have children by the time I'm thirty-five. I don't have to marry this year or next year, but I'd like to get married by the year after that . . . if I have a partner."

Mari thus tried to make the best of the dual markets in her youth; she wished to find work as a regular staff member while she was still able and find a suitable partner and marry so that she could have children. She said that women did not need to marry these days, but when I asked her what was most important in her life, she answered, "Family and marriage [are most important]. At the moment I feel that if I can't marry, I can't do anything." At the time of the interview, Mari had been dating her boyfriend for eight months, and he was not yet ready to marry due to work and family problems. In sum, she felt that marriage was a major goal that she needed to achieve to enter the next stage of her life, and work was of secondary importance.

Her experience replicates that of previous generations of Japanese women. Unlike the previous generations, however, Mari knew that she could not give up struggling to improve her position in the employment market, and she would marry only if she had a suitable partner.

Well-meaning parents, colleagues, and friends encouraged women in their late twenties through early thirties to succeed in both markets. Women were encouraged to capitalize on their university education to take advantage of the new opportunities available to them at work, and they were also expected to secure a husband and start a family. This situation differs from that of their mothers' generation, when women were encouraged to succeed in the marriage market alone. The marriage market itself has changed in that women have higher expectations of their potential mates, while men's expectations of women have changed little. Women hoped that they would be able to succeed in both markets even as they saw tremendous obstacles. In this context, they described strategies that they hoped would allow them to achieve their particular dreams. Next, we consider women in their thirties who continue to struggle in these markets but see that they are unlikely to succeed.

Thirty-Something: Departing from Convention

By their mid-thirties, women realized that their chances of marrying had become slim and that their value in the marriage market continued to decline. A handful of women past their mid-thirties continued to hope for a future that included marriage and family as their primary source of meaning in life. Most women in this age group, however, realized that they did not want to or could not follow conventions to marry as expected by their parents, colleagues, and bosses. These women understood the importance of independence in thought and action and the need to take control of their lives. It may be the case that women who reached their mid- to late thirties without marrying tended to be more independent and questioning of social norms than women who married before this age.

Here I introduce two women in their thirties who questioned conventional paths for women in both work and marriage. Thirty-one-year-old Reiko had just quit a full-time position as a textbook editor at a major publishing firm and was taking freelance jobs while considering her next career move. I met her in her small rented Tokyo apartment, where she was both living and working. She said, "I'm not sure what I'd like to do now. When I graduated from university, I also didn't want to go through the job-hunting process *[shūshoku katsudō]* [which usually takes place during the third and fourth years of university]. The school told us that that's what we should be doing, but I didn't know what that was, and I just couldn't do it. After graduating, for six months I stayed at home and didn't work. I had no idea what it meant for me, as a woman, to work. Also, my mother was a full-time housewife, so she couldn't help me."

Reiko similarly took an unconventional approach to marriage. She said: "I've been seeing my boyfriend for about six years. I'm not interested in getting married. I can't imagine living with him. Our lifestyles would clash. I'm worried that if I lived with him, I would start to feel stress. I would worry, for example, that he's not eating a balanced diet." She uses conventional concerns associated with housewives—for example, to feed her husband properly—to explain why she didn't want to marry. From her words we can see that Reiko would not make decisions about her life course merely because such decisions were expected. Rather, she wanted to consider for herself how each decision related to her life. When I met her for a second interview two years later, Reiko told me that soon after our first interview she had broken up with her boyfriend, a university lecturer, when she realized that he did not have space in his life for her. She had since become engaged to be married to a man who had been her friend for many years, a divorcé who was raising two children. She had not returned to a full-time position at a publishing firm but had continued to work as a freelance editor from her home. She had resisted conventional paths and was happy with her upcoming marriage and with the freedom she exercised in her work. Her sense of satisfaction was achieved through painful self-reflection and thought. She had proceeded at work and in romantic relationships at her own pace and in the face of others' criticism and doubt.

Miki, thirty-four, a high school–educated woman, had also created her own path through life. She had bought her own condominium apartment (manshon) two years earlier in central Tokyo, thus allowing her to move out of a cramped apartment in Yokohama where she had lived with her parents and younger brother. As the prices of apartments had fallen in Tokyo, she was able to find a place within her budget. She was one of only two single women I interviewed who had purchased her own apartment. She did it without consulting her parents. She explained, "I've always done things that surprised my parents. They were also opposed to my studying in the United States for a year. I paid for it myself and studied at a community college. They didn't want me to go. They said that I'd be killed, that I'd be shot. That's the kind of people they are. They're the kind of people who think that girls don't need to go to college. They want me to marry and have children. That's why I make a decision and then tell them what I've decided. That's what I did about going to the United States and about this apartment."

In the marriage market, Miki did not feel pressed to compete, as she felt that she did not need to marry. She had a Canadian boyfriend who lived in the United States and whom she saw a few times a year. She said that they did not get along well when they spent extensive amounts of time together, so it might be better not to marry. Her dreams for the future did not involve marriage and family. Rather, she wanted to buy another apartment and travel around the world. Miki worked for a small, foreign-affiliated company as a regular staff member. She had joined this firm after quitting her job at a previous company, also as a regular staff member, after the company introduced several rounds of layoffs that affected worker morale. She felt that she was lucky to have found her current job after a long search, as she saw that she might not be so fortunate the next time because of her age. She was thinking of studying online for an accounting degree and hoped to one day start up her own business of providing accounting work online for foreign firms.

Both Reiko and Miki broke with convention early in their adult lives. Miki was clearly thinking of how she would adapt to the new economy and was planning to leave the employment market to start her own business. Other women were more reluctant to give up on a conventional life, and they tended to be more passive in their decision making. They were also probably less prepared financially and psychologically for living an independent life. Women in the mid- to late thirties age range had started working when jobs were relatively plentiful and stable. Most had not expected that they would still be single in their thirties, and they had not expected that they would need to strategize and struggle in the employment market. Yet if they remained single, they still had several decades of work ahead of them, and they were still young enough to be able to invest in themselves and adapt to the changing economy. While not all women in this age group had the motivation and initiative of Reiko and Miki, they all understood the need to make plans and prepare for an uncertain future.

After Forty: "We Don't Need Men, but We Do Need Work"

By the time they reached forty, single women were under considerably less pressure to marry, and they were reaching the prime of their working lives. Single women in this age range had mixed views of their success at romance and work. Some still very much wanted to find a romantic partner while others were generally content without a partner. Regarding work, women were better able to judge their own abilities and had learned to appreciate their accomplishments, yet they understood that they were undervalued in the employment market and were concerned about their employment prospects. Single women of this age group also spoke of their plans for caring for their parents and their own elder care.

Noriko, an unemployed forty-six-year-old woman, explained that the transition from youth to middle age brought a decline in the pressure to marry. She said, "When I was twenty-nine, I really felt pressured about marriage. Every night I couldn't sleep from frustration. But after I passed thirty, those feelings went away. It seems that thirty was the big age. All my friends agree that reaching thirty was really awful. Reaching forty was no problem. Some even say that they were glad to reach forty. At that time when you reached thirty, you had trouble finding work. Many [job] advertisements said that they didn't hire women over thirty. It's different now. It may be that now thirty-five is the critical age."

For Noriko, the pressure to marry on schedule was compounded by fears of age discrimination in the employment market. She recalled feeling pressure to marry even though she had decided as a young girl that she need not marry. She was open to marriage but only if the person was someone whom she could respect. Noriko enjoyed her single life, and she had many friends, male and female, who were single. In recent years, she had become interested in Formula One racing and enjoyed traveling to Australia to attend the Australian Grand Prix. At the time of the interview, Noriko did not have a boyfriend, and she and her friends joked that they would enjoy a "Heian-style marriage," in which a man would visit them twice a week but they would keep separate residences.

While content with her personal life, Noriko struggled in the employment market. She had come to Tokyo from Niigata Prefecture to attend university and had lived in Tokyo since her graduation. She had worked for several different companies as a regular staff member but without developing a specialized skill. When changing companies, she was forced to accept salaries that were not commensurate with her work experience. In one case, the company management said it could only pay her the salary of an eighteen-year old if it hired her through normal company policies, although at that time Noriko was already in her thirties and had been working for over a decade. To circumvent this regulation, the company hired her through a regional office that could offer better terms, although she was assigned to work in the company's Tokyo headquarters. The employment market in the 2000s was poor, and regular staff positions for women over thirty were difficult to secure. Noriko's struggles in her career reflect the employment market of the 2000s, in which changing one's place of employment was becoming increasingly common, yet for many older workers, and women in particular, movement was likely to bring a decrease in salary and deterioration of employment conditions. In her last position, Noriko had been transferred from an office job to a factory position in which she supervised the manufacturing of materials used in housing construction. She resigned from the company after a colleague lost part of a finger at the factory. At the time of the interview, she was receiving government unemployment insurance and was studying to obtain a license to sell life insurance.

Women in their forties could ignore pressures to marry, but they could not ignore the realities of the employment market. Sana, a forty-year-old Osaka native, expressed this bluntly as she said, "We don't need men, but we do need work." Sana said that she would like to marry if she met the right person but that employment was more important than men. When I first met her in 2001, she was working as a regular staff computer technician for a pharmaceutical firm that had transferred her to Tokyo from Osaka, where she had been living with her mother and sisters. When rumors circulated that the company would begin laying off workers, she quit, and when I met her in 2004, she had been unable to find another regular staff position. She was working as a temporary staff person at a job that paid significantly less and provided no guarantee of continuous employment and no benefit packages. She said, "It's not good to regret, but now I think that I should have studied harder. If I had an MBA, my life would be better. But what I can do now is to go to interpreter's school. I haven't studied very hard, but I'll study harder. I envy women my age who are managers. Before, we had lifetime employment, but now [one's livelihood] is based on ability. Women can be managers now. The system is now perfor-mance-oriented. When I was younger, I traveled abroad, went drinking with colleagues, and now I'm paying the price." Sana's skills as a computer techni-cian were not sufficiently specialized to bring her job security. As she spoke and wrote English well, she was thinking about further polishing her English to become a professional interpreter.

Noriko and Sana suffered setbacks in the employment markets because they had not sufficiently developed marketable skills but also because of age and gender discrimination in Japanese companies. When they changed com-panies, they found that their career trajectory and value in the employment markets had declined. Both were addressing their employment problems by studying to obtain specialized skills, and they did so because they felt that it was a necessary measure to allow them to survive in the employment market.

Women in their forties had entered the workforce at a time when jobs were abundant and women were not expected to develop specialized job skills. Many had started in entry-level clerical positions and had no intention of remaining in the workforce for several decades. As time passed and they remained single, these women improved their skills and made contributions to their workplaces. In spite of these skills and their experiences, however, women in their forties were concerned about how to remain competitive in the job market, and some were learning specialized skills to be able to contin-ue to support themselves if they lost their current jobs.

In contrast to the employment market, which demanded strategy and initiative, women discussed family and romantic life as being beyond their control. Effort and action did not necessarily lead to a successful romantic relationship, and one could not predict when one's parents would fall ill and require care. In this sense, some women were looking beyond the employment market to a time when family duties would force them into domestic caregiving roles and end the relative freedom of single life.

Conclusion

The 2000s witnessed a decline of the lifetime employment system, the rise of the part-time and temporary work sectors, and greater acceptance of a diversity of lifestyles—including indefinitely delayed marriage. Have these changes improved the lives of women? I suggest that the option of remaining single is a major advance for women because it allows greater freedom of lifestyle and diversity in sexual orientation, personality types, and personal goals. That being said, most single women would have preferred a life that included marriage, family, and work. Women were not finding appropriate partners, and they were not achieving the kinds of careers that brought the job security and recognition that their working experience merited because the primary markets that involved women—the marriage and employment markets—continued to operate on principles that valued women's docility, youth, beauty, and ability to serve men. Pressures for younger women were intense, as they felt that they needed to achieve success in both markets while they were relatively young. As women passed the age of thirty, the pressure in the marriage market decreased, in large part because older women were thought to be beyond the perimeters of the market. Ironically, this brought a sense of freedom and psychological ease for women, especially for those who were not particularly determined to marry. Women in their thirties and forties, however, continued to feel pressure to improve their position in the employment markets as they saw that the market was changing, dividing people into "winners" and "losers." Winners were those with special skills and degrees who could achieve management positions. Losers were those who did not have such degrees or special skills. My informants were concerned that without significant effort and initiative, they would be thrown into the pool of poorly paid part-time and temporary workers.

One might assume that women would be depressed and discouraged when they reached their forties both unmarried and without having successfully established a career. Yet this was not the case. The women I met said that they felt increasingly free and relieved as they aged. At the same time, their actual problems had probably increased as they faced discrimination in the job market, increasing difficulty in finding romantic partners, and concerns about their own and their parents' elder care. Why did women seem to feel increasingly relieved as they aged? It could be that when they reached their forties, they had a clearer idea of what was necessary in their lives and were less moved by others' opinions about how they should live their lives. It may be that women felt a sense of accomplishment in what they had achieved at work, as they had gained recognition and appreciation from others such as bosses and clients. They understood that they had made contributions to their workplaces. One woman talked about how she had changed the corporate culture in her company by refusing to serve tea and asking for drink machines to be installed. Others fought for promotions and against unequal treatment, and they tried to suggest to their bosses and male colleagues that they change their way of treating women. One woman, for example, said that she told her boss that he could ask her about whether she intended to marry, but he should not raise the topic with other women because they would be offended. These changes may be small given the overall structural problems of gender discrimination in Japan, but for the women who initiated these changes and worked every day in these offices, these were not insignificant achievements.

We have seen that single women, particularly those in their forties, were not responding to the requirements of the marriage market that they provide services to men in marriage or use their youth and beauty to marry early. Rather, they were choosing to continue to struggle in the employment market. Yet this market also valued women for youth, docility, and service. Because women saw that they would be marginalized from both markets, they had begun cultivating alternative values and characteristics that would help them survive, such as perseverance, independence, innovation, hard work, and initiative. We have seen in this chapter that women understood that they had to take the initiative to learn new skills, argue for better working conditions, find market niches in which they could contribute, and even educate men about how to value and treat women. Does this represent an emerging new culture in which women in Japan will adopt a new set of values based on individual achievement and strategy? These values are not new or unique to Japan but emerge from globally pervasive neoliberal capitalism. To a certain degree, single women are being forced to acknowledge and adapt to the rules of open-market global capitalism, which has reshaped the Japanese economy in the 2000s. Single women are not, however, entirely committed to playing by its rules because they are not entirely devoted to their work. They wish for something more in life, although they are generally not able to articulate what they want. For the moment, women remain caught between hopes for work and marriage with relatively unsatisfactory results in both. Their overall material conditions may have deteriorated, and they were not attaining the kinds of romantic relationships and recognition they would like. At the same time, in the context of the choices that have emerged in their lives, single women in their thirties and forties continue to choose the difficulties of singlehood over an inappropriate marriage.

Notes

The work described in this chapter was supported by a grant from the Research Grants Council of the Hong Kong Special Administrative Region, China (Project No. CUHK4018/02H). The research was also made possible by a 2001 Summer Grant for Research and a 2001–2002 Direct Grant awarded by the Chinese University of Hong Kong. I thank Moeko Wagatsuma and Chan Yim Ting for their assistance in conducting research.
1. The number of single men has also risen dramatically; 47.3 percent of men in the 30–34 age group were single in 2010, compared to only 21.5 percent in 1980 (Ministry of Health, Labor, and Welfare 2012).
2. In 2010, for example, the mean age of first marriage for women in Tokyo was 29.7, compared to the national mean age of marriage for women of 28.8 (Ministry of Health, Labor, and Welfare 2012).
3. Some examples are *Bus Stop,* which was broadcast on Fuji TV in 2000; *Around 40,* which aired on TBS in 2008; and *Boss,* which aired on Fuji TV in 2009.
4. For example, in 2010, 32 percent of women and 47 percent of men between the ages of thirty and thirty-four were single (National Institute of Population and Social Security Research 2011).
5. My approach is similar to that of Constable, who asks "how love and emotion are intertwined with political economy through cultural logics of desire" (2003, 120).

References Cited

Brinton, Mary. 1992. "Christmas Cakes and Wedding Cakes: The Social Organization of Japanese Women's Life Course." In *Japanese Social Organization,* ed. Takie Lebra, 74–107. Honolulu: University of Hawai'i Press.

Constable, Nicole. 2003. *Romance on a Global Stage: Pen Pals, Virtual Ethnography, and "Mail Order" Marriages.* Berkeley: University of California Press.

Creighton, Millie. 1996. "Marriage, Motherhood, and Career Management in a Japanese 'Counter culture.'" In *Re-imaging Japanese women,* ed. Anne Imamura, 192–220. Berkeley: University of California Press.

Hendry, Joy. 1985. *Marriage in Changing Japan: Community and Society.* New York: St. Martin's Press.

Iwao, Sumiko. 1993. *The Japanese Woman: Traditional Image and Changing Reality.* New York: Free Press.

Lebra, Takie S. 1984. *Japanese Women: Constraint and Fulfillment.* Honolulu: University of Hawai'i Press.

Mathews, Gordon. 2003. "Can 'a Real Man' Live for His Family?: Ikigai and Masculinity in Today's Japan." In *Men and Masculinities in Contemporary Japan: Dislocating the Salaryman Doxa,* ed. James E. Roberson and Nobue Suzuki, 109–206. London: RoutledgeCurzon.

Ministry of Health, Labor, and Welfare. 2012. "International Comparisons." Http://www.mhlw.go.jp/english/database/db-hw/FY2010/dl/live_births05.pdf. Accessed February 9, 2013.

Ministry of Internal Affairs and Communications, Statistics Bureau and Statistical Training Institute (Sōmushō Tōkeikyoku). 2012. *Declining Birth Rate and Aging Population.* Http://www.stat.go.jp/English/data/handbook/c02cont.htm. Accessed February 4, 2013.

Nakano, Lynne. 2010. "Working and Waiting for an 'Appropriate Person': How Single Women Support and Resist Family in Japan." In *Home and Family in Japan: Continuity and Transformation,* ed. Richard Ronald and Allison Alexy, 131–151. New York: Routledge.

National Institute of Population and Social Security Research. 2011. "Attitudes toward Marriage and Family among Japanese Singles." Http://www.ipss.go.jp/sitead/index_english/nfs14/Nfs14_Singles_Eng.pdf. Accessed February 10, 2013.

Ochiai, Emiko. 1997. *The Japanese Family System in Transition: A Sociological Analysis of Family Change in Postwar Japan.* Tokyo: LTCB International Library Foundation.

Ogura, Chikako. 2003. *Kekkon no jōken* (Conditions of marriage). Tokyo: Asahi Shinbunsha.

Ōhashi, Terue. 1993. *Mikonka no shakaigaku* (Sociology of non-marriage). Tokyo: NHK Books.

Rosenbluth, Francis M. 2007. "The Political Economy of Low Fertility." In *The Political Economy of Japan's Low Fertility,* ed. F. M. Rosenbluth, 3–36. Stanford, CA: Stanford University Press.

Sakai, Junko. 2003. *Makeinu no tōboe* (The distant cry of loser dogs). Tokyo: Kōdansha.

Tsuya, Noriko O. 2000. "Women's Empowerment, Marriage Postponement, and Gender Relations in Japan: An Intergenerational Perspective." In *Women's Empowerment and Demographic Processes: Moving beyond Cairo,* ed. H. B. Presser and G. Sen, 318–350. Oxford: Oxford University Press.

Tsuya, Noriko O., and K. O. Mason. 1995. "Changing Gender Roles and Below-Replacement Fertility in Japan." In *Gender and Family Change in Industrialized Countries,* ed. K. O. Mason and A-M. Jensen, 139–167. Oxford: Clarendon Press.

U.S. Bureau of the Census. 2011. U.S. Bureau of the Census Web site. Http://www.census.gov. Accessed August 16, 2011.

Yamada, Masahiro. 1999. *Parasaito shinguru no jidai* (The age of parasite singles). Tokyo: Chikuma Shobō.

CHAPTER 7

The Aging of the Japanese Family

Meanings of Grandchildren in Old Age

SUSAN ORPETT LONG

ONE OF MY favorite feel-good stories after the 3/11 earthquake and tsunami in northeastern Japan was that of the rescue nine days after the quake of eighty-year-old Abe Sumi and her sixteen-year-old grandson Abe Jin. Not only was their survival seen as a metaphor for the ability of Japan to come through the disaster and begin to rebuild, but also the story had a happy ending for the Abe family. After five days recovering in the hospital, Mrs. Abe was reported to be out looking for missing acquaintances, carrying her own bags, and claiming that she was fine. She told a reporter, "'I am eighty years old, and I had a good life,' . . . laughing with a glint in her eye. 'I guess it just wasn't my time'" (Johnston 2011).

The story is also one of my favorites for the questions it raises but does not answer. What was the relationship like between this grandmother and teenage grandson, her son's younger son? Did they live together? Family members having shopped for groceries the previous day apparently allowed the two to survive for nine days on yogurt and water in the rubble of her home. How did they help each other survive? Did they talk? What were grandmother and grandson doing in the kitchen together that afternoon anyway, when the quake hit? What did they mean to each other?

The answers, of course, are individual, yet they are also bound up in the social changes of Japanese society in recent decades. What the grandmother and grandson mean to each other must have to do not only with their own interpersonal history, but also with the cultural meanings of grandchildren and grandparents, with the increasing life expectancies of Japanese seniors, and with the decline in the proportion of elderly who live with their children and grandchildren. Because of the tremendous changes that have occurred, earlier scholarly work on Japanese families provides few answers as we attempt to understand the relationship between the rescued pair in 2011.

This chapter addresses the question of the meaning of grandchildren from the perspective of very old people in Japan in the first decade of the twenty-first century.[1] In what follows, I draw on previous descriptions of grandparent-grandchild relationships and on a series of interviews conducted between 2003 and 2007 among a largely working-class sample of thirty elderly people, mostly women, eligible for long-term care insurance in Tokyo and Akita.[2] The interviewers focused on changes in the respondents' health, daily life, and family relationships over the course of the five-year study, returning to each family every year as long as the family members were able and willing to talk with them. The interviews were not done for the purpose of studying the relationships with extended family. Respondents in general seemed to think of "family" as members of the co-residing household or relationships with spouses and children and sometimes children-in-law. However, the topic of grandchildren sometimes came up naturally in the course of conversational interviews, and the comments and responses to occasional follow-up questions provide suggestive information with which to begin exploring the meaning of these ties in the lives of very old people at the beginning of the twenty-first century. I begin with a brief look at the changes in the Japanese family over the twentieth century. I then turn to the relationships with grandchildren and great-grandchildren the respondents described and discuss their meanings and significance for these elderly Japanese people.

Family and Grandchildren in the First Half of the Twentieth Century

Today's oldest Japanese, those in their eighties and nineties, grew up in the early decades of the twentieth century. Like people everywhere, their understandings and expectations of family have been shaped by their experiences as children and through adulthood, as they and their society changed. To understand what grandchildren mean to them, we begin with a look at the types of family worlds they have experienced in their lifetimes.

The family system of pre–World War II Japan, formalized in national law, was based on an ideal of a stem family household, or *ie*. This type of family did not disappear as parents died and children left home but continued in an unbroken line of descent through time. In each generation, there was a single successor upon whom rested the responsibility for the continuity of the household and for the well-being of its members. Although in reality there were many exceptions and variations to this model, the common assumption was that when possible, the eldest son would be the heir, and his wife would succeed her mother-in-law in a gendered division of labor. Their children would be raised in the household with their paternal grandparents. Relationships with maternal grandparents were recognized and maintained, but regardless of how warm and loving the relationship might be, the grandchildren were seen as part of the stem family of their father.

What were grandparent-grandchild relations like in that era? We have reports from American ethnographers who studied Japan at the time. In describing relationships within a three-generational household, as explained by her Japanese American informants, well-known anthropologist Ruth Benedict wrote that "Children have great freedom with their grandparents, though [the grandparents] are also objects of respect," and she described the way that children might benefit from tension in the mother-in-law–daughter-in-law relationship as mother and grandmother tried to compete for the child's attachment (Benedict 1946, 264). This passage, however, is found in a section on childhood and does not discuss the significance of the relationship for the older generation or possible differences in raising children in non-succeeding, numerically predominant two-generational households.

Ella Wiswell provides us with a more intimate view of grandparents and grandchildren, describing how in the 1930s, people in the village of Suye Mura responded to the pictures she took of them:

> Everyone is pleased to get prints of the photographs I take. They
> pass them from one member of the family to another, old folks put
> on their glasses, and the kids are shown the pictures, repeating with
> great glee, "It's grandpa! It's grandma!" . . . Many ask for extra prints
> to send to relatives or children or grandchildren. Old lady Goto
> wants to have her picture taken for her five-year-old grandson in
> Fukuoka—the one who was so attached to her, she says, when she

was living there. She always tells the same story, about how he would follow her even when she went to the toilet. (Smith and Wiswell 1982, 217)

Smith explains that grandmothers generally took charge of the older sibling when a new baby was born, and co-sleeping with grandmothers and grandfathers was common. Older children typically went to their grandmothers when they wanted money and generally received it (Smith and Wiswell 1982, 228; see also Vogel 1963, 224–226). Thus although grandparents had responsibilities for the care and education of grandchildren of the household, their relationship with at least young grandchildren seems to have been close and fairly indulgent.

Family Change in the Latter Half of the Twentieth Century

Legally, the stem family system ended following World War II, when Japanese family law was rewritten under the Allied occupation, whose goal was to democratize the country. The new laws broke up the stem family system by legalizing free choice of spouse and career, making inheritance equal among siblings, and eliminating the assumption that families continue beyond the lifetimes of the individuals who make them up. In addition to these legal changes, the industrialization of Japan over the course of the twentieth century undermined the stem family system in both urban and rural areas, as most people became more dependent for their future livelihood on the educational system rather than on inheriting the family farm or business. More people moved away from their parents' homes for jobs or for higher education. Corporate workers lived in cramped quarters and were sometimes transferred away from their home areas; rural youth migrated to cities for jobs.

In the last half of the twentieth century, three-generational households continued at a higher rate than in other industrialized countries, but that rate declined dramatically. Even when such a living arrangement was practical for economic or health reasons, providing what Takagi, Silverstein, and Crimmins (2007) call "plasticity" to accommodate social changes, it was no longer the same as the stem family in the earlier period. For more affluent landowning families, some version of co-residence might be a luxury. For working-class families it might be a necessity to share a residence. Co-residence sometimes continued if a grandparent could assist with child care (though many grandmothers "commuted" to this "job" as well) as more women continued working outside the home after marriage. Increasingly, three-generational co-residence that did occur was likely to be a result of the older person moving in with an adult child due to illness or the death of a spouse rather than the middle generation remaining in the family home and raising its children there. Thus the practice of three generations sharing a household continued to exist for some as a practical solution or as an abstract ideal, but for many Japanese families, it was increasingly less practical, less desirable to both the older and younger generations, and thus less compelling. It was no longer the assumed family form; rather it needed to be discussed and negotiated.

Japanese sociologists characterized this change as the nuclearization of the family *(kakukazokuka)*. For all of the reasons noted above, children growing up in the latter half of the twentieth century were less likely to have experienced living in the same home as grandparents than the previous generation, and ideas about what "family" means have changed accordingly. Rather than relying on grandchildren to carry on the family farm or business, most older adults relied on their own savings and pensions for their livelihood in their old age. People came to think of the family not as a work unit, as in the early twentieth century, but as a place for interpersonal ties and the socialization of children. The distinction between maternal and paternal grandparents thus became less significant as people valued emotional ties to daughters and their children as well as to sons and theirs. The increasing proportion of parent-child only (nuclear family) households regularly tracked in government statistics was seen as a measure of Japan's modernity.

Anthropologist Takie Lebra (1984, 37), writing 40–50 years after Wiswell and Benedict, discusses the role of grandparents in the new type of three-generational households, which might look like a pre–World War II stem family in composition but had changed substantially. She describes the grandparental role as both "supplementary to and inhibitory of the parental role." She adds that women sometimes appreciated and sometimes resented the mother-in-law's role as supplementary parent and generally preferred that their own mother play that role (1984, 178–179). Lebra also goes beyond discussing the grandmother's role to examining what it means for an older woman's life. She claims that a woman's role at the beginning of grandparenthood is to make a mother out of her daughter-in-law. "The physical care given to the daughter-in-law seems to be a crucial investment for one's old age; the daughter-in-law thus cared for will not mind nursing the aged mother-in-law's incapacitated body." She identifies a variety of meanings that grandchildren have for the grandmothers she interviewed: as objects of an emotional attachment, as via-ducts for communicating across generations or with spouses, as amusing visi-tors whom they are happy to have come and happy to have leave, as babysitting charges in whom they invest for their own future care, and as important links in household continuity (1984, 263–265). Even when the generations were liv-ing separately, a significant amount of assistance with child care was frequent-ly provided by grandmothers, especially as more married women worked out-side the home (Campbell and Brody 1985).

In recent years, the increased mobility of the population, urbanization, and nuclearization of families mean that grandparents and grandchildren have fewer opportunities for interaction (Thang 2008, 179). Analyzing social survey data, Saito and Yasuda (2009) report that the farther the children live from their grandparents' houses, the less frequently the children have contact with them. Factors that could compensate for the physical distance were not the availability of communication devices (see also Kumagai 2008, 119) but the parents' time and work status. Busy parents found less time to take their children to visit grandparents. Kawano (this volume) points to the contact between grandparents and grandchildren resulting from women's perceived need for child rearing help in a society that remains unfriendly to simultane-ous child-rearing and full-time employment. Unable to get much relief from husbands, mothers of young children turn to their own mothers or, less of-ten, to mothers-in-law for assistance. Survey research has found that younger preschoolers in Japan had more contact with their grandparents than other children because older children may be busy with school and extracurricular activities. Female adult children communicated more often with parents and grandparents than male children and more often communicated with grand-mothers than grandfathers (Tanaka 2001, cited in Saito and Yasuda 2009). Al-though the roles grandparents play are most likely based on the needs of the mother and the age of the grandchild, the *significance* of grandparenthood increased for men with age and remained high for women (Ando 2005). But just what role the grandparents are to play is unclear. In a three-generation survey about grandparents' strengths and needs, the grandparents reported experiencing greater difficulty and more frustration and felt less informed to carry out their grandparental role than their children and grandchildren rec-ognized (Strom et al. 1996).[3]

These descriptions of the roles and interactions of grandparents describe grandparents who are in middle age or early old age, when they are active and grandchildren are babies or school age. But the last half of the twentieth century also brought great demographic shifts that affect the meaning of family.[4] The size of the family has grown smaller due not only to separate residences from grandparents but also to higher rates of divorce and to a declining birthrate. As the cost of raising children grew, more women entered the paid labor force, and people married later. The birthrate in the first decade of the twenty-first century was so low (1.2 children per woman) that the Japanese population was actually experiencing a negative growth rate (−0.2 percent). At the same time, life expectancy increased dramatically, from about forty-three years at the turn of the twentieth century to over eighty at the beginning of the twenty-first century. Thus older people may have fewer grandchildren, but many are living long enough to know their grandchildren as young adults and even to become great-grandparents. What happens to these relationships when grandparents can focus on fewer grandchildren for a longer time? What happens when grandparents become less able to perform grandparental roles culturally defined based on the demographics of an earlier era? As one healthy woman in her eighties expressed, "I took care of my grandchildren while my daughters worked, and now I am helping take care of my great-grandchildren, but I am tired. It's too much now."

Yet there are few descriptive data about older grandchildren and very elderly grandparents, about what the relationship is like from the perspectives of people in these relationships. Historian Norma Field, whose mother was brought up in Japan, offers a sole example. Field's Japanese grandmother is bedridden due to a stroke, barely able to speak, and receiving nutrition through a feeding tube inserted into her nose. Field describes the situation:

> My mother puts on a tape of my daughter [the old woman's
> great-granddaughter] playing Mozart's Andante in C for Flute. It's
> a young girl's playing, faltering and yet charming. My grandmother
> listens avidly, as if she were posing for a statue of Woman Listen-
> ing to Music. When it is over, I ask if she remembers her great-
> granddaughter. She nods, yes. Does she like listening to this tape?
>
> —I love it.
>
> With her eyes, she searches the room for the girl who shares her
> name. (1997, 44–45)

The lack of attention to this phenomenon of very elderly grandparents may be because it is so new. It also may be due to the stigma of being very old, so that the topic seems less significant than other social issues. As Brenda Robb Jenike points out, "The current generation of the oldest-old in Japan is the first cohort to experience an extended period of not only grandparenthood . . . but also great-grandparenthood. Japanese culture and societal expectations for the elderly have not, however, caught up with the realities of this extended longevity" (2004, 217–218). Jenike claims that this new life stage is viewed negatively in part because it has no definition; there is no existing social role applicable to the new demographic situation. This negativity helps to explain the loneliness that many older people feel, their sense of being a burden on their families and on society. Today's grandparents acknowledge a twenty-first-century principle of non-interference with parenting but must find ways to juggle expectations of sometimes contradictory grandparental roles of past and present (Thang et al. 2011). We can hypothesize that as they do so, the current cohort of very old people is helping to create the new cultural expectations of being very old, including what it means to be a great-grandparent and to know their grandchildren as adults. Because there are not yet definable roles or established expectations of twenty-first-century grandparenthood, I thought it would be especially interesting to see what the interview respondents had to say about the meaning of grandchildren and great-grandchildren for them, as a reflection of their past and also of Japan's future.

The Meanings of Grandchildren to Elderly Japanese Today

In our research project, my colleagues and I met people with a variety of relationships with their grandchildren. There were active grandparents who helped care for younger grandchildren and lonely old people who craved meaningful ties with their son's or daughter's young adult children. Others appeared to be fulfilled old people who did have such bonds, elderly great-grandparents glowing with pride in the continuing families they had helped to create, captured in the extended family photographs that appeared in frames on bookshelves or hanging on the wall or (in one case) on a personalized calendar. The grandparents' economic situations varied as well. One family owned a successful business in central Tokyo; another caregiving couple were university-educated artists. In contrast, several elderly couples lived in city-subsidized housing and expressed concerns about personal finances. Most had themselves or through co-residence with their children achieved a lifestyle that would be considered middle class in Japan. At least in our small sample, their relative affluence did not predict the nature of the relationship these elderly people had with their grandchildren. Nor did the geographical and social divide between Tokyo and the more rural Akita samples result in a patterned difference in the meanings of these relationships.

Out of the thirty families we interviewed, nearly all of the older people had grandchildren and/or step-grandchildren. Nine households included a co-residing grandchild (five out of fifteen in Tokyo and four out of fifteen in Akita) at the time of the first interview. Of the nine, one household had two grandchildren, and two (one each in Tokyo and Akita) had a married grandchild who had a child, meaning that the elderly person we interviewed lived in a four-generation household with a co-residing great-grandchild. However, these cases do not all indicate family continuity over the generations as in the early twentieth-century stem family model. In our interviews, we did hear of that intent, particularly in the Akita farm families and in the case of the Tokyo family with a great-grandchild (the family owned a successful business as well as additional land in the vicinity). In other families, however, the grandchildren were young adults who had not yet married and were still living with their parents. In fact, over the course of the project, we heard of their departures from the household for overseas volunteer service, for marriage, and for work (cf. White 2002, 154–163).

In Japanese, a single term, *mago,* is the term for grandchild, regardless of whether the person is male or female or whether the relationship is through a son or daughter, an elder or a younger child.[5] Some of the older people did appear to hold the assumption of the older stem family system that the "inside grandchildren," or the children of the heir to the household, had a different relationship to the grandparents than the "outside grandchildren," who were part of other households. Yet I did not hear these terms used, and although the grandparents sometimes distinguished whose child they were talking about (for example, "my older son's children" or "my second daughter's son") as a way of identifying them, the main way that distinction appeared to impact their relationship with the grandchildren was in the question of co-residence. Yet some cases of co-residence were based on relationships other than eldest son inheritance, such as the families in which the old person was living with a younger daughter or a third son. Bonds with daughters' children were expected even in the stem family system. For example, a new mother was expected to return to live in her parents' household for weeks or months at the time of the birth. This practice continues, if not in the daughter coming home, then in her mother going to her home to assist her with the new baby and older children, providing some opportunity for early bonding with grandchildren through daughters, even if they were considered to have married into another household.

Grandchildren as Sources of Assistance in Old Age

In rare cases, grandchildren in the families we interviewed provided direct assistance in caregiving. A co-residing adult grandson sometimes helped with the physical labor, such as helping to turn his bedridden grandmother. In another family, a young adult granddaughter who was a nurse used her skills to help her mother care for her grandmother with Parkinson's and sometimes took her to doctor's appointments and offered advice. Another woman's grandson had recently become a certified care worker and offered occasional assistance and advice. In one family, the daughter-in-law caregiver had fallen and had difficulty helping the cognitively impaired mother-in-law, so the ninety-four-year-old was moved to the nearby granddaughter's apartment, where she shared a room with her twenty-four-year-old great-grandson. He was apparently a sound sleeper who managed to sleep through his great-grandmother's attempts to find the toilet at night, making things more difficult for his mother (the granddaughter) in the morning.

Interaction across Generations: Long-Term Relationships versus Sporadic Encounters

A few of the people we interviewed had no contact at all with their grandchildren. Others were intimately involved in their lives. Both of these extremes, however, were rare. At one extreme, grandparents with severe cognitive impairment might not be able to remember anything about their grandchildren:

INTERVIEWER: How many grandchildren do you have?
NINETY-SIX-YEAR-OLD WOMAN: Grandchildren? I wonder how many of
them there are. . .

Some saw their grandchildren rarely and then only for holidays or special occasions. Some of the older people complained, or related with apparent disappointment, that the grandchildren came only at obligatory times, formal occasions such as the summer Obon holiday or New Year's, expecting the traditional gift of an envelope of cash. One used the phrase *kao o dashita* (showed their face) to indicate the perceived perfunctory nature of a summer visit. The extent of visiting might vary, however, even among grandchildren in the same family. In one family in which a daughter-in-law was caring for her mother-in-law, the unmarried younger grandson of the ninety-three-year-old came frequently. But the older grandson, who had children of his own, rarely came.

In other families, there was more regular interaction with grandchildren not living in the same house. Some out-of-town grandchildren spent part of their summer vacation in a parent's hometown with the grandparents. Others visited regularly, such as in the family where the granddaughters who did not live in the household frequently visited on Sundays, taking their eighty-eight-year-old grandmother with Alzheimer's disease out for a while. The co-residing daughter-in-law commented, "The nieces come often on Sundays and other occasions. Grandma enjoys being with family, even if she doesn't remember. They take her out for a walk or for tea." Several grandchildren we met or heard about in other families made regular (weekly or monthly) visits to grandmothers in a group home or in a rehabilitation hospital.

Grandparents who lived with their grandchildren or whose relationships were particularly close knew about the grandchildren's lives in detail. In one interview, the eighty-seven-year-old woman showed us a baby *yukata* (cotton kimono) she had hand-sewn for her new great-grandchild. The following year, she and her son were talking about the family and its newest member, his sister's grandson. He began describing the trip in which his sister and her family had included their mother: "[My sister] thought it would be a good change for her. . . . Last year [my other sister] with the grandkids and great-grandkids (now ages five and two) went on a trip. The youngest is the one she was making the *yukata* for last year. His birthday is April 19. She always remembers when the kids were born. She knows the birthdates and years of all of her children, four grandchildren, and two great-grandchildren."

Although there was a lot of variation in the frequency of contact between grandparents and grandchildren, that frequency alone did not determine the nature of the relationship. In one three-generational residence (though the older generation and their son and family lived on separate floors of the house), the grandmother complained, "I told my daughter-in-law that she could trade in my old sewing machine and buy a new one so she could work at home, but the type she uses is expensive. It's good if the mother is home when the children are still small. So [because she is not home with them] I call out [the traditional greetings] to the children when they leave the house to go to school in the morning and when they come home from school."

Later in the interview:

INTERVIEWER: Do the grandchildren come in often?
GRANDMOTHER: Oh, they do. We fight, too. They don't listen to me anymore . . .
INTERVIEWER: What gives you pleasure these days?
GRANDMOTHER: I used to sew and knit, but not any more. I have nothing useful I can do. I used to help with the newsletter at the Women's Association [Fujinkai] and travel a lot. But now, I guess I would say it's my grandkids. . . . Sometimes their grandfather goes upstairs to where they live and plays Go with the grandkids.

In this case, frequent contact led to the grandmother's ambivalence about her relationship with her grandchildren. They did not listen to her, but they were a source of pleasure as her ability to do other things she had formerly enjoyed declined.

On the other hand, there were cases of good relationships even when children and grandchildren did not live nearby, and perhaps when they saw less of each other there was less to complain about (Ruth Campbell, personal communication). For example, a daughter-in-law observed, "Our two daughters come and visit but don't help with caregiving tasks. One lives nearby; the other is in Sendai. The one is working, so not available much. There are five grandchildren [the mother-in-law's great-grandchildren] from their house, and the sister has three grandchildren. That's who's in the big group photo hanging on the wall."

When we asked what the mother-in-law found pleasurable, the daughter-in-law replied, "She waits for people to come, her daughter or the grandkids." At an interview two years later, we noticed a newer photograph on a wall calendar, with the older woman sitting in her wheelchair in the center of a large family, including three great-grandchildren. The daughter-in-law explained that it was taken at her birthday dinner. There were huge trays of sushi and a birthday cake for her as well. She died the next year. All of the children and grandchildren had been to the hospital to see her, where she told them just before she died, "*Minna nakayoku yatte kureta, naa* [You've all gotten along so well (for me)]."

Frequent interaction may make possible a strong positive relationship or be the basis for intensified criticism of grandchildren. Those who interacted primarily in formal, obligatory holiday visits had more distant relationships. Even the traditional grandparental indulgence of the holiday envelope of money gave little satisfaction when the grandparent felt that had been the reason for the visit. In contrast, having contributed to their care as young children, sharing the experience of traveling together, having them come for summer vacations, or visiting informally—these active engagements seemed to create bonds that were closer and more meaningful to the grandparents in their advanced old age.

Grandchildren as Reminders of a Generation Gap

One of the meanings of grandchildren that arose spontaneously in interviews was the sense that grandchildren were different from the grandparents. Generations diverged in the ways they thought and lived as a result of experiencing different conditions and historical events. To some of the old people we interviewed, grandchildren represented a younger group of Japanese whose lifestyles and values were what the grandparents were *not*. One grandmother whose teenage granddaughter lived nearby had grown up during the depression and the long years of Japanese military involvement in Asia and the Pacific. She commented on her granddaughter's requests for money: "Girls these days are into being stylish. Our granddaughter wants a lot of material things." A woman in her nineties expressed gratitude for care by her daughter, son, and daughter-in-law: "They are all good children, and that's something to be thankful for. Children these days are not like this. There are a lot of bad kids. I've had hard times but also have much to be thankful for. My daughter-in-law is a big help, but not the grandkids."

Another woman expressed her sense of difference at a more personal level. She had been widowed in middle age and continued to live alone in her own house for many years. When she became older, her son and family felt it would be better to combine their households before there was a crisis. Her grandchildren were teenagers when they moved in together. She remembers that when they had breakfast together, the grandchildren would finish quickly so they could be off to school. "So I'd be there eating slowly by myself. When I was [living] alone, I only needed to think about myself and do things at my own pace." Over the course of our interviews, including those with this woman, we often heard complaints or observations about generational differences in food tastes, in choices of television shows, and in ideas about free time. It seems that even when relationships with their grandchildren were good, that gap was felt by the oldest generation and sometimes by the women in the middle generation, who had a hard time cooking meals that made everyone happy. The grandchildren served as a reminder to their grandparents that the world had changed around them.

Emotional Bonds

For many of the elderly people with whom we spoke, grandchildren and great-grandchildren were a great source of pleasure and, conversely, a source of worry. Grandparents expressed pride in their grandchildren's accomplishments and sometimes in their mere existence. A few felt strongly supported through the emotional ties they had with grandchildren. The lack of such bonds was a source of disappointment and loneliness to others.

During a follow-up interview that took place at a nursing home, we asked a mentally alert older woman about her family. She had two children, a son who was her primary caregiver and a daughter living a distance away but still within the greater Tokyo area. The interviewer asked, "Does your daughter come to see you here?" She replied, "They haven't told her I'm here." The son, with whom she had been living and who was present during the interview, explained, "We haven't had any contact with her for years." The interviewer continued, "How many grandchildren do you have?" The question was met with silence.

However, even when there was little contact, grandchildren were a source of worry and pride. One example is an elderly rural couple who complained that their grandchildren rarely came and only put in appearances at holidays. Nonetheless, they were pleased that their two grandsons had graduated from college and worried about one who had apparently not passed the national civil service exam he had taken. They proudly took out pictures to show us of a granddaughter, taken at the entrance ceremony to the police academy, where she had recently been accepted. When at one point they had needed a facility for respite care, the couple thought about the nursing home where another granddaughter worked, but their son was concerned about possible conflicts and gossip in their small city and asked his parents to choose another place. The elderly man expressed a wish that he would see the family more. The old couple could depend on their children when they needed instrumental help, but the grandchildren rarely came. I jotted down in my fieldnotes, "They seem lonely, separately."

Another elderly couple told us of their concerns for their teenage granddaughter. She had experienced a difficult life due to domestic violence, her father's death, and her mother's difficult economic circumstances. The grand-daughter was not doing well in school, and the grandparents continued to try to encourage her as they feared for her future.

In stark contrast were the grandparents whose grandchildren brought them great joy, even at a distance. One woman exclaimed, "I'm thankful I'm well taken care of." She said over and over in each interview how grateful she was for those who cared for her. At one point the interviewer asked her, "Is there anything you are not thankful for?" She responded, "Nothing. I'm happy if someone comes, especially the grandchildren [who] are so cute *[mago wa kawaii]!*"

In another situation in which an elderly woman had few physical limitations but moderate dementia, we asked her what made her happy. She replied, "I like day care. The best part is talking with friends there." The daughter-in-law expounded, "But she tells the grandkids that she likes to stay at home, so she's not consistent." In the past, the family had frequently traveled together so that grandparents and grandchildren felt a bond. Now that she was older, she no longer wanted to travel, but her grandchildren made time to be with her. The daughter-in-law described, "The oldest [grandson] lives separately but is not married. He comes about once a month. The other two [grandson and granddaughter] live here. They all go out to dinner together about once a month. The boys each take one of Grandma's arms and walk her, so she likes to go out with them."

Another grandmother told us of her poor relationship with her caregiving husband (Long 2011). In talking about what gave her pleasure, she spoke of how she loved musicals and reported that her daughter occasionally took her out to see them even after she had her strokes. She mentioned how much she enjoyed going to day care. But what seemed to give her the most pleasure was having her young grandchildren, two young sons of her daughter, come over. She was severely disabled and spent much of her day in bed when at home, but the boys would get into bed and play with her, and the physical contact with them was a main source of pleasure in her life. They asked her how she was feeling, she told us, and wondered when she would get better. Her pleasure may have been magnified by the fact that the grandchildren did not have a close relationship with her husband, who said in a separate interview, "The grandkids are everything to her. I can't do anything with them, except give them a little spending money *[okozukai]* now and then." He expressed that he did not like being with old people and clearly wished to deny his own aging. To him, the grandchildren may have represented what he could no longer be. He also saw close family ties as related to gendered kinship roles, of which he wanted no part.

In one family, the grandmother and granddaughter had especially close ties. They knew each other well and, according to the family, had much in common; for example, they all agreed that both were strong-willed. The grandmother and mother had each been widowed early. The granddaughter had spent summer vacations with her grandmother in her home in the countryside, playing with her grandmother at the beach, getting to know her cousins, and had even brought a friend when she was in high school. Like her grandmother, the granddaughter decided to become a nurse, discussing her career plans with her grandmother before enrolling. When the grandmother could no longer manage on her own in the countryside and moved in with her daughter, the granddaughter was still living at home. As mentioned above, she used her nursing skills to assist her mother in her grandmother's care until she moved out at age thirty to get married. Even after that, she continued to visit her grandmother at least once a month. When we asked the grandmother in an interview what had been the best time in her life, she answered, "When my granddaughter was born."

The grandmother had grandchildren through her other daughter as well, and although they lived further away, she saw them and actively kept up with their lives.

She told us that her sixth great-grandchild was about to be born. We also learned from a photograph that the previous winter her two daughters had taken her to Hawaii (with her wheelchair) to visit the older daughter's youngest child, who was married to an American. The worst thing for her, she expressed, was that her husband was not here to see all of the healthy grandchildren. Right after her husband died [she was a young mother at the time] was the saddest time in her life, but now she was happy. "I am happiest when the family is together and laughing." In July, her day-care center celebrated the Tanabata (Star Festival) holiday by having all of the participants write a wish to hang on the specially erected tree in the nursing home. She had written, "*Mago no egao o kansha shite iru.*" (I'm grateful for my grandchildren's happy faces.)

Conclusion

Since the middle of the twentieth century, Japan has undergone dramatic demographic, economic, and cultural changes that have altered the way that people live and the way that they perceive their world and their selves. One of these changes is the creation of a new demographic category, the large numbers of old-old people who have witnessed these changes firsthand. This chapter has asked about the meaning of grandchildren for twenty-first-century elders, whose collective lives are helping to create the new culture of mass longevity (Plath 1980).

With limited data, I have tried to understand their experiences and perceptions of their current lives. Most of the literature on the families of old people has focused on their relations with their children and daughters-in-law, particularly from the younger generation's perspective of the burdens of financial and bodily support. Few have asked about the family from the perspective of the old people themselves. How do relationships with not only children but also with grandchildren contribute to their lives and to what it means to them to be old? Will the increasing social class cleavages of the twenty-first century result in different types of relationships among grandparents and grandchildren in the future?

I suggest that regardless of physical proximity, grandchildren play important roles. Sometimes they can be sources of secondary assistance and support. They cannot be counted upon, but they can potentially help. Grandchildren also contribute to an understanding of who old people are in this brave new world, reminding them of historical and generational changes that have accompanied their own aging. When past relationships, based on helping with child care, shared activities, or other ways of spending active time together, led to close feelings between the generations, grandchildren could also provide a bridge between their grandparents' past and the changing twenty-first-century world. Emotional bonds of love, mutual concern, and pride helped some grandparents continue to have a sense of worth in a society that too often treats them as having outlived their usefulness. We can only imagine what having survived nine days together in the rubble after the earthquake might mean to the grandparent-grandchild relationship of Mrs. Abe and her grandson Jin.

Notes

I am grateful to the families who participated in the longitudinal study of family caregiving under the Japanese public long-term care insurance system instituted in 2000. My work on this project would not have been possible without the leadership of project directors Suda Yūko and Takahashi Ryūtarō and qualitative team members Asakawa Noriko, Asano Yūko, Ruth Campbell, Izumo Yūji, Kodama Hiroko, Muraoka Kōko, Nishida Masumi, Nishimura Chie, and Yamada Yoshiko. Financial support for data collection came from the Japanese Ministry of Education and Science and the Ministry of Health, Labor, and Welfare. Additional funding for data analysis came from the Univers Foundation and John Carroll University. Ruth Campbell and Satsuki Kawano provided helpful feedback on earlier drafts of this chapter.

1. Experts on aging often distinguish between the "young old" and the "old old," but use different ages for the cutoff age between the two groups, ranging from seventy-five to eighty to eighty-five. By using the term "very old" here, I am referring to the advanced age of the people I discuss in this chapter, who were in their late seventies to mid-nineties, while I avoid the technical debate on the definition of "old old."

2. An interdisciplinary research team conducted a series of interviews with thirty elderly people in need of assistance in daily living, along with their family care-givers, as part of a larger study of the public long-term care insurance program that began in 2000. The person in need of care qualified for the program but may or may not have been using its services. In all but one of the families, the main family caregiver was residing in the same household as the elderly person. Our interview sample was chosen to reflect a variety of caregiver–care recipient relationships, including spouses, daughters-in-law, sons, and daughters.

3. The variations in responses in this study were additionally influenced by the gender of the grandchild, the age of the grandchild, whether the generations lived together, the frequency of grandchild care by the grandparent, and the amount of time spent together.

4. Anthropological work on changing Japanese families in the early twenty-first century includes Coulmas (2007), Kumagai (2008), Ochiai (1997), Rebick and Takenaka (2006), and Ronald and Alexy (2011). Changing ideas about old age and the lives of old people are specifically addressed in Izuhara (2006) and Platz (2011).

5. This is one indication that in anthropological terms Japanese kinship is basically bilateral, although patrilineal overlays due to influences from China have also been important. The form of Japanese families has changed greatly over time. The patrilineal stem family model discussed above in this chapter is specific to the last part of the nineteenth and first half of the twentieth centuries, although it had precursors in certain places and social classes earlier.

References Cited

Ando, Kiwamu. 2005. "Grandparenthood: Crossroads between Gender and Aging." *International Journal of Japanese Sociology* 14:32–51.

Benedict, Ruth. 1946. *The Chrysanthemum and the Sword: Patterns of Japanese Culture.* Boston: Houghton Mifflin.

Campbell, Ruth, and Elaine M. Brody. 1985. "Women's Changing Roles and Help to the Elderly." *Gerontologist* 25, no. 6:584–592.

Coulmas, Florian. 2007. *Population Decline and Ageing in Japan: The Social Consequences.* London: Routledge.

Field, Norma. 1997. *From my Grandmother's Bedside: Sketches of Postwar Tokyo.* Berkeley: University of California Press.

Izuhara, Misa. 2006. "Changing Families and Policy Responses to an Aging Japanese

Society." In *The Changing Japanese Family,* ed. Marcus Rebick and Ayumi Takenaka, 161–176. London: Routledge.

Jenike, Brenda Robb. 2004. "Alone in the Family: Great-Grandparenthood in Urban Japan." In *Filial Piety: Practice and Discourse in Contemporary East Asia,* ed. Charlotte Ikels, 217–244. Stanford, CA: Stanford University Press.

Johnston, Christopher. 2011. "Japan's Most Famous Survivor Returns Home in Search for Missing." *Toronto Star,* April 29. Www.thestar.com/news/world/article/ 982838—japan-s-most-famous-survivor-returns-home-in-search-for-missing.

Kumagai, Fumie. 2008. *Families in Japan: Changes, Continuities, and Regional Variations.* Lanham, MD: University Press of America.

Lebra, Takie S. 1984. *Japanese Women: Constraint and Fulfillment.* Honolulu: University of Hawai'i Press.

Long, Susan Orpett. 2011. "Tension, Dependency, and Sacrifice in the Relationship of an Elderly Couple." In *Faces of Aging: The Lived Experiences of the Elderly in Japan,* ed. Yoshiko Matsumoto, 60–86. Stanford, CA: Stanford University Press.

Ochiai, Emiko. 1997. *The Japanese Family System in Transition: A Sociological Analysis of Family Change in Postwar Japan.* Tokyo: LTCB International Library Foundation.

Plath, David. 1980. *Long Engagements: Maturity in Modern Japan.* Stanford, CA: Stanford University Press.

Platz, Anemone. 2011. "Living Apart Together: Anticipated Home, Family and Social Networks in Old Age." In Ronald and Alexy, *Home and Family in Japan,* 254–269.

Rebick, Marcus, and Ayumi Takenaka, eds. 2006. *The Changing Japanese Family.* London: Routledge.

Ronald, Richard, and Allison Alexy, eds. 2011. *Home and Family in Japan: Continuity and Transformation.* London: Routledge.

Saito, Yoshitaka, and Tomoyuki Yasuda. 2009. "An Empirical Study of the Frequency of Intergenerational Contacts of Family Members in Japan." *Journal of Intergenerational Relationships* 7:118–133.

Smith, Robert J., and Ella Lury Wiswell. 1982. *The Women of Suye Mura.* Chicago: University of Chicago Press.

Strom, Robert, Shirley Strom, Pat Collinsworth, Saburo Sato, Katsuko Makino, Yasuyuki Sasaki, Hiroki Sasaki, and Norihiro Nishio. 1996. "Intergenerational Relationship in Japanese Families." *International Journal of Sociology of the Family* 26, no. 2:1–15.

Takagi, Emiko, Merril Silverstein, and Eileen Crimmins. 2007. "Intergenerational Coresidence of Older Adults in Japan: Conditions for Cultural Plasticity." *Journal of Gerontology: Social Sciences* 62, no. 5:S330–339.

Thang, Leng Leng. 2008. "Engaging the Generations: Age-Integrated Facilities." In *The Demographic Challenge: A Handbook about Japan,* ed. Florian Coulmas, Harald Conrad, Annette Schad-Seifert, and Gabriele Vogt, 179–200. Leiden: Brill.

Thang, Leng Leng, Kalyani Mehta, Tsuneo Usui, and Mari Tsuruwaka. 2011. "Being a Good Grandparent: Roles and Expectations in Intergenerational Relationships in Japan and Singapore." *Marriage and Family Review* 47, no. 8:548–570.

Vogel, Ezra. 1963. *Japan's New Middle Class.* 2nd ed. Berkeley: University of California Press.

White, Merry Isaacs. 2002. *Perfectly Japanese: Making Families in an Era of Upheaval.* Berkeley: University of California Press.

CHAPTER 8

Barrier-Free Brothels

Sex Volunteers, Prostitutes, and People with Disabilities

KAREN NAKAMURA

IN 2004, JOURNALIST Kawai Kaori shocked Japan by writing *Sex Volunteers,* a book that chronicled how people with disabilities were being sexually "serviced" by the eponymous sex volunteers for lack of romantic/sexual partners. This sparked a national conversation on the intersectionality of disability and sexuality—and a flurry of books with scandalous titles such as *"I Was a Sex Worker for People with Disabilities."* Feeding into this moral panic were deeper concerns over disability and the family, democracy and social responsibility, and the future of the national health-care system. Various elements within disability communities used this opportunity to push a more sex-progressive agenda— promoting internal conversations, for example, about the appropriateness of using state-provided personal care assistants to take members to "soapland" brothels (see below). The sum of these developments has allowed for new discourses on marginality and inclusion to emerge in the lost decades of the *début de siècle.*

Introduction

One of the subplots in Alejandro González Iñárritu's (2006) Oscar-award-winning film *Babel* involves a Japanese deaf teenager, Wataya Chieko, played by hearing actress Kikuchi Rinko. Emotionally traumatized by her mother's suicide, Chieko has a difficult relationship with her father and is struggling with her growing sexual needs and frustrations. When a police detective comes into her life, she finds herself sexually attracted to him. In one of the critical scenes in the film, Chieko invites the detective into her family home, steps out for a moment, and then returns stark naked.

This scene invokes many of the intersectionalities of sexuality and disability in a dark Japan. Some of the motifs are common to early twenty-first-century Japan, such as the growing gulf between generations and the moral panics over schoolgirl sexuality and values (Leheny 2006; Miller 2004; Ueno 2003). The skill of Iñárritu's directing, however, is that he adds the additional layer of Chieko's deafness. Able to communicate easily only through sign language with another deaf girl, Chieko is cut off linguistically and emotionally from the rest of the world, which floats by as she gazes at it through her father's car window.

Chieko's segment hinges on her deafness. Most viewers (as well as the fictional detective) would not have experienced the same shock value if Chieko had been hearing. The motif of gulfs of communication and desire woven into her story would not have been expressible the same way if Chieko were able to talk with her father, the detective, or the hearing boys her own age whom she found attractive. There are some reverberations within the intersection of sexuality and disability in Heisei Japan that make such a scene powerful.

Even as we enter fully into the twenty-first century, the notion that people with disabilities can have sexuality and sexual needs still seems far from our minds. American documentary films such as *Murderball* (Rubin and Shapiro 2005), which involves young male athletes who become paralyzed—and then remain their former sex-starved, misogynistic jocks while in wheelchairs—are designed to shock and surprise us with the incongruity. More recently, the Academy Award–nominated film *The Sessions* (Lewin 2012) chronicles the true-life story of a man with polio who hires a "sexual surrogate" to lose his virginity. This shock over the notion that people with disabilities might have sexual needs is not just restricted to the West. In this chapter, I will explore how the development of various services in Japan for people with disabilities, such as sex volunteers, sex helpers, and barrier-free brothels, have challenged the idea of people with disabilities as sexually unaware and caused critical conversations about disability and sexuality.

Fight! Takeda Mayumi's Story

In 2001, a twenty-nine-year-old Japanese deaf woman named Takeda Mayumi wrote a short autobiography named *Fight!* The similarities between Mayumi and the fictional Chieko in *Babel* are quite striking. The very real Takeda Mayumi was born on May 27, 1970, in Tokyo. When she was just three years old, she apparently had a high fever and lost her hearing as a result. She learned how to speechread and speak and went to a public elementary school as a mainstreamed student (cf. Nakamura 2006). When she graduated from high school in 1989, she went to a four-year technical college to learn fashion design.

After Mayumi graduated, she started work at a major advertising company but had dreams of going to New York to pursue her fashion design career. In order to do that, she needed to save up some money—more money than her office job would provide. She quit and became a *fūzokujō*, a girl in the sex trade. *Fight!* chronicles her journey through the Japanese sex trade industry, where she became (in her own words) an "extremely popular, idol *fūzokujō*" nicknamed Hyō-chan ("Miss Leopard"). Using the money earned from her customers, Mayumi traveled to New York, where she hooked up with an African American man and gave birth to a daughter. At one level, *Fight!* was a rather simple autobiography, but it had the right mixture of female sexuality, race relations, and disability to catch the imagination of the Japanese public.

At this point, I need to turn briefly to a tangential discussion of prostitution in Japan because without our understanding its quasi-legal nature under Japanese law it will be very difficult to understand the intersectionality of the sex trade and disability.

Prostitution

Prostitution in contemporary Japan is technically illegal, but there are rarely any arrests of prostitutes or their clients (except in the case of underage solicitation). If one goes to a police officer in the red-light district of any major city and asks him where a particular "health center" is by name, he will give directions, even perhaps show a map with the names of all the various brothels marked on it. Touts in the red-light districts openly solicit passers-by with photos of the girls, and neon signs advertise services provided. It's not quite as open as Amsterdam, where the women solicit themselves in windows, but it is fairly close.

In prewar Japan, many forms of voluntary and involuntary sex work were not only legal but also fell into the domain of government promotion and regulation. Soon after the military defeat in August 1945, the Japanese government helped establish the Recreation and Amusement Association (RAA), a system of brothels for the use of American occupation forces (Sanders 2005). The Allied General Headquarters (GHQ) did not express concern over the RAA brothels until the number of prostitutes with sexually transmitted diseases (STDs) rose to unacceptable levels, threatening the fighting readiness of the American forces (Fujime 2006). As a result, the government system of licensed sex work was formally abolished by GHQ decree in January 1946. The decree, however, did not criminalize acts of prostitution where "individuals acted 'of their own free will and accord'" (Kovner 2012, 30). As to why prostitution itself was not abolished in the same decree, the chief of intelligence for the Allied forces, Charles Willoughby, noted at the time that "public sentiment in general [in Japan] is non-committal or in favor of prostitution" (Kovner 2012, 36).

Part of this neutral or slightly positive attitude toward prostitution in Japan is due to a lack of any deep history of moral crusades against it. Neither the Shinto religion nor Buddhism as practiced in Japan have specific proscriptions against prostitution. There were never any laws against prostitution before the twentieth century, although registered prostitution was often restricted to certain "red line" *(akasen)* districts (Iwanaga 2009).

In 1956, four years after the Occupation ended, the Japanese government passed the Anti-Prostitution Law *(Baishun Bōshi Hō)*. Public (and political) sentiment apparently had not changed, as there was not much enthusiasm behind the passing of this law, with the result that one gaping loophole remained: prostitution was narrowly defined in terms of payment for the act of coitus. Thus any sexual act that did not involve an actual penis engaged inside an actual vagina and the simultaneous transaction of money was by definition *not* prostitution. Another loophole was that the 1956 law never stipulated any sort of punishment for the act of prostitution itself, only for the crimes of establishing a brothel and solicitation.

The market quickly responded to the new regulatory environment. Patrons were no longer promised vaginal sex but instead were offered a wide variety of other options: manual stimulation, oral sex, intercrural sex, anal sex, sadomasochism (S&M), role playing, and anything else imaginable (cf. Sinclair 2006). Businesses that provided these services were licensed and regulated by the government as "businesses that affect public morals and practices" *(fūzoku eigyō or fūzokuten)*.

Of course, it would be naïve to assume that coital sex does not ever happen in the establishments. But as anything beyond the standard menu items on the price list is technically a private matter between the sex workers and their clients, soapland operators and their staff are generally shielded from police prosecution.

In the late 1950s, steam saunas, where the female staff would wash down patrons' bodies in private sauna rooms and perform some other services, became popular. The first of these businesses, Toruko Yoshiwara (the Turkish Yoshiwara),[1] opened in the former red-light district of Tokyo in July 1958 (Iwanaga 2009, 108). Other steam saunas opened and identified themselves, as the first one had, as "Turkish baths" *(toruko buro)*. They offered a bath + washdown + nominally non-vaginal sex combination, which became one of the predominant postwar forms of prostitution in Japan. "Turkish baths" became so popular, in fact, that in 1985 there was an aggressive lobbying campaign by the Turkish government to change their appellation in Japan. The new label that was chosen by popular vote was "soapland"—a moniker that remains to this day.

Another type of brothel is the so-called fashion health club. The rooms at the fashion health clubs do not have any bathtub or shower, just a bed, but the same types of (nominally) non-coital sexual services are offered. One variation on the fashion health club is *delivery health,* whereby the women will travel to hotels or homes to perform (again nominally non-coital) sexual acts.

According to Japan's National Police Agency, which regulates and monitors these businesses, in 2010 there were 1,238 soaplands, 836 fashion health clubs, 139 strip joints, 3,692 love hotels, and 303 sex item shops licensed and operating in the country. In addition, there were 15,889 delivery health clubs, almost double the number just four years before. In all of 2010, there were only 4 arrests for managed prostitution (i.e., prostitution in a managed establishment such as a soapland), 246 arrests for streetwalking, and 35 arrests for delivery health services (NPA 2011, 100). Including the crimes of solicitation and providing a place of prostitution, there were 727 arrests for sex work in all of Japan. In comparison, there were 62,688 arrests for prostitution in the United States in 2010, according to FBI data (FBI 2010, table 29).

Although the Japanese National Police Agency report does not break down the statistics by gender, the vast majority of these services were undoubtedly provided by females for male clients. There exist only a very small number of "host clubs," which provide male companionship for women (Takeyama 2005).[2] Host clubs are the male version of the hostess clubs, in which titillating conversation is the main commodity sold on-site; but it is common knowledge that one can take the hosts and hostesses out on dates, with more intimate services provided individually by agreement (Allison 1994; Longinotto et al. 1996; Takeyama 2005).

There was apparently one and only one "soapland for women," which opened in Fukuoka City in February 2007. There, women could purchase a nice bath and sexual services from *ikemen* (good-looking) soapboys. Rates apparently started at ¥30,000 ($300) for ninety minutes—a rare case of economic gender equity. According to a newspaper article, the soapboys described the work as "living hell" because of the emotional and physical needs of the clients. Not surprisingly, though, the club shut down in October, after only eight months in business (RealLive 2007).

Barrier-Free Brothels

The situation for men with disabilities is better than it is for either able-bodied or disabled women who want sexual satisfaction. There are several health clubs and delivery health clubs that specifically target people with disabilities, and they openly advertise their services on the Internet.[3] For example, one "barrier-free delivery health club," La Mer, has a price list on its Web site for a basic course for beginners that includes "hand service" and "lotion service" for sixty or ninety minutes (around $150 and $230 respectively). For a bit more money, there is a special course that includes "all nude; soft-touch; six-nine; kissing; and raw fellatio," with paid options for "lotion play; bare skin; vibrator play; ejaculation in the mouth; and holy water."[4] These prices seem approximately in line with those of regular health clubs, but many people with disabilities in Japan are on social welfare and might have difficulty paying regularly for these services.

Accessible health clubs that I found on the Web include the following: the aforementioned La Mer in Kumamoto City, Tokimeki in Hiroshima, and Delikea in Okayama. Judging from the Web sites, all focus only on providing female services to male clients. There is no mention of male providers to female clients with disabilities or of any gay or lesbian services. Furthermore, all three are in small, regional cities and not in central Tokyo or Osaka. One theory is that perhaps they are located in areas where the police or foreign media will not bring too much attention to them. I think a more convincing argument is that residents of Tokyo and Osaka are more able to request that their personal care attendants take them to regular soaplands and health clubs or that they use regular delivery health services in their own homes or hotels.

FIGURE 8.1

La Mer Web site price list

In 2005, Ōmori Miyuki published a tell-all book titled *I Was a Health Delivery Girl for People with Disabilities*. This was a best-selling biography that chronicled the author's own experiences in the trade. Ōmori had worked in the regular sex trade (soaplands) when she came across an article by the founders of a call-girl service that specialized in people with disabilities that explained why they had created their company. Ōmori's reaction was as follows:

> The article read something like this: "Like the need for food and sleep, everyone has sexual needs but for people with disabilities the reality is that the last item is seen as taboo. Because of this, there are numerous problems in the world of home-helpers [i.e., personal care attendants and home health-care workers] such as clients who touch the breasts or buttocks of the helpers, hug them, or talk incessantly about sexual topics. We created this organization for these types of customers."
>
> At the time that I read this, I thought that my six months of

experience at a brothel [*fūzokuten*] in Tokyo might actually be able to be put to use helping other people. It was perhaps at this point that I decided to work there.

But to be honest, there was another reason why I was attracted to the notion of [catering to] only people with disabilities and that ultimately led to my making up my mind. With able-bodied people, there is always the danger of them using physical force to coerce you to go all the way raw (i.e., without using a condom or other prophylactic). Not only that, but sometimes it even leads to murder. In reality there have been several cases of delivery-health girls that have been killed at hotels.

But in the case of people with disabilities, although there might be some variation, I thought that there was a lower possibility of a person with disabilities violating me by force. In my calculations, I thought that it would be easier for me to run away [from the client] in the event of something happening.

There was another reason why I chose the health delivery industry even though my previous experience in soaplands had been that I didn't have the confidence to get people off unless they penetrated me. I had been hesitant to go into health delivery for able-bodied people for that reason. But I had this feeling that customers with disabilities, in comparison, weren't that experienced with women, so perhaps someone like me, who didn't have really good technique, might still be able to get customers off with just my mouth and hands. That I would be useful to other people [*yaku ni tatsu*] was the second reason, to be honest with you. The primary reasons were that the hourly pay was good and there was less danger of being violated. Although I had never studied nursing care or social welfare—or even expressed any interest in those topics previously or had any occasion to be concerned with them—there was the possibility that I would be able to do something that a normal home-helper couldn't. The thought that I could do something that was of use to others was like a breath of fresh air. (Ōmori 2005, 37–39)

As is clear, Ōmori did not go into the business knowing much about disability issues. Through interactions with her clients, she gained a better understanding of what it meant to have a disability. The timing of the book, however, suggests that Ōmori was simply riding the crest of a booming interest in sexuality and disability that had been spurred by a book that had come out a few months earlier.

Sex Volunteers

The book in question was *Sex Volunteers* (2004), by journalist Kawai Kaori. Kawai herself was not in the sex trade but had become interested in the subject of "sex volunteers." As described in her book, this term encompassed a broad range of activities from people who were merely willing to provide transportation services to soaplands and other brothels to able-bodied people who were having sex with or providing other forms of sexual services for men and women with disabilities. Despite the broad label of "volunteers," the providers included the paid as well as the unpaid, depending on the circumstances.[5]

For example, Kawai followed a seventy-two-year-old man who was dependent on an oxygen bottle after a tracheostomy as he went to soapland with a care attendant. Kawai mused that even though he was putting himself at serious physical risk, this man's actions showed that sex remained one of the basic requirements of life. On the other end of the spectrum, she wrote about a woman with a "congenital dislocation of the hip" who hired a host from a host bar to come to her family home on a weekly basis. With the knowledge of her parents, the host would bathe her and then carry her to her bed, where he would sexually pleasure her. Kawai wrote that this woman waited all week for her Prince Charming to come. This second example, in particular, has angered feminist women with disabilities such as Asaka Yūho (2009), who argues that women (and men) with disabilities need to overcome their self-pity and passivity and take charge of their own sexuality by finding romantic partners who are willing to accept them as they are and have sex with them willingly and not for money or out of pity.

White Hands

To be clear, some of the sites advertising "sex volunteers" on the Internet are not distinguishable from the delivery health call-girl services, except perhaps for the lack of sophistication of their Web sites and the personal services they claim to provide. For example, Sexual Volunteers (SV) Sakura no Kai describes itself as an organization "that helps people with disabilities masturbate [ji'i]." The association's site has a price list for women "volunteers" that ranges between ¥6,000 and ¥7,500 ($75) for a single "care" session in the Tokyo and Osaka areas. Care services can be provided in the handicap-accessible bathroom of the train station if the client doesn't have a private space at home. The association also qualifies that its services are only for people with physical disabilities (mostly cerebral palsy); it does not offer services for people with intellectual or psychiatric disabilities.

There are also organizations such as White Hands (described below) that emphasize the social welfare aspects of their services. Advertising that they are creating "a new sexual public," they offer both masturbation assistance and something closer to what in America is called sexual surrogacy and sexual therapy counseling; White Hands also publishes white papers on the sexual needs of people with (physical) disabilities and manuals for other service providers on the appropriate way to provide masturbation services for people.

In February 2012, I traveled to the remote northern city of Niigata to meet and talk with the president and founder of White Hands, Sakatsume Shingo. Even riding on the Shinkansen super express, it still took me several hours to get to Niigata from Tokyo. This part of Japan was the location for Kawabata Yasunari's

FIGURE 8.2
White Hands Web site

Snow Country (Yukiguni), and true to form, once the train left the tunnel under the Japan Alps, I was greeted by a landscape covered in several feet of snow.

Mr. Sakatsume met me at the train station, and we drove through the snow to his in-laws' house, where we could talk over lunch. While his mother-in-law brought me a traditionally cooked meal and his father-in-law proudly bounced their newborn grandson on his lap, Sakatsume and I talked about his business. He had originally been inspired to study sexuality when he was a college student at the prestigious University of Tokyo, studying under famed feminist scholar Ueno Chizuko. Inspired by one of her seminars, he started doing research into the condition of sex workers and found that many were suffering from social discrimination. Sakatsume thought that he could perhaps change how society viewed sex work by emphasizing its social benefits. In thinking of how to merge the incongruous themes of sexuality and social welfare, he came up with the notion of creating a place where sex workers could cater to the needs of people with disabilities. In an interview for a magazine, Sakatsume noted the following: "There are three aspects to sexual problems: expressions of affection *[rabu],* sexual gratification *[erosu],* and physiological phenomena *[seiri genshō].* Much of the national conversation about the issue of sexual assistance *[seiteki kaijo]* has confused all three issues. White Hands was founded to assist people, such as those with cerebral palsy, who cannot ejaculate on their own, [and it deals solely] with the issue of the physiological phenomena [of ejaculation and not with emotional affection or sexual gratification]. By providing this type of sexual assistance, we hope to be engaging in a socially useful activity" (quoted in Yorimoto 2010).

I asked Sakatsume about his workers and their working conditions. He said that their average age was forty, that they were all women, and that he gave priority to those having Home Helper Level 2 certification or who were registered nurses. He operated under the delivery health model, with his headquarters above his parents' house in Niigata, and he dispatched his staff by telephone to clients all across Japan. Under Japanese law, he was registered as a delivery health prostitution business, a category that rankled him somewhat as it made it difficult for him to both advertise for clients and recruit new workers. One of his main workarounds was to give public lectures and talks at college courses in social work, nursing, and disability studies. Mr. Sakatsume had self-published several manuals on sexual stimulation for people with disabilities by caregivers and had recently finished a book, *The Unusual Passion of Sex Helpers (Sekkusu herupā no jinjō narazaru jōnetsu),* that was published in 2012 by one of the largest publishers in Japan.

The Politics of Sexual Relations

My interest in the subject of sex and people with disabilities had actually been piqued several years earlier. In May 2005, while conducting research on Japanese disability politics, I attended a monthly study group at one of the Kansai area's leading independent living centers for people with disabilities. That month, we were discussing two books that had just come out, the afore-mentioned *Sex Volunteers,* by Kawai Kaori (2004), and *I Was a Delivery Health Girl for People with Disabilities,* by Ōmori Miyuki (2005).

The discussion leader was one of the personal care attendants at this in-dependent living center (ILC). Most of the care attendants were college students or college graduates in their twenties or early thirties. People with severe physical disabilities who were living independently could request personal care attendant services through the government social welfare office. The care attendants were paid to do a wide range of tasks, from simple ones, such as pushing wheelchairs or guiding blind clients, to much more personal ones, such as assisting in eating, toilet, and bathing functions. At this ILC, all clients with disabilities were matched with personal care attendants of the same sex. With the economy in Japan still struggling and unemployment especially high among youth, being a personal care attendant was generally seen as a comparatively well-paying, socially useful occupation versus being a "freeter."

Our discussion leader, Mr. Suzuki,[6] started off by noting that most media coverage of people with disabilities portrayed them as having no sexual desires. Mentioning the film *Josee, the Tiger, and the Fish* (Inudō 2003; cf. Na-kamura 2008), Suzuki said that he felt it was easy for directors to make a "pure" (*junsui*) love story with a disabled protagonist.

In Suzuki's experience as a personal care attendant, many of his clients did not have much sexual information or experience. They might have passed through adolescence in an institution or lived with their families all of their life. Especially people with severe disabilities were always under close super-vision, with very little privacy and unstructured time, a situation that made exploration difficult. This restriction was on top of their functional limitations on self- and other-exploration.

Because the center at which Suzuki worked matched personal care atten-dants with same-sex clients, he could speak only to the experiences of men. Su-zuki was not sure how women with disabilities could achieve satisfaction, but he noted that while "men can go to health clubs, as an attendant myself, I can say that 90 percent of health clubs will not accept someone with disabilities."

Suzuki asked one of his clients why he liked to go to the health clubs. His client responded, "Because the women at the soap clubs will wash my body much cleaner than the staff at the institution. They will even wash underneath my penis. It feels really good to have my penis that clean. [Suzuki], when you wash someone as an attendant, do you pay so much attention when you wash him? There aren't many men who will do it that much."

People with disabilities are often instructed to think of their personal care attendants as a form of assistive technology. Thus they do not need to thank their care attendants each time they do something for them or to feel that they are imposing on them in any way. The care attendants are there to be their legs or their arms or their eyes. You do not thank your arm when it reaches for a glass of water, so why should you thank your care attendant each time you ask him or her to do the same? The goal of such instruction was to overcome the socialized disinclination of people with disabilities to be a "burden" (meiwaku) on other people and to bolster their own sense of agency and independence.[7]

There was discussion in the study group, though, about the appropriateness of asking personal care attendants (who were after all, being paid by the Japanese social welfare system, and thus taxpayers) to take their clients to health clubs or soaplands. Was it okay to ask them to guide them to the entrance? To carry them up the stairs if the entry was inaccessible? To help them undress? To help them with the sexual act itself? At what point did the personal care attendant cease to be the detached legs and arms of a person with disabilities and become someone with his or her own moral strictures and personal feelings? And then there was the issue of legality. Prostitution was illegal (even if there was no punishment defined), a fact that cast a pall over the entire question of using soaplands and health clubs.

But at a more intimate level, if the personal care attendant is the arms of a person with disabilities, would it be okay to ask him or her for help with masturbation? And if so, would we have to think about not only the sex, but also the sexuality of both the client with the disability and the care attendant?

Suzuki also brought up the case of SAR, a social welfare organization in the Netherlands that provides sexual services to people with disabilities. He noted that 90 percent of the clients of SAR were men and that the organization not only advocated that people with disabilities had the right to sex, but also argued a distinction between sex and love. Suzuki raised the question as to whether this meant that people with disabilities were entitled to sex but not love.

Several years later, I asked this question of Sakatsume Shingo of White Hands. He argued that all people were entitled to self-pleasure (i.e., masturbation).

Able-bodied people could self-pleasure whenever they wanted to, but people with severe physical disabilities could not. Thus people with disabilities were entitled to self-pleasure through the "white hands" of his staff. Here, whiteness has multiple connotations, including the use of sterile gloves by his staff, the notion of white-gloved professional service providers such as chauffeurs, and the purity of the act being performed.

Neoliberal Sexualities

Not all in the disability community agree with the philosophy of Sakatsume Shingo and the (paid) sex volunteers of White Hands. Kumashino Yoshihiko is a man with cerebral palsy who founded a registered nonprofit organization called Noir (Noāru), which "supports the sexuality of people with disabilities" by providing links to sexual service providers, social networking, and a blog.[8] In 2001, Kumashino published *A Hurdle of Only Five Centimeters,* in which he wrote about his own sexual experiences, starting with a delivery call girl who helped him lose his virginity.

In January 2012, I interviewed Mr. Kumashino in a café in Tokyo. At the time he was engaged in a crusade to make mainstream soaplands, love hotels, and other venues for barrier-free sex. Kumashino believes that sex volunteers and other organizations such as White Hands operate from a fundamentally wrong attitude of paternalism toward men with disabilities. He sees them as providing a separate but unequal service that feeds off of people with disabilities. Referring to the older average age of White Hands workers (as noted, in their forties), he asked me, "Why do we accept this?" If the market for sexual services was fully accessible, Kumashino felt that people (men) with disabilities would be able to choose more desirable partners than the limited selection at White Hands. I nodded my head but internally wondered about some of the biases that Kumashino was expressing.

Kumashino believes that if White Hands and similar organizations wish to take the high road and be seen as the moral and functional equivalents to personal care assistants for people with disabilities, then ejaculatory assistance provided through such organizations should be done on a same-sex basis. He argues that when able-bodied men masturbate, the hand that performs the act is a male hand; thus it is a same-sex act. When a disabled male calls in assistance, the service provider should be male as he is acting as an extension of the client's will. Otherwise, these organizations should just admit that they are running specialized brothels, as they are in fact doing under Japanese law.

In his book and his blog, Kumashino writes about his experiences with various soaplands and other commercial services. One of Kumashino's side businesses is serving as a paid design consultant to soaplands and love hotel owners who wish to remodel some of their rooms as handicap accessible, "barrier free" in the Japanese parlance.

When I interviewed him, it had been ten years since he had come out with his book. I asked him what had changed in the last ten years, and his face darkened. He said that not much had changed. His call to arms (so to speak) for men with disabilities to be more open and demanding about their need for sexual services met with very little public reaction. While his e-mail box was overfilled with private requests for introductions to amenable delivery health services, very few people with disabilities attended his public talks in person, and none of the mainline disability organizations took him up on his offer to speak at their events. He felt that the fundamental problem was that men with disabilities in Japan just did not have the confidence yet to speak to their caregivers (often their parents) about their needs. They were still too stuck in acting the role of the "good person with disabilities" by not being a burden on other people and not expressing their own needs, especially the baser ones.

Sexual Rights for People with Disabilities

In 2005, Kuramoto Tomoaki put together an edited volume titled *Sexuality and Disability Studies,* which explored the location of sexuality within disability. In his provocative introduction, he pondered whether people with disabilities should be considered "sexually disadvantaged/handicapped" *(seiteki jakusha)* and what the rights of PWDs would be within liberal frameworks such as those proposed by the philosopher John Rawls.

Within the disability community in Japan, there appear to be two ways of viewing people with disabilities in regard to sexual desire. In one view, people like Kuramoto (who is blind) would argue that there is nothing about having a disability that necessarily would make one unable to have sex (in any of its variant forms) or be sexually unattractive to other people. The problem is either internal (psychological) or external (discrimination). This would be the stance that Kumashino of Noir holds as well. The solution is to reduce perceived discrimination against people with disabilities, as well as to make facilities and services fully accessible.

The other view (which Kuramoto notes as well) is that there are certainly some people for whom sex, whether by themselves alone or with someone else, is physically very difficult. Whether it is someone with cerebral palsy whose hands are shaking too much to masturbate or someone who needs assistance to get onto a bed, there are very real physical barriers to full participation. This would be the stance that White Hands takes. In our interview, Sakatsume noted that many men with severe cerebral palsy find it difficult if not impossible to grab their own penis.

From an economic and social justice perspective, Sakatsume noted that many men with disabilities in Japan cannot find work because of their condition and because of social prejudice. As a result, these men are on social welfare and disability pensions and cannot afford regular release through commercial services, which charge at least ¥30,000 ($300) or more for a full session. White Hands thus fulfills a basic social need by providing low-cost release to people with disabilities. This analysis, of course, elides some of the gender issues raised above related to women with disabilities.

Conclusions

Japanese conversations about sexuality and disability in the context of sexual services are possible because of the openness in which prostitution is advertised and available. Because able-bodied Japanese men are able to easily access sexual services, the question of accessibility for men with disabilities becomes a conversation about social equality rather than of morality.

To reiterate the distinctions used by Sakatsume Shingo, the founder of White Hands, there is affectionate love, sexual intercourse, and physiological release. Surveying the list of books on "disability and sex" available in English, I found the overwhelming focus was on sexual intercourse within the context of affectionate love. With the exception of Noonan (1984), very little of the conversation in the United States has been on paid sexual intercourse for physiological release, given the legal constraints on prostitution.

There is also the added dimension of gender. With the exception of Takeda and Asaka, most of the discussion on sexual needs in Japan has been on men with physical disabilities rather than those with intellectual or psychiatric disabilities. The emergence of some dating services for people with intellectual disabilities, as well as the focus of organizations such as Bethel House on safer sex for people with psychiatric disabilities, does indicate some movement in these directions, although nowhere as explicitly as the service provisions for men with physical disabilities.

If we think back to the first part of this chapter, where I discussed the fictional deaf teenage girl in the film *Babel* and the very real deaf woman Takeda Mayumi, who became a soapland worker, the issue of women with disabilities has largely been overlooked by the conversation over men's physiological needs. In many ways, the framing has prevented conversation about women's having any physiological needs. In many ways, Kawai Kaori's discussion of the woman with a congenital hip displacement emphasizes the romantic nature of her weekly "prince's" visit.

Notes

The author wishes to thank Satsuki Kawano, Susan Long, and Glenda Roberts for their critical feedback in shaping this chapter. Research on this topic was conducted with the support of the Waseda University/Yale University 125th Anniversary Asakawa Kanichi Fellowship (2011–2012), Yale Senior Faculty Fellowship (2011–2012), Yale Junior Faculty Fellowship (2007), and Center for Global Partnership Abe Fellowship (2004–2005).
1. Yoshiawara was the name of the red-light district in Edo, the old name for Tokyo.
2. There also exist *onabe* and *okama* (male and female transgender) bars but these fall outside the scope of this chapter.
3. Because of the illegal nature of prostitution in the United States (except in some areas of Nevada), there appears to be little or no advertising of brothel or escort services that are barrier-free or handicap accessible. Instead, sexual service providers in the United States generally specialize as "sexual surrogates" or "surrogate partners," who operate in legal gray zones. These terms were first introduced in Masters and Johnson's 1970 seminal work, *Human Sexual Inadequacy.* In 1984, Raymond Noonan distinguished between prostitution and sexual surrogacy as follows: "The distinctions commonly noted between the two usually rely on the *intent* of the sexual interaction: the prostitute's intent being immediate gratification localized on genital pleasure; the surrogate's intent being long-term therapeutic re-education and re-orientation of inadequate capabilities of functioning or relating sexually." This concept is explored in Ben Lewin's (2012) film *The Sessions,* which is based on an essay by Mark O'Brien (1990).
4. La Mer (2012). For the curious, "holy water" is also known in the United States as golden showers.
5. It should be noted that the Japanese loan word *borantia* (volunteer) in general encompasses both paid and unpaid volunteers, so this is not unusual.
6. "Suzuki" is a pseudonym.
7. Cushing and Lewis (2002) explore the issue of agency in an American home for people with intellectual disabilities.
8. The Web site for Noir is http://www.npo-noir.com/.

References Cited

Allison, Anne. 1994. *Nightwork*. Chicago: University of Chicago Press.

Asaka, Yūho. 2009. *Inochi ni okuru chōjiritsuron: Subete no karada wa hyakuten manten* (A super independence philosophy to give to life: Every body is 100 percent complete). Tokyo: Tarō Jirō.

Cushing, Pamela, and Tanya Lewis. 2002. "Negotiating Mutuality and Agency in Care-Giving Relationships with Women with Intellectual Disabilities." *Hypatia* 17, no. 3:173–193.

FBI Criminal Justice Information Services Division. 2010. "Crime in the United States." Http://www.fbi.gov/about-us/cjis/ucr/crime-in-the-u.s/2010/crime-in-the-u.s.-2010/index-page. Accessed April 12, 2012.

Fujime, Yuki. 2006. "Japanese Feminism and Commercialized Sex: The Union of Militarism and Prohibitionism." *Social Science Japan Journal* 9, no. 1 (April): 33–50.

González Iñárritu, Alejandro. 2006. *Babel*. Film.

Inudō, Isshin. 2003. *Joze to tora to sakana tachi* (Josee, the tiger, and the fish). Film.

Iwanaga, Fumio. 2009. *An Evolutionary Theory of Prostitution* (Fūzoku shinkaron). Tokyo: Heibonsha.

Kawabata, Yasunari. 2011 [1956]. *Snow Country*. Trans. Edward Seidensticker. London: Penguin Books.

Kawai, Kaori. 2004. *Sekkusu vorantia* (Sex volunteers). Tokyo: Shinchōsha.

Kovner, Sarah. 2012. *Occupying Power: Sex Workers and Servicemen in Postwar Japan*. Stanford, CA: Stanford University Press.

Kumashino, Yoshihiko. 2001. *Tatta gosenchi no hādoru: Dare mo kataranakatta shintaishōgaisha no sekkusu* (A hurdle of only five centimeters: The untold story of the sex lives of people with disabilities). Tokyo: Wani Books.

Kuramoto, Tomoaki. 2005, ed. *Sekushuaritī no shōgaigaku* (Sexuality and disability studies). Tokyo: Akashi Shoten.

La Mer. 2012. La Mer Web site pricelist. Http://www.jpr-lamer.com/systems/. Accessed January 12, 2012.

Leheny, David Richard. 2006. *Think Global, Fear Local: Sex, Violence, and Anxiety in Contemporary Japan*. Ithaca, NY: Cornell University Press.

Lewin, Ben. 2012. *The Sessions*. Film.

Longinotto, Kim, Jano Williams, Twentieth Century Vixen, British Broadcasting Corporation, and Women Make Movies. 1996. *Shinjuku Boys*. Film.

Miller, Laura. 2004. "Those Naughty Teenage Girls: Japanese Kogals, Slang, and Media Assessments." *Journal of Linguistic Anthropology* 14, no. 2:225–247.

Nakamura, Karen. 2006. *Deaf in Japan: Signing and the Politics of Identity*. Ithaca, NY: Cornell University Press.

———. 2008. "Film Review of Josee, the Tiger, and the Fish (Joze to tora to sakana tachi), directed by Isshin Inudō." *Asian Educational Media Services News and Reviews* 31 (Winter): 3–4.

Noonan, Raymond J. 1984. "Sex Surrogates: A Clarification of Their Functions." PhD dissertation, New York University.

NPA (National Police Agency). 2011. *Police White Paper* (Keisatsu hakusho). Http://www.npa.go.jp/hakusyo/h23/index.html. Accessed on April 6, 2012.

O'Brien, Mark. 1990. "On Seeing a Sex Surrogate." *Sun Magazine*. Http://thesunmagazine.org/issues/174/on_seeing_a_sex_surrogate. Accessed May 31, 2013.

Ōmori, Miyuki. 2005. *Watashi wa shōgaisha muke no deriherujō* (I was a health delivery girl for people with disabilities). Tokyo: Bookman.

RealLive. 2007. "Zenkokuhatsu no 'josei muke sōpu' heiten de wakatta sōpu bōi no 'ikijigoku.'" (We learned through the closing of the nation's first soapland for women that life for the soapboys was like living hell). Http:// npn.co.jp/ article/ detail/ 75779839/. Accessed April 4, 2012.

Rubin, Henry Alex, and Dana Adam Shapiro. 2005. *Murderball*. Documentary film.

Sakatsume, Shingo. 2012. *Sekkusu herupā no jinjō narazaru jōnetsu*. (The unusual passion of sex helpers). Tokyo: Shōgakkan.

Sanders, Holly Vincele. 2005. "Prostitution in Postwar Japan: Debt and Labor." PhD dissertation, Princeton University.

Sinclair, Joan. 2006. *Pink Box: Inside Japan's Sex Clubs*. New York: Abrams.

Takeda, Mayumi. 1999. *Faito!* (Fight!). Tokyo: Gentōsha.

Takeyama, Akiko. 2005. "Commodified Romance in a Tokyo Host Club." In *Genders, Transgenders and Sexualities in Japan*, ed. Mark J. McLelland and Romit Dasgupta, 200–215. London; New York: Routledge.

Ueno, Chizuko. 2003. "Self-Determination on Sexuality? Commercialization of Sex among Teenage Girls in Japan." *Inter-Asia Cultural Studies* 4, no. 2:317–324.

Yorimoto, Yoshinori. 2010. *Sekkusu "borantia" tte hitsuyō nanoka?* (Are "sex volunteers" necessary?). *Monthly Charger* 5. Http://charger440.jp/kakari/vol43/vol43.php. Accessed January 28, 2012.

PART IV

Making Social Ties

Although the Japanese media have coined the phrase "a society without ties," referring to the waning family and community ties of the 2000s, the two chapters included in this section explore the ways in which people make connections and networks. Kawano's contribution (chapter 9) illustrates attempts by nonprofit organizations to foster networks among mothers of preschoolers, as such networks among kin and neighbors had shrunk significantly by the 2000s. The life course is more diverse, families are smaller, and marriage rates are lower, changes that imply that it is more difficult for a young mother to find a married sibling or fellow mothers of preschoolers in her community of residence. To develop stronger support networks in a community, older women volunteers working for drop-in play centers for preschoolers and their parents help make connections among younger mothers.

Miller's contribution (chapter 10) explores the social world of young women and schoolgirls who consume contemporary divination as a form of social bonding. The market for divination is enormous, but its analysis is often limited; critics often dismiss divination as an exploitative, addictive, or superstitious practice. Rather than examining it as an expression of belief or analyzing its efficacy, however, Miller explores the significance of divinatory practices from the users' perspective. Contemporary divination provides young women and girls with a range of choices that meet their aesthetic tastes and allow them to "play with the occult" with peers. This chapter gives a glimpse into not only the feminized patterns and strategies of consumption, but also the use of the Internet, often accessed through mobile phones, to maintain social ties.

CHAPTER 9

Recreating Connections

Nonprofit Organizations' Attempts to Foster Networking among Mothers of Preschoolers

SATSUKI KAWANO

There are many "refugees" rearing their children here. There are not many places for them.—*Mother of three children, resident of Tokyo*

This center is a place for parents and their young children—for them to get together, relax, and hang out.—*Head of a nonprofit organization who manages a drop-in play center for parents and their preschoolers*

I felt I fit in very well when I came to this center for the first time. And I am deeply into this place, feeling very comfortable. I have no idea what would have happened to me if this drop-in center did not exist.—*Mother of a twenty-three-month-old boy*

UNLIKE IN EARLY postwar Japan (1950s–1960s), mothers of preschoolers in Tokyo today neither have a sense of belonging in their communities nor can easily find support for child rearing among their neighbors. Their communities no longer maintain strong networks of older child bearers who transmit their knowledge of child rearing. Such networks have weakened partly because an increasing number of people remain unmarried, and thus fertility rates have declined. New mothers often stop working in order to rear their children, and as former commuters they tend to be poorly integrated into their communities when their first child arrives. Yet mothers with limited social networks for child rearing are more likely to feel frustrated and dissatisfied with the tasks of parenting. To reduce the extent of mothers' isolation and provide more socially engaging community environments for child rearing, since 2002 the state has been developing drop-in play centers *(tsudoi no hiroba),* where parents and their young children can gather and develop support networks.

Based on participant observation and interviews conducted in Tokyo in January–April 2009, in this study I examine the attempts of organizations that run drop-in play centers to connect mothers of preschoolers and their experiences of using such centers. Thus this chapter provides an analysis of mothers' peer networks, which have received limited attention in the study of mothering and child rearing in Japan (see Holloway 2010). The members of the nonprofit organizations examined here encourage mothers to participate in center activities by using their skills and previous work experiences (e.g., designing a Web site, teaching yoga), thereby inspiring them to create a place of belonging in Tokyo, a city characterized by high mobility, fertility rates significantly below the national average, and a predominance of single-person and nuclear-family households.

The predicament that mothers with young children face as they engage in child rearing is not an isolated problem but is tied to interrelated issues that have been shaped by Japan's postindustrial shift and weak economy following the Lost Decade of the 1990s. An increasing number of new graduates are unable to secure regular employment. The rising number of young people in irregular jobs makes it harder for them to marry and have children, as a stable job is considered necessary for family formation. People's mobility and the development of the service industry have weakened reciprocal ties in communities. The media have sensationalized this crisis of disappearing social ties by using the term "a society without ties" *(muen shakai),* wherein individuals are described as living lonely lives and dying lonely deaths. Along with changing family and work relations, the weakening of community ties has been seen as an expression of Japan's loss of its very essence. Despite the media's predominantly pessimistic portrayals of postindustrial Japan, however, attempts are being made to reconnect individuals to social networks in a range of settings, and nonprofit organizations have provided support to the socially isolated. For example, these organizations have addressed the issues of homelessness; the *hikikomori,* or the socially withdrawn (Borovoy 2008); suicide prevention (Allison 2011); unionization among irregular workers; the elderly who live alone; and socially isolated mothers. Though the range of issues to which nonprofit organizations devote their efforts is vast, many of them share the attempt to reengage individuals in society. This study focuses on one of the many areas of these organizations' activities: the effort to create networks of support for people who are experiencing various levels of social isolation.

Child Rearing, Shrinking Networks of Support, and Anxiety

> The Sameshima grandmother, who lives next door to the Kawabes, came by with the youngest baby in her charge. Mrs. Sameshima is short of milk, and Mrs. Kawabe at once offered her abundant breast. When the old woman said, "Every day I bother you," she said, "What nonsense," and took the baby to her bosom. Her own baby, a very healthy specimen, is carried around by his older brother, who looks after him like a nursemaid. (Smith and Wiswell 1982, 211)

The above description of breast-feeding from an agricultural village of Suye in Kyushu during the mid-1930s clearly illustrates that the mother was not the only person who handled child rearing. A neighbor, a grandmother, and a big brother all played their roles in the endeavor, and although not indicated in the quotation, in fact older children commonly worked as nursemaids *(komori).* Nursemaids were also common in other parts of the nation in prewar Japan (see Partner 2004, 54; Tamanoi 1998). In Nagano Prefecture, for example, Tamanoi (1998, 64) reports that commonly the employer of a nursemaid paid her parents money or rice for her services, and the nursemaid, who was sent to live in her employer's household, received no wages but room and board and some small gifts. This practice also provided young nursemaids with valuable child-care experience.

In contrast, in postwar Japan, child rearing was established as a woman's calling, and the number of stay-at-home mothers increased as wage employment became common, particularly in urban areas. Even in urban areas characterized by the predominance of newly established nuclear-family households, residents who had dependable married siblings could obtain support from them, while those who did not have kin could count on the ties created with neighbors. Demographically, young mothers in the 1960s had many married adult siblings with children who had also migrated to urban areas. Thus a young mother in the Tokyo area was likely to count on a sister or sister-in-law raising her own young children and living nearby. It was not uncommon for mothers to keep in frequent contact with other married siblings who also lived in the Tokyo area, and as a result their children sometimes grew up together as if they were siblings (see Morioka et al. 1968, 263). In her community, a young mother typically found many other young mothers raising small children, as the life course was highly standardized. During the 1960s, therefore, a network of either kin or non-kin was available to provide child-rearing support (Ochiai 2000, 93–95).

Ikuji noirōze, or "child-rearing neurosis," associated with murder-suicides of mothers and their young children, became a social issue as early as the 1970s (Nakatani 2008, 37). In 1982, the psychologist Makino Katsuko drew scholars' attention to a type of anxiety related to child rearing *(ikuji fuan)* that could be observed among mothers of infants and preschoolers and its evident association with mothers' weak social networks. It is worth noting that Makino's pioneering work appeared at a time when the members of the post-transitional cohort, or those born after 1950, came to engage in child-bearing and child rearing (Yamane 2000). Compared with the transitional cohort, born between 1925 and 1950, the post-transitional cohort is associated with the low-birthrate, low-mortality-rate society. In other words, those in the post-transitional cohort grew up in small families, with one sibling closely related in age, and their exposure to younger children was limited. Consequently, by the 1980s, the support network of kin had shrunk, and the parents of the married couple were the typical providers of support (Ochiai 2000, 93–95), a development that significantly diminished the support base for child rearing. The reduction of kin-based and community-based support and the parents' limited exposure to children before the arrival of their own are linked to the growing levels of uncertainty or anxiety related to child rearing (see Harada 2006).

Although community-based support for mothers has weakened, the cultural importance of intensive mothering has not waned during the 2000s. Many married women stop working when their first child arrives so that they can care for their infant. For example, in a national survey among the mothers of children born in May 2010, 79 percent had been employed one year before the arrival of their child, but only 37 percent remained employed six months after childbirth (Ministry of Health, Labor, and Welfare 2013). Fifty-two percent of the mothers surveyed had full-time jobs one year before childbirth, but the figure went down to 29 percent six months after childbirth. The most common reason for quitting jobs among the mothers surveyed was that they wanted to focus on child rearing, although others reluctantly stopped working as balancing family and work was difficult (Ministry of Health, Labor, and Welfare 2013). The above national survey indicates a persisting pattern of interruptions in a married woman's career due to childbirth, even though dual-income families have become more common. The enduring significance of intensive mothering is apparent in the ways in which social institutions are structured. For example, the education system still takes it for granted that mothers volunteer their time and support the schools their children attend (Sasagawa 2006). Commercial child-care services have not grown significantly to compensate for the diminished community-based and kin-based support. Paid caregiving at child-care institutions is seen as unacceptable or inferior at best. Private babysitters are unpopular and uncommon (Holthus 2011).

Moreover, in post-bubble Japan the disparity *(kakusa)* between haves and have-nots is recognized, and raising children can be a very competitive endeavor. A number of books and magazines discuss various methods and experiences of "home education" *(katei kyōiku)* for three-year-old and younger children and are aimed at raising smart children. A stronger emphasis on home education, however, may affect children and their parents negatively by raising their stress levels (Honda 2008, 10–11). While rearing children successfully and sending them to good universities were important concerns among middle-class full-time homemakers in the past (see Lebra 1984), nowadays a greater significance appears to be placed on rearing very young children "successfully."

Critics of child-rearing support often see it as the pampering of lazy mothers who cannot rear their children appropriately and emphasize that their own mothers' generation completed the job without special state or community support. However, the available child-rearing resources—both kin-based and community-based—have diminished, as we have seen, and possibly the standards of rearing very young children are higher today. Roughly one in four mothers has a sister, as many have only one sibling. Moreover, even if a mother has a sister, she might be unmarried and have a full-time job, as life courses are diverse and not all women of child-rearing age are married and have children (see Kurotani and Nakano in this volume). Meanwhile, as noted, new mothers have had significantly less exposure to children and infants before the arrival of their own. In a 2003 survey conducted by Harada (2006, 142) in Hyōgo Prefecture, 54.5 percent of the mothers reported that they had never fed infants or changed diapers until the arrival of their first child. A new mother of the 2000s is expected to do the job well without much experience or support from kin and community. The stress felt by contemporary young mothers of preschoolers, therefore, must be understood as a structural issue.

Studies of child-rearing support illustrate that mothers and their young children increasingly suffer from social isolation in Japan, a condition that negatively affects children's development (e.g., Harada 2006, 98–99; Matsuda 2010). In particular, social isolation is a more serious issue in metropolitan communities, where many mothers live away from their kin and thus can count on them for only limited support (Iwama 2004). Iwama reports that all the eight metropolitan mothers examined in her study lived in nuclear-family households and maintained a division of labor allocating housework and child care to women and wage employment to men (2004, 153). These mothers received limited support from their kin. Their husbands bathed children or played with them on weekends, when they had time. In contrast, the five married women living in Yamagata Prefecture who could reach their natal homes in fifteen minutes on foot or by car received help with child care on a daily basis (2004, 152). Unlike the metropolitan sample, mothers living in Yamagata did not report a sense of isolation as a problem. Similarly, according to a study conducted among a random sample of mothers in five areas of Tokyo (Matsuda 2008, 15, 94), those who lived with their parents or parents-in-law reported lower levels of stress associated with child rearing.

As mothers living in metropolitan areas often live away from their kin, expanding networks among non-kin is particularly important for them to reduce the sense of social isolation and levels of anxiety related to child rearing. Mothers who visit children's centers and those involved in mothers' groups for child rearing *(ikuji sākuru)* are reported to have a wider network of non-kin (Matsuda 2008, 72–73). The social support network of non-kin expands as children grow older and they are sent to child-care institutions (Matsuda 2008, 2010). Conversely, new mothers and stay-at-home mothers of children who are three years old or younger are less likely to have child-care support from non-kin, and the most likely support will come from their parents. Mothers of one child under three living away from their own mothers and mothers-in-law therefore tend to have limited support.

The studies noted above provide us with knowledge regarding the social problems of mothers associated with limited support from non-kin and its negative impact on both the mothers' well-being and their children's development. However, it is still unclear what specific patterns of interaction and strategies of support are effective in expanding mothers' social networks. It is certainly not enough to simply create publicly accessible spaces where mothers with young children can gather; for example, *kōen debyū*, "park début," a phrase referring to a mother and her child's first visit to a neighborhood park, is often accompanied by a sense of uncertainty and tension on the part of the mother, who feels compelled to "blend in" well with the other mothers and children who use the park regularly. By providing a qualitative analysis of the efforts of nonprofit organizations that manage drop-in play centers to create connections among center users and assessing the experiences of mothers who use them, this study thus offers an ethnographic view of new forms of child-rearing support.

Fieldwork

As noted above, in 2009, I conducted participant observation for three and a half months at three drop-in play centers for parents and preschoolers in Tokyo. During that time, I had conversations with mothers and staff. I also took part in the centers' activities. These included educational sessions on child rearing involving the mothers and fathers of young children; a lunch café organized by mothers to serve meals to center users; story time; a potluck dinner for center users, an event hosted by a local municipal office to introduce child-rearing support groups; a volunteers' fair for citizens' groups held to promote the centers' activities to local residents; and a program that trains people to supply child-care providers through Family Support Services (public child-rearing support programs in which local community members provide child care and related services at significantly lower than market rates).

Semi-structured interviews were conducted with five staff members regarding their organizations and activities and with twenty mothers of preschoolers regarding their experiences of using drop-in play centers and the availability of support from kin and non-kin. (All the names of the interviewees used in this study are pseudonyms.) The staff members were local women in various age groups; some had adult children and others school-age children. The majority of the mothers interviewed were in their thirties. Seven were working mothers (five of them were on maternity leave), and the rest were full-time homemakers. Most had only one child. Five mothers had two children, two had three, and one had four. Five of the twenty had a child or children older than three. The majority (thirteen of the twenty) had no ties to child-care institutions such as day-care facilities or kindergarten. All the mothers used drop-in centers regularly and lived close to the center they visited. Usually they walked to or biked to the center.

This study examined mothers of both middle-class and working-class backgrounds, assessments based on their past or current jobs (salesperson, clerical worker, self-employed worker, factory worker, civil servant, yoga instructor, freelance designer, freelance writer, computer systems engineer, flight attendant, and full-time homemaker), as well as their husbands' occupations (construction worker, security guard, restaurant manager, self-employed worker, civil servant, engineer, banker, salaried worker, and medical doctor). I did not recruit an equal number of middle-class and working-class mothers, as the focus of this study was not on social class. Nonetheless, it is worth pointing out that the drop-in centers examined in this study do not necessarily cater only to middle-class homemakers.

As this study employs a small purposive sample of mothers of young children in Tokyo, its results do not represent the typical experiences of young mothers in contemporary Japan. Nonetheless, it provides concrete examples of underexplored new types of child-rearing support—created in response to the demographic and employment changes in contemporary Japan—based on firsthand observation and situated accounts of mothers' child-rearing experiences in their own words. As such, it usefully complements the existing quantitative studies and government surveys on child-rearing support.

The Development of Drop-in Play Centers

The development of drop-in play centers for preschoolers and their parents must be understood in the context of an aging population in postindustrial Japan. During the 1990s declining total fertility rates became a serious issue for the state as it faced a growing number of older persons. The shrinking number of young adults was considered detrimental to the economic and social standing of a future Japan. By formulating national policies such as Angel Plan (1995–1999; see Roberts 2002), New Angel Plan (2000–2004), and most recently the Child and Child-Rearing Support Plan (2005–2009), the state took measures to provide more diverse child-care services and a better social environment for child rearing in the hope of increasing the nation's dwindling fertility rate. The drop-in play center project *(tsudoi no hiroba jigyō),* initiated by the Ministry of Health, Labor, and Welfare in 2002, is one of the specific projects developed by the state in the larger framework of these policies to raise the nation's low birthrates.

Drop-in play centers provide child-rearing support at the community level to families in the area *(chiiki katei)*, and they cater mainly to full-time homemakers and their preschoolers, with a special emphasis upon children up to three years old, who most likely have had no institutional experience. Behind the development of these centers is an understanding that stay-at-home mothers are not necessarily a privileged group that requires no social support, as community networks that used to provide support and child-rearing knowledge to new stay-at-home mothers have deteriorated.

The first drop-in play center was established by the city of Musashino in Tokyo in 1992, before the state formulated the series of policies noted above to increase the nation's birthrate (Kashiwagi and Morishita 1997, 55). Among the people who influenced the founding of this facility were psychologists specializing in child development who had observed the activities of drop-in centers in Ontario, Canada. The play center in Musashino city inspired other people and groups, some of whom started their own play centers. For example, in 2000 a women's group in Yokohama established a privately operated play center (Okuyama and Ōmameuda 2003, 22), which, among other support groups, is said to have influenced the Ministry of Health, Labor, and Welfare to initiate the national drop-in play center project.

In 2010, there were 1,965 drop-in centers nationwide. They are currently classified as *"chiiki kosodate shien kyoten, hirobagata"* (drop-in-center-style bases for community-level child-rearing support) and constitute one kind of facility among several types of children's facilities. Of the 1,965 centers, 592 were directly managed by a city, town, or village; 348 by nonprofit organizations; and 605 by social welfare organizations (Ministry of Health, Labor, and Welfare 2010). Few centers were operated by corporations. There were 125 centers in Tokyo in 2009; among them, approximately two-fifths were open 6–7 days per week; another two-fifths, 5 days per week; and the rest, 3–4 days per week (Ministry of Health, Labor, and Welfare 2009). These centers must be open at least three days per week for at least five hours per day and have at least two staff members with child-rearing knowledge and experience. No special professional qualifications are required to be a staff member. According to a survey of children's facilities (of which the drop-in centers examined in this study are a part) conducted in 2009 by the National Association of Drop-in Centers for Child Rearing, annually an average of 6,676 persons (adults and children) visited each center (Kosodate Hiroba Zenkoku Renraku Kyōgikai 2009).

Drop-In Play Centers: The Physical Settings

A drop-in play center provides an indoor play space for parents and their young children. A center comes with a playroom with a range of toys, big and small, appropriate for children of different ages. Some play centers have several rooms or sections organized according to theme or children's ages. For instance, a center may have areas for books, crafts, blocks, and playhouses. Centers usually have an area set aside for breast-feeding and cribs for children to take a nap. Some have children's washrooms, a low sink, or a diaper-changing table, though many mothers change diapers on the floor, using a

FIGURE 9.1
Mothers and infants at a drop-in play center

special change pad. This practice is not unhygienic, as center users remove their outside shoes when they enter, as is true in homes and many public buildings in Japan. Sometimes a play center also has a play yard, a kitchen, and an eating area for its users.

The size and layout of play centers vary. Play Center A did not have a kitchen, a café area, or a play yard. During lunch, long, low tables and chairs for children were brought out. Adults sat on the floor. Users brought their own lunches. The center provided hot water free of charge to prepare bottles for babies. There was a counter where adults could pay some money and make tea or coffee for themselves. Play Center B had a spacious kitchen/café area with tables and chairs. Users could bring their own lunches, cook something, or order food from neighboring restaurants. This center had a large play yard and a garden. The center also had a multipurpose room that was rented out for special events. Near its office was an area where used children's clothes and gear were sold. Both Centers A and B had message boards where messages from users, notices of various events related to child rearing, and announcements from child-care facilities were posted. Play Center C had a large central room consisting of several areas, including a kitchen, a table area, and an area with toys and structures. There also was a separate room with cribs and futons where children could take a nap. The center did not have an outside play space, but there was a park nearby.

The Role of Staff Members

The presence of regular staff members makes drop-in play centers special. My informants most frequently described a play center as a "homelike" place, which distinguished it from other public play spaces, such as parks or the children's centers called *jidōkan,* which were run by local civil servants who did not interact with visitors in the play area. Mrs. Kanda, a staff member in her sixties, told me, "In this area, many mothers live far away from their natal homes. There are many new mothers who have never cared for young children. They may be unsure about how to raise their first child. We wanted to create a space where mothers could feel relaxed *[hotto dekiru]."*

Staff members act as facilitators who encourage mothers to interact with each other. For example, when they see a new member who seems to have difficulty interacting with other mothers and children, they introduce the new person to a group of regular members and try to open up a conversation involving that new person. Staff members are aware of the importance of the role they play in making connections among parents. Mrs. Kanda told me, "Staff members warmly welcome mothers and connect [tsunageru] them to each other." Their efforts are recognized and appreciated by the users of the drop-in centers. Mrs. Sumi, in her mid-thirties and the mother of a twenty-one-month-old boy, told me, "It is nice that staff members introduce mothers to each other." To get the conversation going for a newcomer, staff members might mention where a regular member lives, her child's age, or in which pre-school an older child is enrolled. The mother of a twenty-three-month-old boy told me, "I felt I fit in very well when I came to this center for the first time. And I am deeply into this place, feeling very comfortable." Such a warm, comfortable atmosphere is created by the efforts of attentive staff members. Several mothers contrasted their experiences at a drop-in play center with those at a children's center where no staff members were present in its play space. Mrs. Hirota, a stay-at-home mother of three, told me, "I use a children's center near my house, but a group of frequent users hang out together in the play area all the time. It is not easy for me to blend in."

Interviewees often pointed out that play center staff also provided knowledge and useful advice regarding child rearing. Mrs. Sumi stated, "I learn a lot from staff members here." Mrs. Miyashita, a thirty-six-year-old mother of a twenty-three-month-old boy, told me that before coming to the center near her house, she had not had a place to go when she had problems related to child rearing. Her mother lives in a city two hours away from her.

Staff members may also connect a mother to child-rearing support providers such as doctors and social workers. A staff member at one play center told me, "We watch hundreds of children and sometimes notice developmental problems before their mothers do. We try to gently guide them to specialists if necessary. Sometimes we encourage the mothers to discuss the issues we see at the three-year-old health examinations." Mrs. Murai, another staff member and the mother of two adult children, said, "Our drop-in center is close to a family support center where specialists work. Some mothers who consult with us want to have formal answers to their questions regarding child rearing, and we refer them to the specialists."

Patterns of Interaction:
Staff Members and Mothers

Most staff and volunteers are women who have older children, and they act as sympathetic supporters to young mothers. When asked, staff members discuss their own experiences or come up with suggestions. However, most frequently they encourage the young mothers to create a discussion rather than passing on their own knowledge and the "right" answer directly. And mothers appreciate the ways in which a staff member offers a piece of advice. For example, at Play Center A, a mother in her mid-thirties told a staff member that her son resisted vigorously whenever she tries to brush his teeth: "My son hates to have his teeth brushed. He runs away from me when I try to do it. I usually have to grab him and hold him with my feet so that he cannot run away from me." She did not like her current method and wanted to know if others used a better one. A staff member in her late forties who used to work at a day-care center replied, "Might it work if you let your son brush his teeth on his own and then you did the touch-up? A song from an advertisement for children's toothpaste includes the phrase 'The mother provides the finishing touch' [she sang that part of the song]." Then the staff asked other mothers how they handled this problem. One mother said she told her son a story, while another one said she used the same method as the mother who had asked the question. The staff member also mentioned a radio show in which a listener shares her problem related to child rearing and other listeners call in to contribute their experiences with the same problem. Then the staff member added, "Well, there is no single right answer [to a problem concerning child rearing]." She did not present herself as a child-rearing specialist but asked other mothers to share their experiences and cited the TV ad and radio show. At the end of the conversation, she made it clear that the suggestions made during this interaction did not work for every child. In these ways the staff member succeeded in creating a forum among mothers in which they shared experiences, thus facilitating peer learning and counseling. The kind of discussion described here did not place a mother in the position of simply receiving support but made her a potential provider of support herself by sharing her own experience, whether positive or negative.

This supportive approach was conscientiously maintained. A staff member told me, "We do not impose our opinions on mothers." As almost all the staff are women with older children, they have the capacity to act as teachers to younger mothers who come to drop-in centers. Yet several staff members told me that they try to listen to the mothers without being critical. Mrs. Murai told me, "We decided not to criticize our center's visitors by using the phrase 'young mothers today.'" An older staff member who works at another center said, "I am done with child rearing [she has two adult children], but it is not a good idea for me to have a sense of superiority and advise this or that to mothers who are in the midst of it." As these older mothers with adult children are seen to have fulfilled their moral obligation of child rearing, they are in a stronger position in relation to the young mothers whom they intend to support. Nevertheless, they strove to avoid presenting themselves as superior and tried to be sensitive to the feelings of those who were receiving the support.

At one center, a volunteer who worked there two days a week made a similar point by telling a story about a mother in her mid-thirties. The mother had told the volunteer that as her son often dropped his toys on the floor in her apartment, she visited the neighbor who lived below her to apologize for the noise he made. The neighbor was critical, saying that she had in fact thought about coming up to the mother's apartment to complain about the noise herself. This unfriendly comment upset the mother. The volunteer suggested that she put a rug on the floor, but the mother did not like this idea, as she loved the wooden floor the way it was. The volunteer also suggested that she have her son just play with soft toys, but the mother looked unsatisfied with this suggestion. At this point the volunteer said, "Then I realized what the mother wanted. She did not want any advice from me about how to reduce the noise level, solve the problem of her son's dropping toys, or handle the neighbor differently, but she wanted me to be sympathetic to her." Other staff members nodded in agreement, indicating that acknowledging a mother's feelings is sometimes much more important than offering her concrete solutions.

By adopting a casual but warm approach, staff members sometimes gain the trust of the mothers, who come frequently to consult with them. At one play center, I observed the interaction between a staff member and a mother in her thirties. Among the staff and volunteers, it was known that she had a medical condition that made it hard for her to keep up with housework, family business, and child care. One day she came in almost in tears and went directly to the window where staff members greet and check in users. A staff member greeted the mother and asked her how she was doing. She told her that she had a ton of work to do. She had to label all her child's clothes because she was sending her to a day-care center in a couple of weeks. She also talked about how she had no energy to do any housework, not even folding laundered clothes. The staff member replied in a gentle tone (as usual), "Oh, you do not have to do everything at once. You do not have to sew your child's name on her clothes; you can just write her name in with a black marking pen and sew it on later when you have more energy to do so. As for the laundry, you can leave the clothes on hangers [dryers are uncommon in Japan] and take down articles when you need to use them." The exchanges continued until the mother seemed a little less distressed and the urgency had disappeared from her voice. The staff member had been accepting and supportive, and the mother seemed to have appreciated it.

In fact, staff members did not feel that what specialists could offer was superior to what they offered at a drop-in play center, even though they did not necessarily possess specialized knowledge—for example, the knowledge possessed by a medical doctor. Mrs. Murai told me, "During three-year-old health examinations some mothers are told by doctors that their children have developmental problems that they had not been aware of. They are often shocked and hurt by specialists' comments, and they come to talk to us. Some of the mothers are in tears. We tell them that children develop at different speeds and that they might want to wait a bit without worrying too much. We listen to these mothers, and many have told us that they felt relieved after speaking to us." Mrs. Murai made it clear that her approach was different from that of a specialist, who might simply give a diagnosis and not necessarily listen to the mothers. By providing emotional support, drop-in play center staff offer a type of support that child-rearing specialists do not.

Networks of Peer Support

At a drop-in play center, mothers exchange a variety of information related to child rearing—for example, about child-rearing goods and equipment, child-friendly coffee shops and restaurants, parks and other play centers, day-care facilities and kindergartens, and pediatricians and child-friendly dentists. When I was conducting participant observation in 2009, my informants frequently discussed the quality of day-care centers or kindergartens and the status of their applications because a new cohort of children is accepted into these institutions in April and many informants were waiting for notice of their child's acceptance. Mothers exchanged not only information but also used clothes and toys. (In some centers, as noted, there is an area where used children's clothes and goods are sold for small amounts of money or given away for free.) Mrs. Hirota told me as she sorted used clothes donated by other mothers to a play center, "Almost all of my sons' clothes come from this center!" Mothers sometimes observed the eating utensils, infant carriers, or pacifier holders used by other children and ask their mothers if they worked well and where they could buy the same items. At one play center, a mother who was interested in buying an infant carrier first tried one used by another mother.

Drop-in play centers are also places where mothers can make so-called *mamatomo* (literally, "mom friends"), or friends who are mothers and with whom they can enjoy getting together with their children. A number of interviewees told me that they had made many friends through their visits to play centers. In some cases, these friends are just people to meet and chat with at the centers, while in other cases they share activities beyond the confinement of a play center—for example, they go on excursions or visit each other's homes with their children. A few interviewees told me that their families also became friends and the husbands also participated in their get-togethers. Mrs. Hirota told me, "I made good friends through the center, and now my family and my friends' families have gotten to know each other very well." Another interviewee told me that she had a group of friends who had parties in the evenings with their husbands and children. At one play center, I heard from a staff member that a group of families who had come to know each other through the center rented a bus to go on a picnic together.

Mothers often chat among themselves about issues of concern, creating a context for sharing experiences and eliciting empathetic comments. At one play center, for example, a mother complained about how she could do no housework the day before because her son had kept following her around trying to get her attention. Other mothers agreed that it was difficult to do housework and care for a child at the same time. Another mother said that her son climbed onto the vacuum cleaner whenever she tried to vacuum her place. Exchanging stories about child rearing was a common way for mothers to get to know each other. Furthermore, sharing experiences was also a way of relieving stress. A number of mothers told me that they felt refreshed after talking to other mothers about child-rearing issues.

Not only recounting their own stories but also listening to the experiences of mothers of older children can guide young mothers. Mrs. Seki, a forty-two-year-old mother of one boy (twenty-one months old), discussed how her son did not share toys with other children when he played at a drop-in play center. Another mother, whose child was three, said to her, "Well, my son is still learning to share toys with others." Mrs. Seki said, with a hint of surprise, "Oh, is that so? Even at the age of three? Would that [sharing] take that long [for kids to learn]?" She was able to use the information she got from another mother to evaluate her current problem and readjust her expectations. Because a three-year-old boy still had a problem sharing toys with other children, perhaps she did not have to worry too much about her own child. A sense of relief that "I am not the only one with this problem" can often result from interactions with other mothers.

Mothers can observe both other children and their mothers at a drop-in play center, an opportunity that may also help them deal with their own issues. They see other mothers' parenting styles and realize that theirs is not the only way of dealing with an issue. They may also encounter a mother whose parenting style and attitude serve as a model for their own. Like consultation with staff and other mothers, the child-rearing knowledge obtained by observing other mothers and children may not necessarily solve a problem, but it can help mothers relativize it and stop worrying too much.

Opportunities for Learning and Exploration

Some drop-in play centers also offer various programs and classes for learning, though it is not a requirement for the play centers to have special events. The frequency of events and classes varies greatly from center to center. Some programs focus mainly on children's development, such as story time, crafts, music, yoga, and rhythmics. Others that target mothers teach child-rearing methods in a formal setting. Breast-feeding specialists, medical doctors, and nurses may be invited to offer classes and consultations. In March 2009, at Play Center A seven events were held, and at Center B, eight events. Some events on child rearing encourage the participation of mothers and sometimes even fathers. Play Centers A and B also hosted a program to train people to become care providers in Family Support Services.

Some of the classes and programs held at drop-in play centers provide child care, and it may serve as a gentle introduction to mothers on entrusting their children to non-family members for the first time. A mother of one boy (twenty-three months old) stated, "I enrolled in a variety of classes and programs with child care at a drop-in center. When I was in a class for the first time for two hours, I was nervous and not sure how my son would react. My son was fine, and that encouraged me to start using temporary drop-off child-care services occasionally at a day-care center near our residence."

Mothers gave mixed evaluations of drop-off child-care provided by non-family members, and several stated that they were afraid of using services that involved leaving their child with a non-family caregiver. Their responses—in particular those of mothers who were full-time homemakers—are not surprising in contemporary Japan; Holthus (2011) notes that even parents who have their children enrolled in day-care centers expressed a reluctance to hire private (non-family) babysitters. Unlike drop-off care, however, interviewees thought child care provided during classes at drop-in centers was "less scary," as it was provided at the same facility where they attended the classes. So if a child had a problem—for example, he or she cried for a long time and kept asking for his or her mother—the mother was nearby to take care of it.

Some centers offer events and classes for mothers that are unrelated to child rearing, such as movies, crafts, and yoga. Some of these classes provide opportunities for mothers to use their skills. A former yoga instructor, for example, taught yoga classes at a drop-in center. She told me, "I am interested in returning to work and have submitted a plan to teach a maternity yoga course at a play center." At one play center, a group of mothers cooked and served meals to the center's visitors at a lunch café several times a month. Some of the group's members were interested in setting up a café in the future, and the center provided a chance for them to hone their skills. Play centers thus also serve as spaces where some mothers can explore future work possibilities.

It is worth noting that nonprofit organizations that manage drop-in play centers consciously make use of mothers' skills and encourage them to participate in the provision of child-rearing support. A mother often stops using a drop-in center regularly when her youngest child gets enrolled in a child-care institution, but she then may take on a new role as a volunteer at the center. Mrs. Funada, a mother of two children aged five and three, told me, "I used to come to this center often before my younger child started attending a kindergarten. Now that he is in kindergarten, I have more time for myself. As I owe much to the center, I started volunteering to give something back to it by doing what I can." Several mothers who have computer skills helped to set up a Web site or produce documents for drop-in play centers. A staff member at one center told me, "It is a good idea to make use of mothers' talents; let them do what they are good at. It is important to give them opportunities to excel. Mothers who visit drop-in centers are not without skills. They often have had various experiences, but they do not have opportunities to make use of them." Indeed, the majority of mothers have had some professional experience prior to childbearing, yet they tend to quit their jobs to rear their children. Drop-in play centers therefore can open up possibilities for them to assume a role different from that of mother and thereby gain a different sense of fulfillment and connectedness.

The Maintenance of Drop-in Play Centers and Issues of Concern

While interviewees commonly reported positive experiences of child rearing as a result of using drop-in play centers, staff members expressed a number of concerns. Funding and budget were frequently discussed issues. A staff member in her thirties told me that the funding system made it difficult to run a play center: "We have to find half of the money we need, and the municipal government gives us the other half. . . . Annually we only get enough to hire one civil servant [though the nonprofit organization spends the money to operate the drop-in play center without hiring a civil servant]. . . . In order to operate a high-quality play center, we need more money—for example, to hire full-time paid staff members." To raise their share of the money, some centers run by nonprofit organizations offer temporary drop-off child-care services *(ichiji azukari)*. A staff member at another center told me, "We receive funding from the ward, and we raise money by offering drop-off services. Then we use half of the money for renting this space and the rest on personnel."

The most common frustration expressed by heads of nonprofit organizations that run drop-in play centers was that the ward, and also the state, which set up the current system, used the nonprofit organizations to cut the public spending on child-rearing support. Their feeling of "being used" by the state cannot be fully understood without considering the status of volunteers and staff at these organizations. Unlike in North America, where volunteering is defined as work without monetary reward, in contemporary Japan, there are "paid volunteers," who are remunerated at below-market rates, and "pure volunteers," who are unpaid. Whether a "volunteer" should always be unpaid is not exactly the focus of my discussion, however. Though there were variations, many "volunteers" I met at drop-in play centers (including regular staff) received some monetary reward, and thus the nonprofit sector often served as a source of irregular "jobs" for them.[1] Several times during my fieldwork, I overheard paid volunteers and staff members refer to a volunteer's involvement in a drop-in center as work *(oshigoto)*. In the context of drop-in play centers, the line between work and volunteering is thus blurred, and "work" at such centers in many ways resembles that regularly available to them in the private sector. Part-time, low-wage jobs without benefits are most commonly available to married women with children, who mainly see themselves as homemakers and would like to make use of their time when their children are in school. Because some drop-in centers are managed directly by a municipality and staffed by full-time civil servants, a staff member hinted that she was not remunerated for her work properly even though she was doing more or less the same job as a civil servant, who is known to enjoy job security and generous benefits. Her sense of frustration, however, was not only about her personal situation but was also about a larger structural issue. She stated, "It is a problem that the ward makes volunteers do what it should take care of and gets the job done by spending little money."

Others expressed the sense of unfairness they felt toward a ward's practices by comparing the centers run by nonprofit organizations with those directly managed by the ward. A staff member in her sixties pointed out, "We have to keep our drop-in center open on a holiday. It's a bit strange, as a center run by the ward is closed on holidays. Even though we keep our place open on holidays, we do not get compensated for it."

The official method of evaluation of drop-in center activities was also an issue. A staff member told me, "The ward only looks at the number of the center's visitors. But what about the quality of support? The question is, which is better, to effectively support ten parents who are experiencing child-rearing anxiety or to hold a special event—for example, a rice-pounding ceremony for the New Year—to attract one hundred people per day? If we have a special event, we can attract many people, but I wonder if that's real support."

Finally, the quality and stability of support provided by their drop-in centers were important issues among staff members. Given that nonprofit organizations running drop-in centers mainly depend upon volunteers who receive little monetary reward for their work, it is not always easy to maintain a sufficient number of dedicated volunteers. Initially they may be eager and excited to engage in the activities of drop-in centers, but their compensation may be so insufficient (definitely below the market rates) that they may rapidly feel burned out. As most of the staff and volunteers are married women with children, they may also stop volunteering as their children grow older and their lifestyles change over time.[2] A staff member in her late forties told me, "The problem is that we have not attracted a new generation of staff members to take over what I have been doing." A staff member at another center said, "People come and go. It is a problem that we have not been able to expand the pool of staff and volunteers."

Conclusion

Drop-in play centers have played a valuable role in connecting mothers of preschoolers who are relatively isolated in their communities of residence, which are now characterized by high mobility, low fertility rates, and the predominance of single- and nuclear-family households. Staff members strive to involve mothers and their children by creating a homelike, warm environment and by encouraging them to participate in the social interactions at the play

centers. When consulted by mothers, staff members listen to them sympathetically and create informal discussions of child-rearing issues by engaging other mothers, rather than by trying to give any single, "right" answer.[3]
Mothers themselves provide support as peers by sharing concerns among
themselves. Users may not necessarily resolve their issues as the result of a
discussion or consultation, yet my informants often told me that they "felt
refreshed" *(sukkiri shita)* or "felt relieved" *(ki ga raku ni natta)* after talking to
a staff member about an issue of concern. Therefore, the interactions that take
place at drop-in centers can reduce the anxiety felt by young mothers.

It is worth emphasizing that the nonprofit organizations encourage mothers to act as helpers and supporters of child rearing rather than being the
passive recipients of support. Drop-in play centers may also inspire mothers
to use their existing skills and experiences and to explore future work possibilities through engaging in center activities. As a result, the involvement
of mothers in a drop-in play center can give them a sense of belonging that
they do not necessarily experience in their daily lives in their communities.
While the nonprofit organizations certainly cannot revive the organic unity of
a given community, it is significant that they are attempting to recreate social
connections in metropolitan communities.

Because most research participants were recruited through the drop-in
play centers, this study does not include the voices of mothers who, for a
variety of reasons, do not use such centers, including those who are reluctant
to meet or talk with others in public settings. It also excludes those who are
not familiar with drop-in play centers. Among these are mothers of newborns
and those who have only recently moved to their communities of residence.
Further research on mothers who rarely use these centers and those who are
not familiar with them would refine our understanding of the existing needs
for child-rearing support. A focus on non-users is also important given that
public welfare services do not always reach the people who need them. Studies
on public services for low-income clients in North America indicate that the
services are often located outside their clients' neighborhoods and cannot be
reached easily by public transportation (e.g., Allard 2009; Peck 2008). None of
my interviewees drove to visit the centers but usually came by bike or on foot.
Thus the lack of an automobile in a family, a factor that is linked to a family's class status, did not necessarily limit access to drop-in centers. Nonetheless, access according to class—geographical or otherwise—remains largely
underexplored and requires further research.

To assess the sustainability of child-rearing support through drop-in play centers run by nonprofit organizations, the following two issues deserve consideration. The first is the matter of quality. As this study illustrates, staff members play important roles in connecting a mother to other mothers and to support providers outside the play centers. Unlike drop-in play centers managed and staffed by municipal bodies, those run by nonprofits depend heavily upon married women volunteers. As noted, some representatives of nonprofit organizations reported that they have not been able to attract a new generation of successors who would be likely to continue their operation. The limited availability of human resources to rejuvenate the existing support staff can pressure the staff to overwork and thus risk lowering the quality of support.

The second issue is a larger structural problem. The increase of drop-in centers run by nonprofit organizations further strengthens the dominant division of labor between married men in the formal employment sector and married women in the informal employment sector or in domestic roles. It is true that drop-in centers can provide opportunities of social engagement for married women during or beyond their child-rearing years, thus encouraging citizen participation in creating better social environments. Nonetheless, the existing easy reliance on nonprofit organizations to fill the social vacuum created by diminishing community ties can be seen as evidence of the state's reluctance to shoulder its responsibility and promote gender equality in patterns of child rearing and employment. The recreation of connections among relatively isolated young mothers is less valuable if it is achieved only at the cost of older mothers who provide the bulk of labor that is remunerated below its market value.

Notes

A Japan Foundation Research Fellowship (2008–2009) funded the fieldwork in Japan for this project. I would like to thank Glenda Roberts of Waseda University for her kindness and generosity as a host researcher during my stay in Japan. I would like to express my deep gratitude to people who participated in this study. I would also like to thank Glenda Roberts, Susan Long, and the anonymous reviewers for their helpful comments on earlier versions of this chapter.

1. Such is the case in many other nonprofit organizations in contemporary Japan. For example, at the organization where I conducted fieldwork for my project on ash scattering ceremonies between 2002 and 2004, regular staff members and volunteers were remunerated, although the monetary rewards were sometimes referred to as "allowances" *(okozukai)* rather than as salaries or wages. See also Nakamura (this volume).
2. A drop-in center must have at least two regular staff members. The number of

staff and volunteers varies greatly from center to center. For example, Play Center B had two regular staff and at least five regular volunteers, while Play Center C had only two regular staff and several occasional volunteers.

3. This pattern of interaction and guidance is also common in classroom settings. See Cave (this volume).

References Cited

Allard, Scott W. 2009. *Out of Reach: Place, Poverty, and the New American Welfare State*. New Haven: Yale University Press.

Allison, Anne. 2011. "Stopping Death as a Politics of Life: Suicide Prevention in Japan." Paper presented at the Death and Desire in Modern and Contemporary Japan Conference at the Università Ca' Foscari di Venezia, Venice, March 7–8.

Borovoy, Amy. 2008. "Japan's Hidden Youths: Mainstreaming the Emotionally Distressed in Japan." *Culture, Medicine, and Psychiatry* 32, no. 4:552–576.

Harada, Masafumi. 2006. *Kosodate no henbō to jisedai ikusei shien* (Changing child rearing and support to raise the next generation). Nagoya: Nagoya Daigaku Shuppankai.

Holloway, Susan. 2010. *Women and Family in Contemporary Japan*. New York: Cambridge University Press.

Holthus, Barbara. 2011. "Child Care and Work-Life Balance in Low Fertility Japan." In *Imploding Populations in Japan and Germany: A Comparison*, ed. Florian Coulmas and Ralph Lützeler, 203–226. Leiden and Boston: Brill.

Honda, Yuki. 2008. *Katei kyōiku no itsuro: Kosodate ni kyōhaku sareru hahaoyatachi* (Home education's narrow path: Mothers who are intimidated by child rearing). Tokyo: Keisō Shobō.

Iwama, Akiko. 2004. "Ikuji kosuto no chiikisa to shakaiteki shien" (Regional variations regarding the cost of child rearing and social support). In *Shōshika no jendā bunseki* (A gendered analysis of low fertility), ed. Meguro Yoriko and Nishioka Hachirō, 150–173. Tokyo: Keisō Shobō.

Kashiwagi, Keiko, and Morishita Kumiko. 1997. *Kosodate hiroba 0123 Kichijōji* (0123 Kichijōji, the drop-in play center). Kyoto: Minerva Shobō.

Kosodate Hiroba Zenkoku Renraku Kyōgikai. 2009. "Heisei nijūichinendo jigyō hōkokusho" (The 2009 activity report). Http://kosodatehiroba.com/08siryou.html. Accessed May 25, 2012.

Lebra, Takie S. 1984. *Japanese Women: Constraint and Fulfillment*. Honolulu: University of Hawai'i Press.

Makino, Katsuko. 1982. "Nyūyōji o motsu hahaoya no seikatsu to ikuji fuan" (Life and child-rearing anxiety among mothers of infants). *Katei kyōiku kenkyūjo kiyō* 3:35–56.

Matsuda, Shigeki. 2008. *Nani ga kosodate o sasaerunoka* (What supports child rearing?). Tokyo: Keisō Shobō.

———. 2010. "Kosodate kiban ni me o mukeru" (Paying attention to the foundation of child rearing). In *Yuragu kosodate kiban* (The foundation of child rearing has been shaken), by Matsuda Shigeki, Shiomi Kazue, Shinada Tomomi, and Suemori Kei, 1–14. Tokyo: Keisō Shobō.

Ministry of Health, Labor, and Welfare. 2009. "Heisei nijūichinendo chiiki kosodate kyoten jigyō jisshi jōkyō" (The 2009 activity report on community-level child-rearing bases). Http://www.mhlw.go.jp/seisakunitsuite/bunya/kodomo/ kodomo_kosodate/ kosodate/ index.html. Accessed May 25, 2012.

———. 2010. "Heisei nijūninendo chiiki kosodate kyoten jigyō jisshi jōkyō" (The 2010 activity report on community-level child-rearing bases). Http://www.mhlw.go.jp/ seisakunitsuite/ bunya/kodomo/kodomo_kosodate/kosodate/index.html. Accessed May 25, 2012.

———. 2013. "Daiikkai nijūisseiki shusshōji jūdan chōsa no gaikyō tōkeihyō" (A statistical summary of the first longitudinal survey on children born in the twenty-first century). Http://www.mhlw.go.jp/toukei/saikin/hw/ shusshoujib/01/ dl/01–4.pdf. Accessed February 22, 2013.

Morioka, Kiyomi, Honma Jun, Yamaguchi Tsuruko, and Takao Atsuko. 1968. "Tokyo kinkō danchi kazoku no seikatsushi to shakaisanka" (The life history and social participation among families living in collective public housing in a Tokyo's suburb). *Kokusai kirisutokyō daigaku gappō IIB: Shakaikagaku jānaru* 7:199–277.

Nakatani, Natsuko. 2008. *Chiiki kosodate shien to hahaoya no enpawāmento* (Community-level child-rearing support and the empowerment of mothers). Nishi, Okayama: Daigaku Kyōiku Shuppan.

Ochiai, Emiko. 2000 [1994]. *Nijūisseiki kazoku e* (To the twenty-first-century family). 5th ed. Tokyo: Yūhikaku.

Okuyama, Chizuko, and Ōmameuda Hirotomo. 2003. *Oyako no hiroba Bīno-bīno* (Bīno-bīno, the playroom for parents and children). Kyoto: Mineruva Shobō.

Partner, Simon. 2004. *Toshie: A Story of Village Life in Twentieth-Century Japan.* Berkeley: University of California Press.

Peck, L. R. 2008. "Do Anti-Poverty Nonprofits Locate Where People Need Them? Evidence from a Spatial Analysis of Phoenix." *Nonprofit and Voluntary Sector Quarterly* 37:138–151.

Roberts, Glenda S. 2002. "Pinning Hopes on Angels: Reflections from an Aging Japan's Urban Landscape." In *Family and Social Policy in Japan,* ed. Roger Goodman, 54–91. Cambridge: Cambridge University Press.

Sasagawa, Ayumi. 2006. "Mother-Rearing: The Social World of Mothers in a Japanese Suburb." In *The Changing Japanese Family,* ed. Marcus Rebick and Ayumi Takenaka, 129–146. London: Routledge.

Smith, Robert J., and Ella Lury Wiswell. 1982. *The Women of Suye Mura.* Chicago: University of Chicago Press.

Tamanoi, Mariko Asano. 1998. *Under the Shadow of Nationalism: Politics and Poetics of Rural Japanese Women.* Honolulu: University of Hawai'i Press.

Yamane, Mari. 2000. "Ikuji fuan to kazoku no kiki" (Child-rearing anxiety and the crisis of families). In *Kazoku mondai: Kiki to sonzoku* (Family issues: Crisis and continuity), ed. Shimizu Shinji, 21–40. Kyoto: Mineruva Shobō.

CHAPTER 10

The Divination Arts in Girl Culture

LAURA MILLER

TWO YOUNG WOMEN, both wearing high school uniforms, were browsing in an accessory shop in the western section of Tokyo. The girl with the short hair and ready smile was a Sagittarius, and she was looking for something very specific: "One of my Lucky Goods for this month is a gold-colored hair ornament. So I'm getting this one," she told me, holding out the sparkly gold clip with a tiny pink skull on it. She had read an astrological horoscope in *Popteen* magazine (one of hundreds of teen magazines with an English name) and wanted to get one of the recommended Sagittarian "lucky" items for the month. What is interesting about her choice is how it illustrates not only the ubiquity of an appropriated Western divination system, but also the manner in which it has seamlessly become enmeshed with the common activity of shopping.

A noticeable escalation of interest in divination and other occult pursuits in Japan was evident during the 1980s, when critics began talking about an *uranai būmu* (divination boom). Many scholars, including Suzuki (1995), Kawano (1995), and Miller (1997), noticed the preponderance of women as consumers of divination schemas and services. Taneda (2000) also described the divination industry as being under the control of women as both producers and consumers of services. Time-consuming and occasionally expensive divination activities have, therefore, been dominated by girls and women for many years. This feminization of fortune-telling results in a preponderance of female aesthetics and tastes being channeled into a diverse range of new or refurbished fortune-telling types and services. While middle-aged and senior women continue to be fascinated by older forms of divination, such as palmistry or the Chinese zodiac, young girls create and consume multiple genres of creolized and occasionally humorous divination. They might use their cell phones to look up Tarot card readings or pay for automated forecasts in booths at entertainment parks.

Since 2002 there has been an expansion of divination themes and images in all forms of popular culture but especially in ways that are intended to appeal to a female consumer. This shift is partly because the majority of divination production is now in the hands of women. Many of the trendy divination salons are owned and run by women, and the divination booths in malls are mainly staffed by women. Women are the primary artists, creators, and producers behind the recent flood of new Tarot card designs, occult goods, Web sites, and divination magazines and books. Although girls and women are now at the forefront of divination production, this chapter will focus primarily on the consumption of divination services and goods.

I am interested in looking at divination not simply because it is a substantial market, but also because it provides recognition of female interests, activities, and economic impact. My aim is not to discover the degree to which girls and young women believe in the efficacy of such practices. There already exist hundreds of surveys that attempt to answer versions of questions such as "Do you think divination is accurate?" Rather, I want to explore the ways that the divination industry has accommodated the aesthetic, social, and entertainment interests of young women and girls.

Exploring Feminized Texts and Spaces

Divination products, media, and services are usually categorized under the term *uranai* (divination). I use the word here to mean practices that intend to predict future events or discover hidden knowledge. Some long-standing and popular divination types in Japan are Western and Chinese astrology, Chinese geomancy or feng shui, Tarot cards, I Ching (Book of Changes), and physiognomy (reading the traits of the face and body). Western-style astrology has been fully assimilated in Japan and is included in most monthly women's magazines, broadcast on TV, and displayed on LCD screens hanging down in subway trains. Chinese feng shui, introduced to Japan many centuries ago, is now popular among young women seeking advice on how best to use specific spaces, such as Itō's (2007) guide to "car feng shui" for female car owners. Itō provides tips for a car's interior design and furnishings that will improve the owner's future prospects and financial success. Specialized feng shui such as the one she proposes are well represented among the thousands of books in this genre. There are, for example, books and courses on workplace feng shui, makeup feng shui, and toilet feng shui.

Some of the schoolgirls and young women with whom I spoke also understood feng shui to include the use of colors to aid in success. One duo I met had yellow charms that they always carried on shopping days because they had read in a shared book that yellow is the color that attracts wealth. A woman in her twenties named Aya told me about a book entitled *Girly Feng Shui Magic Makeup* that she shared with her friend Reiko (Takako and Mirey 2008). The two of them experimented with some of the book's suggestions, such as hairstyles and nail polish colors, that would enhance their careers or relationships. They didn't see the book as something that should be taken seriously; they just thought it might be enjoyable to play around with the ideas in the book, each trying different themes and telling the other what she thought about the results.

Although the Ministry of Economy, Trade, and Industry does not provide statistical information about the divination industry, according to one estimate the industry generates the equivalent of $8.5 billion a year (Brasor 2006). Japanese critics are generally contemptuous of anything related to divination, dismissing it as nothing more than silly "superstition." For example, in an article in the *Asahi Shinbun* (Matsukawa and Ogawa 2011), the writers conflate divination and the occult, warning of dangerous occult dabbling and religious cult entrapment. When we approach the subject from an anthropological perspective, however, we try to understand it on its own terms and from the insider's stance rather than from the perspective of an outsider's norms and ideas. In this case, older men, who are not active participants in girl culture, often project their own ideas and attitudes onto their descriptions of female cultural activities. Unfortunately, most recent news reporting on the popularity of divination narrowly focuses on street fortune-tellers and their potential exploitation of clients. Murata (2012) interviewed only female divination enthusiasts who were characterized as "addicted" to the services provided by street fortune-tellers, noting the escalation in complaints submitted to the National Consumer Affairs Center of Japan. A common stereotype about divination, which reporters such as Murata perpetuate, continues to be that it is a sketchy business provided by stigmatized social groups (resident Koreans at one time made up the majority of street fortune-tellers) who set up temporary tables near high-traffic train stations. Contrary to this portrait, my research reveals a much broader range of services, from upscale and trendy divination salons to corporation-owned stalls in elegant shopping malls, where women and girls enjoy divination not as a type of addiction or irrational belief but as an enjoyable social activity with entertainment value.

In addition, the study of divination in Japan does not fit very well into many scholarly and scientific interpretive frames, in which understanding of religious behavior is often centered on doctrine and individual "belief." There are countless government polls and private-sector surveys of Japanese divination, and these sometimes reflect an obsession with how much people believe in the accuracy of divination types. Furthermore, one common overt or implied message these polls send is that participation in divination activities, which is highest among girls and women, reflects illogical and unscientific thinking. In contrast, this chapter views divination as a behavior that deserves to be understood as a legitimate cultural practice that has value, rather than seeing it as evidence of an unsanctioned ideology.

Divination is a social practice found among many girls and young women who enjoy exploring a multitude of augury styles and types. As one twenty-two-year-old woman told me, "I like Tarot cards, I Ching, and runes because they are ancient types of divination and are also fun to do with my friends." My understanding of divination is based on analysis of texts and fieldwork conducted since 2002. Rather than a concern with individual beliefs about the efficacy of divination, the cultural studies approach used here views it as a meaningful social practice about which we can learn through a variety of media and observations. I spoke to or interviewed ten young women and girls between the ages of fifteen and twenty-two. My encounter with divination in girl culture is also based on observation of behavior in explicitly marked divination booths and shops and derives from participant observation in other venues as well, including shrines, bead shops, bookstores, and game arcades. I often discovered divination subjects and imagery whenever I entered female-oriented consumption spaces. For example, Neko no Mise, a Tokyo café featuring resident cats that customers can play with while sipping a cup of coffee, once offered Tarot card readings a few times a month by a fortune-teller named Ririco. Two women I encountered in the café had originally gone there simply to visit with the cats and catch up with each other's news, but since there was someone on the premises giving Tarot readings, they thought that would be something fascinating to try as long as they were there. After the reading they spent more than thirty minutes talking to each other about what the fortune-teller had said, trying to tie her words to specific events in their lives. Similarly, while doing research on annotated self-photography, I often saw photos on which girls had written their divination blood type (*ketsue-ki-gata*) or Chinese or Western zodiac sign next to their images (Miller 2003, 2005). For example, four girls getting their photo stickers made in an arcade each added the image of their Chinese zodiac animal above their heads. Since there is not much time allowed to add graphics and text to the photos before they are printed, the foursome had decided on adding the zodiac animals before they even got in the booth.

What is it about divination that girls in particular find so attractive? Scholars of religion and ritual in Japan have probed the diverse functions of divination from a variety of perspectives. For example, Kawano (1995) investigated the relationship between single women and their interest in divination during a liminal period spanning the years after graduation and before marriage. She also noted that divination was a social endeavor for women during gatherings or at holidays, a continuing aspect of its appeal. For young women and girls, divination is available as an imaginative activity that readily caters to their tastes and aesthetics. One illustration of this are the many types of Tarot cards designed in Japan on which gothic European landscapes are replaced with adorable animals or endearingly cute scenes (Miller 2011). Divination is also popular among girls because it is something they can do with others, facilitating sharing and bonding. The two girls in the accessory shop described above talked about divination-related charms they ought to buy for friends and family, comparing ideas and assessments about the most appropriate or suitable items that would complement someone's personality and birth date.

Playing with Divinatory Genres

I was talking to a schoolgirl named Naoko about the sheet of stickers with tiny photos on it that she and her friend Tomoko had just printed from a self-photography booth.[1] We were in an arcade in the popular teen-thronged shopping and entertainment area of Tokyo known as Harajuku, a place that was crammed with automated photo sticker machines called "print club" *(purikura)*. Suddenly Tomoko began laughing about something she was viewing on her cell phone. I asked if it was another funny photo perhaps, but she claimed it was only a cute Web site. Pressed, Tomoko revealed that it was an online divination site that provides a forecast based on a person's "cake" personality. The system works as follows: You go to the Cake Divination Web site and enter your name and date of birth, and you are assigned a cake type (such as Chocolate Cake, Chiffon Cake, Baked Cheesecake, or Fruit Tart) that best captures your personality type. For example, someone who is the Shortcake is said to have the qualities of a fashion leader. Although Shortcake folks have a policy of being fashionable, they still aren't gaudy or ostentatious—they are good at casually combining accessories and dressing according to the time, place, and occasion. A Shortcake who entered her birthday on this site was told that in a previous life she was a triceratops dinosaur. Cake Divination can easily be accessed via one's cell phone from the i-mode, SoftBank, and EZweb carriers.[2]

When I asked Tomoko how she came upon Cake Divination, she told me she often found lists of fun divination Web sites and has visited hundreds of them, including Cat Character Divination, Yamanote Train Line Divination, and TV Drama Divination. She said that she occasionally looked at "regular" divination online sites for dream divination, blood typology, and astrology. Cake Divination is one of the popular Internet divination types that have become a large part of girls' cell phone and Internet culture. Indeed, according to Goo Research, Cake Divination is on the top ten "most want to do" list of Internet divination types based on a poll of 1,663 people (56 percent female) in 2005. Other popular Internet sites were Wizard Divination, Conveyor Belt Sushi Divination, Ramen Noodles Divination, and Disney Movie Divination.[3]

The examples of Cake Divination, Conveyor Belt Sushi Divination, and some of the other intentionally amusing types lead us to wonder about methods for organizing or classifying the many forms of divination that are available. How should we group them? Although Tomoko made a distinction between "fun" types such as Cake Divination and older forms such as astrology or blood typology, this manner of classification is problematic because it depends on the classifier's attitudes or belief system. The scholar Suzuki Kentarō (1995) used the distinction of face-to-face or non-face-to-face channels to organize his discussion of contemporary Japanese divination. Face-to-face channels include home fortune-tellers, street fortune-tellers, touring fortune-tellers, and telephone fortune-tellers. Non-face-to-face divination forms are accessed through media: magazines, books, TV, radio, the Internet, and monthly journals. Although nicely human-centered, this system shifts away from the actual form of divination to the manner in which it is consumed.

In looking at how divination is understood in girl culture, I often found that these categories are interwoven in how people think about and use them.

A common scheme for classifying the divination arts in Japan is to use how the divination method operates as the main criterion. This is the way many popular divination manuals and divination schools arrange their descriptions and offerings. For example, a vocational school in Ebisu named Akademeia College, which trains students to be professional fortune-tellers, divides the "divination arts" into categories depending on whether or not there is use of the person's birth date, the person's physical traits, or involves the manipulation of objects.

Divination that begins with the seeker's birth date is found in many older forms as well as newer types. Conservative author and TV personality Hosoki Kazuko is one of the most well known, and perhaps most vilified, of the divination experts who often appeared on TV in the 2000s. She has authored more than one hundred books that use the birth date as the basis for a modified Chinese-style astrological system called Six Star Astrology (Rokusei Senjutsu). Dorman (2007) has tracked the ways that Hosoki manipulated her system in order to make it more appealing to conservatives and those concerned about the loss of "Japaneseness." Hosoki is one of many so-called "charisma fortune-tellers" esteemed among the older crowd, but most girls told me they thought she was creepy or old-fashioned. Whenever I browsed through the divination sections of bookstores in Tokyo, I rarely saw women under twenty reaching for any of the Hosoki books. Instead, they thumbed through cute editions describing newly invented divination types such as Penguin Divination (Ono 2007a), Panda Divination (Midori 2007), or White Bear Divination (Ono 2007b).

One birth-date-based divination craze popular among young women and girls is Animal Divination (Dōbutsu Uranai), a new zoomancy that is quite different from the borrowed Chinese zodiac, which also aligns animals with birth years. In this new system, the twelve animals are pegasus, elephant, lion, cheetah, tiger, wolf, monkey, koala, black panther, sheep, raccoon dog, and fawn, and each is associated with one of four elements (earth, sun, full moon, and new moon). The comic artist Kubo Kiriko (1999 and several subsequent years) created adorable illustrations for a series of Animal Divination books that sold millions of copies. There is even a cell phone application for accessing one's Animal Divination fortune from Noracom. Animal-type divination systems are so popular among girls that there are always new ones being created. Another animal system uses typical zoo creatures: gorilla, panda, elephant, penguin, giraffe, alligator, cheetah, polar bear, zebra, hippo, and owl (Primavera 2008). The seeker finds out her (or his) zoo type by consulting a chart that lists zoo animal types by birth year and date.

A second classification for divination uses traits of the seeker's body or physical components. The popular indigenous typological system called *ketsueki-gata* is based on personality characterization according to blood types A, B, AB, and O. This type of classification had its origin during the Taishō era (1912–1926) and became popular in later decades when it was proposed as a reliable method for understanding personality types. It has had immense cultural impact: numerous schools, corporations, and other institutions once used the system to organize work or study groups, and many ask for the applicant's blood type on job applications.[4] Every girl and young woman I have ever met in Japan knows her own blood type. One may buy condoms, Hello Kitty good luck charms, and diet pills geared to each of the four blood types. In many of the girl spaces I frequented as part of my research, blood typology often emerged as a motif or gimmick. One divination fad that several girls mentioned to me as a droll, non-serious sort that they did with their friends was Gundam (Gandamu) fortune-telling, in which characters from the famous animation series are paired with blood types A, B, AB, and O to yield forty-eight personality types (Gandamu Uranai Chō Seisaku Iinkai 2001).

A third method for organizing divination uses objects such as cards or stones that are manipulated or selected at random and are thought to be material manifestations of prophecy. Older and imported divination forms such as I-Ching, Tarot cards, and crystals are examples of this object-based category. While I was hanging around a divination shop named Wiz Note, located in a northern area of Tokyo popular for dining and entertainment (see below), I saw two schoolgirls spend almost thirty minutes debating about whether or not one of them should buy a deck of "rune" Tarot cards, a good example of this category. They left the shop but returned a few minutes later to buy them. The alphabetic runes have long been associated with divination in Europe, and this deck, created by charisma fortune-teller Kagami Ryūji (2000), was antique-looking, with Renaissance-style art together with the Nordic runes. One tells fortunes with the twenty-four cards by placing them face down and selecting three at random that will suggest future outcomes.

Magazine companies, government agencies, university researchers, and marketing firms all routinely conduct surveys to determine people's beliefs about the efficacy of divination. A poll conducted by Goo Research (2010), a private Internet marketing research firm, shows that all these divination methods are considered reliable. People who participated in the poll, which asked them which divination system they thought had the greatest chance of predicting the future, ranked palmistry as the most reliable (see table 10.1). The 2010 Internet poll had 51.1 percent female respondents, nearly half of them under thirty. Two types, Four Pillars Divination and Name Divination, tied for the number two spot. Four Pillars Divination (Shichū Suimei) was originally from China and uses the year, month, day, and hour of birth to predict the seeker's future. The well-known divination celebrity Hosoki Kazuko, mentioned above, created a technique she calls Six Star Astrology based on this borrowed Chinese system, and it is ranked number four. Name Divination (Seimei Handan) can take different forms, but most often it is a type of numerology derived from the character strokes found in the seeker's written name.

In addition to there being divination forms that rely on the seeker's birth date or physical traits or the manipulation of objects in this top-ten list, there are also types of divination that originate in Japan, China, and Europe listed here as well. Such an eclectic mix illustrates another problem in the classification of divination: many of the types that are most popular among girls are hybrid forms that exploit multiple strategies and current interests. Consider Cat Characters Divination (Tomono 2007). The seeker starts with his or her Western zodiac sign and cross-checks it against his or her blood type; the

TABLE 10.1	*Which divination type do you think has the highest predictive value?*
1	Palmistry
2	Four Pillars Divination
2	Name Divination
4	Six Star Astrology
5	Tarot Cards
6	Blood Typology
7	Geomancy (feng shui)
8	Physiognomy
9	Dream Interpretation
10	Western Zodiac

cross-check yields one of twelve alphabet letters. Depending on one's sex, the seeker looks up his or her type under the assigned letter to determine which of twelve possible cat characters represent the forecast. The cats are *manga* characters such as Yume, Michael, Yukipon, Kuro, and Fukufuku. *Manga* drawings for each character are found throughout the book, and the presentation suggests that girls are the primary target for the book.

One particularly interesting system is Korean Food Divination (Kankoku Fūdo Uranai), an Internet Web site that determines one's personality type and forecast based on an assigned Korean dish. In this scheme, which is a hybrid of three different ways of categorization, the seeker uses a chart to locate his or her birth month and cross-references it with both blood type and Chinese astrological sign. This yields a number that one uses to check against a list of famous Korean foods and their linked forecasts.[5] Three women in their twenties who had traveled together to South Korea told me they liked this divination system not only because it was humorous, but also because it reminded them of the trip they took. During their time in Seoul they first ate many types of Korean food that were new to them, so playing Korean Food Divination was a way to remember their experience and also to display to others their knowledge of Korean food types.

Another example that illustrates the way divination products and services are often linked to other fads is the combination of systems used to create Korean Wave Face Divination (Yanagi 2005). This system introduced Korean-style face reading, originally a divination system from China, with famous Korean pop stars as examples of particular facial types. The term "Korean Wave" was coined to describe the influx of Korean popular culture into Japan, especially hit TV dramas, and the increase in fans of Korean cultural products from 2003. There are associated fortunes based on variation in eyebrow shape, nose type, ear type, mouth shape, eye shape, facial structure, and hairline pattern. One schoolgirl named Masako told me she liked the Korean Wave Face Divination book because the illustrations reminded her of the main character in the TV drama series *Dae Jang Geum* (Jewel in the Palace in English titling), a historical series that follows the life of the first female imperial physician in Korean history. The book also includes information and maps for visiting divination cafés in Seoul, with directions and explanations of the types of divination services found in different specialized coffee shops. This aspect of the divination industry—combining other amusements with fortune-telling—characterizes how divination is frequently consumed in tandem with other leisure pursuits.

Divination Entertainment

On a sunny day in October, three schoolgirls were buying paper lottery oracles *(omikuji)* at Kameido Tenmangū, a Shinto shrine dedicated to Tenjin, the god of scholarship. The oracles are small slips of paper drawn at random, each with a Chinese character denoting different levels of luck. In the past these fortune slips were most often simple papers that might contain a poem and a brief forecast for travel, study, finance, and personal relationships. At this shrine, there are two options for the oracles: a typical one for ¥300 and a more elaborate one for ¥500. The expensive alternative comes tied together with a small origami doll of a girl in a kimono.

I wondered if perhaps a young female shrine attendant *(miko)* had come up with the idea of using such a variety of divination forms and a cute wrapping in order to appeal to young female visitors. When I asked, however, no one in the shrine kiosk that sells amulets and other goods even knew when these new-style oracles got started. But they did say that these origami-style oracles were proving to be extremely popular, especially with young women and schoolgirls.

The oracle itself, however, is also of interest because it lists several different types of divination forecasts, including Chinese astrology, Western astrology, blood typology, and Japanese directional divination *(katatagae)*. The schoolgirls paid for the more expensive oracle, a decision I asked them about. They thought the cheaper one would be just as legitimate, but it was not as cute. One

FIGURE 10.1

Paper lottery oracle from Kameido Tenmangū

of them said it would be nice to glue the origami doll into their photo journals, with a shot of the trio standing in front of the shrine. Their divination experience was part of a shrine visit in which they engaged in other typical rituals, such as writing votive plaques and buying amulets. The visit to the shrine itself was rooted in a day-long excursion to the far reaches of Tokyo that included shopping and eating out at a new restaurant.

As scholars of Japanese religion have often pointed out, activities at temples and shrines are frequently embedded in touristic sightseeing (Nelson 1996; Reader and Tanabe 1998). Divination as a part of girls' entertainment is most explicit at Namco Namja Town, an indoor theme park complex in northern Tokyo. It houses several discrete recreational areas along with alleys that zigzag through them. Most are food-oriented experiences, such as Gyoza Stadium, a laneway with retro-style dumpling stalls that sell famous potsticker types from around Japan. One distinct section is named Soothsayer Street (Uranai-shi Sutoriito; see figure 10.2). Here, customers purchase divination forecasts in automated booths for ¥500, with a choice of eleven virtual experts in Chinese astrology, Kabala, Tarot, South Asian astrology, and other occult sciences.

One of the featured booths is dedicated to a famous street divination provider named Kurihara Sumiko. Her booth, labeled "the Shinjuku Mother" (Shinjuku no Haha), derives from the nickname she earned after reading palms, doing physiognomy, and forecasting Chinese astrology in an area of Tokyo known as Shinjuku since the 1950s (she was born in 1930). Kurihara has been the subject of intense media attention, including an autobiography, a *manga,* a television drama series, and a documentary. She also has a Web site and an Android cell phone application. A young woman who paid for Kurihara's in-person divination service (the Shinjuku Mother charges a flat fee of ¥5,000) told me that she felt more optimistic, uplifted, and happier after speaking with the warm and engaging Kurihara, regardless of how "real" or accurate the divination may have been. Younger women and girls who cannot afford the actual service from Kurihara herself think the Namco Namja Town booth falls in the realm of campy retro and hold the opinion that the game complex booth version of the Shinjuku Mother is not only affordable, interactive, and fun, but also less time-consuming and more comfortable to visit when one is with friends. Asked if she would like to visit the real-life Shinjuku Mother instead of the video booth imposter, a young woman named Naoko said, "It would be a little scary. And then there's such a long wait. It's a pain. Coming here is more convenient."

On many visits to Namco Namja Town I observed groups and pairs of girls entering Soothsayer Street, where they first purchased tokens to use in one of the booths. The area is decorated in shabby faux Arabian artifacts and drapery, with tacky lamps and arabesque architectural bits scattered around. Each booth had a bench that might seat two or three people in front of it. I rarely saw a person enter Soothsayer Street alone, and men and boys seemed to enter only if they were accompanied by a female partner. This was a fun activity that girls appeared to enjoy, and each booth yielded a printed sheet with forecasts on it at the conclusion of the session that customers could take home with them.

Divination is regularly provided as a fun activity at many other venues. Examples include the "butterfly divination" display at the Insect Knowledge

FIGURE 10.2

Entrance to Soothsayer Street

Festival and Carnival at the Itami City Insect Museum and divination tables at many seasonal outdoor and indoor festivals. In Osaka there was an indoor theme park named Dōtonbori Gokuraku Shōtengai (now closed) that featured Taishō era (1912–1926) recreations of stylized cafés and restaurants. On the fifth floor there were several retro-style divination booths. There are also "divination tours" from Japan to Hong Kong, Taipei, and Shanghai. The tour companies pitch the trips as an opportunity to explore the birthplace of Chinese-style divination. For example, the Kinki Nippon Tourist Company advertised a visit to Taipei's teeming divination sector in its July 2008 brochure, which promised to provide translators and guides for a safe and smooth experience.

Walking around Tokyo one may easily stumble upon new divination boutiques and shops where girls and women purchase Tarot cards, crystals, Chinese divination compasses, amulets, and other goods. During 2008 I visited many of these sites to speak to divination specialists and to observe the type of services and goods being offered, as well as the interactions between providers and clients. I also found many divination booths in chic shopping malls; these are usually called "divination corners." Most of the booths are operated by corporations that have a stable menu of divination experts who rotate among booths at different malls on different days of the week. One of the better-known companies is Mari Fortune, which has seven booths in upscale malls around Tokyo. The schedules are easily accessed online and list multiple types of divination, from the old-fashioned to newer hybrid or New Age types. Each booth seats one to three diviners, and there is a standardized price structure based on time. Having uniform and posted fees has made these businesses quite successful and especially attractive to girls and young women, who do not need to worry about being bamboozled. Unlike the street soothsayers maligned by Murata (2012), these clean and bright divination booths never generate complaints about fees or services.

One woman with whom I spoke at a booth in north Tokyo said she always went to a nearby Mari Fortune location whenever her favorite divination specialist was doing a rotation there. She told me that Mitsuhana Maya Sensei provided a type of Tarot card reading called Inspiration Tarot, which she found especially attractive and meaningful. This variety of Tarot incorporates the seeker's affect together with the reader's interpretations to predict the short-term future. Mitsuhana offers other divination services, including Chinese Nine Star astrology, palm reading, directional divination, and I-Ching Tarot readings. There are many divination providers like Mitsuhana who have a solid reputation and a loyal fan following. Their followers always address or refer to these divination specialists with the title *sensei* (teacher).

In addition to the booths found in malls there are also small divination shops located in office buildings and along busy streets. They sell goods and provide readings and other services. One place that was particularly appealing to schoolgirls and young women was a trendy shop named Wiz Note. It was later relocated to an office building, but in 2008 it was crammed in among other businesses found on the main pedestrians-only shopping street in the northern section of Tokyo called Ikebukuro. The shop was always crowded with foot traffic because of its location near a popular store and shopping center. Wiz Note offered divination services and carried a variety of occult goods, including crystals, Tarot cards, Chinese feng shui compasses, and amulets. The store was owned and managed by two women and was packed with female shoppers every time I visited. I often saw uniform-wearing schoolgirls inside rummaging through the Tarot decks and occult goods that crowded the store's shelves. Two women in their twenties who were seated at a very tiny

FIGURE 10.3
Wiz Note divination shop in Tokyo

round table, where one of them was preparing to have a Tarot card reading, talked to me about what they found most attractive about the shop. They liked that it was a welcoming space for women and that the all-female staff were always there to answer their questions in a warm and kind manner. They also doubted that some of the items they found most intriguing or edgy, such as a deck of Gay Tarot cards, would ever be found in more "traditional" retail spaces in Japan (see figure 10.3).

Reinvented Historical Divination

One of the earliest forms of divination in Japan, thought to have arrived with immigrants from the continent during the Yayoi era (traditionally 300 BCE~250 CE), is called scapulimancy *(futomani)*. Although I have yet to find any girls using this method, which directs fire or heat onto deer shoulder bones or tortoise shells in order to produce cracks that can be interpreted to portend the future, I have found other ancient forms of divination reemerging in contemporary girl culture. My friend's daughter Emiko often manipulates and admires some unique divination and magical objects she bought because of her interest in the legendary Heian era (794–1185) wizard or *onmyōji* (literally, yin yang master) named Abeno Seimei. Emiko, like millions of other girls and women, became enchanted with the figure of Seimei after reading wizard novels and *manga* and then seeing a feature film about him. Female infatuation with Seimei created an enormous boom in books, CDs, games, films, *manga,* anime, and toys (Miller 2008). Shinto shrines dedicated to the wizard also experienced an increase in the number of visitors, who came to pay respect and to buy newly designed amulets and charms.[6]

During several visits to Seimei Shrine in Kyoto (see figure 10.4), I had casual conversations with some of the girls and women who had made pilgrimages to its narrow but refurbished grounds. I talked to one young woman in the shrine's souvenir kiosk, where she had loaded up on many Seimei goods, such as a music CD, a notebook, a cotton hand towel, and several cell phone straps decorated with the shrine's pentagram symbol and that she planned to give to friends. She related how she had never learned anything about Seimei in school, and it was initially the novels featuring him, written by the science fiction writer Yumemakura Baku, which she had read in the early 2000s, that sparked her interest in this Japanese-style wizard. Afterward she sought out anything having to do with Seimei and was especially interested in any type of divination related to his craft. She told me his style of divination was attractive

FIGURE 10.4
Women and girls visiting Seimei Shrine, Kyoto

because it was so ancient and mysterious. Emiko had traveled from Tokyo with two friends and her aunt to visit the Kyoto Seimei shrine a year before I spoke to her, and afterward she hunted for books and games related to the sorcerer. Similar to Emiko, many girls and women have gained a renewed interest in forms of magic and divination associated with the Heian period wizard, including directional divination, use of scapegoat paper effigies for purification or to cast out bad energy, and Taoist spirit writing on paper amulets. Several authors have benefited from this interest and tailored their books to include divination and magical objects that girls could cut out, assemble, and use in their own wizard practice.

One of the most prolific of these writers is Kuyōgi Shūkei, who has produced several boxed sets that contain occult objects (Kuyōgi 2001, 2002). *The Abeno Seimei Codes: The Wizard's Craft, Circumvention of Directional Taboos, and Charms for the Prevention of Bad Luck* (Kuyōgi 2003) come packaged with two patterns to assemble divination dice, eight cards with images of Taoist gods, templates for making paper effigies, Taoist spirit writing papers to copy, and a feng shui compass. Other Seimei-themed boxed sets have cardboard cosmographic divination boards included with them (Taguchi 2002). Emiko has several of these boxed sets and appreciates the tactile participation in Seimei fandom they allow her. The tactile and aesthetic appeal of the new forms of divination and how they are packaged are a few of the reasons this business has penetrated girl culture, yet critics rarely attend to these critical points.

Conclusion

The spectrum of divination-driven activities or divination-oriented goods and entertainment has generated enormous profit, yet it remains an industry that receives little attention in mainstream business reporting. I believe that we should pay attention to aspects of divination since 2000 that are new or different. Girls and women are a force behind many financially lucrative markets, but this trend is often overlooked because of the "feminized" nature of these cultural products and services. For example, in my study of the beauty industry (Miller 2006), I found that in 2003 there were 173,412 documented beauty shops. By contrast, that same year there were 7,530 wedding and funeral services, 67,789 auto repair shops, and 14,136 software businesses, economic domains that have been the intense focus of scholarly and business reporting and interest, while the beauty industry remained virtually invisible. Although the divination industry is similarly gendered, it is almost always the focus of negative reporting in the Japanese media, where it is trivialized or demonized.

The two girls with whom I spoke in the Shibuya accessory shop about the astrological charm referred to *Popteen* as the inspiration for the selection of such an object. The role of print media, especially magazines and *manga,* is critical to understanding the escalation of interest in divination and the occult among girls and young women. Monthly *manga* magazines and publications include special free insert giveaways called *furoku.* Prough (2011) has discussed how these are used by *manga* publishers to entice readers. But various magazine publishers also include these inserts, and since 2000 many of the inserts have taken the form of punch-out divination goods, oracle cards, or Tarot cards. Several mid-twenties women who were avid connoisseurs of beautiful Tarot card decks said they became interested in studying this art because their girlhood magazines often carried tear-out *furoku* sheets of colorful and unusual Tarot cards that fascinated them. They recalled that the free cards were something they and their friends talked about and shared.

By looking at some of the newer forms of divination, particularly varieties of borrowed, hybrid, and reinvented occult practices that have emerged in recent years, we attend to an under-analyzed and gendered industry. Additionally, I hope we might understand the function of divination as a form of entertainment or social play. Thomas (2007) has written about how Miyazaki anime films are a conflation of religion and entertainment. I also see "occult play" as an aspect of the revitalized divination industry.

Similar to divination systems everywhere in the world, the ones consumed by girls and women in Japan are presented in such a way that the prognoses might suit almost anyone. Rather than advocating the efficacy of their forecasting results, many girls and women told me that whether or not divination is true or accurate, they were able to gain some useful insight into a personal situation just by virtue of thinking about it in a focused manner. When they talk about their worries and concerns with someone, such as a divination provider or their friends who participate in a divination activity with them, they feel that they have taken a step toward understanding the issue from a more dispassionate stance, and this step in turn aids them in decision making. Thus talking about their worries within the framework of the divination activity is seen as a legitimate move rather than a self-centered monopolization of a conversation. When the divination activity is framed as a fun, entertaining friendship activity, it also shifts the orientation away from behavior that might otherwise be seen as egotistical self-involvement.

Notes

1. All the names used for those I interviewed or spoke to are pseudonyms.
2. Cake Divination (Kēki uranai) at http://u-maker.com/17010.html. Accessed December 11, 2011.
3. Goo Research, "Ranking of Divination I'd Like to Try" (Yatte mitai netto uranai rankingu), at http://ranking.goo.ne.jp/ranking/010/net_uranai/. Accessed December 11, 2011.
4. There is a theory in Japan that one reason for the popularity of this native blood typology system is that there is a distribution of the four blood types among the Japanese population that is much less skewed than in some other populations. According to Fujita, Tanimura, and Tanaka (1978), it is 29.25 percent O, 38.65 percent A, 22.15 percent B, and 9.95 percent AB. Compared to Anglo-American and some European populations, the frequency of the four blood types in Japan is much less bunched into one or two categories as it seems to be in those

populations. However, in terms of worldwide distributions Japan is not unique in this regard. Among Latvians, Hungarian Rom, Egyptians, Persians, and other populations the blood type frequencies are similar to those found in Japan.
5. Korean Food Divination at http://www.k-plaza.com/life/ life_uranaitop.html. Accessed January 22, 2008.
6. In 2012, the Seimei Shrine announced on its Facebook page that it was selling a special pretty blue combination amulet–lottery oracle created to celebrate the summer Tanabata festival and only available for a few months.

References Cited

Brasor, Phillip. 2006. "Weekly Magazines Joust over Trillion-Yen Fortune Telling Trade." *Japan Times,* March 12.
Dorman, Benjamin. 2007. "Representing Ancestor Worship as 'Non-Religious': Hosoki Kazuko's Divination in the Post-Aum Era." *Nova Religio: The Journal of Alternative and Emergent Religions* 10, no. 3:32–47.
Fujita, Yoshiko, Masako Tanimura, and Katsumi Tanaka. 1978. "The Distribution of ABO Blood Groups in Japan." *Japanese Journal of Human Genetics* 23, no. 2:63–109.
Gandamu Uranai Chō Seisaku Iinkai. 2001. *Chō! Gandamu uranai* (Super! Gundam divination). Tokyo: Wani Books.
Goo Research. 2010. Tekichūritsu ga takai to omou uranai rankingu (Rankings for divination we think has the highest predictive value). Http://ranking.goo.ne.jp/ranking/010/ fortune_cometrue_2010/. Accessed December 11, 2011.
Itō, Yumi. 2007. *Kei kā fūsui* (Easy Chinese geomancy for your car). Tokyo: Taiyō Shuppan.
Kagami, Ryūji, 2000. *Shinsei rū-n tarotto senjutsu* (Divination art of the sacred runes). Tokyo: Gakken.
Kawano, Satsuki. 1995. "Gender, Liminality and Ritual in Japan: Divination among Single Tokyo Women." *Journal of Ritual Studies* 9, no. 2:65–91.
Kubo, Kiriko. *1999. Dōbutsu uranai* (Animal divination). Tokyo: Shōgakkan.
Kuyōgi, Shūkei 2001. *Abeno Seimei hiden: Onmyōji "shikigami" uranai* (The secrets of Abeno Seimei: Divination with the wizard's "spirit helpers"). Tokyo: Futami Shobō.
———. 2002. *Abeno Seimei higi: Onmyōdō jusengu shihō shinsho* (Abeno Seimei's secret tricks: Writings on the Four Treasures and tools of the way of the wizard for spells and incantations). Tokyo: Futami Shobō.
———. 2003. *Abeno Seimei Gokui Onmyōdō, katatagae, yakuyoke jusen* (The Abeno Seimei codes: The wizard's craft, circumvention of directional taboos, and charms for the prevention of bad luck). Tokyo: Futami Shobō.
Matsukawa, Atsushi, and Naoki Ogawa. 2011. "After Aum 1: Occult Subculture Makes a Comeback." *Asahi Shinbun.* Http://ajw.asahi.com/article /behind_news/ social_affairs/ AJ201112070063a. Accessed December 7, 2011.
Midori, Mayu. 2007. *Panda uranai* (Panda divination). Tokyo: Orange Page Mooks.
Miller, Laura. 1997. "People Types: Personality Classification in Japanese Women's Magazines." *Journal of Popular Culture* 31, no. 2:143–159.
———. 2003 "Graffiti Photos: Expressive Art in Japanese Girls' Culture." *Harvard Asia Quarterly* 7, no. 3:31–42.

———. 2005. "Bad Girl Photography." In *Bad Girls of Japan*, ed. Laura Miller and Jan Bardsley, 127–141. New York: Palgrave Macmillan.

———. 2006. *Beauty Up: Exploring Contemporary Japanese Body Aesthetics.* Berkeley: University of California Press.

———. 2008. "Extreme Makeover for a Heian-Era Wizard." In *Mechademia: An Annual Forum for Anime, Manga and the Fan Arts,* issue 3: *Limits of the Human,* ed. Frenchy Lunning, 30–45. Minneapolis: University of Minnesota Press.

———. 2011. "Tantalizing Tarot and Cute Cartomancy in Japan." *Japanese Studies* 31, no. 1:73–91.

Murata, Satoru. 2012. "Fortunetelling Addiction Spreads among the Insecure." *Asahi Shinbun,* April 11. Http://ajw.asahi.com/article/behind_news/social_affairs/AJ201204110003.

Nelson, John K. 1996. "Freedom of Expression: The Very Modern Practice of Visiting a Shinto Shrine." *Japanese Journal of Religious Studies* 23, nos. 1–2:117–153.

Ono, Toden. 2007a. *Pengin uranai.* (Penguin divination). Tokyo: Orange Page Mooks.

———. 2007b. *Shirokuma ōra uranai* (White bear aura divination). Tokyo: Orange Page Mooks.

Primavera, Marie. 2008. *Dōbutsuen uranai* (Zoo divination). In *Seda* (Mook), pp. 30–37. Tokyo: Hinode Publishing.

Prough, Jennifer. 2011. *Straight from the Heart: Gender, Intimacy, and the Cultural Production of Shōjo Manga.* Honolulu: University of Hawai'i Press.

Reader, Ian, and George Tanabe. 1998. *Practically Religious: Worldly Benefits and the Common Religion of Japan.* Honolulu: University of Hawai'i Press.

Suzuki, Kentarō. 1995. "Divination in Contemporary Japan." *Japanese Journal of Religious Studies* 22, nos. 3–4:249–266.

Taguchi, Shindō. 2002. *Abeno Seimei chokuban uranai* (Abeno Seimei cosmic board divination). Tokyo: Futami Shobō.

Takako and Mirey. 2008. *Gārii fū sui majikku meiku* (Girly feng shui magic makeup). Tokyo: Takeda Random House.

Taneda, H. 2000. "Fortune-Telling and Women: Contemporary Characteristics of Fortune-Telling in Japanese Society." *Journal of UOEH* 22, no. 4:351–362.

Thomas, Jolyon Baraka. 2007. "Shūkyō Asobi and Miyazaki Hayao's Anime." *Nova Religion* 10, no. 3:73–95.

Tomono, Kōji. 2007. *Neko kyara uranai* (Cat characters divination). Tokyo: Kōdansha.

Yanagi, Watei. 2005. *Onna o ageru! Hanryū "kao uranai"* (Just for women! Korean wave style face divination). Tokyo: Goma Books.

Persisting Patterns and Continuities

Despite the shifts toward differentiation and an amplified sense of uncertainty that have been examined in this volume, people's lives remain embedded in some persistent patterns of culture and of social interactions. Yet these patterns are more than cultural remnants; they are incorporated into the experiences of everyday life and reinterpreted in the new contexts of globalization, recession, and mass longevity. Part V features three chapters that highlight certain enduring institutions, practices, and ideas in Japan's twenty-first century. Despite the state's efforts to "internationalize" Japanese education by introducing English classes in elementary schools and encouraging more individual and exploratory learning, Cave (chapter 11) reveals certain lasting institutional arrangements and patterns of social interaction that characterize the Japanese school system from elementary to high school. For example, we find the familiar emphasis upon developing students as whole persons and a reluctance to divide students into classes according to their academic performance. As students mature, they find themselves in a much more hierarchical educational system, with only a small group of them proceeding to top-ranked, competitive high schools and then to prestigious post-secondary institutions.

Roth (chapter 12) examines the relationship between the rising popularity of K-cars *(keijidōsha),* known for their fuel efficiency and compact size, and the increasing number of female drivers. K-cars became particularly widespread in Japan's recessionary economy during the first decade of this century, as they are less expensive and let their owners enjoy special tax savings. Women drivers have embraced these lightweight cars to fulfill their domestic roles, rather than departing from feminine roles and neutralizing formerly masculine images of driving.

Kawano (chapter 13) explores the significance of ash scattering, a new mortuary practice in contemporary Japan, by examining the mortuary choice made by a seventy-three-year-old woman. Although by the 2000s new alternatives to the conventional interment of cremated remains in a family grave have gained social recognition, the conventional practice remains the norm. A family grave accommodates urns of multiple family members and is passed on from generation to generation. By scattering the remains of their family dead at sea or on a mountain, the survivors are not required to inherit and maintain a memorial site, and thus ash scattering is often seen by its critics as a rejection of the family grave system and the associated values of family continuity and respect for ancestors. However, as Kawano illustrates, the adoption of ash scattering does not straightforwardly imply its supporters' refusal to participate in conventional mortuary practices and care for the family dead.

CHAPTER 11

Education after the "Lost Decade(s)"

Stability or Stagnation?

....

PETER CAVE

STORIES OF CHANGE generally attract more attention than narratives of continuity. But as Baker Street's fictional detective once said, sometimes the remarkable event is what did not happen. Over the last twenty-five years, there have been significant attempts to change Japanese education, as might have been expected, given the new challenges that have arisen during that time; yet these have had limited success. This chapter examines how far new departures and challenges have affected schools and considers what the state of education can tell us about the state of Japan. At the elementary and junior high levels, I focus especially on three movements during the late 1990s and 2000s: the attempt to encourage more autonomous and creative learning; the subsequent reemphasis of conventional academic attainment; and the promotion of small class sizes and differentiated learning. Ironically, these movements have left Japanese compulsory education not so very far from its starting point in the early 1990s. This raises the question of why relatively little change has occurred. Does this represent stability or stagnation? Is it a sign of a sensible approach to change and a willingness to recognize the strengths of existing structures and practices, contrasting with the sometimes frenetic whirlwinds of initiative and counter-initiative that have often left teachers elsewhere in the world bewildered and cynical? Or does it signify uncertainty, indecision, and paralysis, a disabling inability to respond to new needs and circumstances? I will first give an ethnographic view of the different stages of school education in contemporary Japan before examining this larger question.

Elementary Education

Japan's elementary and junior high schools have been subjected to conflicting movements over the last two decades. During the 1990s and early 2000s, policymakers focused on two goals: encouraging more autonomous learning and creativity while promoting children's healthy development through engagement with the social and natural worlds around them (Cave 2007, 16–19, 195–196). In 2002, this culminated in the move to a five-day school week, the slimming down of hours for traditional academic subjects, and the introduction of a major new program at the elementary and junior high levels, Integrated Studies (Sōgō-Teki na Gakushū), intended to achieve both the above goals through exploratory learning. Yet even before 2002, there were attacks on the new curriculum, both from conservatives worried about slipping academic standards and from progressives concerned that a focus on exploration would favor middle-class children and widen inequality (Cave 2007, 19–21). In response, the government promoted smaller class sizes and learning differentiated according to proficiency. Both of these initiatives were innovative, in a system with a maximum class size of forty at the elementary and junior high levels and long-standing aversion to differential treatment of children.[1] Deepening public and media concern about falling academic standards during the 2000s led to schools increasingly refocusing on "basic academic attainment" as the decade progressed, culminating in a new curriculum revision that once again increased hours for academic subjects from 2011–2012.[2] Here, I illustrate the effects at three elementary schools in Sakura, a city of one hundred thousand people in the Kansai region of Japan, visited in 2008 and 2010.[3]

It is 8.30 a.m. at Shinmachi Elementary School on a late September morning in 2008, and teachers are making their way to the classrooms. Each elementary class has its own teacher, who teaches almost all subjects to the children—nationally, 63 percent of elementary teachers are women and 37 percent men (Monbukagakushō 2011a). Once the teacher has arrived, the two monitors for that day call the class to order and start the morning meeting. Monitor duty rotates daily around the class, so every child must take on this task—one aspect of a set of responsibilities that children learn to fulfill. Each child is a member of multiple small groups within the class, and responsibilities for different activities are rotated around the groups, so that all take their turn. Primary duties are serving lunch and cleaning the school daily. At lunch time, the members of the responsible group don aprons, caps, and masks for hygiene purposes; wheel the pans of food to their classroom on a trolley; and then serve it to their classmates. Later in the day, all children spend twenty minutes cleaning the school, from classrooms to corridors and toilets, using brooms, dustpans, and floorcloths. They thus learn to take responsibility for their own environment; there are no cleaning staff for these duties.

Most children will already have experienced small groups and some rotating responsibilities at preschool, attended by 95 percent of Japanese children, most commonly from ages three to six (Cave 2011a, 247–250; Lewis 1989). Japanese preschool teachers resemble elementary school teachers in preferring a low authority profile that lets children learn to work out their own differences. These approaches are strongly influenced by memories of children's lives in Japan up to the 1960s or so, before affluence, motor cars, and computers, when children tended to learn social skills by playing outside for hours in neighborhood groups, largely unsupervised by adults (Tobin, Hsueh, and Karasawa 2009, 154–156). This nostalgia for aspects of the past is expressed by Shinmachi's principal, who tells me that the human heart *(kokoro)* has worsened more than anything else in Japan, as seen in poor manners and failure to keep rules; moreover, he says, children lose their motivation when life is easy *(raku)*, as he thinks it is today. Such concerns, fueled in the late 1990s by moral panics about heinous crimes, classroom indiscipline, and sexually open school girls, resulted in turn-of-the-century emphasis by government and schools on "education of the heart" *(kokoro no kyōiku)* (Higashi 2008), a movement that has led to stress on the social and emotional development aspects of Integrated Studies, as we shall see.

The elementary curriculum includes Japanese, mathematics, physical education, music, and arts and crafts through all grades. Social studies and science start from third grade and home economics from fifth grade. In the first two years of school, children take a subject called "Life Studies," in which they learn about various aspects of the world around them. Children take Integrated Studies from third grade, and in today's lesson at Shinmachi, the fifth graders are reflecting on the rice harvesting they did the week before. They talk about how tiring it was, how it made them think about how people used to live, how much the rice had grown in a short time, and various physical features of the rice plant. The teacher is particularly keen to reinforce what the students say about how hard it is to grow and harvest rice and how they need to be thankful to the farmers—in other words, the moral lessons the children learn from their experience. The next day, the children brainstorm things about rice that they would like to research in more depth. The two lessons show teachers using Integrated Studies both to encourage students' inquiry learning, which was its original curricular purpose, and also to have children think about the moral and social implications of their experiences. The new program is thus being used not only for innovative purposes, to encourage individuality and creative thought, but also to have children reflect on the demands of life and what they owe to others—a more long-standing educational aim, brought into renewed prominence by stress on "education of the heart."

Senior teacher Mr. Sanada tells me that the Shinmachi school survey shows that the children are unenthusiastic about Integrated Studies, unlike children at Satoyama, his previous school in Sakura. The difference, he thinks, lies in the contrasting environments of the two schools. Shinmachi is a large school in a fast-developing but nondescript suburb, whose local environment offers no obvious focus for Integrated Studies projects. Satoyama is a small school in a traditional semi-rural district of the city, where children can study the local lifestyle of small-scale arable farming and cultivation of the mountain foothills. For Shinmachi, Mr. Sanada says, it will be good to have less Integrated Studies and more academic teaching from 2011, not least because the latter matches the demand for basic academic attainment at the local public junior high school, to which almost all Shinmachi children progress. In 2008, the educational trend is very much to emphasize conventional subjects rather than the interdisciplinarity of Integrated Studies, he observes.

Shinmachi also provides a good example of how elementary schools implement small-group teaching (usually in mathematics). Small-group teaching and proficiency-related learning have been promoted by the Ministry of Education and Science since 2001, but Shinmachi's teachers use them selectively, in some textbook units and for some classes. For the unit I observe, two classes have been divided into smaller groups of fifteen students each (ignoring individual proficiency). However, the third class is not divided, so that all children can benefit from listening to the ideas of the few in the class who are good at mathematics. This peer learning (*oshieai*) in a larger group is felt to be more valuable than extra teacher attention in a smaller group, an attitude consistent with observations in the 1990s (Cave 2007, 145–146). On the other hand, teachers are ready to teach some units in smaller groups differentiated by proficiency if this is effective; units focused on number topics such as fractions and decimals are thought suited to this approach. Teachers continue to believe strongly in the value of a strong class group that enables children of different proficiencies to learn from one another (Cave 2007, 100, 145–146), and their attitudes to differentiated learning are cautious though pragmatic. According to the teacher of the third class, Ms. Hara, many students in the class showed not only low mathematical proficiency but also little confidence overall; she implied that this was sometimes linked to difficult family situations, in an area of the city experiencing rapid growth, as many families move in from elsewhere in Japan.

We now fast forward two years to September 2010 at two more of Sakura's elementary schools, Aoba and Shukuba. The lessons observed here vividly illustrate how teachers are seeking to respond to demands for solid academic attainment alongside moral and social awareness and investigative ability. First comes a sixth-grade Japanese class at Aoba, a school opened about a decade earlier to serve a large private housing development. Female teacher Ms. Izumi starts by showing the children a series of Chinese character *(kanji)* flashcards, in response to each of which the whole class chants the reading together. She next has the class read a famous passage from Confucius' *Analects,* aloud three times in unison from a handout and twice more reading from a wide-screen television. After this, Ms. Izumi introduces two new Chinese characters; she shows the children how to write them on the blackboard and has them write the characters in the air with their fingers, counting the strokes as they do so aloud in unison; then they read the compounds that use the characters listed in their book aloud in unison; then they write the characters several times in their books and go to Ms. Izumi's desk to have their books checked. All this is conducted at a good pace in just twelve minutes. During the rest of the lesson, the class starts a new textbook unit entitled *The Town Where We All Live Together (Minna de ikiru machi).* Ms. Izumi gets the children to think about the grammar of the title, and they then read the first page of the text and underline what they consider the key phrases; the children's most popular choice is "each of us has the duty *[gimu]* to do what we can." Ms. Izumi tells the children that living together in a town is not just about getting but also about paying and that in the following lessons, they will think about how to make their town a better place and put forward two proposals to the Sakura Children's Council (Kodomo Gikai). Moral and social development is thus incorporated into Japanese language lessons, as well as into Integrated Studies.

Later, senior teacher Ms. Yoshioka tells me that Ms. Izumi emphasizes the basics and that her teaching style is rather different from that of many Sakura teachers, as she has recently moved to the city from Osaka. Ms. Yoshioka comments that the current trend is to use the textbook more than she herself used to in the 1990s, when I observed her lessons at Nakamachi Elementary School (Cave 2007). While acknowledging the importance of basic attainment, she suggests that it is also important to develop children's abilities to apply what they learn, gently implying a potential tension between the two demands. Nonetheless, thinking for oneself is not off the agenda; later, Ms. Izumi tells me how her class staged debates, like those I had witnessed at Nakamachi in the mid-1990s (Cave 2007, 104–106).

Three days later, I visit Shukuba, a small elementary school in a rural corner of Sakura. I observe a fifth-grade Japanese class on the unit "People's Relationships with Things" *(Hito to mono to no tsukiaikata)*, which is about recycling. It is a very different lesson to the one at Aoba; the children spend most of it scattered among the classroom, the library, and the computer room, doing investigative learning in preparation for writing. Later, the female teacher tells me that the current textbooks for Japanese contain many more investigative learning exercises than those she used as an elementary student in the late 1980s. However, such exercises are somewhat curtailed in the new textbooks recently published for use from 2011. Instead, these books feature short readings from famous works of classical literature, such as the *Pillow Book* and the *Tale of the Heike*. Mr. Sanada, who is now vice-principal at Shukuba, suggests that this is linked to a recent fashion for having children learn to recite poems and other short passages by heart, an exercise that is supposed to be good for the brain—helping to explain the rationale behind the recital of the *Analects* at Aoba. (Table 11.1 summarizes information about the elementary and junior high schools discussed.)

The variety of learning activities in these lessons from 2008 and 2010 shows how elementary schools are responding to resurgent demands that children have a firm grasp of academic basics, a strong moral sense, and a firm grounding in the local community. Integrated Studies has been used for social and moral education as well as to encourage self-motivated exploratory learning. Yet schools have not abandoned the promotion of investigation and thinking for oneself, the major concerns of the 1990s and early 2000s. Exactly what approaches are used at a particular school depends on teachers' assessments of the most suitable response to local children's needs, though there is a significant degree of commonality among schools in a locality because of the regular transfer of teachers. Thus, within Sakura, small schools in more stable, traditional, and rural communities, such as Satoyama and Shukuba,

TABLE 11.1	Elementary and junior high schools in Sakura discussed in the text	

NAME	LEVEL	DESCRIPTION
Shinmachi	Elementary	Large suburban school of roughly 750 students, in a district with relatively high numbers of families who have moved in from elsewhere in the prefecture or other parts of Japan.
Aoba	Elementary	Medium-sized suburban school of roughly 550 students, opened about 2000 to serve a private housing estate.
Shukuba	Elementary	Small rural school of roughly 200 students, in a district with many long-established families.
Yoneda	Junior high	Medium-sized rural school of roughly 400 students, in a district with many long-established families.

have tended to place greater emphasis on investigative learning, while a school like Shinmachi, in a rapidly growing suburb with significant social strains, has focused more on securing children's basic academic attainment. Such commonalities and variations are also illustrated by the research of Shimizu Kōkichi and his team on effective elementary schools in areas of social disadvantage.[4] Shimizu points to the variety of strategies used, describing Fukuoka and Osaka schools that employ small-group and differentiated learning and Osaka schools that emphasize the creation of a strong school and classroom community, learning from peers in class, and strengthening children's sense of togetherness and achievement through class singing and "human pyramids" at sports day (Shimizu 2004; 2008, 31–72). He argues that these features are particularly characteristic of Kansai schools (Shimizu 2004, 232–233)—and they can also be seen in the more middle-class Kansai environment of Sakura (see above and Cave 2007)—though Nancy Sato (2004, 17, 89, 97) documents class singing and "human pyramids" in a working-class school in Tokyo, suggesting how widely such strategies are diffused. Yet there is not homogeneity; Shimizu (2004) shows that schools serving similarly disadvantaged populations vary widely in their approaches and results, while Boocock (2011) describes an Osaka school subjecting its socially disadvantaged children to dull, drill-focused teaching that deviates from more commonly reported styles of elementary teaching and fails to stimulate learning.

Elementary education generally emphasizes learning to help others, cooperate, and see oneself as part of an interdependent community, not just as an individual. By sharing responsibilities, children learn that everyone can and should contribute to the general welfare. Lessons are also based strongly on a belief in the efficacy of learning from one another. This does not exclude individual difference and originality. Most teachers welcome and encourage the expression of different ideas. In recent years, Integrated Studies has been used both to encourage individual learning projects and to promote moral and social education. By selective use of small-group teaching and differentiated learning, teachers have sought to respond better to the academic needs of individual children, especially in the context of a renewed focus on basic academic attainment. However, the fundamental belief in interdependence and cooperation remains, and many if not most schools see strong classroom cohesion and peer learning as vital for academic progress.

Junior High Education

The emphasis on cooperation and team spirit continues during the three years of junior high school, the second stage of the nine years of compulsory education in Japan. This emphasis is exemplified by preparations for the cultural festival of October 2007 at Yoneda Junior High, a school of about four hundred students in a rural district of Sakura (see figure 11.1). Like the sports day held a few weeks before, this major event involves every student in the school. One message of this inclusiveness is that everyone matters. Being a good contributor is more important than being a star. A second message, frequently repeated at every level of Japanese schooling, is that if everyone combines powers *(chikara o awaseru),* great things can be accomplished. Working together, not the brilliance of isolated individuals, is presented as the key to success. After lessons end, the Yoneda students work in groups to create artworks from everyday materials, such as plastic bottles or drinks cans, and build versions of fairground games from wood and painted cardboard.

However, the Yoneda cultural festival also offers individuals the opportunity

FIGURE 11.1

Students preparing for the cultural festival at Yoneda Junior High School

to shine, particularly in the plays that each grade performs. These performances allow the dramatically inclined to declaim before the entire school, as well as providing major responsibilities for students who act as directors. The cultural festival is also the time when members of the school art club put their works on display for the rest of the school to view.

Extra-curricular club activities *(bukatsudō)* also mix emphases on common endeavor and individual talent. Such activities are a major feature of Japanese junior high and high schools (Cave 2004). Although not mandated by the national curriculum, they are ubiquitous, absorbing huge amounts of students' and teachers' time and energy. Schools generally offer a range of both sports and cultural clubs. Popular sports clubs include baseball, soccer, track and field, swimming, volleyball, basketball, table tennis, tennis, kendo, and judo. The most popular culture clubs are generally the brass and woodwind band and the art club. Top-level high schools tend to offer a wider range of culture clubs, springing from the interests of the students themselves. With the exception of the band, culture clubs are often run in a relaxed way, meeting just once or twice a week. Sports clubs, however, expect dedication, usually practicing for an hour or two on weekdays and generally on one if not both days of the weekend. Because practice takes place almost every day all year round (including most of the vacations), a student cannot join more than one sports club; and though changing clubs is usually possible, it is not encouraged. The implicit, and sometimes explicit, messages are that students should be devoted to a single thing *(hitotsu no koto ni uchikomu)* and should keep going to the end *(saigo made ganbaru),* deeply held values in Japan. An important side effect is that students cannot be all-round stars—regardless how talented they are athletically; for example, they cannot join both the baseball and soccer teams. Such a restriction might seem hard on the highly talented, but on the other hand, it allows more students the chance to take a leading role. It is thus a system that favors encouraging the talents and efforts of many, rather than a few outstanding athletes. Yet this does not deny recognition to individuals, for it is individual performance that decides which students are chosen to play in the regular inter-school tournaments.

Junior high is also the start of serious individual academic assessment. Midterm and end-of-term tests become a major feature of school life, largely determining grades. Students also know that progress to high school, the next stage of education, depends on their performance as individuals in the high school entrance exam.

In today's first period at Yoneda, one second-year class has a social studies lesson. Having studied geography during the first year, students are now studying history and will study civics in their final year. The class is nearing the end of the textbook, which starts in prehistory, about five million years ago, and gives a compact chronological account reaching up to the present day in about 230 pages. Generally speaking, the content of two textbook pages is to be covered in each fifty-minute lesson, a pace that does not allow the teacher, Mr. Kasuga, much time. Today's lesson deals with the latter stages of World War II. Mr. Kasuga spends the first ten minutes questioning the students about the basic facts covered in the textbook, using projections of a map of the war zone and a photo of fighting on Saipan. There are always several students ready to raise their hands and answer. He then gives out a copy of a letter relating war memories from a book entitled *Onnatachi no taiheiyō sensō* (Women and the Pacific War), reads it out, and then talks about what he has heard from his grandparents about their war experiences, ending with the words *sensō akan* ("war is no good" in Kansai dialect). He encourages the students to ask their own grandparents about their war experiences. Next, he moves on to the invasion of Okinawa, the southernmost islands of the Japanese archipelago and the only part of Japan to be invaded during the war. He talks about how school students were recruited to serve the war effort, specifically mentioning the Himeyuri Butai (Star Lily Corps), a group of female students recruited as field hospital nurses, most of whom were killed in the fighting (Watanabe 2001, 143–145). After writing on the blackboard a few key points for the students to copy down, Mr. Kasuga talks about the untruthful way that the war was reported to the Japanese people, so that they were encouraged to fight to the end. He hands out a copy of part of the well-known graphic novel *Hadashi no Gen* (Barefoot Gen), explaining that many people in Okinawa killed themselves, as shown in the *manga,* and that some claim they were instructed to do so. Having spent about twenty-five minutes using these supplementary materials to deepen students' appreciation of the content outlined in the textbook, for the remaining fifteen or so minutes he reverts to his earlier approach, asking students a series of questions about the section on the defeat of Italy and Germany and then writing key points on the blackboard for them to copy down. The lesson is probably fairly typical of history teaching in Japan's junior high schools (Cave 2003). With so much material to cover in so little time, teachers generally find it difficult to engage students in analysis and discussion. Nonetheless, most teachers do their best to interest students in the subject matter and deepen their understanding by introducing information and materials additional to those in the textbook.

Besides acquiring basic historical knowledge and understanding, students are gaining disciplined study habits. They learn to take notes—some social studies teachers explicitly teach students strategies for organizing their notes—and later use the notes to revise for tests and examinations.

As it happens, this lesson was not the first time the second-year students had encountered the story of the Star Lily Corps, as it had been the subject matter of the play performed by the third-year students at the previous year's cultural festival and had made a big impact on the audience, some of whom had been in tears as they watched. The anti-war message that has featured strongly in Japanese culture since the end of World War II (Orr 2001) can thus be conveyed in various ways in schools.

Integrated Studies was introduced into junior high schools in 2002, as into elementary schools (Bjork 2011; Cave 2011b). Most junior high teachers greeted it with caution or skepticism, being unused to teaching beyond their own subjects and worried that the kind of active learning Integrated Studies demanded would threaten school discipline, a major concern at this stage of education. Moreover, as teachers at Yoneda and other junior high schools in Sakura explained, responsibilities for subject teaching, pastoral care, discipline, and clubs left very little time for the cooperative planning, curriculum creation, and resource preparation that Integrated Studies needed. In the words of Yoneda's Integrated Studies coordinator, Mr. Mori, "Schools don't have the time, and I don't think teachers have that level of capacity. . . . We've only just got our heads above water." As a result, schools tended to fill much Integrated Studies time by expanding existing activities, such as workplace experience, careers study, and preparatory study for the third-year school trip. At Yoneda, first-year students also undertook a research project about their chosen aspect of the prefecture's history, culture, life, or natural environment, including visits to sites such as museums or nature study centers. As at elementary schools, Yoneda and other junior high schools used Integrated Studies in part for social and moral education, trying to get students to think about the good of society and empathize with the needs of others. As part of the Integrated Studies curriculum at Yoneda, first-year students visited local welfare facilities for the elderly or people with disabilities. Meanwhile, third-year students studied "universal design," an approach to making the built environment easy for all to use. Hamamoto (2009, 130–145, 193–195) reports similar activities at two junior high schools in low-income areas of Osaka, though unlike schools in Sakura, the Osaka schools also spent time studying marginalized communities with an important presence in Osaka, such as Koreans or *burakumin;* some teachers framed all these studies of groups subject to discrimination or disadvantage (including the elderly and those with disabilities) as "human rights education," interpreted as learning to understand the feelings of others and care for them. Junior high teachers have been more comfortable using Integrated Studies for these kinds of long-standing aims than for the 2002 curricular reform's aims of fostering exploratory, self-motivated learning, which teachers have tended to see as impractical, whether in Sakura, Niigata (Bjork 2011), or Osaka (Hamamoto 2009). The reduction of Integrated Studies time to allow more hours for academic subjects in the curriculum revision implemented in 2012 (Cave 2011b, 160) was an acknowledgment that the new initiative had not fulfilled government expectations.

Teachers have been much more positive about small-group teaching (usually implemented in mathematics and English), funded by the Ministry of Education and Science from 2001 onward. At Yoneda, students learned mathematics and English in classes of 15–20 students, half the size of classes in other subjects, for two of their three years at the school. Teachers welcomed the increased attention they could give students and the accompanying improvement in student motivation, although there was little evidence of changes in teaching methods to take advantage of the more favorable conditions. The ministry has also encouraged differentiated learning in proficiency groups, but like elementary schools, many junior high schools have been cautious about this, introducing it mainly in mathematics and generally in a minority of lessons (Monbukagakushō 2009). At Yoneda, students were taught in proficiency groups for only the more demanding latter section of each textbook unit and were allowed to choose which group to join, subject to advice from the teacher, an approach that seems widespread (Cave 2008). Many teachers continued to be uncomfortable about treating students differentially, partly out of long-established egalitarian beliefs and partly because of fears that any gains might be canceled out by loss of motivation and lower expectations among students in lower proficiency groups.

During the nine years of compulsory education, the vast majority of Japanese children attend their local public schools, experiencing little differentiation and considerable emphasis on solidarity and cooperation. At the same time, the structure of the educational system and the organization of learning at junior high individuate students within a competitive structure. Students must take an entrance examination to progress to high school. For most, this will be the prefectural public high school exam, which is set in five subjects—Japanese, English, mathematics, science, and social studies. The exam for each subject takes 40–50 minutes, depending on the prefecture. Since students can usually apply to only one public high school, and they do so before the exam takes place, it is important for them to estimate correctly how good their exam performance will be. Because of the possibility of failure, they also need to apply to a less demanding private high school as a backup. Some students, especially in major cities, also apply to a high-ranking private school as their first choice and take the entrance exam set by that school. Guiding students through this complex process is part of the job of junior high teachers.

For those who want extra help with studies, *juku* (private tutorial and test-preparation schools or programs) offer extra tuition at evenings and weekends (Roesgaard 2005; Rohlen 1980). Children may not feel they understand school lessons well enough, or their parents may be dissatisfied with their study habits. *Juku* are diverse. Most provide tuition aimed at passing high school entrance exams *(shingaku juku),* often using a didactic teaching style much like lessons at school and in similar-sized classes. Others *(hoshū juku)* focus on helping slower learners understand material already studied at school, providing more individually oriented tuition. Some teachers are full-time employees, while others are part-timers—often university students or even retired schoolteachers. To enroll in a top *juku,* students must often pass an entrance exam. While schools emphasize group solidarity, *juku* have a contrasting focus on individual aspiration and achievement. A typical exam-focused *juku* will offer junior high students a package of three compulsory evening lessons a week, one each in mathematics, Japanese, and English, often rising to five lessons a week (adding science and social studies) in the final year. This package may cost about ¥25,000–35,000 ($300–420 at $1 = ¥80) a month. The cost is manageable for many families, a fact that helps to explain why *juku* enrollment rates are so high—according to Benesse, a major producer of educational materials with its own research institute, 43 percent of junior high students attended *juku* in 2006 (Benesse Kenkyū Kyōiku Kaihatsu Sentā 2006). However, lower-income families can find such fees an unmanageable strain (Slater 2010, 147). An alternative is to use study aids such as Benesse's own Shinken Zemi exercises, which are produced at different levels, from basic through regular to challenging, and in different versions tailored to each of Japan's forty-seven prefectures. Benesse claims that one in five junior high students uses Shinken Zemi; in 2012 a monthly subscription cost just over ¥6,000 ($75 at $1 = ¥80) (Benesse Corporation 2012).

It is often argued that *juku* are a major means of class reproduction in Japan and that middle-class students who can better afford them use them to develop "strategies for maximization which improve their chances of high exam scores" (Slater 2010, 151). This is a plausible argument. However, research by Kariya (2010) finds that test scores are better correlated with cultural capital than with *juku* attendance, suggesting that *juku* may often reinforce learning competencies that ultimately stem from habits and cultural knowledge acquired through the family. What both Kariya and Slater show is that there are stark differences in study behavior and academic aspiration among Japanese children, and these are strongly associated with family background, whether theorized in terms of greater or less cultural capital (Kariya) or in terms of social class (Slater). Meanwhile, Shimizu (2004) finds that some Osaka junior high schools serving socially disadvantaged populations with low *juku* attendance outperform other schools in better-off areas with high *juku* attendance. Shimizu (2004, 231–234) suggests that such schools have a strong critical awareness of the impact of social class and cultural capital on children and purposefully seek to redress the balance, unusual in a country where education has tended to avoid confronting social class issues. These studies draw attention to the diversities within junior high education.

High School: The Great Divide

Though the Japanese high school system differentiates students according to academic performance (Okano and Tsuchiya 1999, 62–109; Rohlen 1983), within each high school there continues to be great stress upon the solidarity of all, with little or no differential treatment (tracking or setting) within programs. Most high schools offer a regular academic program. Nominally, all such programs follow the same curriculum, but there are large differences between the level of difficulty of regular programs at higher-ranking and lower-ranking schools. Students generally choose either the arts stream or the science stream from the second year onward. Besides regular academic programs, there are also vocational programs, usually provided by dedicated vocational high schools (most commonly commercial, industrial, and agricultural). Vocational programs and schools have been a feature of the Japanese education system for over a century. While such schools used to be a popular choice for students, producing well-trained graduates who went on to good careers, their popularity has declined in recent decades as credential inflation has taken place, and more and more students aspire to progress to university (Okano and Tsuchiya 1999, 65–66, 101–108). It has become much more difficult for vocational high schools to attract academically able students, although the best still occupy a mid-ranking place in the high school hierarchy; there is regional variation here too, with technical high schools stronger in Kyushu than in the Tokyo region, for example (Hida et al. 2007). A small number of high schools also offer specialized programs in subjects such as science and mathematics, English, music, and art. Such programs are an innovation of the last twenty years, part of the attempt to offer a more diverse range of educational options that allow students to develop individual interests and strengths (Okano and Tsuchiya 1999, 214).

The extremes of high school education can be illustrated by history lessons observed at three Tokyo schools. The first takes place at perhaps the most academically successful school in Japan, a national high school for boys that is attached to a national university. A high proportion of its students enter Tokyo University, Japan's most prestigious. During this lesson, the teacher gives an interesting and intellectually sophisticated lecture on how historians have dealt with the Meiji period, when Japan modernized in the late nineteenth century. The lesson ignores the students' history textbook; later, the teacher tells me that the students are bright enough to understand the textbook content without any extra explanation, allowing him to treat more advanced topics in the lessons. Some of the students seem interested, others less so; the teacher does not engage them in discussion or invite their questions, nor do they offer any. There is no school uniform, and the school buildings are unremarkable; judging from externals only, a visitor would never guess that this is one of the nation's academic powerhouses. (Table 11.2 summarizes the high schools I discuss.)

The second lesson takes place at Ikegaoka, a private school for boys that is only slightly less academically successful than its national rival but shares the features of a somewhat shabby school building and no school uniform. In fact, one of the boys taking the history lesson in the hot summer weather wears nothing more than a pair of shorts. There is no reprimand; Ikegaoka is well known for its liberal ethos. This lesson deals with the ancient civilizations of the Indus Valley. Unlike the lesson at the national school, this lesson deals with a textbook topic in a relatively orthodox way; similar lessons on this subject, taught in a similar lecture style, could be observed at other high schools throughout Japan, though not necessarily as well taught and at such a high level. The teacher is a graduate of Tokyo University and himself a contributing author to a high school history textbook. Though Ikegaoka is one of Japan's top private schools, the fees are relatively modest—less than ¥800,000 yen ($9,600 at $1 = ¥80) annually—though still unaffordable for a low-income family.

TABLE 11.2	*List of high schools discussed in the text*	
NAME	LOCATION	DESCRIPTION
Tokyo National	Central Tokyo	A national boys' "laboratory" high school with a liberal ethos; among the most academically successful schools nationwide.
Ikegaoka	Central Tokyo	A private boys' high school with a liberal ethos; among the most academically successful schools nationwide.
Shimoda	Tokyo suburbs	A public co-educational high school of below average academic level.
Terakawa	Kansai suburbs	A public co-educational high school; among the most academically successful in the prefecture.

The third lesson takes place at Shimoda, a low-level Tokyo public school. The topic is the 1815 Congress of Vienna. It is clear that the subject holds little or no interest for many of the students. Two girls have large mirrors open on their desks; with their lightly tanned skin, dyed brown hair, short skirts, and loose socks, they follow the then fashionable style for more rebellious high school girls. Five minutes after the lesson starts, another girl arrives and unceremoniously takes her seat at the back, sitting cross-legged on her chair (she is wearing tracksuit bottoms underneath her skirt) in a style that is decidedly not approved as feminine in Japan. She takes from her bag another large mirror and an equally large makeup case and spends the next twenty minutes carefully making herself up. After about ten minutes, the teacher comes by her seat and rather feebly suggests that she attend to the lesson, but his presence is ignored, and he moves away. It seems clear that this teacher, at least, has more or less given up the struggle to capture or compel all his students' attention in the somewhat recondite subjects that the curriculum obliges him to teach them, though in another lesson that I observe the same day, I see a politics and economics teacher who is much more energetic and successful in engaging his students. Nonetheless, the episode vividly illustrates two important aspects of education in Japan. The first is the inflexibility of the curriculum and the paucity of choice for students. Even at high school level, teachers' ability to decide what they will teach is significantly limited by the constraints of a one-size-fits-all national curriculum designed on the assumption that all high school students should learn roughly the same content. The exceptions are those teachers (probably rather rare) who are sufficiently strong-minded to skip over parts of the textbook and focus in more depth on other parts. The assumption underlying the high school curriculum is that all students require education in certain basic subjects—including mathematics, English, science, and (as we have seen) world history; moreover, the content of the curriculum should fundamentally be the same for all, even down to what might seem unlikely topics, such as the Congress of Vienna. This assumption may have made sense when the national curriculum was first enforced at the end of the 1950s, when less than 60 percent of students went on to high school, but since the proportion of students going on to high school exceeded 90 percent in the mid-1970s (Monbukagakushō 2011a), it has become much more questionable, and it means that significant numbers of students are forced to endure lessons in subjects regarding which they have little or no aptitude or interest. This also means that students who really want to study particular subjects are hindered from doing so because teachers are obliged to tailor their lessons to the entire class of 30–40 students, including those who are only there on sufferance.

The second point illustrated by this episode is the reluctance of teachers to exert stringent discipline. This may seem an odd comment, given the common reputation of Japanese schools as places of strict control (Kerr 2001, 282–306). Certainly, in some respects Japanese schools do pay significant attention to discipline. At junior high school, in particular, there are generally thoroughgoing efforts to ensure punctuality, dress codes, and good order in general. Many high schools also pay attention to these things, especially those below average in the hierarchy. Yet if students remain unresponsive to teachers' cajoling, berating, visits to parents, and so on, there is generally great reluctance on the part of the school to take the final step and expel the student (a step that is in any case illegal during compulsory education). As Slater (2010, 154–158) illustrates, teachers at low-ranking high schools generally do all they can to enable students to graduate, and strive against daunting odds to maintain a sense of the school as a "moral community" and a place of meaningful learning. Schools tend to take the view that because exclusion will benefit neither an individual student nor society in the longer term, such an extreme measure should only be taken when a student is so disruptive as to cause serious problems for the education of others. Teachers tend to consider that as long as a student is connected to the school and the social network that it represents, there is a continuing chance that he or she will reform. This may be a sensible view, given that some criminological theories argue that disaffection and delinquency among young people are often a passing phase from which they can emerge given time and patience (Downes and Rock 2003, 148–149; Sato 1991, 157–177). Certainly the approach has been linked with continued low crime rates throughout the post–World War II period (Hamai and Ellis 2006).

As shown by Kariya and Dore (2006, 143–147) and Slater (2010), socioeconomic status and high school attendance are strongly related. According to one study, 76 percent of students at top private schools like Ikegaoka had professional and managerial parents, and only 6 percent had parents who were manual workers, while at the lowest-ranked high schools, the proportions were 35 percent and 22 percent respectively (Kariya and Dore 2006, 144). This relationship between social class and academic attainment seems to be strengthening, as discussed below.

Inequality and the "Disparity Society"

Significant disparities in motivation and achievement have been a feature of Japanese high schools for decades, but since the 1990s, such disparities have widened and have spread downward to the junior high and even elementary level, causing serious concern. According to one survey, the proportion of second-year junior high students who do not study at all outside school increased significantly between 1989 and 2001, with the greatest increase (43 percent to 59 percent) among students with poor basic life habits (such as not eating breakfast, brushing teeth, or sleeping at a set time); test scores in mathematics and Japanese also dropped (Kariya 2008, 37–49). Another survey of second-year students at eleven high schools found that the proportion of students who reported not studying at all outside school rose from 22 percent in 1979 to 35 percent in 1997 (Kariya 2008, 74–84). Recent surveys indicate a strong relationship among cultural capital, learning competencies, and performance in mathematics and Japanese (Kariya 2010), and repeat surveys at Tokyo high schools in 1979 and 1997 show a strengthening relationship between the socioeconomic status of a student's family and the high school attended (Kariya and Dore 2006, 145). Though this relationship between social class and academic attainment was clear even in the 1970s (Kariya 2010, 109–111; Kariya and Dore 2006, 145; Rohlen 1983), Kariya (2010, 110) argues that it has strengthened from the 1990s onward. Whereas there was relatively little public focus on inequality during the 1970s and 1980s, a period dominated by a sense that affluence was spreading and life chances were becoming more equal, inequality and the "disparity society" *(kakusa shakai)* have become major issues in the 2000s, as poorly paid, dead-end jobs become a permanent reality for many young people and socioeconomic polarization becomes more evident (Kariya 2010, 87–92).

The exact reasons for widening disparities in motivation and achievement at school need further research. What is clear, however, is that significant numbers of Japanese students no longer feel that it is worth putting in the hard work of studying. In part, this is likely to be due to a paradoxical combination of increasing affluence for many along with a sense of narrowing opportunities and increasing deprivation for some. The sense of narrowing opportunities results from the increasing difficulty that academic low-achievers face in securing a permanent job with good prospects and benefits, caused in turn by the stagnation in the Japanese economy since 1990 that has led firms to cut back on secure jobs in favor of contract and temporary positions, often with poor pay, conditions, and career prospects (Kariya 2010, 90–91). The increased deprivation comes not only from the direct pressures on youth employment, but also the squeeze on the pay and conditions of many older workers and the increased family pressures faced by many, especially as a result of rising divorce rates, which often leave the remaining parent (usually a working mother) in poverty or near poverty (Abe 2008). However, increased deprivation for some has gone along with increasing affluence in Japanese society as a whole, as a result of which Japan has become gradually more consumerist over the last quarter century; in Japan's cities and suburbs, there are more and more shops, cafés, restaurants, and places of entertainment, filled with an ever-increasing range and variety of enticing goods and offering services undreamed of by the more diligent students of the 1970s, ranging from DVDs and Internet to video games and smart phone apps. In short, never have there been more temptations to forego deferred gratification in favor of having fun right here, right now, and even the considerable social and moral forces brought to bear by families and schools in Japan are insufficient to ward off such temptations completely.

Low motivation and academic achievement do not necessarily rule out education beyond high school, however. The proliferation of universities in

Japan, the majority private, combined with plummeting numbers of children, has left lower-level universities in a parlous situation in which some are willing to take even low achievers in order to come closer to filling their programs (Goodman 2010). Since Japanese universities tend to be very reluctant to fail students once they are admitted, even low achievers can often achieve a university degree. How much such a degree will ultimately benefit them is another matter, however, as employers are well aware of universities' relative standing, and they recruit accordingly. Entering a prestigious university, in contrast, is achievable only through ability and effort; high-level universities recruit almost all their students via demanding entrance examinations, rather than using the softer methods, such as school recommendations or interviews, which are widely employed by lower-level institutions ("Iyoku aru gakusei erabu niwa" 2011). This difference does not mean that prestigious universities' examination procedures are unproblematic. On the contrary, they remain largely dominated by multiple-choice and short-answer questions that test knowledge and understanding more than the ability to articulate ideas or analyze arguments, just as in the 1980s (Rohlen 1983, 94–95), and this examination method in turn has a deep effect on teaching at the high school level. For high-achieving students, therefore, little has changed in the educational landscape over the last twenty years, though the post-2008 global economic crisis has made the job market even more competitive, with no guarantees of a stable path to success. For low achievers, however, pressure has relaxed in the sense that mediocre or even poor school performance is no longer much of a barrier to higher education, even if the cachet the resulting degree brings is largely illusory.

Internationalization and Foreign Language Education

One of the buzzwords of Japanese educational reform in the 1980s was "internationalization" *(kokusaika)* (Goodman 2007). Yet a quarter-century later, there is still good reason to think that the education system fails to equip Japanese people well enough for international engagement. The average performance of Japanese students in the Test of English as a Foreign Language (TOEFL) has been among the lowest in Asia (Ogawa 2011). The falling numbers of Japanese students studying abroad has also caused concern (Fukushima 2010; Nae and Fraysse-Kim 2012). Such is the case despite government initiatives to improve the situation, such as the Japan Exchange and Teaching (JET) Program, which has placed thousands of native-speaker language assistants in schools each year since the late 1980s, and the Super English High School (SELHi) program, which funded about 150 high schools across Japan to undertake action research into improved English teaching (Aspinall 2011, 135–136). Since the early 1990s, a limited number of high schools have set up specialized programs for students who wish to focus on English study. Such programs may allow students to spend as many as ten or more hours a week studying English by their second or third year, and they usually include special events such as weekend "English camps" and opportunities for short-term or long-term study abroad.[5] Such programs do result in better teaching and improved English abilities for some students. However, they are not necessarily found at the top-level high schools that take Japan's most able students. The opportunities for the latter can be illustrated by two lessons observed in fall 2011 at Terakawa, a top-level public high school in the Kansai region. The first is a regular lesson for first-year students, taught by a young teacher who is himself a graduate of a specialized English high school program and who speaks English well. Despite the teacher's qualifications, a major feature of the lesson is memorization and repetition of the reading text being studied. Students are hardly required to produce any English of their own, whether written or spoken. The number of students in the class—close to forty, as is standard—does not help. The second lesson is a third-year elective English lesson. This is very different; a mere ten or so students work in pairs, debating in English using their pre-prepared notes and switching partners every few minutes. Though their English is not perfect, they communicate successfully and enthusiastically. However, there are only two or three hours a week of electives, meaning that English lessons like this one are the experience of a small minority. It seems clear that the improvement of foreign language standards at the high school level still has a long way to go.

Overall, Japan's foreign language education continues to be inadequate; the reluctance of university students to study abroad is the result partly of this inadequacy and partly of employers' surprising apparent lack of interest in the qualities gained through overseas study.[6] The introduction of "English activities" for one hour a week in the fifth and sixth grades of elementary school from 2011 (Ogawa 2011) is a half-hearted measure whose timidity speaks volumes about the deep ambivalence within Japan toward engagement with the outside world (Aspinall 2011). Similarly striking is the apparent lack of any sense that foreign language education in schools might need to encompass the teaching of Chinese, the language of Japan's giant neighbor and surely one of the major global powers of the next century.

Stability or Stagnation?

As stated at the start of this chapter, what has changed over the last quarter-century in Japan's schools is less striking than what has not. Efforts to promote more exploratory, interdisciplinary, and self-motivated learning at elementary and junior high schools have met with some success in elementary schools, but at the junior high level the response of teachers has generally been tepid or worse. These reform efforts coincided with slippage in the performance of Japanese students in the PISA (Program for International Student Assessment) academic attainment tests, providing ammunition for criticisms of the reforms and demands that schools get "back to basics" (Cave 2007, 20–21; Takayama 2008); in consequence, the revised school curriculum implemented from 2011 onward has cut back on hours for Integrated Studies, which was intended to promote independent thinking and self-motivated learning. Funding smaller class sizes in selected subjects has probably helped students who struggle academically by allowing them more teacher attention, but teaching methods may not have changed. At the high school level, meanwhile, there have been even fewer changes for most students, though the introduction of programs that allow some students to specialize in particular subjects has had a limited effect in increasing diversity. In part, this lack of change can be seen as recognition of the real strengths of the existing education system in combining solid academic training with attention to human development. Yet Japanese education can also be strongly criticized, especially at the secondary level, for failing to develop students' particular strengths and for neglecting inquiry learning and the development of analytical, critical, and creative abilities (Cave 2011a, 253–254), while foreign language education remains a disaster area (Aspinall 2011). The limited attempts to tackle these problems over the last two decades have suffered from poor implementation, but there are more fundamental reasons for their lack of success and, indeed, for the fact that more ambitious measures have not been considered. At the junior high level, teachers are so busy fulfilling the heavy institutionalized demands upon them to provide academic basics, pastoral care, and discipline that they have minimal time or energy for pedagogic innovation (Cave 2011b). The same is true at high school, where the university entrance exam structure—which is largely outside state control—also stifles curricular or pedagogic change. Perhaps the most fundamental reason for the relative lack of change, however, is uncertainty on the part of the government and nation about what kind of society and state Japan should become in the twenty-first century. This uncertainty has been strikingly reflected in the dramatic changes of direction in education policy over the last two decades. Increased emphasis on individuality, autonomy, and exploration, focused on Japan's envisioned future needs, was first modified in the light of a "moral panic" about the supposed threat of social and moral disintegration to emphasize community and "education of the heart"; then, after a fierce debate about standards of academic attainment, came a partial reversion to the educational content and methods of earlier decades. Regardless of the rights and wrongs of these decisions, they are evidence of powerful nostalgia for the values and practices of the past—a past differently constructed by different people but generally featuring a highly selective and idealized picture of well-socialized, energetic, and bright-eyed youngsters full of motivation, living in warm families, and spending their free time exploring the natural environment or interacting with the local community.[7] In short, there is a desire to return to the imagined "glory days" between the start of the "high-growth period" in 1955 and the bursting of the bubble economy in 1990, and it is this desire—albeit generally unexpressed in such direct terms—that has been most influential in driving the actions of teachers and the arguments of pundits. What this fails to recognize is that schools alone cannot adequately provide the resources for human development that used to be provided by children's social and natural environment, especially without a significant change in the proportion of national wealth that goes into education.[8] The resulting lack of vision or direction, moreover, leaves education in danger of aimless drift and unable to equip Japan's children as might be desired for the challenge of adapting to a fast-changing future. Arguably, what children are likely to need are habits of inquiry, exploration, and proactive problem solving, along with the creative ability to come up with new ideas and the critical rigor to test such ideas to destruction. In the existing education system, such habits and abilities are not as well developed as they could be. Moreover, the system as it stands is also failing to equip children to operate internationally, even though it is now twenty-five years since Prime Minister Nakasone Yasuhiro's Education Council made "internationalization" a key goal of educational reform (Goodman 2007).

I would suggest, therefore, that the state of education in Japan is an index of the state of Japan itself. In many respects school education continues to be excellent, developing children's social and emotional capacities alongside their intellectual abilities. Yet like the wider society, schools are grappling with problems of increased inequality, and a loss of confidence about Japan's future has resulted in inward- and backward-looking tendencies that have strongly affected education. School education in Japan has a stability and strength of quality that many other countries might envy, but without greater willingness to confront the challenges of the future, this stability stands in real danger of turning into gradual stagnation. The extent to which it changes will tell us much about what kind of country Japan wants to be.

Notes

1. The Japanese public school system is noted for a relatively high degree of nation-wide standardization of facilities and academic attainment within compulsory education (elementary and junior high school) (Okano and Tsuchiya 1999, 60). In the Ministry of Education and Science's 2007 National Academic Achievement Tests in Japanese and mathematics, for example, average total scores for junior high students in forty-one of Japan's forty-seven prefectures were within 10 percent of the average total score nationwide (286.1 out of a maximum 400). Scores were not generally affected by degree of urbanization, though the top scores were in rural prefectures (Fukui, Toyama, and Akita) ("Osaka 45-banme, Akita, Fukui toppu" 2007).
2. The details of the curriculum revision are available on the Ministry of Education and Science Web site: http://www.mext.go.jp/a_menu/shotou/youryou/main4_a2.htm. Accessed January 3, 2013.
3. Sakura is a pseudonym, as are the names of schools and teachers. Like many "cities" *(shi)* in Japan, Sakura includes an urban core and suburban and semi-rural surrounds. Income in its prefecture is close to the national average, and education levels a little higher. Eighty percent of the city population live in owner-occupied dwellings, higher than the national average of 60 percent. The Kansai region includes the six prefectures around the major cities of Osaka, Kyoto, and Kobe.
4. At the schools studied by Shimizu (2004, 2008) and Boocock (2011), there are significant numbers of children from the *burakumin* community, "a castelike minority group" (Nabeshima 2010, 109) that has suffered from severe discrimination and whose children have academic achievement well below the national average.
5. For examples, see the Web sites of Ina Gakuen High School in Saitama Prefecture (http://www.inagakuen.spec.ed.jp/comm2/htdocs/?page_id=78) and Kokusai Jōhō High School in Shiga Prefecture (http://www.kokujo-h.shiga-ec.ed.jp/).
6. For example, in a letter to the Asahi Shinbun (July 7, 2011), one 2007 university graduate tells how her year's study abroad made job-hunting harder, as companies saw her delayed graduation at the wrong time of year (September) as problematic.
7. For examples of significant documents infused by such nostalgia for an imagined past, see the 2000 report by the National Commission for Educational Reform, set up by former prime minister Obuchi Keizō (http://www.kantei.go.jp/foreign/education/report/report.html; accessed May 17, 2012); Fujiwara Masahiko's (2005) best-seller *Kokka no hinkaku*; Prime Minister Abe Shinzō's (2006) book

Utsukushii kuni e; and the First Report of the Education Rebuilding Council (2007), set up by Abe during his first administration. Much of the debate about educational reform since 1989 has also critiqued the present by contrasting it with a supposedly better past (Cave 2007, 14–23).

8. According to the OECD (2011, 221), in 2008 Japan spent $8,301 per student in primary, secondary, and post-secondary non-tertiary education, slightly above the OECD average of $8,169. Its spending was very similar to that of Canada ($8,388) and Finland ($8,068); lower than the Netherlands ($9,251), the United Kingdom ($9,169), and the United States ($10,995); but higher than Germany ($7,859) and South Korea ($6,723). According to the Japanese Ministry of Education and Science (Monbukagakushō 2011b, 36), in 2009 there were 14.5 children per teacher in lower secondary education (12.2 in upper secondary) in Japan, compared to 16.6 (14.7) in Canada, 10.1 (16.6) in Finland, 15.1 (13.9) in Germany, 19.9 (16.7) in South Korea, 16.1 (12.3) in the United Kingdom, and 14.3 (15.1) in the United States (OECD average, 13.5). Thus Japan devotes similar levels of resources to school education as do comparable countries. Japan may be unusual, however, in the very high expectations on its teachers to provide substantial guidance and support for human development, an effort that takes time away from pedagogical engagement (Cave 2011b). In short, Japan may be expecting much more than other countries from similar levels of resources, and these expectations may be unrealistic.

References Cited

Abe, Aya. 2008. *Kodomo no hinkon* (Child poverty). Tokyo: Iwanami Shinsho.

Aspinall, Robert W. 2011. "Globalization and English Language Education Policy in Japan: External Risk and Internal Inertia." In *Reimagining Japanese Education,* ed. David Blake Willis and Jeremy Rappleye, 127–145. Oxford: Symposium Books.

Benesse Corporation. 2012. "Shinken zemi chūgaku kōza" (Shinken zemi junior high course). Http://chu.benesse.co.jp/. Accessed May 21, 2012.

Benesse Kenkyū Kyōiku Kaihatsu Sentā. 2006. *Dai-yon-kai gakushū kihon chōsa/ kokunai chōsa: Chūgakusei-ban* (Fourth basic survey of study in Japan: Junior high section). Tokyo: Benesse Corporation. Http://benesse.jp/berd/center/ open/ report/gakukihon4/ hon/index_chu.html. Accessed May 21, 2012.

Bjork, Christopher. 2011. "Imagining Japan's 'Relaxed Education' Curriculum: Continuity or Change?" In *Reimagining Japanese Education,* ed. David Blake Willis and Jeremy Rappleye, 147–169. Oxford: Symposium Books.

Boocock, Sarene Spence. 2011. "The Schooling of *Buraku* Children: Overcoming the Legacy of Stereotyping and Discrimination." In *Minorities and Education in Multicultural Japan,* ed. Ryoko Tsuneyoshi, Kaori H. Okano, and Sarene Spence Boocock, 44–76. Abingdon: Routledge.

Cave, Peter. 2003. "Teaching the History of Empire in England and Japan." *International Journal of Educational Research* 37:623– 641.

———. 2004. "*Bukatsudō:* The Educational Role of Japanese School Clubs." *Journal of Japanese Studies* 30, no. 2:383–415.

———. 2007. *Primary School in Japan: Self, Individuality and Learning in Elementary Education.* Abingdon: Routledge.

———. 2008. "Equity at the Japanese Chalkface." Paper presented at the annual meeting of the Comparative and International Education Society, New York, March 17–21.

———. 2011a. "Learners and Learning in Japan: Structures, Practices, and Purposes." In *Handbook of Asian Education: A Cultural Perspective,* ed. Yong Zhao, 247–264. New York: Routledge.

———. 2011b. "Explaining the Impact of Japan's Educational Reform: Or, Why Are Junior High Schools So Different from Elementary Schools?" *Social Science Japan Journal* 14, no. 2:145–163.

Downes, David, and Paul Rock. 2003. *Understanding Deviance.* 4th ed. Oxford: Oxford University Press.

Education Rebuilding Council. 2007. *Education Rebuilding by Society as a Whole: First Step toward Rebuilding the Public Education System. First Report.* January 24. Http://www.kantei.go.jp/jp/singi/kyouiku/houkoku/eibun0124h.pdf. Accessed May 17, 2012.

Fujiwara, Masahiko. 2005. *Kokka no hinkaku* (The dignity of the state). Tokyo: Shinchō Shinsho.

Fukushima, Glen S. 2010. "Reverse Japan's Insularity." *Japan Times,* April 8. Http://www.japantimes.co.jp/text/eo20100408gf.html. Accessed May 14, 2012.

Goodman, Roger. 2007. "The Concept of *Kokusaika* and Japanese Educational Reform." *Globalisation, Societies and Education* 5, no. 1:71–87.

———. 2010. "The Rapid Redrawing of Boundaries in Japanese Higher Education." *Japan Forum* 22, nos. 1–2:65–87.

Hamai, Koichi, and Thomas Ellis. 2006. "Crime and Criminal Justice in Modern Japan: From Re-Integrative Shaming to Popular Punitivism." *International Journal of the Sociology of Law* 34, no. 3:157–178.

Hamamoto, Nobuhiko. 2009. "Japanese Middle Schools' Adaptation of the Integrated Studies: A Case Study." PhD dissertation, Rutgers University.

Hida, Daijirō, Mimizuka Hiroaki, Ōtawa Naoki, Sim Choon Kiat, and Hori Takeshi. 2007. "Kōgyō kōkō no gendai-teki yakuwari to reribansu ni kan suru kenkyū" (Research on the contemporary role and relevance of technical high schools). Paper presented at the fifty-ninth annual conference of the Nihon Kyōiku Shakai Gakkai, Ibaraki University, Mito, September 22–23.

Higashi, Julie. 2008. "The *Kokoro* Education: Landscaping the Minds and Hearts of Japanese." In *Social Education in Asia,* ed. David L. Grossman and Joe Tin-Yau Lo, 39–56. Charlotte, NC: Information Age.

"Iyoku aru gakusei erabu niwa: Suisen/AO nyūshi kokkōritsu-dai no ugoki" (To select motivated students: National and public universities' movements regarding recommendations and admissions office entrance exams). 2011. *Asahi Shinbun,* July 8, 25.

Kariya, Takehiko. 2008. *Gakuryoku to kaisō* (Academic achievement and social class). Tokyo: Asahi Shinbun Shuppan.

———. 2010. "From Credential Society to 'Learning Capital' Society: A Rearticulation of Class Formation in Japanese Education and Society." In *Social Class in Contemporary Japan,* ed. Hiroshi Ishida and David H. Slater, 87–113. London: Routledge.

Kariya, Takehiko, and Ronald Dore. 2006. "Japan at the Meritocracy Frontier: From Here, Where?" In *The Rise and Rise of Meritocracy,* ed. Geoff Dench, 134–156. Oxford: Blackwell.

Kerr, Alex. 2001. *Dogs and Demons: The Fall of Modern Japan*. London: Penguin.
Lewis, Catherine C. 1989. "From Indulgence to Internalization: Social Control in the Early School Years." *Journal of Japanese Studies* 15, no. 1:139–157.
Monbukagakushō. 2009. *Heisei jūkyū/nijūnendo zenkoku gakuryoku/gakushū jōkyō chōsa tsuika bunseki hōkokusho* (Report on a national survey of study and attainment in 2007–2008). December. Http://www.nier.go.jp/ 07_08tsuikabunsekihoukoku/. Accessed February 8, 2012.
———. 2011a. *Monbukagaku tōkei yōran* (Digest of educational statistics). Http:// www.mext.go.jp/b_menu/toukei/002/ 002b/1305705.htm. Accessed May 17, 2012.
———. 2011b. *Kyōiku shihyō no kokusai hikaku* (International comparison of educational indicators). Http://www.mext.go.jp/b_menu /toukei/data/kokusai/ __icsFiles/ afieldfile/ 2012/ 03/27/1318687_01_1.pdf. Accessed May 25, 2012.
Nabeshima, Yoshiro. 2010. "Invisible Racism in Japan: Impact on Academic Achievement of Minority Children." In *Challenges to Japanese Education: Economics, Reform, and Human Rights*, ed. June A. Gordon, Hidenori Fujita, Takehiko Kariya, and Gerald LeTendre, 109–130. New York: Teachers College Press; Yokohama: Seori Shobō.
Nae, Niculina, and Soonhee Fraysse-Kim. 2012. "Nurturing Internationally Minded People through Overseas Programs." *Nagoya University of Business and Business Administration Journal of Language, Culture, and Communication* 13, no. 2:13–27.
OECD. 2011. *OECD Factbook 2011–2012: Economic, Environmental and Social Statistics*. Paris: OECD.
Ogawa, Hiroki. 2011. "Why English Is Tough in Japan." *The Diplomat*, May 13. Http:// the-diplomat.com/a-new-japan/2011/05/13/why-english-is-tough-in-japan/. Accessed May 14, 2012.
Okano, Kaori, and Motonori Tsuchiya, eds. 1999. *Education in Contemporary Japan: Inequality and Diversity*. Cambridge: Cambridge University Press.
Orr, James J. 2001. *The Victim as Hero: Ideologies of Peace and National Identity in Postwar Japan*. Honolulu: University of Hawai'i Press.
"Osaka 45-banme, Akita, Fukui toppu." 2007. *Sankei Shinbun*, October 25, 1.
Roesgaard, Marie Højlund. 2006. *Japanese Education and the Cram School Business*. Copenhagen: NIAS Press.
Rohlen, Thomas P. 1980. "The *Juku* Phenomenon." *Journal of Japanese Studies* 6, no. 2:207–242.
———. 1983. *Japan's High Schools*. Berkeley: University of California Press.
Sato, Ikuya. 1991. *Kamikaze Biker*. Chicago: University of Chicago Press.
Sato, Nancy E. 2004. *Inside Japanese Classrooms*. New York: RoutledgeFalmer.
Shimizu, Kōkichi. 2004. "Teigakuryoku kokufuku e no senryaku: 'Kōka no aru gakkō' no shiten kara" (Strategies for overcoming low academic attainment: From the standpoint of 'effective schools'). In *Gakuryoku no shakaigaku* (A sociology of academic attainment), ed. Kariya Takehiko and Shimizu Kōkichi, 217–235. Tokyo: Iwanami Shoten.
———. 2008. *Kōritsu gakkō no sokojikara* (The latent power of public schools). Tokyo: Chikuma Shinsho.
Slater, David H. 2010. "The 'New Working Class' of Urban Japan: Socialization and Contradiction from Middle School to the Labor Market." In *Social Class in*

Contemporary Japan, ed. Hiroshi Ishida and David H. Slater, 137–169. Abingdon: Routledge.

Takayama, Keita. 2008. "The Politics of International League Tables: PISA in Japan's Achievement Crisis Debate." *Comparative Education* 44, no. 4:387–407.

Tobin, Joseph J., Yeh Hsueh, and Mayumi Karasawa. 2009. *Preschool in Three Cultures Revisited: Japan, China, and the United States.* Chicago: University of Chicago Press.

Watanabe, Morio. 2001. "Imagery and War in Japan: 1995." In *Perilous Memories: The Asia-Pacific War(s),* ed. T. Fujitani, Geoffrey M. White, and Lisa Yoneyama, 129–151. Durham, NC: Duke University Press.

CHAPTER 12

Lightweight Cars and Women Drivers

The De/construction of Gender Metaphors
in Recessionary Japan

JOSHUA HOTAKA ROTH

LET ME START with a vignette from the mid-1990s, when I was a twenty-eight-year-old graduate student doing dissertation research on Japanese Brazilian migrants in Japan. My fieldsite was Hamamatsu, Shizuoka Prefecture. I had rented a car to drop a friend off at Narita Airport and was returning to Shizuoka, passing through the mountains around Hakone late on a Saturday night. I forget what I had rented—a Nissan Sentra or a Toyota Corolla. It was not a sports car, but it was managing the winding road reasonably well when out of nowhere a car raced up behind me and passed me on a curve. I could not believe it. And before I knew it, another car whizzed by, and another. I tried to keep pace, my pulse racing, but very soon realized it was impossible. Before I made it out of the mountains, several more groups of cars raced by me. I made a mental note that there was some crazy driving going on around Hakone and continued on my way to Hamamatsu. Little did I know I would be thinking about it more than fifteen years later for my current project on car cultures in Japan.

It was in the early and mid-1990s when the *manga Wangan Midnight* (Kusunoki 1994, 1997) and *Initial D* (Shigeno 1995) documented the culture of street racing that had developed in the liminal time space of the late-night mountains encircling Tokyo and on urban highways. These long-running *manga* spun off anime series, video games, and live-action films. The main protagonist in each is a lower-middle-class high school boy, one living in his own apartment after his parents divorced, another growing up with his father. Each is immersed in a schedule of school, part-time work, and a home life lacking in emotional warmth. They are *hashiriya,* good kids who achieve an emotional high through speed, as opposed to *bōsōzoku,* kids who specialize in loud roars, ostentatious modifications, and harassment of other drivers and entire neighborhoods for its own sake.

One of the minor characters in *Wangan Midnight* is a mechanic who has retired from street racing but whose passion is rekindled when encountering the main protagonist and his early model Nissan Z on the highway one night. This mechanic is drawn back to racing despite the fact that his wife is pregnant—or perhaps because of the pregnancy and his urge to deny imminent fatherhood. Several other characters ask themselves why they do what they do as they roar along urban highways at breakneck speeds. While none of them explicitly laments the superficiality or meaninglessness of their lives, the thrill of speed clearly provides a heightened experience that compensates for some unstated lack.

Sociologist Stephen Lyng (1990) has written about the emergence of extreme sports and other forms of voluntary risk taking in the context of highly disciplined industrialized societies. He theorizes risk taking as a kind of "edgework," allowing people living in an overly disciplined and bureaucratized world to explore existential questions. At the least, edgework allows people to experience a temporary high, a fleeting transcendence of the obligations with which they are encumbered in the rest of their lives.

Cotton Seiler (2008) offers a comparable reading of the impact of automobility more broadly in the United States. If risk taking provides some transcendence of the drudgery of daily existence, automobility more broadly offered Americans a means by which they could express a new form of individualism at the turn of the last century, when the increasing bureaucratization of daily life and the Taylorization of workplaces posed a substantial threat to the republican model of selfhood, conceived in terms of "productive labor and the stewardship of its fruits" (Seiler 2008, 29).[1] As the self-reliant individual became increasingly pinned down by the new economic order, the individualist ethos found an outlet in the sphere of consumption. More than the automobile itself, however, Seiler writes that it was "*driving's* sensations of agency, self-determination, entitlement, privacy, sovereignty, transgression, and speed

... [that were] instrumental in establishing automobility as a public good. ....
Driving provided the means by which the transition . . . from character to personality; from inner-direction to other-direction; from utilitarian to expressive
individualism; from sovereign to social selfhood . . . could be both dramatized
and expiated" (41; emphasis in original).

While collectivism, rather than individualism, has been central to con-
structions of Japanese society and culture, the eager embrace of the personal
automobile during the 1960s at the start of what has been called the My-Car
era (Plath 1992) suggests that the taste of individual autonomy could be allur-
ing to those who had never before experienced it, much as it had been to those
Americans who had felt a need to regain what had been lost.

In both the U.S. and Japanese contexts, however, women were seen as de-
pendents rather than sovereign individuals, so we may not expect that driving
served the same function of providing an alternate viable form of selfhood for
them to compensate for the denial of sovereign selfhood in modern industrial
society. But we should not assume that all women have been satisfied with
their lot. In fact, Seiler shows that women in the United States from very early
on were drawn to the promise of the open road and the sensations of agency
and speed.

But if automobility has represented a kind of freedom from the constraints
and obligations of both workplace and home, people have experienced it in
different ways. In Japan, I argue that automobility itself is distinctly structured
into the bifurcated styles of power and speed, on the one hand, and civility
and safety on the other. In Japan, it may have offered men fleeting moments
of transcendence of the everyday through sensations of power, speed, flow,
and transgression, but it offered women only more of the kinds of expectations that have shaped other aspects of their lives. Many women drive tiny
K-jidōsha, K-cars, and these cars themselves serve as a metaphor that yokes
women to their everyday routines and to their roles as mothers and wives.

In this chapter, I will draw on ethnographic data, as well as the online social
networking site Mixi, to suggest the ways in which the gender associations of
certain cars and driving styles support the larger gender system in Japan. Moreover, I will examine what happens when these associations start to break down.

K-Cars

No more than 11.15 feet long and 4.86 feet wide and with a 660 cc engine,
K-cars are the smallest class of cars in Japan. These specifications have

increased somewhat since the category of the K was first established in 1950, reflecting the increase in size and power of cars in general. In that year, the Transportation Ministry specified K-cars as those not exceeding 9.84 feet in length and 4.32 feet in width, with a tiny 300 cc engine (Ozeki 2007, 13). The next year the limit on engine size was increased to 360 cc. But it was not until 1955, when Ks started to be taxed at a substantial discount compared to larger cars, that manufacturers began making them in substantial numbers. Since then, the number of Ks has increased rapidly.

The category of Ks was feminized beginning with the rapid increase in the number of women drivers from the early 1970s, as the ideal of the female homemaker took hold in Japan. In 1969 women comprised just 17 percent of all license holders. Their share had risen to 29 percent by 1980 and 42 percent by 2004 (National Police Agency 2005). In some two-car families, there may be a larger sedan that the husband will drive and a K (marked by the yellow license plate) for the wife (see figure 12.1). In the Mixi interest group called "Do

FIGURE 12.1

A husband and wife. The yellow license plate (right) indicates a K-car.

not make fun of K-cars!" a woman claims that she is very happy with her K, that it gets great mileage, and that it feels roomy on the inside. She writes that the one drawback of the K, "compared to my husband's sedan, is that other cars on the road do not give way to me."

Ks represent practicality and economy. They do not represent the exciting potential of other kinds of cars. Their speed is limited. They generally cannot go on highways. They are perfect for puttering about city streets to go shopping or for taking kids to and from music or English lessons or play dates with schoolmates. While many mothers may take their preschoolers to school on the backs of their bicycles and older kids generally walk to school, cars are important for many child-centered activities, especially in suburban areas such as in Hamamatsu City, Shizuoka Prefecture, where I did my dissertation research in the mid-1990s, as well as in Kawagoe City, Saitama Prefecture, where I did car-related research in 2007. One mother on a Mixi site wrote that she had logged more than twenty-seven thousand kilometers in the last two and a half years going back and forth to her child's preschool and that the K was serving as "the legs of the family in place of the bicycle." Rather than providing a release from their roles as wives and mothers, Ks help women fulfill those roles. Gender schema helps compartmentalize the conflicting discourses on manners and speed by making it seem natural for men to speed and women to give way. And it makes it seem natural that men drive sports cars and women drive Ks.

The association of Ks with women drivers is evident in the numerous posts on the "Don't make fun of K-cars" interest group on Mixi about how women view men who drive Ks. In addition, there is an entire interest group with over eight hundred members called "What's the Problem with Men Driving Ks?" Some posts express anxiety about whether driving a K makes one an undesirable marriage prospect. One person replies to such a post noting that he "dated someone that turned up her nose at anyone who didn't drive a BMW but that after driving here and there together for a year in [his] Suzuki Alto, they ended up getting married, and the Alto continues to be [their] beloved car to this day." Another writes that "In this ecological age, it is nonsense to judge a man by the size of the car that he drives." Yet in their denials of the rationality of judging a person by his or her car, they implicitly acknowledge that many people continue to do so. One writes more explicitly that "I don't think marriage or dating is impossible just because someone drives a K. But as others in the community have written, I think there is still the tendency for people to think that 'it is just not possible that a man drive a K.'" As we see, even if some men drive Ks and some women drive full-sized sedans or sports cars, both those types of cars continue to be associated with the other gender and thereby lend support to official gender ideology.

K-Cars as Metaphor of Gender and Driving Styles

Differences in the domain of gender relate analogically to differences in the domain of cars. Men are to women as sports cars are to economy cars. If, as Sapir (1977, 22–30) has explained, analogies are built upon metaphors, then sports cars are like men and economy cars are like women. And, as Fernandez (1977, 1986) suggests, metaphors may further motivate performance, as men race their cars and women give way. Thus we have a set of dichotomies (see table 12.1).

My analysis here is inspired in part by the kind of obsessive attention to binary oppositions that Claude Lévi-Strauss developed in his mid-twentieth-century structural anthropology (1963, 1966), which has long been criticized as a projection of his own habits of logical thought onto a far messier and fluid cultural reality.[2] Despite the criticism, certain basic tenets of structuralism

TABLE 12.1 *Gender Analogies*

In these paired dichotomies, the vertical axes consist
of metaphors upon which the overall analogies are built

men	:	women
sports cars	:	economy cars
aggressive driving	:	considerate driving
flow	:	stop and go
mastery	:	ineptitude
transcendence	:	quotidian

continue to inform many anthropologists today, even those (like myself) who generally devote much more attention to the messiness of daily life. One key tenet is that people do not perceive meaning in isolated phenomena but in the relation of phenomena to each other, ultimately creating distinct systems of meaning that constitute cultures. The key difference between classical structural analysis and later structuralism-inspired (including post-structural) analyses today is that the former imagined these meaning systems as crystalline totalities, while the latter make allowances for blurred boundaries and the possibility of change.

I use this method of analysis to suggest that Japanese understand the meaning of sports cars in relation to K-cars, of men in relation to women, and of driving with power and speed in relation to consideration and safety. Yet I acknowledge that the abstract coherence of these sets of oppositions is more complicated in lived experience and subject to change over time.

As in the United States, a gendered bias associates men with mastery and speed and women with consideration and safety. In many articles on driving manners from car magazines in the 1960s and '70s, considerate driving was exemplified by the term *yuzuri-ai,* or mutual giving way, and was central to a widespread discourse on driving manners (Roth 2012). Aggressive driving, in which drivers tailgated and frequently passed others, was described as *gatsu gatsu unten* or *ōbō unten.* These articles linked considerate driving to safety and in doing so framed consideration as gender neutral. But such a style of driving takes on a somewhat feminine aspect when contrasted to the discourse on speed so pronounced in car related *manga,* anime, video games, movies, and motor sports. The discourse on speed allowed some of the men with whom I interacted to interpret considerate driving, and the stop-and-go manner in which many women drove Ks, as a kind of *noro noro unten* (lethargic driving), which impeded traffic and caused frustration for other drivers.

When we consider the ways in which gender schema structures the domain of automobility, however, we need to recognize that not all Japanese women drive in a stop-and-go manner. Some love to drive fast and are perfectly able to weave through traffic at high speeds with the best of the guys, as was the case with one of my neighbors in Kawagoe. In college she enjoyed taking car trips with friends and fondly recalled the accolades she received for her quick reflexes and good sense for mountain roads. Later she redirected her love of speed toward a mastery of road networks in various delivery jobs, a formerly male-dominated occupation into which women have entered in substantial numbers since the 1980s. The metaphorical work of the K-car helps to explain the durability of the stereotype of women drivers—both the positive one of women as considerate drivers who give way and the negative one of women as lethargic and inept drivers who just get in the way—in the face of abundant counterexamples of confident and fast women drivers.

Driving in Inner and Outer Spaces

Gender ideology maintains itself despite the diverse individual experiences and subjectivities of women drivers. Claudia Strauss (1997) has explored how people either integrate or compartmentalize conflicting discourses. Conflicting discourses sometimes engender widespread debate that can lead to compromise and resolution, on the one hand, or to discord and rupture on the other. But at other times these conflicting discourses may continue undisturbed, compartmentalized into separate mental spheres. Such compartmentalization occurs not only when people are exposed to multiple conflicting discourses, but also when a single discourse comes into tension with lived experience.

One example of this compartmentalization is the cognitive structuring of space in Japan into *uchi* (inner) and *soto* (outer) realms that may allow women to modulate between different modes of behavior and even thought, depending on context. Such a structuring may permit women to find an equilibrium between official and unofficial attitudes without experiencing them as contradictory. Jane Bachnik (1992), Dorinne Kondo (1987), and authors of a whole line of studies going back to Doi Takeo (1973) and Nakane Chie (1970) have shown how distinct modes of being are conceptually mapped onto inner and outer realms. While it is permissible and expected for one to express one's true feelings *(honne)* within the inner realm, it is more appropriate to cover these over with social propriety *(tatemae)* in the outer realm.

Such compartmentalization is what Ashikari Mikiko (2003) found in her study of Japanese women's use of foundation to whiten their faces. She writes that middle-class urban women's almost universal use of foundation when they move through outer spaces ends up sustaining official ideologies that require women's greater formality in self-presentation, even though they are much more relaxed within the more intimate inner spaces of the home.

As Amy Borovoy (2001, 2005) has argued, however, women's experience of inner space is not necessarily one of intimacy and freedom to be "oneself." Rather, the housewife has been expected to attend to her husband's every need, even to the point where she has enabled his alcoholism and found it difficult to draw a line between a destructive codependency and a culturally valued dependency.

Ashikari's understanding of inner space is too sanguine. And her understanding of outer space may also be overly simplistic, for such spaces can be read very differently, and these differences can lead to conflict when men and women drivers encounter each other on the road.

Women's use of K-cars for shopping and for transporting children around town associates these cars with domesticity, and one might think of the neighborhood within which the K navigates as an extension of the inner space. Certainly it is a very different kind of space from the mountain roads and highways that are the province of the late night activity of street racers. And yet men navigate these same neighborhood roads on their way between neighborhoods. For them, Ks may appear like women in outer spaces without their whiteface. Ks are like women walking around outside with their aprons on.

Perhaps such an interpretation also informed those men who commented to me that Ks drive in a sluggish manner, disrupting the flow of traffic, and should be taken off the road. There is much opportunity for men and women to contest the status of neighborhood spaces—women defining them as extensions of inner space and men defining them as outer space. It is in this contest that men may berate women just for being on the public roads, as if these roads were their own private spaces. For their part, women may berate men for their aggressive attitudes that violate the expectation of decorum in outer spaces and the consideration expected in inner spaces.

Many women noted a stark difference in treatment when they drove Ks compared to when they drove full-sized cars. One woman in her mid-thirties mentioned that when she drove a K, she was tailgated much more frequently (*yoku aorareru*) than when she drove a larger car. One complained that men assumed that larger cars had priority over Ks. She described one instance when she turned off a main road onto a smaller alley, one of many in Japan open to traffic in both directions but wide enough for just one car to pass. There, she had a standoff with an oncoming taxi, arguing about who should back up. The male taxi driver invoked the common stereotype that women did not know how to back up. In this case, however, the woman would have had to back up into a busy street. More than anything else, the taxi driver's attitude galled this woman, who took down his license plate number and phoned in a complaint.

Male aggression toward women drivers takes its most extreme form when criminal gangs target them. One woman described an experience with an *atariya* (accident faker) where one car tailgated her and another car in front stopped short on purpose. She was able to stop without hitting the car in front. Nevertheless, a "scary looking" guy got out of one car and accused her of hitting him and demanded compensation. When she threatened to call the police, the other cars drove off, but she said that other women could easily be intimidated into handing over money.

Some women are clearly able to resist male aggression directed toward themselves and their Ks on neighborhood roads. Such resistance rejects the masculinist disparagement of feminine driving styles and critiques the especially aggressive masculine styles that violate norms of safety and consideration. Such resistance suggests that the cognitive compartmentalization of different styles of driving appropriate for the inner and outer realms is contested as men and women have different understandings of neighborhood spaces. This contestation, however, does not deny that there may be a legitimate difference between masculine and feminine styles of driving, where men may drive in a fast, flowing, masterful way without aggression and where women may drive considerately without getting in the way of others. Moreover, some women, rather than rejecting gendered differences, embrace and enhance the feminine dimensions of the K, selecting pastels and pinks; adorning it with frilly curtains, cushions, and stuffed animals; and creating interior spaces of feminine sociality and solidarity that indifferently rebuff masculinist critiques of Ks as obstructing traffic.

Driving in Drag

But what of women who drive fast and aggressively? If bifurcated styles of driving support gender ideology, do not women street racers undermine it? In the *manga Initial D* and *Wangan Midnight,* there have been a few female racers. However, they have all been single young women unattached to families, and we may consider them to have been playing masculine roles in contrast to the majority of female characters whose role is to care for, wait for, worry about, or fall in love with the male drivers. On the one hand, these female racers present the possibility that women can define themselves apart from the domestic ideal. On the other hand, they can end up reinforcing the gender ideology by fulfilling a recognized gender ideal, albeit a masculine one that is not normally associated with women, rather than fashioning a more radical alternative.

The multiple interpretive possibilities in the case of female street racers are in some ways similar to those of the female actors who specialize in male roles in the all-female Takarazuka Theater. In her study of Takarazuka, Jennifer Robertson (1998) highlights this ambiguity. At one level, these female specialists in male roles *(otokoyaku)* do not challenge the heterosexual gender norm in which romance is possible only between masculine and feminine gendered characters. Indeed, many in the audience find in Takarazuka a fulfilling representation of their heteronormative romantic fantasies (Nakamura and Matsuo 2003). And yet at another level, the audience is quite aware that the actors are women and that these actors are able to create male roles that are somehow different from and more desirable than men in the real world. To some degree, Takarazuka acting has led to a lesbian fan subculture centered around the dashing and romantic female specialists in male roles (Robertson 1998).

Yet the comparison between Takarazuka's male role specialists and female street racers holds only to a certain point. Women who drive in drag—women who reject Ks for other kinds of cars that allow for much more masculine styles of driving—may end up reinforcing gender stereotypes in a less ambiguous way than do the Takarazuka's actors. After all, cars encase and obscure the driver, rendering the sex of the driver irrelevant in a way that is not the case with Takarazuka, where the knowledge of drag facilitates an interpretation that potentially directly conflicts with official gender ideology. The relative anonymity of confident and aggressive women drivers dampens, if not precludes, such an effect.

A more significant threat to official ideology would be if more and more women and men started driving Ks in an aggressive way. Such driving would represent a radically different stance on the part of an object that is gendered female and serves as a metaphor for female drivers, in a way that an unseen woman driving a masculine-gendered car in an aggressive fashion cannot express. Likewise, official ideology could be destabilized if both men and women drove larger, more powerful cars in a more polite and less aggressive manner.

Gender Schema and Driving
Metaphors in Recessionary Japan

Sales of K-cars have exploded with the onset of the long-lasting recession in Japan. The K's proportion of total car ownership has increased from a low in 1980 of 17 percent to a high in 2010 of 35 percent, with the rapid increase in market share occurring since 1990 (Ozeki 2007, 156). Not only do Ks cost substantially less than do other cars, but also they continue to enjoy a lower tax status, they are often exempt from the rule that requires purchasers of cars to show proof of having a parking space *(shako shōmei)* when registering the car, and their fuel economy has become a greater advantage in this era of high gas prices. While many Ks are trucks and minivans used for business purposes and are not gendered in the same way as K sedans, the proportion of K sedans has risen from just 11.22 percent of the K market in 1990 (Ozeki 2007, 156) to 65.59 percent in 2010 (Zenkeiren 2010).

The increased number of Ks in itself may not have been sufficient to transform their gender associations, but it laid the groundwork. Increased engine size and efficiency have complemented the increased numbers. As noted, engines have expanded from just 300 cc in 1950 to 660 cc in 1990. Greater efficiency also means that substantially more power is harnessed even from a modest increase in combustion. Today, Ks have a lot more pep than they used to, allowing people to drive them much more aggressively than before. In the past, people thought it would be too dangerous to drive Ks on highways. Now, even without modifications they can more than keep up with high-speed traffic.

Many posts on several K-car-related Mixi interest groups record the surprise of the drivers of normal sedans when Ks are able to shake tailgaters or pass other cars. One K owner recounts driving home from work stuck behind a slow moving car: "When I moved into the other lane to pass, I found that there was a line of ten or so cars, but it wouldn't look good to return and I couldn't if I wanted to, so I just floored it and passed the entire line. . . . The drivers I passed must have thought, 'What, a K?!'" One woman writes that she drives a thirteen-year-old MOVE: "Although it is a K, I'm an idiot who tailgates normal cars."

With the emergence of modified, turbo-charged Ks, the focus of the monthly magazine *Hot-K,* launched in November 2009 (see figure 12.2), we have the further breakdown of the dichotomy of sports cars and K-cars. Japan's long recession has affected street racers as much as anyone, and some have switched to racing K-cars, which are much cheaper to maintain. In addition to the lower sticker price and lower taxes, many parts for Ks cost significantly less than they do for other cars. Those who practice drifting on the mountain roads, spinning their wheels as they go around tight turns, generally have to replace their tires every week. K tires cost half as much as standard-sized tires, a savings that quickly adds up.

The transformation of Ks may mean that at least this dimension of automobility will no longer offer the same metaphorical and analogical buttressing to official gender ideology. Of course, the transformation of the K's metaphorical function will not in itself transform gender in Japan. In fact, Naomi Quinn

FIGURE 12.2

The monthly magazine Hot-K began publication in November 2009.

(1997, 141–161) argues that people use most metaphors opportunistically to express ideas that are already shaped by underlying cultural schemas. She argues against Lakoff's (1987) understanding of metaphors as shaping thought itself, noting that people use a wide range of metaphors, often mixing metaphors in order to get across what they already wanted to say. From her perspective, Ks never supported gender ideology so much as they expressed it. Thus if the K's metaphorical function was no longer available, Quinn would argue that the underlying gender schema would easily find alternative means of expressing itself.

There is evidence, however, that the large-scale economic transformations that have given new prominence to Ks and contributed to the shift in their metaphorical value are simultaneously putting pressure on the underlying gender schema. As in many other countries, more and more jobs in Japan have been outsourced to part-time labor forces or sent overseas. The gender schema was based in part on differentiated labor conditions, with men working in full-time, permanent jobs and women in part-time jobs and in the home, but more and more of the jobs in the new economy are precarious, like those that have traditionally been associated with women. Fewer men than before are able to fulfill the ideal of working for prestigious and stable companies. And fewer women than before are interested in the old ideal of marrying and having children.

It would be a mistake to assume that economic shifts ultimately determine metaphor, cognitive schemata, and all other cultural ephemera. The recession could easily lead to a retrenchment, as well as to a reformulated gender system. And even if the gender system were to become more egalitarian, it could do so in any number of ways that are unrelated to economic context. In Japan, the gender schema and metaphors about cars and driving styles enabled the coexistence of mutually contradictory discourses, one about speed and power that flourished in popular culture primarily among men and the other about giving way that flourished in the official project of controlling driving behavior associated primarily with women. A shift in gender schemata may lead to more conscious linkages of the conflicting discourses, breaking down their cognitive compartmentalization and forcing some resolution. If the bifurcated driving styles of speed versus manners are no longer compartmentalized by the gender schema, any number of new combinations may open up. Will women bring a new kind of sociality to speed, integrating speed and safety by keeping racing to racetracks and off public roads? We may be witnessing in Japan a shift from a somewhat integrated and durable cultural system to one characterized by uncertainty and change (Strauss and Quinn 1997, 111–136). While uncertainty may be disquieting for some, it also brings with it the potential for building a better future.

Notes

1. Taylorization refers to the application of the "principles of scientific management" as laid out by Frederick Taylor (1911). As artisanal production, in which individual craftsmen have control over all steps in the production process, gradually gave way to the increasingly minute division of labor, Taylor pioneered

the scientific study of human motion with the goal of maximizing efficiency and reducing injury. As workers are reduced to repeating a very limited number of motions within a larger production process, it is more likely that they become alienated from the product of their labor and lose a sense of autonomy.

2. It is no surprise that Lévi-Strauss is not known for doing in-depth fieldwork. Rather, he preferred to work with mythology and objects of art collected by others, which he could more cleanly subject to his structural analysis.

References Cited

Ashikari, Mikiko. 2003. "Urban Middle-Class Japanese Women and Their White Faces: Gender, Ideology, and Representation." *Ethos* 31, no. 1:3–37.

Bachnik, Jane. 1992. "The Two 'Faces' of Self and Society in Japan." *Ethos* 20, no. 1:3–32.

Borovoy, Amy. 2001. "Recovering from Codependence in Japan." *American Ethnologist* 28, no. 1:94–118.

———. 2005. *The Too-Good Wife: Alcohol, Codependency, and the Politics of Nurturance in Postwar Japan.* Berkeley: University of California Press.

Doi, Takeo. 1973. *The Anatomy of Dependence.* Tokyo: Kōdansha.

Fernandez, James W. 1977. "The Performance of Ritual Metaphors." In *The Social Use of Metaphor: Essays on the Anthropology of Rhetoric,* ed. J. David Sapir and J. Christopher Crocker, 100–131. Philadelphia: University of Pennsylvania Press.

———. 1986. *Persuasions and Performances: The Play of Tropes in Cultures.* Bloomington: Indiana University Press.

Kondo, Dorinne K. 1987. "Creating an Ideal Self: Theories of Selfhood and Pedagogy at a Japanese Ethics Retreat." *Ethos* 15, no. 3:241–272.

Kusunoki Michiharu. 1994. *Wangan Midnight.* Vol. 3. Tokyo: Kōdansha.

———. 1997. *Wangan Midnight.* Vol. 6. Tokyo: Kōdansha.

Lakoff, George. 1987. *Women, Fire, and Dangerous Things: What Categories Reveal about the Mind.* Chicago: University of Chicago Press.

Lévi-Strauss, Claude. 1963. *Structural Anthropology.* New York: Basic Books.

———. 1966. *The Savage Mind.* Chicago: University of Chicago Press.

Lyng, Stephen. 1990. "Edgework: A Social Psychological Analysis of Voluntary Risk Taking." *American Journal of Sociology* 95, no. 4:851–886.

Nakamura, Karen, and Hisako Matsuo. 2003. "Female Masculinity and Fantasy Spaces: Transcending Genders in the Takarazuka Theater and Japanese Popular Culture." In *Men and Masculinities in Contemporary Japan: Dislocating the Salaryman Doxa,* ed. James Roberson and Nobue Suzuki, 59–76. London: RoutledgeCurzon.

Nakane, Chie. 1970. *Japanese Society.* Berkeley: University of California Press.

National Police Agency (Keisatsuchō). 2005. "Hyō 1–13, Menkyo hoyū jinkō no suii, 1955–2004" (Figure 1–13, license holders 1955–2004). *Keisatsu hakusho* (Police Agency white paper). Http://www.npa.go.jp/hakusyo/h17/hakusho/h17/figindex.html. Accessed August 14, 2010.

Ozeki, Kazuo. 2007. *Nihon no keijidōsha* (Japan's lightweight cars). Tokyo: Miki Shobō.

Plath, David. 1992. "My-car-isma: Motorizing the Showa Self," In *Showa: The*

Japan of Hirohito, ed. Carol Gluck and Stephen R. Graubard, 229–244. New York: Norton.

Quinn, Naomi. 1997. "Research on Shared Task Solutions." In Strauss and Quinn, *A Cognitive Theory of Cultural Meaning,* 137–188.

Robertson, Jennifer. 1998. *Takarazuka: Sexual Politics and Popular Culture in Modern Japan.* Berkeley: University of California Press.

Roth, Joshua Hotaka. 2012. "Heartfelt Driving: Discourses on Manners, Safety, and Emotions in the Era of Mass Motorization in Japan." *Journal of Asian Studies* 71, no. 1:171–192.

Sapir, J. David. 1977. "The Anatomy of Metaphor." In *The Social Use of Metaphor,* ed. J. David Sapir and J. Christopher Crocker, 3–32. Philadelphia: University of Pennsylvania Press.

Seiler, Cotton. 2008. *Republic of Drivers: A Cultural History of Automobility in America.* Chicago: University of Chicago Press.

Shigeno Shūichi. 1995. *Initial D.* Vol. 1. Tokyo: Kōdansha.

Strauss, Claudia. 1997. "Research on Cultural Discontinuities." In Strauss and Quinn, *A Cognitive Theory of Cultural Meaning,* 210–251.

Strauss, Claudia, and Naomi Quinn, eds. 1997. *A Cognitive Theory of Cultural Meaning.* Cambridge: Cambridge University Press.

Taylor, Frederick Winslow. 1911. *The Principles of Scientific Management.* New York: Harper and Brothers.

Zenkeiren (Zenkoku keijidōsha kyōkai rengōkai) (National Association for K-Cars). 2010. "Kei san/yon rin sha oyobi zen jidōsha hoyū daisū no nen betsu shu betsu suii" (Changes in the numbers of three- and four-wheel K-cars by year and type). Http://www.zenkeijikyo.or.jp/statistics/. Accessed August 17, 2010.

CHAPTER 13

The Story of a Seventy-Three-Year-Old Woman Living Alone

Her Thoughts on Death Rites

SATSUKI KAWANO

"I've decided to have my cremated ashes scattered at sea. I have had a contract drawn up and deposited the fees," Mrs. Noda, a seventy-three-year-old woman living in a city near Tokyo, told me as we enjoyed tea and sweets one afternoon in February 2003. She felt relieved that everything had been set up. I asked her, "What did other people say about the scattering?" Mrs. Noda replied, "No one said, 'That's so nice.' Everybody was, like, 'Why would you or should you?' But when I told my kids, my son agreed to take care of it. He did not say anything or complain." At first, Mrs. Noda's story seemed to be a happy case of having a supportive adult child who promised to realize the wish of his parent. Soon after this exchange, however, I discovered that the son was not her own but the child of her husband's deceased first wife. Indeed, a much more complex story about Mrs. Noda's choice to have her ashes scattered gradually emerged over more than a year of my fieldwork in Tokyo.

The scattering of cremated ashes is a relatively new practice that developed since the early 1990s with the formation of a citizen's movement, the Grave-Free Promotion Society of Japan (Sosō No Jiyū O Susumeru Kai; GFPS). The founder of this group is Yasuda Mutsuhiko, a former *Asahi Shinbun* journalist whose career focus prior to the birth of the movement was on water-conservation issues. The organization had approximately sixteen thousand members in 2011. All the data for this chapter were collected during my fieldwork conducted at the GFPS between 2002 and 2004.

In contemporary Japan, the norm is to inter the cremated ashes of multiple family members in a family grave (the so-called *iebaka*) with a single underground structure to hold the urns. This practice is sometimes seen as "traditional," evoking the timeless past. However, it is in fact a relatively new development in Japan's history (Fujii 1993, 18; Makimura 1996, 112). Before World War II, burial and cremation were both practiced, but burial was more common (Kawano 2010). After the war cremation rapidly replaced burial in many parts of Japan. By the 1990s, cremation was taken for granted, facilitating the establishment of a family grave to accommodate the ashes of multiple family members.

A number of previous studies that have examined mortuary practices in Japan since the 1990s highlight the changes and diversification in the practices (e.g., Boret 2012; Inoue 2003; Kawano 2010; Mori 2000; Rowe 2006, 2011; Suzuki 2000; Tsuji 2006). Among a variety of factors examined in previous studies, demographic shifts and changing family relations have been examined in depth (e.g., Inoue 2003; Kawano 2010; Makimura 1996). Some older persons today do not have culturally preferred caretakers of their family graves—typically a married son and his wife. As families are smaller, some people have no sons. An increasing number of younger people remain permanently unmarried, and people with permanently unmarried sons might find it difficult to secure a ritual caretaker once their sons have passed away. Divorce is not uncommon, and depending on who takes custody of a child, a divorce could lead to the loss of a future caretaker. New burial systems, such as ash scattering and graves with permanent ritual care *(eitai kuyōbo)*,[1] provide practical alternatives to people in diverse family situations who cannot secure a future ritual caregiver. Although the family, rather than an individual, is the unit for acquiring and using a conventional family grave, these new mortuary systems allow for individuals to secure their own posthumous destinations. Moreover, these alternatives are much less expensive than conventional family graves. In particular, with the GFPS, volunteers, rather than funeral or religious specialists, help conduct ash-scattering ceremonies for members or their kin, and they cost much less (often less than $1,000).

While it is not difficult to see new and old practices as opposites or new ones as replacing the old, some studies have highlighted the ways in which survivors combine a new mortuary practice with more conventional ones followed to venerate the deceased (Kawano 2004). By examining Mrs. Noda's case, this chapter will examine the adoption and meaning of ash scattering as seen from a social actor's viewpoint and will illustrate that a person who adopts ash scattering does not necessarily reject the conventional mortuary practices. Mrs. Noda frequently visits her marital family grave, where her deceased husband as well as his parents and his first wife rest. She has also conducted conventional Buddhist memorial rites for the family dead with the help of a Buddhist priest. Nonetheless, she has chosen not to burden her stepchildren with the responsibility of her memorial care by electing ash scattering. Although she has provided memorial care to deceased family members for many years, she does not wish to receive the same care from her stepchildren, even though she is on good terms with them. Rather than exploring her case of ash scattering mainly as an expression of personal religious faith, this chapter thus examines her attitudes toward death rites that are embedded in the larger context of her family relations and lifestyle choices.

This chapter illustrates that a new mortuary practice such as ash scattering can be a strategy to manage a sense of distance felt by a person in non-normative family situations. Because new burial systems such as ash scattering and graves with permanent ritual care provide a person with a posthumous destination away from his or her family, these systems are sometimes used to resist the persistent gender or family ideologies that limit women's mortuary choices (Inoue 2003; also see Kawano 2003). It is thus that married women who have endured unhappy marriages can get "divorced" after death or single women can express their sense of independence through the choice of their own posthumous residence.

Mrs. Noda, however, does not fundamentally challenge the gender and family ideologies like women seeking posthumous divorce, though we do find an expression of agency in her selection of ash scattering. On several occasions during my fieldwork, I heard about adult children rejecting the interment of their stepmothers' ashes in their family graves because they felt that their stepmothers were not part of their families. Mrs. Noda's is the only case of a stepmother declining to join her husband's family grave.

Living Alone in Late Adulthood

"The present is the best time of all," was Mrs. Noda's reply when, after an extended interview, I asked her to identify the best period of her life. The reply came without the slightest hint of hesitation. After learning that she lives by herself, one might wonder why. In early postwar Japan, parents often lived with a married child and his (or sometimes her) spouse and children. Three-generational households provided elder care in a society that lacked a mature social security system (see Hashimoto 1996). Daughters-in-law were typically the caregivers, and caregiving was seen as a woman's duty as well as an expression of her femininity (Harris and Long 1993; Jenike 1997; Lock 1993, 2002; Long 1996; Rosenberger 2001). The family-based elder-care system was associated with the respect and affection owed to the elderly, and a social stigma was attached to the non-family caregiving provided in elder-care institutions.

By the 2000s, however, a number of changes had occurred in the elder-care system. In 2000, a long-term care insurance program was introduced by the state, and the elderly could now hire nursing-care assistants. This professionalization of elder care brought a more neutral image to caregiving by non-family members (Jenike 2003, 183–184). Furthermore, prolonged life expectancies, the limited availability of co-resident daughters-in-law, and new ideas about caregiving have led to the diversification of caregivers. Many people wish to have their daughters rather than their daughters-in-law as caregivers, although such a preference was already clear before 2000 (see Long 1987, 2008). Women over sixty years old and even a growing number of sons and husbands now serve as family caregivers (Harris and Long 1999; also see Kawano 2010). Despite the rapid professionalization of elder care, an older person living alone is still associated with vulnerability—in both physical and emotional terms. In the 2000s, the media sensationalized the phenomenon of the elderly dying alone *(kodokushi)* as a grave social problem; a partly mummified body, lying unnoticed for months by neighbors or faraway kin, grimly symbolized the breakdown of community and family ties that used to support the elderly.

The elderly themselves, however, do not always accept the negative images associated with living alone in late adulthood. A number of people prefer to live alone because by doing so, they do not need to worry about the difficult human relationships associated with three-generational living arrangements. For example, Mrs. Noda chose to live alone even though her married stepson had intended for her to live with him after the death of her husband. She has been living in a three-room unit in an old *danchi* (a community consisting of low-rise condo buildings) for the past thirty years, both with her husband and after his death, except for a brief period during his hospitalization and right after his death, when she stayed with her stepson and his family. Looking through the large sliding windows of her tatami-matted living/dining room, I could see a public school and flowering plum trees. Mrs. Noda told me, "Birds come and visit." In the small kitchen, a table, which Mrs. Noda had bought for her husband when she was caring for him, was now used to hold an ancestral altar. This small, black, cabinet-like altar accommodated her deceased husband's tablet *(ihai)*. It was early March, and an electric carpet still remained in the middle of the living room. Central heating is uncommon in homes in the Tokyo area, and an electric carpet is convenient in tatami-matted rooms, where people sit on the floor. It is thus that in Mrs. Noda's living/dining room there were no sofas or chairs.

Mrs. Noda went to live with her married stepson in a nearby city during the time when her husband was hospitalized, while her stepdaughter's family moved into the vacated condo unit. At that time the stepson thought her move was a permanent one, although it turned out to be temporary, as we will see below. Every day she commuted to her husband's hospital to look after him. Because Japanese hospitals used to be understaffed, it was common for a family caregiver to supplement the professional medical care provided by nurses and doctors (see Caudill 1961). Though for the past two decades understaffing has not been a major issue, the presence of a family caregiver at a hospital is still seen as an indication of strong family support and highly valued interdependence, despite the fact that hospitals are supposed to maintain a "complete" care system. Mrs. Noda told me, "When my husband passed away sixteen years ago, I stopped going to the hospital. I no longer had a place to go [during the day]. Then I came back to this *danchi*. My stepson told me that I was selfish [to have done so]. I did not like living with him and his family because I felt stressed by having to maintain smooth relations with them. . . . Also, when I was living in my stepson's home, I had no neighbors to talk to, as I knew no one there. . . . [Since I've moved back to this unit], I am relaxed, living without worries."

As a long-term resident, Mrs. Noda finds the condo community a convenient place. A bank, a supermarket, a park, and schools are all within a few minutes' walk. One afternoon, she took me to the supermarket. She walked into the store and quickly found what she was looking for—tofu, clams, salted *shishamo* (a kind of fish), and tuna. In addition to its convenience and familiarity, the community is a good place for Mrs. Noda, as she knows many neighbors. Some invite her to end-of-the-year parties, which she enjoys greatly. She goes to a public bathhouse during the winter months, not because her residence lacks a bath, but to socialize and enjoy the large, relaxing setting; she loves to chat with other regulars. She has given a house key to her neighbor next door so that she can check on Mrs. Noda: "I told her to open the door of my unit if she sees newspapers piling up outside the door." Having a younger neighbor in her sixties to depend on makes Mrs. Noda feel better about living alone. In short, the long-standing community network in her neighborhood provides her with social and emotional support, thereby allowing her to manage the vulnerability of living alone in late adulthood satisfactorily.

Mrs. Noda told me that she likes to use her body and move around. Every day, she would take a one-hour walk to a seaside park. There is a nice trail, and many people take walks or walk their dogs there. While we were walking together along the trail one day, she mentioned that she participated in the cleaning of nearby beaches as a volunteer: "Every year I find strange objects, and last year I found a huge box." After talking about her volunteering experiences at a nonprofit organization for a few minutes, she proudly told me, "Several younger volunteers [in their sixties] caught cold and did not come to a meeting last week. I have not caught a cold for the past ten years! I take a walk every day and get exposed to cold air. That's why I am full of energy *[genki]*." She continued: "My favorite activity used to be work. I used to work as a part-time cleaner." She told me that she never skipped work. She was tough and committed to it; she disliked complaining about physical pain: "I went to work even when I had all my teeth pulled."[2] She laughed: "The next day [after all the teeth had been removed] my face was swollen, but I still went to work. My husband called me crazy."

Although Mrs. Noda loved to work, after working long enough to qualify for a pension, she eventually quit her job to travel. Since the death of her husband, she has taken many trips, including ones to Mexico, Hawaii, Egypt, and Mongolia. During our interview, she told me that she planned to go to the Silk Road the following year.

Mrs. Noda is still active, but her memory is not as good as it used to be. Sometimes she cannot follow a TV show. She loses track of conversation in a group setting; she does not get a joke when others burst into laughter. She told me, "My daughter says that a hearing aid would help, but I went to a doctor and he said I am still fine without it." She has a thorough health examination every year. She said, "My doctor tells me not to drink, but I drink one bottle of sake (180 ml) once a week anyway. I love it warm. I would rather shorten my life than not drink at all!"

Mrs. Noda's life has not been easy. She told me, "I was determined to live alone. I didn't think of getting married." When I asked her why, she replied, "When I was young, I was very ill for a long time." Mrs. Noda was born in 1930. When she was a young girl, marriages were typically arranged, and a social stigma was attached to illness. She continued: "Since I was a daughter, my parents wanted to cure me without surgery. An operation leaves a large mark on the body [which was seen as damaging to her marriageability]. But a doctor told us that I had only half a year to live, so my parents agreed to an operation. Luckily it went well and I recovered."

Mrs. Noda married a man who had lost his wife. He had two young children by the first wife and was twelve years older than Mrs. Noda. On the ancestral altar in her home, a photograph of her and her husband was displayed. The husband was seventy years old and she was fifty-eight when a friend took the photograph. Mrs. Noda raised her stepchildren, and they are now married and have their own married children. Both of the stepchildren live in nearby cities, and the stepdaughter occasionally visits her. She said, "I do not have children of my own. I refer to my stepchildren with the suffix 'chan' but not my grandchildren." This suffix can be used to refer to one's own children in an affectionate manner, although it is certainly not a requirement. The suffix is also an affectionate but polite way of referring to the children of one's friends or neighbors. By always adding the suffix, Mrs. Noda is thus expressing her distance from the stepchildren. If the children were her own, she would not need to use it consistently. (Listening to her remark, I realized that my own step-grandmother always used the same suffix when she referred to me, whereas my blood grandmother did not always use such a suffix.)

Although Mrs. Noda was a second wife, she rapidly became part of her husband's network of kin. He had twelve siblings and many relatives. Mrs. Noda told me, "My husband's sisters all loved to sing and dance. They came with their children and we had parties together. We went to a nearby beach to dig clams and ate them together. My husband loved to have guests and often invited his colleagues to our home. He didn't worry about not having a special dinner for guests. He used to say, 'Just add some *nappa* [an inexpensive leafy vegetable] to a hot pot!'"

Mrs. Noda's husband used to be in the army. Many of his relatives had jobs related to the military. When she showed me his picture, I said, "What a handsome young man!" She replied, "He had delicate features, and in the army he was mistaken for a gay. Homosexuality was not uncommon in the military. . . . Once he complained to me that he was such a handsome man but that I was not very feminine." She laughed and added, "I am not very feminine or sexy; I was a tomboy [otenba]!" Her husband's remark does not necessarily indicate a marriage without affection, however, as people in the older generations avoid openly praising their spouses. To do so would be considered bad manners and embarrassing. Moreover, in contrast to today's new marital ideals (see

Mathews, this volume), in Mrs. Noda's youth marriage was primarily about having children and maintaining the household rather than about a romantic bond between two individuals attracted to each other (see Borovoy 2005). Therefore, it makes sense that despite his unkind comment, Mrs. Noda still made positive comments about her husband:

> I am not sure exactly why, but my husband decided to go to Manchuria to test his luck when he was young. Once established, he was planning to get married and take his new bride to Manchuria. However, the Russians captured him. He got to know another Japanese man while he was captive. When my husband was finally released, he offered to go to his acquaintance's home in Kanagawa Prefecture and tell the family that their son was alive. The family had a large, prosperous business, and to thank my husband for delivering the great news, the family offered him a job. But my husband turned it down, saying that his wife-to-be was waiting for him and he had to return to her. When I heard this story, I thought it was really nice that he came back to his wife rather than focusing on his career.

Thus Mrs. Noda praised her husband's character; he had kept his word and returned to his spouse.

When her husband grew old and ill, Mrs. Noda cared for him. She bought special elder-care equipment in order to keep him at home. She said, "I used to bathe my husband. I remember that he really loved it." When her husband's condition worsened, he was hospitalized, and, as noted, she moved temporarily to her stepson's house to commute to the hospital every day. When her husband passed away, she was depressed for a while. Sixteen years after her husband's death, however, she feels happy with her life once more. She told me, "I did not think that I would ever feel that way or that I would be able to enjoy late adulthood."

In fact, Mrs. Noda feels that now is the best time of her life. She survived World War II, overcame her long-term illness, raised her stepchildren and married them off, and took care of her husband and sent him off to the world of the dead. Now that her duties as a married woman had been fulfilled, she had her remaining life to enjoy. She was financially self-sufficient, as she had a pension. She told me, "In my parents' generation, it was taken for granted that adult children would care for their parents. Yet the society has changed, and one does not need to depend on children any more. It is so much better now."

Tending the Family Dead

While Mrs. Noda provides no more care to family members who are alive, she is not free from her caring duties, for she takes good care of the family dead. Ritual activities for the family dead are often associated with Buddhism. Yet when asked about their personal faith in religion, many people in contemporary Japan deny feeling any personal commitment to religious organizations or teachings. Nevertheless, they still take part in certain ritual activities, as they center on the well-being of the family dead and their communities (Kawano 2005; Traphagan 2004). Mrs. Noda is such a person. When asked about religion, she said, "I am not very religious. Yet I offer tea at the household altar every morning. When I cook rice in the morning, I offer rice too. Every morning, I recite mantras at the altar. My natal family's religion was Shin Buddhism, but I am not concerned about being reborn into a Buddhist paradise. Reciting mantras is like greeting [the family dead]."

When I visited Mrs. Noda's residence, she cooked a delicious meal for me, and when the rice was cooked, she offered a small amount to the ancestral altar before serving me. A cup of tea, beautiful flowers, and a dish of fruit were also placed near it. Mrs. Noda said, "My husband told me to offer him rice wine, so I do that as well." The ancestral altar is the medium through which the bereaved communicate with deceased family members by making regular offerings, joining hands, praying, chanting sutras, or simply thinking of the deceased. The act of "feeding" the deceased by regularly offering food and drink creates a ritual presence of the deceased in the survivors' lives. The social and cultural importance of ancestral altars is well documented in anthropological studies conducted in early postwar Japan (Plath 1964; Smith 1974). Ancestral altars have not disappeared from people's homes, although those of contemporary design have been developed to match consumers' tastes today, and thus there are more choices (Nelson 2008). Despite some changes and new developments, tending the family dead remains an important part of Japanese social life.

A funeral is only the beginning of a long ritual cycle that a deceased person has to go through to become a benevolent ancestor, and memorial rites are commonly held up to thirty-three or fifty years after a person's death (Smith 1974). The ritual efforts of the survivors are considered essential for the deceased's peaceful rest. Deceased persons without family are considered to become pitiable homeless spirits, as they lack the support and ritual care from the living that they need to achieve their transformation into benevolent ancestors. Whether dead or alive, a person's well-being rests on support from the family. Some people in contemporary Japan may not believe in the existence of ancestral souls, but they still value caregiving for the family dead as an expression of family bonds. For instance, Mrs. Noda said to me, "I visit my husband's grave at least once a month, on the anniversary of his death, and during the New Year holidays. His grave is only thirty minutes away from my place. Many more memorial anniversaries need to be performed for my husband, but I have already asked my stepson to take charge of them. We hold anniversary rites at a Buddhist temple. My stepchildren and their children all attend the rites. We have recently conducted my husband's thirteenth-year anniversary rite. We are already done with the thirty-three-year anniversary ritual for his first wife." (These periodic memorial rites are typically performed to mark the first, third, seventh, thirteenth, seventeenth, twenty-third, twenty-seventh, and thirty-third anniversaries, though there are variations; see Smith 1974, 95.)

Despite the postwar legal changes that equalized inheritance among siblings, memorial assets such as household altars and family graves, which are used by generations of family members, cannot be divided or shared. Only one person, most commonly a married male child, inherits the right to use a family grave, and along with his wife he is responsible for maintaining it. An in-marrying bride gains the right to use her husband's family grave. Therefore, as a bride who married into her husband's family, Mrs. Noda is obliged to maintain his family's grave and is supposed to join his family in that grave after death. However, though she tends her husband's family grave very conscientiously, she herself is not planning to join this family after death. Her situation is not simple, as she is a second wife without children, and below I shall return to this issue.

In addition to maintaining her husband's family grave, Mrs. Noda also cares for her natal family's grave in her hometown in northern Japan, a duty that is not typically the responsibility of a married-out daughter. Although she continues to venerate her parents at the natal family grave when possible, she is not its primary caretaker; that responsibility often rests on the shoulders of her married brother and his wife. During the festival of the dead held in August, when people are expected to venerate their deceased kin at family graves in many parts of Japan, Mrs. Noda takes a bullet train and returns to her hometown. She told me, "My parents and my brother are gone, and I am the only one left [in my family]. No family member is left in my hometown, and if I do not visit the grave, no one will. I visit my parents' grave at least three times a year, during the festival of the dead and on the equinoxes. . . . In this region, it is customary to offer flowers at acquaintances' graves. Everyone carries a large basket full of flowers. When I return to my hometown to visit my parents' grave, there are many people walking around with baskets, and I get to talk to some of my acquaintances." As Mrs. Noda's brother passed away without producing children, she is the only descendant left to provide her parents with ritual care. Although she has more than her ordinary share of ritual duties, she was not resentful about this task.

Mrs. Noda regularly visits her husband's sister's grave as well. Apparently, she was a very nice person. Every time Mrs. Noda went to see her, the sister-in-law told her not to come to her funeral or the grave. Mrs. Noda said, "I guess she did not want to be a burden, as her family's grave is far from my place, and there is a very steep path leading up to it." Despite the sister-in-law's multiple reassurances that it was unnecessary, however, Mrs. Noda continues to visit her grave.

Although Mrs. Noda herself has chosen an unusual way of disposing of her ashes, she closely follows the typical pattern of memorializing the family dead—for example, by maintaining the household altar and her husband's family grave. She also took on the additional responsibility of caring for the natal family dead. Nonetheless, as the next section will reveal, she is concerned about overburdening her stepchildren—a concern that played a role in her selecting ash scattering for her own ending.

Choosing Ash Scattering

I read about the Grave-Free Promotion Society in a major newspaper, cut out the article, and kept it for a long time. Let me see. . . . I think I still have the article. [Mrs. Noda produced the article and handed it to me.] . . . But this was not the first time I thought about ash scattering. When I was younger, I read about a person whose ashes were scattered in the Ganges River. The story touched my heart. However, when I was talking with a friend and her husband about the story and my interest in ash scattering, the husband told me that something like that [scattering ashes in the Ganges River, an act that is associated with philosophical sophistication] is for an *interi* [educated person]. Then I forgot about it. Much later, I read the article on the GFPS and contacted the organization regarding membership. About a year after receiving the membership information, I joined the GFPS. . . . Once

I had joined the organization, I had a chance to observe a collective scattering ceremony held at sea near Tokyo and decided to have my scattering ceremony at sea.

I asked Mrs. Noda why having her ashes scattered at sea was attractive to her. She said she liked the idea of scattering at sea better than scattering on a mountain because no traces were left.

One might wonder why Mrs. Noda does not want to leave traces of herself behind, particularly because she does venerate ancestors at family graves that preserve the remains of the deceased—something some GFPS members do not do because they do not believe in the afterlife or in souls resting in graves. Mrs. Noda is not very religious, though like many other religiously uncommitted persons in contemporary Japan, she finds visiting graves socially meaningful. And most GFPS members routinely take part in Buddhist-style veneration practices at death and ancestor rites for their relatives, colleagues, or neighbors. Occasionally I met members who strictly avoided Buddhist-style ritual practices—for example, joining hands at an altar to venerate the deceased—but they still expressed their respect toward the deceased through a moment of silence or closing their eyes, for instance. Ritual occasions for the deceased thus are concerned with their performers' ties with the dead, and this line of thinking makes sense when considering Mrs. Noda's point that reciting mantras is like greeting the deceased as social rather than supernatural beings. In short, Mrs. Noda's caring for the family dead reveals her embeddedness in a web of family relations. Toward understanding why she wishes to leave no traces of herself after death, her own comments on others' graves give us some ideas. When Mrs. Noda and I visited the famous Iwasaki family mansion in Tokyo (the family that founded the Mitsubishi conglomerate), I told her that I had seen the family's grave in a cemetery in Tokyo but noticed there were no flowers there. She responded: "Well, that is a pity. If no one comes to a grave, it would be much better not to have one." Later it occurred to me that perhaps she had selected ash scattering partly to avoid wondering whether her stepchildren would memorialize her at the family grave.

On another occasion, Mrs. Noda told me a story that revealed her thoughts on memorial care given to the deceased at a family grave. The story was about a friend's friend, an older woman who had passed away several months earlier. Her husband had already died a while before, and an urn containing his cremated remains was placed in his family's grave. When his wife passed away, however, her ashes were placed in her natal family's grave. Her marital family had an excuse that the family grave was full, but it is a highly unlikely reason to turn down the ashes of a full-fledged family member. After all, the grave is a person's house after death. By using a lack of space as the reason to reject the wife's ashes, her marital family declared that she was not one of them. Mrs. Noda saw this message behind the excuse and said, "It is a pity that her ashes were not placed in the husband's family grave on the grounds that she had not had children." When a husband dies after a short period of marriage, it is not unusual for his in-marrying bride, if childless, to "return" to her natal family. By giving up her marital family name, which is tied to her husband's family, and her consequent right to be buried in his family grave, she reassumes her membership in her natal family, thus gaining an opportunity to seek another marital partner. However, in the story told by Mrs. Noda, the husband's kin wrongfully rejected his wife's ashes, probably against her wishes. Because of her long marriage and by keeping her husband's name after his death, the woman was certainly entitled to be buried with him. Mrs. Noda said to me several times that the woman was pitiable, and I wondered if she was thinking about her own situation. Although she was also a childless older woman, her husband's family or stepchildren had not rejected the placement of her ashes in their family grave. Nevertheless, she might have thought that scattering ashes without trace would be better than interment with little ritual care, perhaps given reluctantly or resentfully by those left behind. Mrs. Noda did not want to be a burden. She clearly felt that depending on her stepchildren for memorial care would be an imposition. Her family situation had certainly shaped her choice of a different posthumous destination away from her husband, as well as the husband's parents, former wife, eldest son, and his wife.

Although old age in Japan is a time for dependency and Japanese people highly value interdependence, nonetheless overdependency is deeply feared (Traphagan 2004). Mrs. Noda's preference to leave no traces, which will make her less dependent on others after her death, is consistent with her wishes to avoid overdependency in old age. She told me a story of her stepdaughter's husband's sister's co-resident mother-in-law. This woman loved to play gateball (*gētobōru*; a team-based ball game popular among the elderly in Japan). One day she came home after her practice and went to her room to take a nap. When her daughter-in-law went to call the mother-in-law to dinner, she was gone. Mrs. Noda said, "What a great ending—to die after having done something she loved to do. . . . I really want to die without causing a nuisance to others."

Furthermore, when Mrs. Noda and I once visited a Shinto shrine, she washed her hands at a purification sink, proceeded to the shrine, threw a coin into the donation box, and joined her hands together with her eyes closed. Then she told me she made visits to shrines to wish for a shorter life. In preindustrial Japan, long life was a common wish made at shrines and temples, so Mrs. Noda's wish indicated Japan's postindustrial shift: now, longevity is taken for granted and strongly associated with long-term suffering and overdependence on family caregivers (Long 2005). In Japan's postindustrial context of dying, older persons routinely discuss and desire not being a burden on others. Such a longing is also expressed in the religious realm. There are Buddhist temples, known as sudden-death temples, that are supposed to grant people a swift death (Long 2005, 55; Wöss 1993). These attract elderly visitors. Rather than a sign of depression or elder abuse, however, a petition for a sudden death among the elderly indicates a desire for self-sufficiency and concern for family caregivers.

Mrs. Noda had already made mortuary arrangements by herself, though prearranging mortuary ceremonies and obtaining a grave plot while one is still alive are not unusual in the mainstream society. She said to me, "I am not complicated. Soon after I observed a scattering ceremony conducted by the GFPS, I had a contract made for my own scattering ceremony. It's been paid for." A funeral specialist with whom she contracted will take charge of her scattering ceremony. She continued: "I decided against having a funeral when I pass away. [As ash scattering is conducted in lieu of the interment of cremated remains, some GFPS members do choose to have a funeral.] Though my husband received a posthumous name from a Buddhist priest, I decided not to receive one." A Buddhist priest commonly gives a posthumous name to the deceased as a sign of becoming a Buddhist disciple, though in contemporary Japan this practice does not necessarily indicate a personal commitment to Buddhism. The rank of a posthumous name and the scale of a funeral both reflect the socioeconomic standing of the deceased's family in a tightly knit community. However, among newer residents in urban centers like Tokyo, some people do without them. It is certainly not unusual for GFPS members to skip a Buddhist funeral or do away with a posthumous name. The reasons for omitting these steps vary. Common explanations were "They are expensive"; "They are an empty formality"; "I do not want to make a Buddhist priest richer"; and "I am not religious." The late 1990s and the 2000s saw open, lively debates in the media on the meanings and appropriateness of contemporary Buddhist funerals and other mortuary practices (e.g., the conferring of posthumous names, the interment of cremated remains in a family grave, and the performance of memorial rites) (see, for example, Covell 2008). In such a context of candid, critical discussions of mortuary practices, Mrs. Noda's plan for a simple scattering ceremony without a posthumous name hardly sounds revolutionary, particularly in an urban center.

Because the interment of cremated remains in a family grave continues to be the mainstream practice imbued with the cherished value of honoring ancestors, GFPS members' families do not always support their choice of ash scattering (Kawano 2010). Opposition from family members is not unusual and can cause serious friction. I asked Mrs. Noda, "What was the reaction of your stepchildren to your decision to have an ash-scattering ceremony?" She said she did not encounter any opposition from them:

> When we got together to conduct a memorial anniversary ritual for my husband, I announced that I would have my ashes scattered at sea. There was a moment of silence. Then, my eldest son said he understood and would scatter my ashes on a famous mountain in my hometown. So I quickly told him that one is not allowed to scatter ashes freely without the landowner's permission. [She laughs.] My stepson did not oppose my choice or complain; he remained calm—the way a man should. My stepdaughter was surprised, as she had never heard of ash scattering. My stepchildren are going to take care of my scattering ceremony [with a funeral specialist's help]. My granddaughter also told me that she would do it for me. Yet another grandchild was completely against scattering because not finding his grandmother in the family grave would make him sad when he visited. I was moved by his remark that he would miss me even though I am unrelated to him by blood.

I asked Mrs. Noda what she would have done if her stepson had been against ash scattering. She said with a smile, "I would probably have it done anyway!"

Mrs. Noda is hesitant to ask for help from her stepchildren partly because she wants to spare them strain, worry, or awkwardness. When she filled out the contract form with a funeral specialist, she wrote down her stepdaughter's name. She told me that she was concerned about making it awkward for her stepson, as it is customary for a son to take charge of a mortuary ceremony. She is attentive to her stepchildren's feelings, a position that seems to cause her stress at times. She tends not to consult them, and this is the case with both mortuary and nonmortuary matters. For example, when she decided to go on the trip to Mongolia, she did not tell her stepchildren about it until a couple of days before her departure so that they would not worry. Another GFPS member commented on Mrs. Noda's maintaining distance (enryo suru) from her stepchildren: "It seems that her stepdaughter is a nice, warm person, and she might feel better if Mrs. Noda relied on her more often."

Mrs. Noda's wish to minimize her dependence on her stepchildren, however, is not the only reason she chose ash scattering. The GFPS idea of rejoining nature after death is appealing to her. As noted, she takes walks regularly and enjoys the beauty of nature. While we were walking together in her neighborhood, she said to me, "I've seen a kingfisher here [a bright blue bird commonly found near water]. It is gorgeous! Some people try to feed kingfishers." When we came to a point overlooking the ocean, she said, "A sunset from this spot is amazing. Sometimes you can even see Mount Fuji [the highest mountain in Japan, known for its beauty] from this park." She was eager to share her impressions and observations. She continued: "I love to share my feelings when I see beautiful things, and I try to talk to strangers walking nearby. But they do not always respond with a similar level of excitement."

Mrs. Noda told me that a good way to die would be to be walking around on a mountain, as she loves to do, and to pass away at one point during the walk. Leaves would pile up on her body, and later snow would cover her. She said, "That way, I would fertilize the surrounding nature. I always thought that kind of ending would be great. Yet, in reality, police officers would come, and it would create a scene if I pursued my ideal. I would not be able to have that kind of ending."

Mrs. Noda's trip to Mongolia left a lasting impression on her. She had a chance to stay in a tent. Animal dung was used for heat, a method she thought was great, as it is not wasteful. She told me, "I saw dead animals in Mongolia and thought that it was a real shizensō [a natural mortuary rite]." Indeed, shizensō is the mortuary practice that the GFPS promotes; the group is against a mortuary practice that is destructive to nature. The organization is opposed to the building of large-scale cemeteries because they necessitate the cutting down of trees and the spreading of pesticide to keep the cemeteries neat. Interring cremated remains in a concrete underground structure is "unnatural," as it prevents the remains from reverting to nature.

While the GFPS encourages people to have their cremated remains scattered on a mountain or at sea, members sometimes praise other "natural" mortuary practices such as burial, which also allow the remains to return to nature. Mrs. Noda's comment on the dead animals she saw in Mongolia addresses this ideal propagated by the GFPS: "I thought it was nice that the animals died and perished in nature or got eaten by other animals." She continued: "When I take a walk, I often see ducks. They are cute. I say to them in my mind, 'Someday we will be together again [in nature].' My ashes will be scattered at sea. The ducks might even drink the water containing my ashes." Becoming part of nature after death is not discussed as an alienation from kin, though critics might hold such a view of ash scattering. Rather, to its supporters, a return to nature offers a comforting, aesthetically pleasing image of posthumous existence that is an alternative to the conventional idea of resting in peace in a family grave. The idea of returning to nature through ash scattering allows its supporters to construct new scripts of afterlives.

Discussion and Conclusion

Although ash scattering is sometimes seen as an ideological challenge to the taken-for-granted Buddhist mortuary authority, a closer examination reveals a far more complex picture of this relatively new mortuary practice from its users' perspective. The case of Mrs. Noda demonstrates that ash scattering can be used as a way of managing the sense of distance that one might feel in relation to one's potential ritual caretakers. Mrs. Noda has chosen to live away from her married stepson, who had expected her to come and live with him and let him care for her ritually. And now she has decided to have her ashes scattered at sea rather than having them interred in a family grave. She is concerned about overburdening her stepchildren, particularly because she is not related to them by blood. Similarly, other GFPS members with whom I talked also emphasized their desire to reduce their dependence on children—particularly those who are without married sons and have only married-out daughters. Asking a daughter to care for the natal family grave would entail doubling her ritual care responsibilities if she was already responsible for looking after her husband's family grave. Ash scattering, therefore, provides a memorial strategy for people who lack a culturally preferred caretaker to maintain a family grave (Kawano 2010).

The feeling of an absence of family solidarity can also lead a family member to opt for ash scattering. In fact, seeking a separate resting place through ash scattering is not unusual among GFPS members—in particular those who have structurally weaker positions in their families (Kawano 2010). For example, adoptees and in-coming brides are expected to adapt to their adoptive or marital family traditions and prove themselves in the eyes of their family members. In particular, in a family without a male heir, it is not totally unusual for the family to adopt a daughter's husband as the heir (called the *mukoyōshi;* this practice used to be much more common when the society's economy was based on agriculture, as the adopted heir took charge of the family's farm), but he has a low status in the family, and usually his wife has the upper hand. Like an in-marrying bride, he must take his wife's family name, and he is expected to join his wife's family grave. Ash scattering is sometimes chosen when adoptees or brides find their family situation oppressive. In this context the practice can be a release from strained family relations. A discussion of posthumous divorce through ash scattering is not uncommon: women who are unhappy in their marriages want to "divorce" their husbands after death and have a separate resting place. As Inoue (2003) points out, graves with permanent ritual care that can accommodate individuals rather than families are sometimes chosen by would-be divorcees. Mrs. Noda's case, however, differs from such cases of posthumous divorce. Although her stepson assumed that her remains were to be interred in the family grave, she does not have a strong sense of belonging to her marital family as she has no natural children of her own.

A collective ash-scattering ceremony, conducted for multiple, unrelated families to scatter the ashes of their deceased kin, often costs less than $1,000 per family, and a single-family ceremony may cost around $2,000. In contrast, establishing a new, centrally located grave in the Tokyo area may easily cost more than $25,000. Ash scattering is certainly an inexpensive alternative to acquiring a new family grave in Tokyo. Nevertheless, I reject the argument that people's choices are determined simply by the low cost of scattering ceremonies. If new memorial alternatives such as ash scattering were chosen based purely on individuals' financial circumstances, the GFPS would then predominantly have economically disadvantaged members. However, this is not the case, as I encountered a number of middle-class members, such as former salaried employees, professionals, and civil servants, as well as members with working-class backgrounds. The cost of ash scattering, however, did have a role in shaping members' mortuary choices. One characteristic of the GFPS members was that they tended not to be part of a long-standing community in which generations of their ancestors had lived. Many of them were relatively new migrants in their urban communities of residence. As such, they tended to see their own endings as private issues rather than public affairs signifying their family's social standing in their community (Kawano 2010). A social actor makes a consumption choice by assessing the value of a ceremony in the existing cultural, social, and historical context. The cost of ceremonies matters not because the majority of GFPS members could not afford expensive graves but because they could define the option of ash scattering as a private consumption choice that did not damage their family's status. In Mrs. Noda's case, her natal family no longer existed; her marital family had a grave of its own. She did not worry about the watchful eyes of her neighbors and relatives, who might judge her marital family's reputation by scrutinizing the scale of her mortuary ceremony.

Mrs. Noda's case reveals that her choice of ash scattering does not necessarily lead to a rejection of conventional mortuary customs. She feels that old and new practices can coexist without any sense of incoherence. Her case thus challenges common assumptions held by critics—for instance, that GFPS members "throw away" their ancestors' ashes and thus neither respect those ancestors nor perform conventional memorial rites for the family dead. Contrary to such assumptions, Mrs. Noda maintained a busy schedule of tending to the family dead in both her natal and her marital families. She valued the expression of care and concern through visiting graves and chanting mantras to the deceased. What she did for others, however, was not what she wanted to impose upon others. Rather than obliging her stepchildren to care for her, she chose a path to reduce the extent of her dependence in the posthumous world.

It is worth emphasizing that Mrs. Noda's mortuary choices reflect her ability to make personal decisions on her own; these, however, are made by considering, rather than disregarding, her relationship with her stepchildren. She wishes to minimize her dependence on others while recognizing her ties to others, rather than maximizing her independence by presenting herself as an autonomous individual free from social and family relations. The distinction between minimizing dependence and maximizing independence might seem subtle, but it is significant culturally and analytically. Too often, critics claim that ash scattering illustrates the ever-expanding "individualistic" orientations prevalent in today's Japan, and the new mortuary practice is often contrasted with the waning group-oriented ancestor worship that symbolizes interdependence and group solidarity. As Mrs. Noda's case reveals, however, the relationship between the old and the new is much less straightforward.

Notes

I would like to thank Mr. Mutsuhiko Yasuda of the GFPS, volunteers at its Tokyo office, and other GFPS members who allowed me to participate in their activities and conduct my research. A Social Science Research Council–Japan Society for the Promotion of Science postdoctoral fellowship (2002–2004) made it possible for me to conduct extended fieldwork in Japan for this project. Glenda Roberts of Waseda University kindly served as a host researcher during the tenure of my fellowship. I am grateful for thoughtful comments provided by Glenda Roberts and Susan Long as well as anonymous reviewers on earlier versions of this chapter.

1. The Japanese term for "graves with permanent ritual care" has also been translated as "eternal memorial graves" (Rowe 2003, 110) and "eternally worshipped graves" (Tsuji 2002, 188).

2. Mrs. Noda seems to have been unlucky. Her dentist told her to get dentures and to make several appointments to remove her remaining teeth (she insisted on having them all pulled out during one visit). This dentist removed even her healthy teeth and made her buy a very expensive denture, for his profit. This radical practice of pulling perfectly good teeth used to be more common in early postwar Japan. During the 2000s, however, this kind of dentist is no longer typical.

References Cited

Boret, Sébastien. 2012. "An Anthropological Study of a Japanese Tree Burial: Environment, Kinship and Death." In *Death and Dying in Contemporary Japan,* ed. Hikaru Suzuki, 177–201. London: Routledge.

Borovoy, Amy. 2005. *The Too-Good Wife: Alcohol, Codependency, and the Politics of Nurturance in Postwar Japan.* Berkeley: University of California Press.

Caudill, William. 1961. "Around-the-Clock Patient Care in Japanese Psychiatric Hospitals: The Role of the Tsukisoi." *American Sociological Review* 26, no. 2:204–214.

Covell, Stephen G. 2008. "The Price of Naming the Dead: Posthumous Percept Names and Critiques of Contemporary Japanese Buddhism." In *Death and Afterlife in Japanese Buddhism,* ed. Jacqueline I. Stone and Mariko Namba Walter, 293–324. Honolulu: University of Hawai'i Press.

Fujii, Masao. 1993. "Gendai no bochi mondai to sono haikei" (Contemporary problems concerning graves and their backgrounds). In *Kazoku to haka* (Families and graves), ed. Fujii Masao, Yoshie Akio, and Komōto Mitsugi, 6–24. Tokyo: Waseda Daigaku Shuppanbu.

Harris, Phyllis Braudy, and Susan O. Long. 1993. "Daughter-in-Law's Burden: Family Caregiving and Social Change in Japan." *Journal of Cross-Cultural Gerontology* 8, no. 2:97–118.

———. 1999. "Husbands and Sons in the United States and Japan: Cultural Expectations and Caregiving Experiences." *Journal of Aging Studies* 13, no. 3:241–267.

Hashimoto, Akiko. 1996. *The Gift of Generations.* Cambridge: Cambridge University Press.

Inoue, Haruyo. 2003. *Haka to kazoku no henyō* (The transformation of graves and families). Tokyo: Iwanami Shoten.

Jenike, Brenda Robb. 1997. "Gender and Duty in Japan's Aged Society: The Experience of Family Caregivers." In *The Cultural Context of Aging: Worldwide Perspectives,* 2nd ed., ed. Jay Sokolovsky, 218–238. Westport, CT: Greenwood.

———. 2003. "Parent Care and Shifting Family Obligations in Urban Japan." In

Demographic Change and the Family in Japan's Aging Society, ed. John Traphagan and John Knight, 177–201. Albany: State University of New York Press.

Kawano, Satsuki. 2003. "Finding Common Ground: Family, Gender, and Burial in Contemporary Japan." In *Demographic Change and the Family in Japan's Aging Society*, ed. John Traphagan and John Knight, 125–144. Albany: State University of New York Press.

———. 2004. "Scattering Ashes of the Family Dead: Memorial Activity among the Bereaved in Contemporary Japan." *Ethnology* 43, no. 3:233–248.

———. 2005. *Ritual Practice in Modern Japan*. Honolulu: University of Hawai'i Press.

———. 2010. *Nature's Embrace: Japan's Aging Urbanites and New Death Rites*. Honolulu: University of Hawai'i Press.

Lock, Margaret. 1993. *Encounters with Aging: Mythologies of Menopause in Japan and North America*. Berkeley: University of California Press.

———. 2002. *Twice Dead: Organ Transplants and the Reinvention of Death*. Berkeley: University of California Press.

Long, Susan O. 1987. *Family Change and the Life Course in Japan*. Ithaca, NY: China-Japan Program, Cornell University.

———. 1996. "Nurturing and Femininity: The Impact of the Ideal of Caregiving in Postwar Japan." In *Re-imaging Japanese Women*, ed. Anne Imamura, 156–176. Berkeley: University of California Press.

———. 2005. *Final Days: Japanese Culture and Choice at the End of Life*. Honolulu: University of Hawai'i Press.

———. 2008. "Someone's Old, Something's New, Someone's Borrowed, Someone's Blue: Changing Elder Care at the Turn of the 21st Century." In *Imagined Families, Lived Families*, ed. Akiko Hashimoto and John W. Traphagan, 137–157. Albany: State University of New York Press.

Makimura, Hisako. 1996. *Ohaka to kazoku* (Graves and families). Tokyo: Toki Shobō.

Mori, Kenji. 2000. *Haka to sōsō no genzai* (Graves and mortuary rites at present). Tokyo: Tokyodō Shuppan.

Nelson, John K. 2008. "Household Altars in Contemporary Japan: Rectifying Buddhist 'Ancestor Worship' with Home Décor and Consumer Choice." *Japanese Journal of Religious Studies* 35, no. 2:305–330.

Plath, David W. 1964. "Where the Family of God Is the Family: The Role of the Dead in Japanese Households." *American Anthropologist* 66:300–317.

Rosenberger, Nancy. 2001. *Gambling with Virtue: Japanese Women and the Search for Self in a Changing Nation*. Honolulu: University of Hawai'i Press.

Rowe, Mark. 2003. "Grave Changes: Scattering Ashes in Contemporary Japan." *Japanese Journal of Religious Studies* 30, nos. 1–2:85–118.

———. 2006. "Death by Association: Temples, Burial, and the Transformation of Contemporary Japanese Buddhism." PhD dissertation, Princeton University.

———. 2011. *Bonds of the Dead*. Chicago: University of Chicago Press.

Smith, Robert J. 1974. *Ancestor Worship in Contemporary Japan*. Stanford, CA: Stanford University Press.

Suzuki, Hikaru. 2000. *The Price of Death*. Stanford, CA: Stanford University Press.

Traphagan, John. 2004. *The Practice of Concern*. Durham, NC: Carolina Academic Press.

Tsuji, Yohko. 2002. "Death Policies in Japan: The State, the Family, and the

Individual." In *Family and Social Policy in Japan,* ed. Roger Goodman, 177–199. Cambridge: Cambridge University Press.

———. 2006. "Mortuary Rituals in Japan: The Hegemony of Tradition and the Motivations of Individuals." *Ethos* 34, no. 3:391–431.

Wöss, Fleur. 1993. "Pokkuri-Temples and Aging." In *Religion and Society in Modern Japan,* ed. Mark R. Mullins, Susumu Shimazono, and Paul L. Swanson, 191–202. Berkeley: Asian Humanities Press.

GLOSSARY

Japanese Entries

akasen 赤線 official red-light districts in postwar Japan; the 1958 Anti-Prostitution Law abolished them

aoru あおる to follow another vehicle at an unsafe distance; tailgate

arubaito アルバイト part-time work performed by young people who are either still in school or who have not yet secured a regular job

atariya あたりや accident faker

baburu sedai バブル世代 cohort of Japanese who came of age during the economic "bubble" in the late 1980s and early 1990s

Baishun Bōshi Hō 売春防止法 Anti-Prostitution Law of 1958 (*baishun* refers to prostitution; it literally means "the selling of spring")

bakkuyādo バックヤード backyard, or the backroom of a convenience store that serves as an office, rest space, and storage area

bentō; obentō 弁当 often works of art, these Japanese-style boxed lunches are available at convenience stores, train stations, or food stalls; also prepared at home to be taken to work or school

bōsōzoku 暴走族 "tribes" or gangs of youth who drive around in ostentatiously modified cars, including those with removed or modified mufflers; they make loud and high-pitched sounds with the goal of harassing other drivers and entire neighborhoods

bukatsudō 部活動 extracurricular school club activities

burakumin 部落民 caste-like minority of ethnic Japanese that has suffered long-standing discrimination in Japan

-chan ちゃん affectionate but polite suffix commonly attached to a child's first name

chiiki katei 地域家庭 families in the local area

chiiki kosodate shien kyoten, hirobagata 地域子育て支援拠点広場型 drop-in-center-style base for community-level child-rearing support

chikara o awaseru 力を合わせる to combine powers

chōkōrei 超高齢 the old old; usually referring to those over seventy-five or eighty

chōnan 長男 eldest son; in the Meiji legal code, the son who would most likely inherit and carry on the family line *danchi* 団地 community consisting of low-rise or high-rise condo buildings

dankai no sedai 団塊の世代 cohort of Japanese who were born within ten years after the end of World War II (roughly between 1946 and 1954)

Dōbutsu Uranai 動物占い Animal Divination, a system created by *manga* artist Kubo Kiriko

eitai kuyōbo 永代供養墓 grave for an individual or unrelated individuals that requires no maintenance by successors; commonly used by people without descendants

enryo suru 遠慮する to maintain a social distance by not depending on others

erai hito えらいひと important person or people

furītā フリーター part-timer; a young worker not currently engaged in education who works part-time jobs as opposed to having full-time, salaried employment

furoku 付録 free insert giveaways found in magazines and *manga*

fūzoku 風俗 public morals, often specifically sexual morals; often used as a euphemism for the sex trades

fūzokujō 風俗嬢 woman who works in the sex trade industry

gachi gachi de ガチガチで frozen with fear

gakudō hoiku 学童保育 after-school day-care program

gakureki shakai 学歴社会 education-credentialist society

ganko oyaji 頑固親父 stubborn old man

gatsu gatsu unten がつがつ運転 aggressive driving

genki 元気 energetic

gētobōru ゲートボール gateball; team-based ball game popular among the elderly in Japan

gimu 義務 duty

haken 派遣 shorthand for *haken shain;* temporary staff

haken shain 派遣社員 worker who is employed by a dispatch company to do specific tasks at another firm for a fixed period, usually with fewer benefits than those given to regular employees or with no benefits

hashiriya 走りや street racers who achieve an emotional high through speed

hidari uchiwa 左団扇 to be wealthy (that is, so wealthy as to have a servant fanning you at your left hand)

hikikomori ひきこもり the socially withdrawn; the term refers to young people who are not attending school or are unemployed and lead socially isolated lives

Himeyuri Butai ひめゆり部隊 Star Lily Corps

hitogara 人柄 personality

hitotsu no koto ni uchikomu ひとつのことに打ち込む to devote oneself to one thing

hoikuen 保育園 day-care center

honne 本音 inner feelings

ichiji azukari 一時預かり temporary drop-off child-care services

ichioku sōchūryū shakai 一億総中流社会 all-middle-class society; a society where just about everyone is middle class; commonly used by Japanese to refer to their society during and after the high-growth economy of the 1960s until the recession of the 1990s

ie 家 the multigenerational stem family model that was the legal basis for families and households in late nineteenth- and early twentieth-century Japan; a stem family household was a social unit of production and consumption that continued through time through the succession of one heir (often the eldest son) and his/her spouse, who would take over the responsibilities for the gender-appropriate roles in each generation; changes to family law after World War II eliminated the legal status of the *ie,* and as industrialization increasingly undermined the household as a unit of production, the economic basis for the stem family declined gradually over the twentieth century in both urban and rural areas; optional multigenerational residence continues to a limited degree for a number of practical and ideological reasons in contemporary Japan

iebaka 家墓 family grave; a single underground structure with a single gravestone bearing a family's surname and accommodating multiple urns containing the cremated remains of the family dead

ihai 位牌 ancestral tablet; often a dark, lacquered wooden tablet bearing the posthumous name of the family dead

ikemen イケメン good looking

ikigai 生きがい that which makes one's life worth living

ikuji fuan 育児不安 child-rearing anxiety

ikuji noirōze 育児ノイローゼ child-rearing neurosis

ikuji sākuru 育児サークル mothers' voluntary social groups for child rearing

interi インテリ educated person

ippanshoku 一般職 clerical track or position(s) in Japanese corporations with no or few opportunities for advancement; such positions are usually given to women who are known as "office ladies"; their positions include full-benefit packages and continuous employment contracts

ippōteki 一方的 unilateral; one-sided

jidōkan 児童館 children's center; facility for children's welfare and healthy development based on Child Welfare Law; staffed by those with appropriate qualifications to guide children who use the facility

jojo kakusa 女々格差 "female-female disparity," or economic and social disparity among Japanese women that began to develop in the 1980s based on women's individual educational and professional achievements

juku 塾 extracurricular private tutorial and test-preparation schools or programs (full-time, after-school, or summer programs); for remedial or advanced tutelage to assist children in passing entrance exams for higher schooling; sometimes translated as "cram schools"

kaigo fukushishi 介護福祉士 caregiver for the elderly infirm; literally, "caregiving welfare expert"

kaigo hoken 介護保険 the public long-term care insurance program

kaizen 改善 continual improvement in production through worker innovation *kakarichō* 係長 sub-section chief

kakukazokuka 核家族化 the nuclearization of the family; Japanese sociologists use this term to refer to the transition *(ka)* over the course of the twentieth century from a household structure based on a multigenerational stem-family model to one based on a "modern" nuclear family *(kakukazoku)* composed only of parents and their children

kakusa 格差 disparity (See *kakusa shakai*)

kakusa shakai 格差社会 disparity society; often used to refer to Japanese society after the 1990s

kanji 漢字 Chinese character(s); ideograms

kao o dashita 顔をだした showed one's face, put in an appearance; some grandparents lamented that their grandchildren merely put in an appearance on holidays or other obligatory occasions and that they thus did not have much of a relationship with them

katei kyōiku 家庭教育 home education

keijidōsha 軽自動車 K-cars; lightweight cars whose engines and body sizes fall within specified limits and are taxed at a lower rate than other cars

keppekishō 潔癖性 very neat and tidy person; a compulsively tidy person

ketsueki-gata uranai 血液型占い indigenous Japanese divination system based on blood type

kodokushi 孤独死 dying alone; refers to the death of a socially isolated person; often used to convey waning community and social ties in contemporary Japan

Kodomo Gikai 子供議会 Children's Council

kōen debyū 公園デビュー park début; the occasion on which a (new) mother takes her young child to a park for the first time; a rite of passage for the mother and the child to join other parents and children in the neighborhood

kokoro 心 heart

kokoro no kyōiku 心の教育 education of the heart

kokusaika 国際化 internationalization

komori 子守り nursemaids

konbini コンビニ Japanese abbreviation for the English term "convenience store"

konkatsu 婚活 spouse-hunting activities; shortened form of *kekkon katsudō* (marriage activities), which refers to the practice of actively searching for a spouse through participating in matchmaking and dating activities

mamatomo ママ友 "mom friends"; a mother's friends who are also mothers

mazushii kokoro 貧しい心 literally, to have a poor heart; to be miserable, to feel one has no love to spare for anyone

meiwaku 迷惑 nuisance or bother to others

mikirihanbai 見切り販売 "time sales"; the practice of discounting food items nearing their consume-by date

miko 巫女 female Shintō shrine attendant

mottainai もったいない literally, "what a waste" or "what a shame"; a phrase of

Buddhist origin used to express pity or dismay when something is not properly used, cared for, or appreciated

nenjūmukyū 年中無休 open twenty-four hours per day, all year round; the hallmark of convenience store operations

nikushokukei joshi 肉食系女子 carnivorous women; media-generated term that describes women who purportedly actively pursue sex and marriage

nobi-nobi のびのび carefree, without inhibition

noro noro unten のろのろ運転 lethargic driving

obentō お弁当 see *bentō*

oden おでん hot stew containing various hearty marinated ingredients; popular in winter months but thanks to convenience stores, now available year-round

okusan 奥さん literally, "person in the interior"; the housewife, especially as counterpart to a salaried-employee husband

omake おまけ gift or service used to curry favor with customers

omiai お見合い arranged meetings; meetings arranged for the purpose of helping women and men find a spouse

omikuji おみくじ paper lottery oracles sold at temples and shrines

omote 表 front stage, the public arena

onigiri おにぎり rice ball; Japan's convenience store industry is credited with industrializing this compact food and helping make it a favorite

onmyōji 陰陽師 literally, "Yin Yang master"; a wizard or sorcerer

osanazuma 幼妻 young wife

oshieai 教え合い peer learning

otenba お転婆 tomboy

otokoyaku 男役 female specialists in male roles; associated with the Takarazuka (all-female) Theater

otsukaresama お疲れさま thank-you for your hard work

parasaito shinguru パラサイトシングル parasite singles; unmarried adults who live with their parents

pāto パート irregular employee; one without the benefits associated with regular employment and with much lower wages; may or may not work part time

purikura プリクラ literally, "print club"; automated photo sticker machines

raku 楽 easy; comfortable

rojōseikatsusha 路上生活者 literally, "person/people living on the street"; often used as an alternative to terms like "homeless person" or "vagrant"

rosu ロス literally, loss; a term commonly used in Japan's consumer industry to refer to food products that are nearing or have reached their expiration date and are removed from store shelves for disposal in some form

rosu chāji ロスチャージ literally, "loss charge"; a royalty fee embedded in the price of a product that, under Japan's current convenience store practices, the franchise owner pays when a food item is not sold and is subsequently discarded

sābisu zangyō サービス残業 unpaid overtime

saigo made ganbaru 最後まで頑張る to persevere to the end

seishain 正社員 regular staff; staff with corporate benefits packages and job security

sengyō shufu 専業主婦 full-time homemakers

senmongakkō 専門学校 post–high school two-year technical school

senmonshoku 専門職 specialist positions in Japanese corporations requiring technical expertise

shizensō 自然葬 ash-scattering ceremony; a mortuary practice that is considered to return the remains of the deceased to nature without damaging the environment; the mortuary practice coined and promoted by the Grave-Free Promotion Society

shōhikigen 消費期限 consume-by date

shōmikigen 賞味期限 best-before date

shunin 主任 level of supervisor before sub-section chief

shūshoku katsudō 就職活動 job-hunting activities that generally take place during a student's third and fourth year at university

sōgōshoku 総合職 professional track or position(s) in Japanese corporations with opportunities for advancement

Sōgō-Teki na Gakushū 総合的な学習 Integrated Studies

sōshokukei danshi 草食系男子 herbivorous men; media-generated term that describes men who purportedly are not actively interested in sex and marriage

Sosō No Jiyū O Susumeru Kai 葬送の自由をすすめる会 Grave-Free Promotion Society of Japan (GFPS)

soto 外 outer; outside

tatemae たてまえ outer display

teikei 提携 face-to-face relationship between producers and consumers developed in the 1970s in the domain of organic agriculture in Japan as a resistance against the market; it is a non-market form of community-supported agriculture

tekazashi てかざし healing technique in Mahikari-kyō (a religious sect) involving the raising of the palm of the healer's hand to emit spiritual light

tsudoi no hiroba つどいの広場 drop-in play centers where parents and preschoolers gather and socialize; supported by the state to build a sense of community and networks among parents and their young children

tsudoi no hiroba jigyō つどいの広場事業 national drop-in center project initiated by the state to build drop-in play centers for parents and their preschoolers in their communities

tsukaisute shakai 使い捨て社会 disposable society

tsunagari つながり links; connections

tsunageru つなげる to connect

uchi うち inner; inside

ura 裏 back stage, the private arena

uranai 占い divination

uranai būmu 占いブーム divination boom
yakeato sedai 焼け跡世代 cohort of Japanese who spent their childhood in the
    "burnt ruins" immediately after World War II
Yasuda Mutsuhiko 安田睦彦 founder of the Grave-Free Promotion Society
yorozuya 万屋 general store; it was common in many parts of Japan during the 1960s
    and 1970s; it is uncommon in Tokyo today
yuzuri-ai 譲り合い mutual giving way

English Entries

Angel Plan (1995–1999) エンゼルプラン
Child and Child-Rearing Support Plan (2005–2009) 子供子育て応援プラン
The Democratic Party of Japan 民主党
Equal Employment Opportunity Law of 1986 (EEOL) 雇用機会均等法
Family Support Services ファミリーサポートサービス
Hyōgo Prefecture 兵庫県
Japanese Organic Agriculture Association (JOAA) 日本有機農業研究会
Kanagawa Prefecture 神奈川県
kindergartens 幼稚園
Kyushu 九州
Lehman Shock (of 2008) リーマンショック
Liberal Democratic Party of Japan 自由民主党（自民党）
life-time employment 終身雇用
Lost Decade 失われた十年
Ministry of Education and Science; Ministry of Education, Culture, Sports, Science,
    and Technology (MEXT) 文部科学省
Ministry of Health, Labor, and Welfare (MHLW) 厚生労働省
Musashino City 武蔵野市
New Angel Plan (2000–2004) 新エンゼルプラン
oil shock オイルショック
Osaka City 大阪市
the postwar period 第二次世界大戦後、1945年–
three-year-old health examinations 三歳児検診
salaryman サラリーマン
seniority-based wage 年功序列賃金
Suye Village 須恵村
Yamada Masahiro 山田昌弘
Yamagata Prefecture 山形県

CONTRIBUTORS

Peter Cave is Lecturer in Japanese Studies at the University of Manchester. He is the author of *Primary School in Japan* (Routledge, 2007) and most recently "Japanese Colonialism and the Asia-Pacific War in Japan's History Textbooks: Changing Representations and Their Causes" (*Modern Asian Studies* 47, no. 2 [2013]: 542–580).

Satsuki Kawano is Associate Professor of Anthropology at the University of Guelph, Canada. Her research interests include ritual, death and dying, aging, family and kinship, and child rearing. She is the author of *Ritual Practice in Modern Japan* (University of Hawai'i Press, 2005) and *Nature's Embrace: Japan's Aging Urbanites and New Death Rites* (University of Hawai'i Press, 2010).

Sawa Kurotani is Professor of Anthropology at the University of Redlands, California. Her primary areas of scholarly interest have been globalization, gender, and Japanese studies, as exemplified in her first book, *Home Away Home: Japanese Corporate Wives in the United States* (Duke University Press, 2005). Her current research centers on the lived work experience of Japanese female professionals and the impact of the social, economic, and legal changes in the Japanese workplace. She also has a monthly column in *Daily Yomiuri*, one of the largest English-language dailies published in Japan.

Susan Orpett Long received her PhD in anthropology from the University of Illinois, Urbana-Champaign. She served as John Carroll University's first coordinator of East Asian Studies and is currently Professor of Anthropology there. Her research interests include comparative medical systems, family change, care of the elderly, and the cross-cultural study of bioethical issues. She is the author of *Final Days: Japanese Culture and Choice at the End of Life* (University of Hawai'i Press, 2005) and *Family Change and the Life Course* (Cornell University East Asia Papers, 1987). She edited *Lives in Motion: Composing Circles of Self and Community in Japan* (Cornell University East Asia Papers, 1999) and *Caring for the Elderly in Japan and the U.S.: Practices and Policies* (Routledge, 2000).

Gordon Mathews is Professor of Anthropology at the Chinese University of Hong Kong. Among other books, he has written *What Makes Life Worth Living? How Japanese and Americans Make Sense of Their Worlds*, *Global Culture/Individual Identity: Searching for Home in the Cultural Supermarket*, and *Ghetto at the Center of the World: Chungking Mansions, Hong Kong*, and he co-edited *Japan's Changing Generations: Are Young People Creating a New Society?*

Laura Miller is Ei'ichi Shibusawa-Seigo Arai Endowed Professor of Japanese Studies and Professor of Anthropology at the University of Missouri–St. Louis. She has published widely on Japanese popular culture and language, including topics such as the wizard boom, girls' slang, and print club photos. She is the author of *Beauty Up: Exploring Contemporary Japanese Body Aesthetics* (University of California Press, 2006) and co-editor (with Jan Bardsley) of *Bad Girls of Japan* (Palgrave, 2005). She also co-edited (with Jan Bardsley) *Manners and Mischief: Gender, Power, and Etiquette in Japan* (University of California Press, 2011) and (with Alisa Freedman and Christine Yano) *Modern Girls on the Go: Gender, Mobility, and Labor in Japan*.

Karen Nakamura is a cultural and visual anthropologist at Yale University whose research focuses on disability and minority social movements in contemporary Japan. Her first book, *Deaf in Japan: Signing and the Politics of Identity* (Cornell University Press, 2006), was awarded the John Whitney Hall Prize from the Association for Asian Studies. Her second book, *A Disability of the Soul: An Ethnography of Schizophrenia and Mental Illness in Japan,* was published in 2013 (Cornell University Press). She is currently working on a project involving the intersections of disability and sexuality.

Lynne Y. Nakano received her doctorate in anthropology from Yale University and is a professor in the Department of Japanese Studies at the Chinese University of Hong Kong. Her research focuses on the emergences of new social identities in East Asian societies, including volunteers in Japan and single women in Japan and urban China. Her current research compares the experiences of single women in Tokyo, Hong Kong, and Shanghai. She is the author of *Community Volunteers in Japan: Everyday Stories of Social Change* (Routledge, 2004).

Glenda S. Roberts, who received her doctorate in cultural anthropology from Cornell University, is Professor and Director of International Studies at Waseda University, Graduate School of Asia-Pacific Studies. Her research focuses on gender, work, and family in contemporary Japan, as well as on immigration policy and the reception of newcomer foreign residents in Japan. Her publications include "Salary Women and Family Well-Being in Urban Japan" (*Marriage and Family Review* 47 [2011]: 571–589) and *Staying on the Line: Blue-Collar Women in Contemporary Japan* (University of Hawai'i Press, 1994).

Nancy Rosenberger has a PhD in cultural anthropology from the University of Michigan and is a professor of anthropology at Oregon State University. She specializes in gender, food, and cultural change in Northeast and Central Asia. She is the author of *Gambling with Virtue: Japanese Women and the Search for Self in a Changing Nation* (University of Hawai'i Press, 2001) and *Seeking Food Rights: Nation, Difference, and Repression in Uzbekistan* (Cengage Learning, 2012). Rosenberger participates in food system activism in Oregon with a focus on local food for low-income people.

Joshua Hotaka Roth is Professor of Anthropology at Mount Holyoke College. He is the author of *Brokered Homeland: Japanese Brazilian Migrants in Japan* (Cornell University Press, 2002). His research on car cultures in Japan extends to the history of driving manners; discourses about emotions and driving; and Japanese map culture, sense of place, and way finding.

Gavin Hamilton Whitelaw is Associate Professor of Anthropology at International Christian University (ICU) in Tokyo. He is also the coordinator of ICU's Japan Studies Program. In 2004–2005, he conducted ethnographic research on Japanese convenience stores, communities, and small shop culture. In 2013, he curated a special exhibition on convenience store material culture for ICU's Yuasa Memorial Museum. He is currently revising a book manuscript titled "At Your Konbini."

INDEX

Topics in this index refer to the nation of Japan, unless otherwise noted. Topics and titles beginning with numbers are listed as though spelled out. For example, the "3/11 Earthquake" is listed under "T". Tables are indicated by "t." following the page number. Page numbers in italic type refer to figures.

"health clubs" providing sex services, 206–207. *See also* health clubs
"bubble economy," 1, 3, 33, 46, 100. *See also* economic growth
bubble generation (*baburu sedai*), 1, 19, 81, 84, 85; women of, 3, 19, 81, 83, 86, 90, 99–103
Buddhism: Buddhist-style funerals, 327, 329–330; priests, 70–71
burakumin (minority) community, 282–283, 295n4, 339
Burawoy, Michael, 54
burial, 11, 20, 317, 318, 331. *See also* mortuary practices

Cabinet Office of Japan, 14, 57
capitalist market system, 4, 7, 9, 82, 111, 119, 127, 129, 180; global capitalism, 2–3, 53, 165, 180. *See also* consumerism; consumption; economic growth; economic recession
car cultures, 20, 300; gender metaphors and, 305t., 305–307. *See also* K-cars (*keijidōsha*); street racers (*hashiriya*)
career women, 5, 19, 56n23, 89, 95, 108, 130, 204; of the bubble generation, 81, 83–85, 99–100; efforts to combine career and marriage, 97, 99, 166, 169, 171, 172, 179–181, 227; narratives of self-construction, 101–102; rejecting marriage for careers, 130
caregivers: daughters (especially unmarried) as, 74, 94–95, 191–192, 325; daughters-in-law as, 192, 193, 319; diversification of, 196, 319; for the elderly, 200n2; son (especially eldest) as, 94, 317
"carnivorous women" (*nikushokukei joshi*), 166, 343
Cave, Peter, 10, 13–14, 20, 57n30, 269, 271, 272, 274, 275, 276, 277, 278, 280, 281, 283
chains, 142–143, 156. *See also* franchise stores; retail food regulations and practices
Chiba University, 156
Chieko, Wataya (deaf teen in *Babel*), 202–204
Child and Child-Rearing Support Plan, 230
child-rearing anxiety, 226, 228, 242–243; insecurities and stresses, 114, 225–229, 242, 243, 341
child-rearing, positive experiences, 240. *See also* networks of young mothers
child-rearing support: commercial services, 227; critics of, 227–228; non-family caregivers (emergence and trust issues), 11, 15, 239–240, 319; pre-war family assistance disappearing, 225–227; specialists, 234, 237; state services (*See also* drop-in play centers), 224, 227, 230–231; structural shifts in, 227–229; studies of, 188, 223, 228–230. *See also* drop-in play centers; networks of young mothers
children's centers (*jidōkan*), 228, 233
Chinese language teaching, 292
class reproduction, 19, 45, 90, 102, 284–285; private test-preparation (*juku*) and, 284–285. *See also* social class

class-specific *habitus*, 86. *See also habitus*
class stratification, 4, 42, 43, 54n2, 56n20, 86, 90, 127, 199, 289; disadvantaged populations, 165, 171, 216, 278, 285, 333. *See also* social class
clerical positions and clerical-track jobs (*ippanshoku*), 5–6, 85, 86–90, 170, 341
cognitive structuring of space, 306, 307, 344
collectivism, 302; collective action, 155
communication devices, 188, 222, 248, 252
communicator, men's new role as, 64, 68
community, 118, 221, 224, 226, 229, 276, 294; condominium community, 320–321; weakening of community ties, 221, 224, 226, 244
Constable, Nicole, 181n5
consumerism, 19, 135, 343. *See also* consumption; retail systems
consumer-farmer relationships (*teikei*), 114–117
consumption, 8–12, 247; affluence and, 5; emerging new services and, 8–12
convenience store diet, 146, 147, 149
convenience stores (*konbini*): as a cultural form, 155–157; "food fight" among, 138, 155–156; globalizing standards, 157; just-in-time distribution practice, 142; as meeting places, 149–150; "observant participation" study of, 140, 146; super-saturation of, 138. *See also* franchise stores; loss (*rosu*) in retail businesses; retail food regulations and practices; waste (*mottainai*)
cooperative relationships, 31, 120, 169; JOAA ideal of, 127
corporations, 90; chains (*See also* franchise stores), 142–143, 156; corporate benefits, 1, 170, 344; corporate subsidiaries, 93; rules on disposal of waste (*mottainai*), 143. *See also* white-collar workers
Coulmas, Florian, 2, 200n4
cram school (*juku*), 284–285
cremation, 316, 317. *See also* ash-scattering ceremonies (*shizensō*)
criminal gangs, 308–309
cross-generational relations: generation gap, 195–196; grandparent-grandchild relationship, 183, 188–190, 192–195
cultural capital (Bourdieu), 19, 42–43, 53, 95, 99, 285, 289
cultural schemas, and metaphors, 305–306, 310–313
culture clubs, 280
curriculum and changes to, 272–274, 286–287, 288, 295n2. *See also* educational system
Cushing, Pamela, and Tanya Lewis, 218n7

Dae Jang Geum (Korean film), 256
Daichi Co., 113
Daily (a convenience store): evening shift at, 135–138, *137*; retail practices at, 138–140, *140*, 144, 145, 147–148, 157. *See also* convenience stores (*konbini*)

daughters, 33, 47, 49, 70, 102, 122, 123, 187, 191–192; father-daughter relationship, 122, 123; married-out daughter, 12; unmarried daughters, 94–95, 163, 187. *See also* family
daughter's husband as heir (*mukoyōshi*), 333
daughters-in-law, 11, 17, 185, 187, 199; as caregivers, 192, 193, 319
day care center (*hoikuen*), 11, 32, 45, 46, 198, 235–237, 239, 340
day laborers, 8
death, self-sufficiency in, 329. *See also* mortuary practices
death rites. *See* mortuary practices
debates, school, 276, 292
Democratic Party, 1, 345
demographic changes: aging of population (*See also* aging), 2, 3, 166–167, 230; declining fertility rates, 16, 166, 224, 230, 242; declining population, 1, 189. *See also* single women
dependency, 16, 52, 328
deregulation: of prostitution, 205; of public programs, 11, 46; workplace, 5, 11, 27
disability: disabled rights movement, 216–217; independent living and, 213; intersections with sexuality, 202–203, 216–217; politics of, 213. *See also* men with physical disabilities
disadvantaged populations, 165, 171, 216, 278, 285, 333
disasters. *See* Fukushima Nuclear Power Plant; 3/11 Earthquake; tsunami
disparity (*kakusa*): female-female disparity (*jojo kakusa*), 6, 102, 341; income disparity, 5, 6, 14, 37–38, 86, 227, 290; male-female disparity (*danjo kakusa*), 6, 55n14, 102, 180. *See also* social class
"Disparity Society" (*kakusa shakai*) discourse, 1, 4, 289–290, 342
"disposable society" (*tsukaisute shakai*), 137, 344
divination (*uranai*), 5, 20, 222, 250–251, 256; aesthetic appeal of, 9, 222, 248, 251, 264; boom in practices of (*uranai būmu*), 247; female social bonding and, 9–10, 222, 251; feminization of, 248–251; girl culture and, 247–248, 253, 262; Goo Research poll on, 252, 254–255; as an industry, 10, 247–248, 249, 256, 264, 265; online sites, 252, 256, 260, 266n5; ratings of efficacy, 255. *See also* girl culture; occult pursuits and objects
divination (*uranai*), forms of: animal systems, 253–254; based in body traits, 254; birth-date-based, 253; blood-type divination (*ketsueki-gata uranai*), 251, 252, 254–256, 255t., 257, 265–266n4, 342; Chinese-derived, 248, 249, 251, 253, 255, 256, 257, 258, 260–261; Gundam fortune-telling, 254; Korean divination forms, 256, 266n5; older forms, 248, 254; using objects such as cards or stones, 254; Western-style astrology, 248–249
divination market, 10, 222, 256

divination shop (Wiz Note), 254, *261*
division of labor: based in gender, 77, 84, 88, 102, 185; in marriage (traditional), 2, 3–5, 9, 15, 21n3, 56n9, 84, 225–226, 228; structural problem of, 244; Taylorization and, 56n19, 313–314n1
divorce, 60–61; rates of, 171
drag, driving in, 309–310
driving styles: gender metaphors and, 300, 306–313. *See also* K-cars (*keijidōsha*); sports cars
drop-in play centers (*tsudoi no hiroba*), 223, 242–244, 344; assessing sustainability of child-rearing support, 243–244; comments of staff and mothers at, 233, 234, 235, 237; critics of, 228–229; events and classes at, 233, 239–240, 245n3; increasing nonprofit support of, 224, 229, 231, 240–244, 244n1; number of nationwide, 231; Ontario, Canada centers, 231; physical settings, 232–233, *232*; quality of, 237, 241, 242, 244; specialists like doctors and social workers, 234, 237; staff members interaction with mothers, 233–237, 244–245n2; state project to develop (*tsudoi no hiroba jigyō*), 224, 227, 230–231; volunteers at, 229, 234, 236, 240–242. *See also* child-rearing; networks of young mothers
drop-off child-care services (*ichiji azukari*), 241, 340
dying alone (*kodokushi*), 319, 342

earthquake (2011). *See* 3/11 Earthquake
economic growth, 54n5, 107, 131; "the bubble economy," 1, 3, 33, 46; the "economic miracle," 3, 83, 86, 89; government policy and, 106, 111; opposition to, 111, 129. *See also* bubble generation; neoliberal economy
economic instability, 1, 27–28
"economic miracle," 3, 83, 86, 89. *See also* "bubble" economy; "bubble" generation
economic recession, 1–2, 4, 5, 6–7, 19, 25, 43, 45, 82, 83, 269, 341; effects of changes on lifestyle and livelihood, 6–7, 27, 43, 45, 51, 52–53, 84, 92, 130; gender structures and, 300, 310–313; post-bubble economy, 5, 14, 51, 84, 86, 90, 227, 294; post-2008 global economic crisis, 1, 2, 27, 345; sales of K-cars increase and, 270
economic recovery, 3–4
Economy, Trade, and Industry, Ministry of (METI), 138, 249
educational capital, 21n3, 94, 95, 99, 100, 102
educational institutions. *See* elementary education; high school education; junior high school; universities
educational reform, 20, 291, 293–294, 296n7. *See also* foreign language education; "internationalization"
educational system, 12–18, 271–272, 291, 293–295; "back to basics" effort, 293; curriculum and changes to, 272–274, 286–287, 288, 295n2;

dual structure of, 10; expenditures on, 296n8; Integrated Studies (Sōgō-Teki na Gakushū), 272, 274, 282, 293; is an index of the state of the nation, 294–295; "learning competency" concept, 42–43, 53, 285, 289; nationwide standardization and compulsory education, 285n1; pedagogical approaches, 13; teachers, 272–276, 278, 280–284, 288–289, 293–294, 295n3

education-credentialist society (*gakureki shakai*), 42

"education of the heart" (*kokoro no kyōiku*), 273, 274, 294, 342

Education and Science, Ministry of, 274, 283, 296n8; National Academic Achievement Tests, 295n1

EEOL (Equal Employment Opportunity Law), 81, 83, 88, 95–99

elder care, 11, 95, 176, 319, 342; system of, 319

elderly. *See* aging; older people; older women

eldest son (*chōnan*), 12, 111–112, 341; performing mortuary duties, 330

elementary education, 272–273, 274–278; curriculum, 273–274; schools, 277t.

emotional bonds: of older people to grandchildren, 187, 192–194, 195–196. *See also* cross-generational relations

emotional development, 273, 294

emotional support, 65, 237, 321

employment: income and types of, 36, 55–56n15; outsourcing jobs, 4, 313; part-time work, 2, 15, 46, 63, 122, 130, 144, 164, 165, 170, 179, 241, 313, 339; seniority-based advancement system, 1, 98, 171, 345; temporary work (*haken*), 2, 165, 170, 179; work conditions, 5–8, 27; youth irregularly employed ("freeters"), 6, 213. *See also* lifetime employment; non-regular or irregular work; unemployment; working men; working women

employment benefits, 38

employment markets for single women, 163, 170–172, 177–179

English language study, 61, 291, 292

environment (natural), 82, 107, 110, 119, 122, 128, 132, 143

Equal Employment Opportunity Law. *See* EEOL

ethnic minority (*burakumin*), 282–283, 295n4, 339

ethnographic research, 18–19; fieldwork techniques and experiences, 3, 5, 21, 241, 314n2, 316–318; interviews, 18–19, 28, 61, 143–144, 163, 184, 200n2, 224, 229; participant-observation, 18, 146–148, 158n1, 224, 229–230, 237, 250

everyday life, 18, 65, 131, 144, 147, 269, 301, 306

expired food, 139–140, 141, 146, 156. *See also* retail regulations and practices

exploratory learning, 13, 269, 272, 276, 283, 293

extracurricular activities, 188; club activities (*bukatsudō*), 280

family, 184, 198–199; family members (*see* daughters; daughters-in-law; grandchildren; grandparents; husbands; in-laws; sons; wives); national law and, 185, 186; nuclearization of (*kakukazokuka*), 187–188, 342; population mobility and, 188; postwar model of breadwinner and homemaker, 2, 3–5, 9, 15, 21n3, 56n9, 84, 225–226; of pre–World War II, 175; spousal role changes, 62, 186–187; urbanization and, 188; weakening of family ties, 186–188, 226. *See also* cross-generational relations; marital relationship; multigenerational households; stem family model (*ie*)

family business, 3, 87, 89–90, 157, 162, 236

family caregivers. *See* caregivers

family farm, 3, 186, 187, 333

family grave (*iebaka*), 12, 18, 270, 317–318, 325–330, 332, 333, 341

Family Support Services, 229, 239, 345

farming/farmers: conventional or traditional, 109, 110, 112, 118, 125, 127; "eco-farmers," 114. *See also* organic farmers

fashion health clubs, 206. *See also* prostitution

father-daughter relationship, 122, 123

female-female disparity (*jojo kakusa*), 6, 102, 341

female specialists in male roles (*otokoyaku*), 309–310, 343

female volunteers, 229, 234, 236, 240–242

femininity, nurturance as, 5, 20, 319

feng shui (geomancy), 248, 255t.; *Girly Feng Shui Magic Makeup*, 249

fertility rates, decline in, 16, 166, 224, 230, 242

Field, Norma, 189–190

fieldwork techniques and experiences. *See* ethnographic research

Fight! (Takeda), 204, 217

five-day school week, 272. *See also* educational system

food: industrialization of, 157, 343; large distribution companies, 113–114; management of freshness, 136, 139, 140, 143; retail food regulations and practices; organic farming; self-sufficiency (*jikyū*) issue, 11, 106, 114; shelf life, 135

food consumer groups (*teikei*), 114–117

"food fight," 155–156. *See also* franchise stores

food safety, insecurity over, 114, 138

foreign language education, 61, 291–292

Four Pillars Divination, 255t.

franchise contract, 8–9, 82, 136, 141

franchise stores, 8, 137, 138, 142–143, 152, 155–156

freshness, management of, 136, 139, 140, 143

frustration, 72, 241; around women's status, 75, 175; economic, 6–7, 241–242

Fu, Huiyan, 2, 55n6

fuel efficiency, 270. *See also* K-cars (*keijidōsha*)

Fujii, Masao, 317

Fujii family: Ami (daughter), 47–48, 54; Atsuko

(daughter), 45–47; blue-collar family of
Kansai, 25, 28–29, 39–42; Masaji (husband
and father; his illness and death), 30–32, 39,
52; meeting and marriage of Sachi and Masiji,
30–32; Sachi (mother and wife) (see Fujii
Sachi); social class across generations, 42–45;
upwardly mobile aspirations, 32–33; Yūji
(son), 49–52, 54, 57n29
Fujii Sachi (blue-collar wife and mother): her
concerns over the past and future, 52–53; her
efforts to progress on the job, 33–37; her life
as an irregular employee, 37–39; her rural to
urban migration, 29–30; meeting Masiji and
marriage, 30–32. See also Fujii family
Fukushima Nuclear Power Plant: explosion, 1, 127;
radioactive contamination concerns, 107, 114,
127–128, 131, 132n4
full-time homemakers, 21n3, 56n19, 63, 172, 174
Furuichi, Noritoshi, and Tuuka Toivonen, 6

Genda Yūji, 51
gender and work. See working women
gender ideologies and schemas, 304–310, 312, 313,
318; gender metaphors, 300, 310–313; K-cars
and gender, 305t., 305–307
gender-segregated roles: lessening of, 62–67, 77–78,
306; as breadwinner and homemaker (postwar
marriage ideal), 2, 3–5, 9, 15, 21n3, 56n9, 84,
225–226
generation gap, 6, 195–196. See also cross-
generational relations
GFPS. See Grave-Free Promotion Society of Japan
(GFPS)
Giddens, Anthony, 4
Gill, Tom, 8
girl culture: aesthetic tastes, 9, 222, 248, 251, 264;
interest in divination (uranai), 247–248, 253,
262; leisure and social bonding, 9–10, 222,
251, 256–258. See also divination (uranai);
Namco Namja Town
glass ceiling, 34, 85, 99
global capitalism, 2–3, 53, 165, 180. See also capitalist
market system
global consumer culture, 129, 155
global food system, 114–115, 119, 131–132
globalization, 2–3, 83, 269
"golden eggs" (kin no tamago), 30, 54n5
Goo Research poll, 252, 254–255. See also divination
(uranai)
government economic policy, 106, 111, 157
grandchildren, meaning of (to older generation),
184–186, 187–188, 190–192, 199; providing
caregiving assistance, 192–195
grandparent-grandchild relationship, 183, 185–186,
188–190, 196–198; co-residence, 191–192;
emotional bonds, 196–198; living proximity
and, 188
grandparents, maternal or paternal, 187

Grave-Free Promotion Society of Japan (GFPS),
316–317, 326–327, 329, 331, 345; fieldwork
conducted at, 317; members' self-perceptions,
333–334
grief, traumatic, 37, 203

habitus, 83, 90, 103, 145; Bourdieu's theory of,
42–43, 85–86; family habitus, 43
Hadashi no Gen (Barefoot Gen), 281
Hamamatsu, Shizuoka Prefecture, 300, 304
handbooks on contemporary Japan, 20
Harada Masafumi, 226, 228
harassment on the job, 37, 98
Hashimoto, Akiko, and John Traphagan, Imagined
Families, Lived Families, 20, 319
"health clubs" (sex services), 206–207; not accepting
disabled men, 213–214
health examinations, for three-year olds, 234, 237,
345
Health, Labor, and Welfare, Ministry of, 2, 17, 166,
181n1, 181, 227, 231–232
heir: daughter's husband as (mukoyshi), 333; eldest
son as (commonly), 12, 120, 185, 191, 341
Higashi, Julie, 273
high-school educated women, 44, 169, 175
high school education: academic performance differentiation in, 285–286; curriculum, 286–287;
discipline at, 288–289; school as a "moral
community," 288; schools, 287t.
"high-skill society," 42
Himeyuri Butai (Star Lily Corps), 281, 282, 340
history studies, 286, 288
Holloway, Susan, 224
Holthus, Barbara, 15, 227, 239
"home education" (katei kyōiku), 227
homeless people (rojōseikatsusha), 148, 225, 343
Hook, Glen D., and Hiroko Takeda, 2
Hosoki Kazuko, 253
Hot-K magazine, 311, 312. See also K-cars
(keijidōsha)
housing allowances, 1
human capital, 42–43
"human pyramids," 277
"human rights education," 282
husbands: erosion of breadwinner role, 62–64; extramarital affairs, 75; increased participation in
household work , 40–41, 54n3, 61, 62, 63, 67,
75–76, 228; marital satisfaction, 73; relational
expectations of, 64–66, 75, 77; valued for
status and income, 21n3, 61, 71, 72, 102, 169.
See also family; men's experiences

I-Ching, 254, 260
Ichiraku. See Teruo, Ichiraku
identity, 107–108
Ikegaoka High School, 286, 287t., 289
Imamura, Anne, Re-imaging Japanese Women, 21
immigration, 3

Iñárritu, Alejandro González, *Babel,* 202–203, 218
income: average, 55n14; of individuals and families, 3–4, 31–32, 37, 38, 44, 46, 50–51, 56n27, 95, 129; low-income population, 243, 282–286; marital experiences and, 63, 66, 71–73, 152–153, 169–170, 227; types of employment and, 36, 55–56n15
income disparity, 5, 6, 14, 37–38, 86, 227, 290. *See also* disparity (*kakusa*); social class
independence: for disabled people, 213; for older people, 11, 319, 334; as a value, 6, 8, 106, 125, 130, 165; for women, 55n7, 117, 120, 172, 174, 176, 180
independent living centers (ILCs), 213
individualism, 301–302
individuality, 4, 70, 274, 294
industrialization, 186, 341; advanced industrial society (*see* postindustrial society); of food, 157, 343
inequality, 272, 290, 294–295. *See also* income disparity
inheritance laws, 325
Initial D (Shigeno), 300–301
in-laws: daughter-in-law, 11, 17, 199; daughter-in-law (as caregiver), 192, 193, 319; daughter's husband as heir (*mukoyōshi*), 333; mother-in-law/daughter-in-law relationship, 185. *See also* family
inner realm (*uchi*), 306, 344; women's experience of, 307–308
Inoue, Haruyo, 317, 318, 333
insecurity and uncertainty: about food, 114, 138; entrepreneurial, 139, 155; in livelihood, 2, 3–5, 8, 27–28, 84, 176, 269; marital, 167, 172, 304; over the future, 1, 53, 84, 293–294, 313; regarding child rearing, 114, 225–229, 242, 243, 341
instructors, notes to, 19
Integrated Studies (Sōgō -Teki na Gakushū), 272, 274, 282–283; reduction of, 293
interdependence, as a value, 101, 278, 320, 328, 334
interdisciplinary learning, 293
Internal Affairs and Communications, Ministry of, 164, 166
"internationalization" (*kokusaika*), 291–292, 294, 342
Internet, 207, 222, 252, 254, 255, 256, 290, 302. *See also* technology
irregular workers. *See* non-regular or irregular work
Ishida, Hiroshi, and David H. Slater, 20, 54n2, 56n20
Ishida and Slater, *Social Class in Contemporary Japan,* 20
Ishiguro, Kazuhiko and Kieko, convenience store couple, 151–154
isolation. *See* social isolation
IT industry, 283. *See also* technology
Iwama, Akiko, study of metropolitan mothers, 228
Iwasaki family mansion, Tokyo, 327

Japanese language lessons, 61, 275
Japan Exchange and Teaching (JET) Program, 291
Jenike, Brenda Robb, 9, 11, 190, 319
JOAA (Japanese Organic Agriculture Association), 9, 105, 110–113, 117, 118, 119–122, 124, 125; ideal of cooperative relationships, 127. *See also* organic farmers
junior high school, 278–285, *279*

Kagami Ryūji, 254
kakusa shakai. See "Disparity Society" (*kakusa shakai*) discourse
Kana (organic farmer), 105–106, 108–110, *109,* 111, 113, 114–116, 125–127
Kansai family. *See* Fujii family
Kansai schools, features of, 277–278
Kariya, Takehiko, 42, 285, 289, 290; and Ronald Dore, 289, 290
Kawagoe City, Saitama Prefecture, 304
Kawai Kaori, *Sex Volunteers,* 202, 210, 213, 218
Kawano, Satsuki, 188, 223, 247, 251, 270, 316, 317–318, 319, 324, 330, 332–333; fieldwork conducted at GFPS, 317
K-cars (*keijidōsha*), 10, 20, 270, 302–304, *303,* 342; fuel efficiency and, 270; gender analogies of driving and, 305t., 305–309, 311–313; *Hot-K* magazine, 311, *312;* interest groups about, 311; more females driving (*See also* women drivers), 270, 302, 308, 310; turbo-charged, 311
Kelly, William, 4, 130
kindergartens, 45, 116, 230, 237, 240, 345
Kondo, Dorinne, 307
Korean popular culture: divination websites, 256, 266n5; influx of, 256
Korean residents, 250, 281–282
Kosugi, Reiko, 52–53
Kumagai, Fumie, 73, 188, 200n4
Kumashino Yoshihiko, *A Hurdle of Only Five Centimeters,* 215
Kuramoto Tomoaki, *Sexuality and Disability Studies,* 216
Kurihara Sumiko, 258
Kurotani, Sawa, 5–6, 19, 81, 83, 85, 227
Kuyōgi, Shūkei, *The Abeno Seimei Codes,* 263–264

Lakoff, George, 312
La Mer (sex site for disabled men), 207, *208*
Lareau, Annette, 42–43
"learning competency," 42–43, 53, 285, 289
Lebra, Takie S., 187–188
Lehman Brothers bankruptcy ("Lehman Shock"), 1, 2, 27, 345
Lévi-Strauss, Claude, 305, 314n2
Lewin, Ben, *The Sessions,* 203
Liberal Democratic Party, 1, 345
life course or path (*shinro*), 86, 163; changes in, 12–18, 61–62, 77, 89; counter to mainstream,

National Consumer Affairs Center of Japan, 249
National Institute of Population and Social Security
    Research, 164, 168, 169
national law on the family, 185, 186. *See also* family
National Police Agency, 206–207
national policies. *See* Angel Plan; New Angel Plan
    Child; Child-Rearing Support Plan
native blood typology system, 264n4
natural environment. *See* environment
neighbors, ties with, 221, 226, 337
neoliberal economy, 3, 5, 7, 37, 52, 53, 180
neoliberal sexualities. *See* sexuality
networks of young mothers: "mom friends"
    (*mamatomo*), 238, 342; mother's groups for
    child rearing (*ikuji sākuru*), 228; "park début"
    (*kōen debyū*), 229; peer support and, 237–239;
    play-center learning opportunities, 239–240;
    play-center spaces for, 233–234; positive
    child-rearing experiences and, 241–242. *See*
    also drop-in play centers (*tsudoi no hiroba*);
    social networks; young mothers
NGOs. *See* nonprofit organizations
1990s period (Lost Decade), 4, 5, 224, 271
Noda, Mrs., 316, 318, 319–321, 335n2; caring for the
    family dead, 324–326; familial relationships,
    322; her choice of cremation and ash-scat-
    tering, 316, 326–332; life of, 316, 321–323;
    thoughts on mortuary care, 327–328
Noir (Noāru) nonprofit website, 215, 216, 218n8
non-family caregivers, 11, 15, 239–240, 319. *See also*
    child-rearing support
nonprofit organizations, 156, 321; providing
    child-rearing support, 224, 229, 231, 240–244,
    244n1
non-regular or irregular work, 2, 4, 5, 6–7, 48, 241;
    agency work (*haken*), 55n6; gender asym-
    metry and, 16, 37–39, 48, 54, 55n7, 56n17;
    irregular employee (*pāto*), 29, 225, 243; many
    young people in, 6, 52, 57n29, 224; unioniza-
    tion of, 225
Noracom, cell-phone application, 253–254. *See also*
    divination
nostalgia, 273, 294, 295–296n7
nuclearization of the family (*kakukazokuka*),
    187–188, 224, 225–226, 228, 242, 342
nuclear power fallout. *See* Fukushima Nuclear Power
    Plant
nursemaids (*komori*), 225, 342

occult pursuits and objects, 20, 222, 247, 248, 249,
    258, 261, 263, 264–265. *See also* divination
Ochiai, Emiko, 14, 167, 200n4, 226
OECD, 296n8
Ogasawara, Yuko, 6, 55n12, 84, 101
Ogawa, Naohiro, et. al., 16, 17, 73, 249, 291, 292
Ogura Chikako, 164, 167, 169
Ōhashi, Terue, 167
oil shocks of 1973–1974, 3

Okano, Kaori, and Motonori Tsuchiya, 285–286,
    295n1
Okinawa, invasion of, 281
older children, 56n24, 186, 188, 192, 225
older people: emotional bonds to younger genera-
    tions, 187, 192–194, 195–196, 199; emotional
    needs and vulnerability of, 319, 321; employ-
    ment discrimination against, 170; the frail
    elderly, 5, 20, 162, 183; increase in longevity,
    20, 162, 190, 199, 269, 329; independence for,
    11, 319, 334; lives of, 190–191, 200nn4–5;
    living alone, 316, 318, 319–320; the very
    old (or old old—*chōkōrei*), 2, 184–185, 190,
    198–199, 200n1, 340; the "young old" and the
    "old old," 200n1
older women, 32, 56n17, 179, 248; disadvantaged,
    165; employment discrimination against,
    170, 171; and marriage, 179; as volunteers,
    221–222; as workers, 6, 56n17, 165, 170–171
old vs. new middle-class, 7–8, 52
Ōmori Miyuki, "I Was a Health Delivery Girl for
    People with Disabilities," 208–210, 213
online sites: for divination, 252, 256, 260, 266n5;
    social and interest networks, 302, 303, 304,
    311
organic agriculture association. *See* JOAA (Japanese
    Organic Agriculture Association)
organic farmers: life of Kana, 105–106, 108–110,
    109, 111, 113, 114–116, 125–127; pioneers,
    113; women as, 5, 19, 121–125. *See also* Kana
    (organic farmer)
organic farming, 105, 108–110, 112, 114; food
    consumer groups (*teikei*), 114–117; as a life-
    style, 105, 113, 119–121; relating to the local
    farming community, 125–127
Orr, James J., 282
Osaka City, 148, 260, 345
Osaka University, 148
Osawa, Mari, 2, 21n1
outer realm (*soto*), 307, 344
outsourcing jobs, 4, 313

paid volunteers, 218n5, 241
palmistry, 248, 255t. *See also* divination (*uranai*)
paper lottery oracles, 257–258, *257*
parenting, 42, 190, 224, 239
part-time work, 2, 15, 46, 63, 122, 130, 144, 164, 165,
    170, 179, 241, 313, 339. *See also* employment
paternal grandparents, 185. *See also* cross-genera-
    tional relations; family
pedagogical approaches, 13
peer learning (*oshieai*), 235, 274, 278, 343
people with disabilities. *See* disability; men with
    physical disabilities
performance-based evaluations: academic, 285, 289;
    job-related, 2, 178
personal care attendants for disabled men, 213–214
physiognomy divination, 248, 255t., 258

Pierre Bourdieu: theory of *habitus,* 42–43. *See also*
    habitus
PISA (Program for International Student Assess-
    ment), 293
Plath, David W., 14, 66, 302, 324
Point of Sales (POS) terminals system, 140
politics of sexual relations, 213–215
pollution, postwar growth and, 114
population: mobility of, 188; period of negative
    growth, 189. *See also* demographic changes
post-bubble economy, 5, 14, 51, 84, 86, 90, 227, 294.
    See also economic recession
post-bubble generation professional women, 85–86;
    clerical track, 86–91; tech jobs, 91–95
post-bubble Japan. See economic recession
posthumous events: divorce, 318; naming, 329
postindustrial society, 2, 4, 162, 224–225, 230, 301,
    329. *See also* capitalist market system
post-structuralism, 306
post-2008 global economic crisis, 291; "Lehman
    Shock," 1, 2, 27, 345
postwar period, 1, 17–18, 21n2, 86, 114, 156, 325;
    baby boom, 76; earlier (1960s and 1970s), 3,
    12–13, 16, 143, 319, 324, 335n2; the "econom-
    ic miracle" (1980s), 3, 83, 86, 89; lifestyle and
    life course, 131, 161, 206, 319, 324, 335n2
poverty, 84, 290
preindustrial society, 329
preschool, 11, 234; preschool teachers, 273
preschoolers, 16, 20, 188, 221, 223; mothers of. *See*
    young mothers
private tutorial and test preparation (*juku*), 284–285
professional women. *See* career women
proficiency groups, 283
proficiency-related learning, 274
prostitution (*fūzoku*), 217–218; "health clubs"
    and sites for sex services, 206–215; licensed
    sex work, 205; one service for women, 207;
    prostitutes working with disabled people,
    202–204, 208–210; red-light districts (*akasen*),
    205, 218n1, 339; sex volunteers, 10, 202,
    203, 210–212, 213; system for American
    occupation forces (RAA), 205; voluntary and
    involuntary sex work, 205
psychiatric disabilities, 217

Quick News media conglomerate, 96–98, 100
Quinn, Naomi, 311–312

RAA (Recreation and Amusement Association), 205
radioactive contamination, 107, 114, 132n4. *See also*
    Fukushima Nuclear Power Plant
Radish Bōya Co., 113
recession. *See* economic recession
religion, marital conflicts over, 69–70
resistance, organic farming as, 107–108, 117–119
retail food regulations and practices: "best-before"
    dates, 139, 157; food waste management

programs, 156; just-in-time distribution, 142;
    management of freshness, 136, 139, 140, 143;
    rules on disposal of waste (*mottainai*), 143;
    "time sale reduction" (*mikirihanbai*), 142–143;
    time sale reduction practice, 142–143. *See also*
    chains; convenience stores (*konbini*)
retail systems: chains, 142–143, 156; franchise con-
    tract, 8–9, 82, 136, 141; headquarters royalty
    fee, 142; product bar codes, 140. *See also* retail
    food regulations and practices
retirement, 12–18, 60; early retirement, 27, 28,
    36–38, 152
rice balls (*onigiri*), 139, 141, 146, 151, 155, 343;
    plastic-wrapped, 157
rice harvesting, 273
risk taking, 301
Roberts, Glenda S., 25, 27, 32, 39, 40, 44, 54n2,
    55n10, 55n12, 64, 85, 95, 100, 230
Robertson, Jennifer, 309–310; *A Companion to the
    Anthropology of Japan,* 20
Roesgaard, Marie Højlund, 284
Rohlen, Thomas P., 10, 284, 285, 290, 291
romantic love, 168
Ronald, Richard, and Allison Alexy, *Home and
    Family in Japan,* 20, 200n4
Rosenberger, Nancy, 81, 105
Rosenbluth, Francis M., 167
Roth, Joshua Hotaka, 300
Rowe, Mark, 317
Rubin, Henry Alex, and Dana Shapiro, *Murderball,*
    203

Sachi. *See* Fujii Sachi (blue-collar wife and mother)
Saito, Yoshitaka, and Tomoyuki Yasuda, 188
Sakai Junko, *The Distant Cry of Loser Dogs (Makeinu
    no tōboe),* 166
Sakatsume Shingo, 211–212, 215; *The Unusual
    Passion of Sex Helpers (Sekkusu herupā no jinjō
    narazaru jōnetsu),* 12
salarymen, 3, 93, 99, 124, 345; concepts of masculin-
    ity, 78n2; and homemaker (household model),
    14, 33, 42, 56n19, 108, 152; new middle-class
    and, 7–8. *See also* white-collar workers;
    working men
SAR (Netherlands) sex service, 214
Sato, Nancy E., 277, 289
Satoyama school, 274, 276
schoolgirls, 21–22, 203, 251, 256
school system. *See* educational system
Seiko (bubble-generation professional woman),
    career aided by EEOL, 95–99, 101, 102
Seiler, Cotton, 301–302
Seimei, Abeno, 262, 263–264
selfhood, women's, 101–102, 302
"self-responsibility" trend, 2
seniority-based advancement system, 1, 98, 171, 345
seniors. *See* older people; older women
service sector, emerging new services, 8–12